INCARNATION

Northwestern University
Studies in Phenomenology
and
Existential Philosophy

INCARNATION

A Philosophy of Flesh

Michel Henry

Translated from the French by Karl Hefty

Northwestern University Press
Evanston, Illinois

Northwestern University Press
www.nupress.northwestern.edu

English translation copyright © 2015 by Karl Hefty. Published 2015 by
Northwestern University Press. Originally published in French in 2000 under
the title *Incarnation: Une philosophie de la chair*. Copyright © 2000 by Éditions
du Seuil. All rights reserved.

Printed in the United States of America

10 9 8 7 6 5 4 3 2 1

Library of Congress Cataloging-in-Publication Data

Henry, Michel, 1922–2002, author.
    [Incarnation. English]
    Incarnation : a philosophy of flesh / Michel Henry ; translated and with a
preface by Karl Hefty
        pages cm. — (Northwestern University studies in phenemenology and
existential philosophy)
    Includes bibliographical references and index.
    ISBN 978-0-8101-3125-5 (cloth : alk. paper) — ISBN 978-0-8101-3126-2
(pbk. : alk. paper)
    1. Incarnation. 2. Flesh (Theology) 3. Theological anthropology—
Christianity. 4. Phenomenology. 5. Phenomenological theology. I. Hefty, Karl.
translator, writer of preface. II. Title. III. Title: Philosophy of flesh. IV. Series:
Northwestern University studies in phenemenology & existential philosophy.
    BT701.2.H42413 2015
    128—dc23
                                                        2015004450

Contents

Translator's Preface

Incarnation: A Philosophy of Flesh is a book that aims to elucidate what Michel Henry calls "incarnation," or existence-in-the-flesh. To be incarnate, for Henry, does not mean to *have* a body, but to *be* one, and not just any kind of body, but a living one that feels itself, suffers, enjoys itself, and moves itself. The living body, or "flesh," is capable of sensing. It can touch a body in the world, but can also be touched by one—and it can touch itself. This power to feel itself will forever distinguish it from all other bodies. To say something about existence in the flesh, then, is not to say anything about the world of things it makes possible, the "sensible world" and everything in it, but rather to say something about what comes before flesh and makes *it* possible. How does life come in flesh? That is the unusual question that will become the primary motif of the phenomenology of incarnation.

And yet, as the reader will soon discover, the life that comes in flesh and makes it living is not some mysterious principle that by a flick of the magic wand comes to animate an inert mass already there. Life "reveals itself" in flesh in a way that no act of thought, philosophical or otherwise, can do, since it is only by being alive that we know, with an invincible certainty, what life is. In the immanence of life in flesh, all of life's modalities are revealed—as what they are: hunger and thirst, but also satiety; suffering of all kinds, but also joy. In the sense in which Henry means it, life in flesh is real life in real flesh, the life that allows each of us at every moment to say, and say with certainty, "I am alive."[1] Such a proposition, in Henry's view, is possible only on the basis of a prior relationship of every flesh with the life that gives it, in a singular way, life. To elucidate the original form of that relationship, one might say, is the subject and task of this book. *That* is the life *Incarnation* is about.

What, then, does this book aim to achieve? Can philosophy tell us who we are? The book's subtitle reads, "a philosophy of flesh." But why is a philosophy of flesh needed if philosophy cannot add anything to what life itself has already said in flesh? What can its intellectual elaboration offer to the humble, the poor, or the suffering, who may well bear the weight of life far better than an erudite philosopher? If the death of philosophy (and of the human sciences too) is indexed by its near-total social, cultural, intellectual, and practical impotence today, perhaps this is only the natural consequence of the original impotence of philosophy, of any thought, before life. And yet, reading the subtitle in reverse, starting from flesh, an entirely different agenda emerges, and a different picture of philosophy. It is clear that Henry endeavors to initiate a renewal of philosophy itself, and a renewal so complete that it will require philosophy "to rethink everything, if one can think reality."[2]

Michel Henry (1922–2002) was one of the great French philosophers working within, and also in some ways against, the tradition of philosophy known as "phenomenology," inaugurated by Edmund Husserl (1859–1938) at the beginning of the twentieth century. Henry's contribution to that tradition, and to philosophy as a whole, is only at the early stages of its appraisal, but its impact is already beginning to be felt: "Life," for Henry, is "phenomenological." By this he does not mean that life is one thing among others, appearing in world alongside other phenomena. Rather, life is phenomenological "in the sense that it denotes phenomenality itself, givenness itself." And far more, "the givenness of givenness."[3] Totally unique in the way that it gives itself, life can in no way be reduced to the "world" or to anything "in" the world. Life gives itself originally in itself; life and self-givenness are one. By redefining its most basic concept, Henry has not merely suggested a new region or subfield for phenomenology to consider, he has altered in an essential way what phenomenology is and does.

In the first part of *Incarnation*, Henry offers a critical rereading of historical phenomenology, framed within a global indictment of the whole of modern Western philosophy from Galileo to Heidegger. The reappraisal of phenomenology in this part of the book comes to a point in Henry's engagement with Husserl, since it is perhaps to Husserl that Henry remains closest, and thus also perhaps in relief against Husserl that the stakes of Henry's argument appear in their finest distinction. Husserl saw a necessary connection between givenness and life, but his fatal mistake, in Henry's view, was made from the beginning. In place of life in its originary givenness, Husserl substitutes the self-constituting ego, and through this process of substitution, replaces life's singular living reality with its "essence." Not only is the reality of the "impression" lost in this substitution, Henry claims, but the reality of time itself is too. Since flesh is by definition impressional, these critical remarks in part 1 are prerequisite to the phenomenology of flesh that Henry then develops in a positive way in the second part.

Before discussing the argument he offers in part 2, it is worth making several additional remarks about Henry's reading of Husserl. An important distinction between them has to do with the form of the relation of the ego to its own life, and thus also to itself, and to the time that it constitutes. Husserl says that the phenomenological reduction opens me to "the whole stream of my experiencing life [*erfahrenden Lebens*]," which is "continually there *for me*" and given "with the most originary originality as it itself."[4] "Reflecting, I can at any time look at this original living and note particulars [. . .]," he says, and "the world experienced in this reflectively grasped life goes on being for me (in a certain manner) 'experienced' as before."[5] But does it? Henry does not think so. The first gap opened up by reflection tears life away from its originary living reality, turning life's pathos-filled "embrace" into a synthetic, constituted unity. As Henry sees it, everything is at stake in the difference. Not only is the method of phenomenology decided here, but philosophy itself, and indeed life's meaning, hang in the balance.

Many that follow in Husserl's wake, Heidegger notably, but also Sartre, Merleau-Ponty, and others, refuse to follow the so-called transcendental turn Husserl makes in the *Ideas*. One might think this is because they preferred a phenomenology rooted firmly in time, in all of its historical, existential, and perceptual dimensions. Henry is distinctive in that he *does* remain faithful to Husserl on this issue: "Phenomenology is a transcendental philosophy."[6] But what does "transcendental" mean in this context? In Husserl's sense, it means all that Descartes means by the word *cogito*: "the being of the pure ego and its *cogitationes*, as a being that is prior in itself, is antecedent to the natural being of the world."[7] Henry's position differs from Husserl's, however, in that for Henry the sense of "transcendental" is not an ideal one. It describes life as such, and to that extent also flesh. An entirely new meaning is assigned to the idea of a "transcendental" philosophy. It cannot be said to abstract from time, because only in life is time real. And yet, in so far as it is a living present, life in itself has no past or future. To "reverse" phenomenology thus means: with respect to the series of impressions that together give form to time, it is not a question of what comes after an original impression makes its presence felt, but of what comes before an original impression and makes it effective.

The second part of *Incarnation* allows Henry to explore what a true phenomenology of flesh implies, and to test how far it is capable of thinking life's *own* self-givenness, in its living actuality, in flesh. The central task in this part of the book is to distinguish a phenomenology of the sensing body, a body that has the power to move itself and to touch itself, from what philosophy has understood under the ambiguous heading "sensible body." To explain what is capable of sensing itself and feeling itself by reference to something else that is sensed *by* it is to fail to understand what sensing means, and what it involves. A totally different conception of the body is needed, precisely in so far as it is living. Only the generation of flesh in absolute Life, Henry insists, is capable of rendering intelligible the original powers of flesh, in their living, phenomenological reality. In this context, Henry's critical rereading of Condillac and Maine de Biran, two French counterparts to the British empiricists, is a highly important contribution to the history of modern philosophy.

The phenomenological analysis of flesh in part 2 opens onto a phenomenological analysis of incarnation in part 3. In a surprising and even hidden way, it is in this part of the book that the question of freedom intervenes in Henry's argument, under the form of the anxiety of flesh that gives from its own power. The intrinsic connections between the various parts of his analysis are here perhaps most difficult to decipher: power, freedom, anxiety, sin, desire, passivity, eroticism—how do these themes hold together under the sub-heading "salvation in the Christian sense"? And how does the answer to that question hold together with Henry's foregoing analyses? However those questions are answered, it cannot be said that Henry's argument here amounts to an uncritical recourse to theology (as if that were a disqualification of it). To uncritically assume *that* conclusion is to submit philosophy to dogmatic prejudice, and then philosophy becomes what it opposes. A completely distinct rethinking of the relationship between the phenomenology of life and theology is needed, and to reduce that relationship to preconceived determinations is to fail to understand it.

In view of the broader development of Michel Henry's philosophy, *Incarnation* can, in a sense, be seen as a crowning achievement. With the original edition appearing in French in 2000, it is the last book he published during his lifetime. (Although he lived to complete the full manuscript of *Words of Christ* [2002],[8] it was published a few months after his death.) Considering his work as a whole, *Incarnation* is situated within several conjoining contexts. Most immediately, it belongs together with *I Am the Truth: Toward a Philosophy of Christianity* (1996)[9] and *Words of Christ* as the second of a final trilogy of books that together forge an approach to Christianity within philosophy. In treating the question of flesh, it also returns full circle to an issue raised at the end of his first book, *Philosophy and Phenomenology of the Body* (published in 1965, though its composition was completed in 1949), where he poses for the first time "the problem of incarnation."[10] There the problem of incarnation and the problem of flesh come together in the question of finitude, and it is this question, one might say, that *Incarnation* develops most fully.

Finally, it must be said that *Incarnation* also tests how far the phenomenology of life can treat, and indeed resolve, another question that occupies Henry from the beginning: the question of intersubjectivity. In the 1953–54 academic year, Henry taught a course at Aix-en-Provence on the question of the "experience of the other" in Hegel, Husserl, Sartre, and Scheler. His notes for the course show detailed treatment of many of the same topics that appear in *Incarnation* (corporeality, sexuality, "being-with," etc.), all working toward an experience of the other in the first person.[11] Readers will be aware that Henry addresses the problem of intersubjectivity directly in *Material Phenomenology* (1990), but in his introduction to that book, Henry writes that "a systematic study of intersubjectivity will be the subject of a *subsequent* work."[12] *Incarnation* is undoubtedly the later work he has in mind. In an interview contemporaneous with the publication of *Incarnation*, Henry confirms, with respect to the question of the other, "I wanted to see, as a challenge, if my phenomenology of life could resolve the problem that no one had resolved, in my opinion."[13]

It will be up to his readers and generations of interpreters to determine whether *Incarnation* is situated within or beyond what has traditionally been understood as the modern world. Henry takes up anew the central problems and questions that determine modern empiricism and rationalism (and in some sense all philosophy), and he addresses these problems as they persist through the birth and development of historical phenomenology. Yet Henry does not simply refute the theses of his philosophical predecessors, nor does he merely substitute one premise or prejudice for another. Instead, by reformulating their same questions, he gives them a new inflection, and because he cuts straight to what is fundamental, it is difficult to overestimate what is at stake if his arguments succeed. The phenomenology of life, as Henry says, "implies a revival of philosophical questioning in its entirety" and "offers a future to phenomenology and to philosophy itself" and "at the same time, discovers a new past."[14] So if *Incarnation: A Philosophy of Flesh* engages in an epic battle with the modern world, perhaps it is not only in order to destroy it, but also to open a way for the breath of life in it.

In the following translation, we have sought to render Henry's French as faithfully as possible, balancing the need to maintain the author's conceptual rigor and style with the unique demands of English prose. If, despite every effort at peaceful resolution, those two priorities have remained in conflict, the preference has been given to the need for conceptual accuracy. The author pushes the limits of what French can do, and perhaps even exceeds those limits at times, and it is those moments, and their peculiar grammatical character, that have given the most difficulty. Several particular terms and constructions are worth mentioning.

In a frequent and important formulation, Henry says that life *s'éprouve soi-même*. The verb *éprouver* means "to feel" or "to experience," but also "to suffer," "to sustain," "to test," "to put to the test," and even "to afflict" or "to distress." The dynamic tension between active and passive meanings is not accidental, and in Henry's construction the term is not merely reflexive, but exceedingly so, and no single English verb can do justice to the richness of the original French. Henry does not exactly mean that life "experiences itself," as if life were an object of experience, nor that life is the "experience of oneself," as if a substantial self were there prior to it that it would then experience. The sense is something more like what experiencing *it*self undergoes. So most often, we have chosen the still-inadequate but approximate locutions "to undergo experiencing itself" or "experiencing undergoing itself."

Several other decisions also deserve mention in this context, since they also pertain to Henry's definition of life. Henry speaks of an *épreuve de soi*, where *l'épreuve* has the sense of a "trial" or "test" or "ordeal." We have translated this as equally "self-trial" or "trial of oneself." But Henry also employs another term with juridical connotations: *le procès*, meaning a "(legal) action," "trial," "court proceeding," or even "lawsuit." It may also mean "process," in the linguistic or anatomical sense, but French also has available *processus*, and Henry usually does not use this word. In order to preserve its wider meaning, and since it occurs in the context of discussing life's self-generation, we have elected to translate *procès* most often by the term "proceeding." Something like a trial or ordeal is meant, and any connotation of a process is in some sense secondary. Finally, Henry's "*la venue*" we have rendered both as "arrival" and "coming," without significant conceptual distinction, but with some preference for the former, since it avoids the feel of a nominalization. Occasionally, where decisions have been made (or avoided), we have included the original French term in brackets.

For ease of reference, the philosophical or theological works cited most often in the text have been gathered in the "Abbreviations to Frequently Cited Works." Where authoritative or recent critical editions are available, we have adopted them. Where they are not available, or not recent, we have translated directly from the French, as cited by Michel Henry. Scripture references have been given from the New Revised Standard Version. In a number of instances, both philosophical and biblical, standard translations have been modified, and these instances have been indicated parenthetically. In no case have the modifications altered the sense. These small changes have been made either to preserve consistency with Henry's usage, or to preserve the flow of his sentences, which often cite selectively. Husserl's *Ur-impression*, for example, has been rendered not "primal impression," as with the standard English translation, but "originary impression." The footnotes throughout the text correspond to Henry's own footnotes in the original French edition.

The work on this translation would not have been possible without the support and encouragement of many. I would like to express my gratitude to Henry Carrigan at Northwestern University Press, for his exemplary professionalism throughout the translation process, and for his encouragement and patience as I worked to complete it; and also to Martin Coleman whose careful work on the English copy helped to correct errors and clarify ambiguities; the final work is better for his efforts. I am especially grateful to Anne Henry for her generosity, encouragement, and hospitality, which have brought me closer to the author of this book; and I would like to thank Jean-Luc Marion, whose indefatigable passion for the essential is a gift to us all. Most of all, I am grateful for my family, who has labored with me, and especially for Victoria Hefty, to whom I dedicate this translation.

Notes

1. Edmund Husserl, *Ideen zu einer reinen Phänomenologischen Philosophie, I. Buch: Allgemeine Einführung in die reine Phänomenologie* (The Hague: Martinus Nijhoff, 1976) / *Ideas Pertaining to a Pure Phenomenology and to a Phenomenological Philosophy*, trans. F. Kersten (Dordrecht: Kluver, 1998), Hua III-1 §46, 86 / 100.

2. Michel Henry, *Phénoménologie matérielle* (Paris: Presses Universitaire de France, 1990), p. 12 / *Material Phenomenology*, trans. Scott Davidson (New York: Fordham University Press, 2008), p. 6.

3. "Le corps vivant," in Michel Henry, *Auto-donation. Entretiens et conférences* (Paris: Beauchesne, 2004), p. 127; originally published as "Le corps : sujet ou objet," in *Les Cahiers de l'École des sciences philosophiaues et religieuses*, no. 18, 1995, pp. 71–97, and republished as "Corps" in *Préntentaine*, no. 12–13, March 2000: 13–35.

4. Edmund Husserl, *Cartesianische Meditationen und Pariser Vorträge* (The Hague: Martinus Nijhoff, 1950) / *Cartesian Meditations*, trans. Dorion Cairns (Dordrecht: Kluwer, 1999) Hua 1, I, §8, 59 / 19.

5. Ibid.

6. See §13, p. 77, below.

7. Hua I, I, §8, p. 61 / p. 21.

8. Michel Henry, *Paroles du Christ* (Paris: Seuil, 2002) / *Words of Christ*, trans. Christina M. Gschwandtner (Grand Rapids, MI: Eerdmans, 2012).

9. Michel Henry, *C'est moi la vérité* (Paris: Seuil, 1996) / *I Am the Truth: Toward a Philosophy of Christianity*, trans. Susan Emanuel (Stanford: Stanford University Press, 2003).

10. Michel Henry, *Philosophie et phénomenologie du corps* (Paris: Presses Universitaires de France, 1965) / *Philosophy and Phenomenology of the Body*, trans. Girard Etzkorn (The Hague: Martinus Nijhoff, 1975).

11. Henry proposed for its title "Communication of Consciousnesses and Relations with the Other." His previously unpublished course notes have been made available thanks to the commendable work of the recently established Fonds Michel Henry, under the direction of Jean Leclercq, at the Université catholique de Louvain. They are gathered and presented, together with an excellent critical introduction, in Revue Internationale Michel Henry, no. 2, 2011: 71–178.

12. Michel Henry, *Phénoménologie matérielle* (Paris: Presses Universitaire de France, 1990), p. 12 / *Material Phenomenology*, trans. Scott Davidson (New York: Fordham University Press, 2008), p. 6, our emphasis.

13. Michel Henry, "Interview with Virginie Caruana," in *Entretiens* (Arles: Sulliver, 2005), p. 121.

14. Michel Henry, *Phénoménologie matérielle* (Paris: Presses Universitaire de France, 1990), p. 12 / *Material Phenomenology*, trans. Scott Davidson (New York: Fordham University Press, 2008), p. 6.

Abbreviations to Frequently Cited Works

Frequently cited references appear parenthetically in the text. The following authors and works are cited according to their original edition first, followed by the pagination of the standard English language edition, where available.

René Descartes

AT / PW   *Œuvres complètes.* Adam and Tannery (Paris: Vrin, 1996) / *The Philosophical Writings of Descartes,* ed. and English trans. John Cottingham, Robert Stoothoff, and Dugald Murdoch (Cambridge: Cambridge University Press, 1985–1991).

Edmund Husserl

Hua I   *Husserliana I. Cartesianische Meditationen und Pariser Vorträge,* ed. Stephen Strasser (The Hague: Martinus Nijhoff, 1950) / *Cartesian Meditations: An Introduction to Phenomenology,* English trans. Dorion Cairns (The Hague: Martinus Nijhoff, 1960).

Hua II   *Husserliana II. Die Idee der Phänomenologie. Fünf Vorlesungen,* ed. Walter Biemel (The Hague: Martinus Nijhoff, 1950) / *The Idea of Phenomenology,* English trans. Lee Hardy (Dordrecht: Kluwer Academic, 1999).

Hua III   *Husserliana III. Ideen zu einer reinen Phänomenologie und phänomenologischen Philosophie. Erstes Buch. Allgemeine Einführung in die reine Phänomenologie,* ed. Karl Schuhmann (The Hague: Martinus Nijhoff, 1976) / *Ideas Pertaining to a Pure Phenomenology and to a Phenomenological Philosophy: First Book— General Introduction to a Pure Phenomenology,* English trans. Fred Kersten (Dordrecht: Kluwer, 1983).

Hua IV   *Husserliana IV. Ideen zu einer reinen Phänomenologie und phänomenologischen Philosophie. Zweites Buch: Phänomenologische Untersuchungen zur Konstitution.* ed. Marly Biemel (The Hague:

Martinus Nijhoff, 1952) / *Ideas Pertaining to a Pure Phenomenology and to a Phenomenological Philosophy: Second Book—Studies in the Phenomenology of Constitution*, English trans. Richard Rojcewicz and André Schuwer (Dordrecht: Kluwer, 1989).

Hua VI   *Husserliana VI. Die Krisis der europäischen Wissenschaften und die transzendentale Phänomenologie. Eine Einleitung in die phänomenologische Philosophie*, ed. Walter Biemel (The Hague: Martinus Nijhoff, 1976) / *The Crisis of European Sciences and Transcendental Philosophy*, English trans. David Carr (Evanston: Northwestern University Press, 1970).

Hua X   *Husserliana X. Zur Phänomenologie des inneren Zeitbewusstseins (1983–1917)*, ed. Rudolf Boehm (The Hague: Martinus Nijhoff, 1966) / *Leçons pour une phénoménologie de la conscience intime du temps*, French trans. H. Dussort (Paris, PUF, 1964) / *On the Phenomenology of the Consciousness of Internal Time (1893–1917)*, English trans. John Barnett Brough (Dordrecht: Kluwer Academic, 1991).

Martin Heidegger

SZ   *Sein und Zeit* (Tübingen: Max Niemeyer, 2006, 19th ed.) / *Being and Time*, English trans. Joan Stambaugh (New York: State University of New York Press, 1996).

Søren Kierkegaard

SKS 4   *Begrebet Angest, Søren Kierkegaards Skrifter*, Vol. 4, ed. Niels Jørgen Cappelørn et al (Copenhagen: Gads Forlag, 1997) / *The Concept of Anxiety*, English trans. Reidar Thomte (Princeton: Princeton University Press, 1980).

Tertullian

CC I   *La Chair du Christ*, Vol. I, ed. Jean-Pierre Mahé (Paris: Cerf, 1995).

INCARNATION

The Question of Incarnation

Incarnation takes place at the center of a constellation of problems that we intend to treat in this essay. In its first sense, incarnation concerns all living beings on earth since these are all incarnate beings. This first very general remark already confronts us with enormous difficulties. The distinguishing characteristic of incarnate beings is that they have a body. But the entire universe is composed of bodies, which common sense, many philosophers, and almost all scholars have long regarded as material bodies. Is the body that belongs to living beings the same as the material body that quantum physics investigates, and that serves as a support for the other hard sciences of chemistry and biology? Many people think so today, which is precisely the age of science, and yet an abyss separates forever the material bodies that fill the universe, on the one hand, and the body of an "incarnate" being such as man, on the other.

In order to throw light on this abyss, we will make an initial decision to leave living beings other than human beings outside the field of our investigation. A decision like this is not arbitrary. It is justified by a methodological choice to speak of what we know rather than of what we do not. For everyone, every man and every woman, at every moment of their existence, has the immediate experience of their own body—feels the difficulty the rise in the sloped lane brings, or the pleasure of a cold drink in summer, or of a light breeze on their face—while their relation to animal bodies such as infusoria, shrimp, or insects is of another order. So much so that certain thinkers, and not the least of them, have regarded all such living beings, with the exception of man, as if they were like computers that understand nothing of what they do. But the increasingly widespread idea that the human body can be comprehended in this way, as though it were a computer too, just more developed and a "generation" more advanced, comes up against a major objection.

Here the abyss widens. An inert body like those we find in the material universe—or that we can construct using material processes torn from it, by organizing them and combining them according to physical laws—such a body senses and feels nothing. It does not sense itself and does not feel its own feeling, it neither loves nor desires itself. Even less does it sense or feel or love or desire any of the things around it. According to Heidegger's profound remark, the table does not "touch" the wall against which it is placed. What is proper to a body such as ours, on the contrary, is that it senses every object that is close to it; it perceives each of its qualities, it sees its colors, hears its sounds, breathes in a scent, determines the hardness of the soil with a foot, and the smoothness of a fabric with a hand. And it senses all of this, the qualities of all these objects that make up its environment, it feels the world that presses on it from all sides, only because it feels its own feeling first, in the effort it exerts to ascend the lane, and in the impression of pleasure that sums up the cool of the water or wind.

We will now fix in appropriate terminology this difference between the two bodies we have just distinguished—our own, which feels itself at the same time it senses what surrounds it, on the one hand, and the inert body of the universe, on the other, whether it be a stone on the path or the micro-physical particles that supposedly constitute it. We will call the former *flesh*, reserving usage of the word *body* for the latter. For our flesh is nothing other than what *feels itself, suffers itself, undergoes itself and bears itself, and thus enjoys itself according to impressions that are always reborn.* For this reason, it can feel the *body* outside it, and touch it as well as be touched by it—and this is what the external body, the inert body of the material universe, cannot do in principle.

The first topic of our investigation will be the elucidation of flesh. We want to speak of the incarnate beings we are, we men and women, and of this singular condition that is ours. This condition, the fact of being incarnate, is nothing other than incarnation. To be incarnate is not to have a body, to put oneself forward as a "corporeal" and thus material being—an integral part of the universe, which one awards with the same qualifier. To be incarnate is to have flesh, and, perhaps more precisely, to be flesh. Thus incarnate beings are not inert bodies that neither sense nor feel anything, conscious neither of themselves nor things. Incarnate beings are suffering beings, shot through with desire and fear, feeling all the impressions that are bound together with flesh because they are constitutive of its substance—which is thus an impressional substance, *beginning and ending with what it feels.*

Defined by everything a body lacks, flesh should not be confused with the body, but is instead, if one may say so, the exact opposite. Flesh and body are opposed as sensing and un-sensing—that which enjoys itself on the one hand; blind, opaque, inert matter, on the other. This difference is so radical that, though it may seem obvious, it is very difficult, even impossible, actually to think it. And this is because it is a difference between two terms, one of which ultimately escapes us. If it is easy for us to know our flesh, to the extent that it never leaves us and adheres to our skin in the form of numerous impressions of pain and pleasure that constantly affect us—so that each of us actually knows quite well, with an absolute and unbroken knowledge, what his flesh is (even if he cannot express this knowledge conceptually)—our knowledge of the inert bodies of material nature is quite different and vanishes on arrival, ending in complete ignorance.

Here it is not a question of difficulties of the technical sort that are encountered in quantum physics, where each "measure," at the very location of what it seeks to apprehend, interferes with or makes indeterminate the very parameters selected for this purpose. A metaphysical and final aporia bars our way, because the ultimate physical element must still reach us somehow and there is no way around this final order of things: A flash on a screen, for example, is interpreted as the collision of a photon, a sensation of light that arrives in our flesh nowhere else but where this flesh impresses upon itself. Outside this inevitable reference, it remains unknown and unknowable what the object of physics, the "thing in itself," or what Kant called the "noumena," would be.

The analysis of the body can never become an analysis of our flesh, or eventually its explanatory principle; rather, the contrary is true: Our flesh alone allows us to know, within the limits prescribed by this inescapable presupposition, something like a "body." Thus the contours of a strange inversion already stand out before our eyes. The man who knows nothing, nothing but the hardship of all the suffering in his bruised flesh—the poor, and the "little ones"—probably knows much more than an omniscient mind situated at the end of the ideal development of science, for which, according to an illusion that was widespread in the nineteenth century, "the future and the past alike would be present to its eyes."

Systematically elucidating the flesh, the body, and their enigmatic relation will allow us to address the second subject of our inquiry: Incarnation in the Christian sense. It is founded on John's astounding proposition: "And the Word was made flesh" (1:14). This extraordinary utterance will haunt the consciousness of all who will endeavor to think it, from the eruption of what we will call Christianity onward; the first reflections of Paul, the evangelists, the Apostles and their messengers, the Fathers of the Church, the heretics and their opponents, and the councils—in short, an entire spiritual and cultural development perhaps without equivalent in the history of humanity—all witness to this. The importance of this decisive sequence of philosophy and theology, which in the early Christian period were mixed together, cannot be obscured by the fact that many of the intellectual works composing it have disappeared, victims of a gigantic shipwreck along with the majority of texts from antiquity. Its importance stems from the fact that where the speech of Incarnation is pronounced, an inevitable confrontation is provoked that very soon becomes almost obsessive, between those who will strive to understand it, even if they still do not have the means at their disposal to do so, and those who reject it unconditionally as incompatible with their philosophy, which is nothing more and nothing less than Greek philosophy!

The former are converts, Jews, Greeks, and pagans of all sorts, who want to understand that in which they have just put their faith. The others are the "Greek," which now means those who, whether Greek or not, continue to think as Greeks, and accordingly are unable to think what is said in John's mysterious word.

On the one hand, the Greek Logos displays its essence outside the sensible world (and everything pertaining to it, whether animality or inert matter), exhausting this essence in the timeless contemplation of an intelligible universe. That the contemplation of a pure intelligible makes the world of things comprehensible and supplies its archetype changes nothing about the fundamental situation, from which the opposition between sensible and intelligible that will come to govern Western thought originates.

On the other hand, the radical incompatibility between the Greek concept of Logos and the idea of its possible incarnation reaches its apogee as soon as it assumes the meaning it will have in Christianity, as conferring salvation. This is indeed the thesis of Christian dogma that one can truly call "crucial," and it is the principle of its entire "economy."

Greek thought opened before man the royal road of a possible, if not plausible, salvation. Man, according to this thinking, is an animal endowed with Logos. By his animality, by his natural body, he falls within the province of the sensible, which itself is subject to becoming. In this respect, he is a perishable being, destined for decomposition and death. But endowed with Logos, and thus with the capacity to contemplate the intelligible archetypes of things and, through these, the light of the Absolute that illuminates them, he also has a soul, or rather "he is nothing apart from its soul" (*Alcibiades*, 38c). When the soul turns away from the sensible world to be united to the eternal *nous* and lost in the contemplation of the Intelligible, the soul will, like the Intelligible, be eternal. These originally Platonic schemas, which will be taken over by Gnosticism, were known to all Greeks.

And here Christianity situates its salvation in the body. This material body, subject to putrefaction, which falls prey to becoming, and even more the seat of sin, the organ of sensory attraction, and the victim predestined for every illusion and every idol, is appointed to snatch us from death! As we acquire the means to do so, we will offer an analysis of this strange economy of salvation that caused hilarity among the Greeks. When on the Areopagus in Athens Paul sought to explain to them how human immortality rests on the resurrection of the body, his listeners, as we know, went away sneering: "We will hear you again about this" (Acts 17:32).

As extraordinary as the doctrine was the attitude of those who immediately and unreservedly accepted it, and, further, agreed *to risk the fate of Christianity on its most implausible thesis.* It is true that the paradox was far from being the same for everyone. The "Christian" Jews, those who had recognized in Jesus the Messiah, and in a general way all who were of Jewish culture, did not share the Greek conception of the dualism between the soul and body. In Judaism, man is not cut into two distinct substances and is not a result of their synthesis, which in any case is incomprehensible; so no hierarchy is set up between them. Man is a unitary reality endowed with diverse properties, all of which define a single condition. Far from being the object of certain discredit, and even if it remains subject to the rigorous prescriptions of the Law, what is of the flesh (paternity or maternity, for example) represents a fulfillment for Jewish man, and a fulfillment of his highest desire.

The identity that exists between the conceptions relating to flesh in Judaism and those in the new religion (which in the beginning is only a heretical sect) will nevertheless be broken when this new religion emerges. The motive for this divorce, which has all the character of a tragic battle, is two-fold. In the first place, there is the idea Judaism has of God and his creation. God created the world outside himself, and he is separated from it in the same way that he is separated from man, whom he drew from the matter of this world. Even before the arrival of Hellenism, Judaism contains within it, connected to the idea of a *terrestrial* body, a notion of man as destitute and destined for death. Only a gratuitous act of God, of his all-powerful will, allows his servant to hold out hope that he will not be delivered over to Sheol. It was nearly as difficult for a Jew to believe in the resurrection (and many did not) as it was for a Greek. A terrestrial creature fashioned in the silt of the earth, he seemed destined, by his origin as much as by his sin, to return to it. "Remember that you are dust [. . .]" (Genesis 3:19).

The second motive for the brutal rupture between Judaism and the sect of Christ stems precisely from Incarnation. That the Eternal, the distant and invisible God of Israel—the one who always hides his face in clouds or behind bushes, whose voice one hears at most (of whom, incidentally, is it the voice?)—comes into the world and takes on an earthly body to subject it to the torment of an ignominious death reserved for villains and slaves, is in the end something as absurd for an erudite Rabbi as for a sage of pagan Antiquity. For this most destitute man to pretend to be God is the greatest blasphemy, which indeed deserved death.

If the Jewish refusal—the refusal of the Temple priests, high priests, scribes, Sadducees, and Pharisees—is in the end (despite the secret conversion of numbers of them, and despite the idea that they had of flesh as the organic totality of man) as violent as the Greek refusal stemming from dualism, we are then brought back to our initial observation, to the extraordinary character of the unconditional faith that all the Jewish, Greek, and pagan converts would place in the Incarnation of the Word, which is to say, in Christ.

It is in hindsight that, not content to constitute the substance of the life of the first communities gathered around the sacred meal, Incarnation in the Christian sense becomes the object of a specific intellectual reflection—even if the "human battle," actually a succession of terrible persecutions, "Jewish" first, then Roman, continues to accompany the "spiritual combat." Very great thinkers, the Fathers of the Church, will devote themselves to this reflection. We have already seen how, having assumed the Christian paradox that posits the coming of God in a mortal body as the metaphysical condition of human salvation, they were forced to fight on two fronts: against the Jews and against the Greeks.

Against the Jews, as shown for example in the debate between Justin and Rabbi Trypho, who precisely could not understand how the Christians placed their hope "in a man who was crucified."* But it is the transcendence of the God of Israel that ultimately makes his incarnation unintelligible. Yahweh is a jealous God. Jealous of his divine essence, the power to exist—"I am Who I am" (Ex. 3:14)—which exists only in him and is not shared. Hence the pretension of a man to be himself God indeed seems absurd. Jewish monotheism is flawless. The jealousy of the God of Israel toward men, or rather toward all their idols (women, money, power, foreign gods, etc.), toward everything that would claim to be a substitute for Yahweh as an object of worship, is only the consequence of this primary ontological jealousy, which is the jealousy of the Absolute. And it is true that a plural God, if you will, is inconceivable for a thought of Being for which everything that is or can be comes from the only Being that truly exists, the one who has in himself the strength to be. We will see how the great councils of the Church, as well as its most remarkable thinkers (before the Aristotelian invasion of the thirteenth

*Justin Martyr, *Dialogue avec Tryphon*, French trans. G. Archambault (Paris: Picard, 1909), X, 3; I, 49 / *Dialogue with Trypho*, English trans. Thomas B. Falls (Washington, D.C.: Catholic University of America Press, 2003), p. 18.

century), surreptitiously abandon every form of ontology (and particularly the ontology that had the most remarkable theoretical flourishing in Greece), keeping only its language. This was the price to pay, or the decisive step to take, in order to safeguard the founding intuition of the Incarnation. So Hellenism will tend to disappear or occupy only a secondary place to the extent that the "philosophy" of Christianity will become more adequate to its object. According to Bernard Sesboüé's profound appraisal concerning the Council of Nicaea, the Hellenization of language goes hand in hand with a de-Hellenization of the faith;[*] as we will claim, however, this occurs first with respect to thought itself.

This is the singular ideal sequence that we can situate historically through the Fathers of the Church and the great councils, but the content of it is the result of the internal development of antagonistic presuppositions. As soon as Christianity escapes its Hebraic origins, and by virtue of its desire for universalism, it is confronted with a culture that is, for the most part and from the intellectual point of view, Greek culture. That culture thus has to accept what is most antithetical and incomprehensible for it, and to put it now more accurately, it has to accept *the reality of Christ's body in the Incarnation as a condition for the identification of man with God.* So from Greek concepts they seek to understand the most anti-Greek truth there is. This is the contradiction the Fathers and councils will confront more than once.

In the ancient context, an approach that is as paradoxical as what it strives to understand is not only motivated by proselytism. Christianity itself does not have adequate concepts for its highest Truth. This is not because of some intellectual poverty that would be proper to Christianity, as if the early Christians were infant thinkers needing only to be instructed by real philosophers—Greek philosophers! It is for a more radical reason: *The Truth of Christianity is not of the intellectual order.* And the genius of the Church Fathers (whether Greek or not), the striking character of the sequence of ideas that weaves its way little by little through their dazzling intuitions, was precisely this—They grasp the Truth of Christianity in its most baffling affirmation: the Incarnation. In fact, it is not grasped in an affirmation (which would still be only mental, or at least would be open to the judgment of the mind); it is grasped in what escapes every thought: *In a body and a flesh.*

---

[*] Bernard Sesboüé, "Jésus Christ dans la tradition de l'Église," in *Jésus et Jésus Christ*, no. 17 (Paris: Desclée, 1993), p. 100: "The peculiarity of the council of Nicaea is to profess in a trenchant manner the radical difference between the mystery of Jesus Christ and Greek philosophy. The paradox is that this de-Hellenization takes place at the very moment the language of faith is Hellenized."

The fight the Fathers took up and pursued relentlessly, from the end of the first century through the following centuries and successive councils, does seem extraordinary. It is the fight to affirm, defend, and demonstrate by every means available (but also with the help of new insights and sudden illuminations) that Christ had a real body and a real flesh like our own, and that the possibility of salvation takes place in it and in it alone. We said that it is a fight waged against Greek thought, and its devaluation of the sensible and the body.* The aim of this critique, however, is not directed toward the past. It unmasks everywhere around it the achievements of Greek culture, its resurgences and oblique substitutes, before with a sudden horror it recognizes them in itself: In all who, although they accept the idea of the coming of the Word of God on earth, do not accept a real incarnation. Even if an incarnation is not conceivable without a flesh being assumed, without a coming in a body in whatever form that may be, the flesh of Christ could still be only an apparent one. Or it may be that the matter of this flesh is not that of which man is made. It is an astral, "psychic," or even "spiritual" matter. Actually, his flesh is better described as a soul, a flesh-soul or a soul-flesh, etc.

All this debris of Greek thought (or of more ancient prejudices) is not only refused across the different forms of Gnosticism; it is pieced together immediately as a compact block: heresy. "Heresy" means everything that, under various masks and through spurious and false constructions, denies the truth (in other words the reality) of Incarnation. Gnosticism becomes a heresy in the eyes of Christianity in as much as it rejects the central Christian affirmation. Irenaeus: *Against the Heresies: On the Detection and Refutation of the Knowledge Falsely So Called.* Tertullian: *The Flesh of Christ*, and *The Resurrection of the Flesh.* Athanasius: *The Incarnation of the Word: Against the Arians*, etc. Is it an accident that the most violent denunciation of Gnosticism arises in the very text in which the Incarnation is affirmed categorically, in which we find the dazzling pronouncement "And the Word was made flesh" (John 1:14)? For John also says: "Many false prophets have gone out into the world. This is how you will know if the Spirit of God inspires them: every spirit that proclaims that Jesus Christ has come among us in the flesh is from God" (1 John 4:1, 2; translation modified).†

Yet we must remember the meaning this unconditional affirmation of the incarnation of the Word of God assumes, not only in John, but

---

*Does one need to recall here that the idea taken up by Nietzsche and spread everywhere, according to which Christianity teaches the contempt of the body, is a crude untruth?

†And again: "Many who would seduce you have gone into the world: they do not profess the faith in the coming of Jesus Christ in the flesh." (2 John 7).

throughout the Gospels and the so-called canonical writings, as establishing the possibility of salvation. But how? Why and how would coming in a mortal flesh be a token of eternity? Despite the paradox, many reasons converge here, a network of implications so tight and on this point so essential that they belong to the "core" of Christianity. We will list them quickly before later proposing an explanation.

The Incarnation of the Word is constantly given in Christianity as *the manner in which the Word became man.* And this evidently implies a first condition that is constantly reaffirmed in the Fathers, namely that *the flesh of Christ is like ours.* This is the thesis that supports the enormous set of impassioned critiques directed against the heretics—all those who, as we have seen, strive to erase, minimize, and denature in every way the reality of Christ's flesh, and first of all its identity with our own. Thus, rejecting the theses of Marcion, the heirs of Valentinus, and Apelles, according to which Jesus did not have flesh, or had a flesh different from ours, or "of a particular quality," Tertullian, on the contrary, asserts that "the Christ would not be called man without having a flesh" and "a flesh like our own," a flesh that cannot be composed of anything other than human flesh.[*]

But if the Incarnation of the Word, its coming in flesh, and in flesh like ours, means that it comes in our human condition, and takes custody of it, it is because another thesis is also enveloped in John's profound affirmation: *man is defined as flesh.* For the Word [*Parole*] does not say that the Word [*Verbe*] took on the human condition and for this reason was endowed with flesh, among other human attributes; the Word says that it "was made flesh," and that is truly why, in and by this flesh, it was made man.

Is there any need to repeat how much this definition of man is opposed to the Greek conception, to the point of shattering it? For the Greeks the flesh defines only animality; there is no man, in his specific difference from the animal, except to the extent that added to this flesh is the capacity to form meanings, to speak, to perceive Ideas, in short, the Logos that the animal by itself lacks. But then it is not only the Christian vision of man (for which the human condition occurs only in and through the flesh) that brutally confronts the Greek conception. The two interpretations of the Logos are equally opposed, and are no less different. To be made flesh, for the Greek Logos (by which we mean: *to be made in itself flesh*), would not mean to be made man, but exactly the opposite, to get rid of its own essence, to close off the human condition, to be nothing more than animal. We will have to come back to this deci-

---

[*] Tertullian, CC I, V, pp. 231, 229, respectively.

sive point, but we see already that an entire intellectual universe hangs in the balance.

With the definition of man as flesh, a new implication follows. If the Incarnation of the Word means its coming into the human condition, the *relation of God to man* is also at stake, in so far as the Word is God's own. As long as this relation is established on a spiritual plane, extending from the "soul," the "psyche," "consciousness," reason, or the human spirit toward a God who is himself Reason and Spirit, this relation is conceivable. It becomes much more difficult to explain if man draws his own substance from flesh. Where does the possibility of an *internal* relation between this carnal man and God reside when the latter is clearly identified with the Logos? Doesn't this two-fold definition, resting at the heart of John's Word [*Parole*] *as a definition of the God–man (or man–God) relation*, encounter the disjunction Hellenism institutes between the "sensible" and "intelligible"?

The difficulty increases vertiginously if, examining the word of John with more attention, one recognizes that not only the general relation between God and man is here proposed under the absolutely new form of a relation between the Word and flesh, but also that this paradoxical relation is placed *within one and the same person, namely the Christ.* With this confrontation and precipitous antagonism between its constituents, the internalization of the God–man relation, which has become the Word–flesh relation in the person of Christ, calls radically into question its internal possibility—the very being of Christ is challenged. Can a God be made man in the form of the Word being made flesh, and do so in one and the same person? How should we treat an existence at the juncture of two heterogeneous substances? Is someone like the Christ conceivable?

This will constantly preoccupy the Fathers and will be the subject of all the great councils. The eminent participants that they gather through the early centuries will reflect endlessly on the person of Christ, on the possibility that he could unite in his existence two different natures, one divine, the other human. The very word *person* is one of the terms retained in order to affirm the real existence whose possibility is in question: The real, concrete, effective, singular, and actual existence of the One who, uniting in himself the two natures, remains "one and the same" as man and as God. This appeal to Greek terminology (person comes from the Greek *prosopon*, from which the Latin *persona* is derived, and this word denotes, as we know, the mask worn by theater actors) will not be the only one. The recourses to the Greek system of conceptualization, and through it to Greek ontology, multiply as the problem of the nature of Christ is posed with greater acuity. For with the Fathers it will never be a question of skirting the issue beneath a word, but of producing its intelligibility as far as can be done. Beyond the factual existence or dogmatic affirmation of Christ, the continuous effort of the councils is oriented toward the internal possibility of this existence. Could this effort succeed within the horizon of Greek culture?

The problem in any case is posed in an ever more precise manner. The union of the two natures must be the union of their properties, more precisely of two series of properties, some belonging to God, and others to man. From Nicaea to Constantinople, it is the question of the appropriation of properties or (since this is how it is stated in Greek) the appropriation of idioms. In what sense can Christ, as God, appropriate human properties? In what sense is he capable, as man, of appropriating divine properties? As difficult as it is to grasp the union or unity of the two series of properties in Christ, their parallelism also counts as an explication of his mysterious existence. As God, for example, the Christ knows all things; as man, he cannot foresee the future. Thus the series of antitheses, which always results when a divine property is brought together with its absence or limitation in man, is resolved *a priori*. An infinite understanding in God, yet "a finite understanding like our own," Kant will still say. On the one hand, the impassibility of a timeless God, as impervious to the blows of becoming as to the tribulations of history. On the other hand, *possibility*, fragility, vulnerability, hunger, thirst, sufferings, and the horrific story of Christ's *passion—his death.*

Here again Incarnation crosses the path of our thought. For as long as man defines himself through Reason, just like the Greek God in the end, the capacity for the first to appropriate the properties of the second, to participate in it, at least through "the best part of his being," is posited in principle. The communication of properties, certain ones in any case, is a virtual *a priori* that everyone will make an effort to realize in himself. With the definition of man as flesh, the two series of properties have become irreducible to one another; an uncrossable distance separates them. Does one imagine the *noûs*, eternally lost in the contemplation of the archetype, a pure crystal illumined by its light, suddenly straining with fatigue, demanding a pillow, beginning to weep upon learning of his friend's death, or marveling at the perspicacity of a woman who has just sat down by his side to listen to him, leaving her sister to care for the cooking?

Worse, does one imagine that this arch-archetypal God, the beyond of the essence, is born in the dripping womb that midwives and doctors manipulate, "a clot of blood among the refuse"? It is these unsavory representations that Gnosticism rejects; they, or what they awaken, are what Tertullian opposes with furor against Marcion in his diatribe against him: "Exposing from the exordium your hatred of birth, let us now hold forth on this filth the genitals have put into the womb, these hideous clots of blood and water . . . describe us this womb then, more monstrous by the day, weighed down . . . unleash yourself . . . against the obscene organs of a woman in labor" (CC I, IV, 223). It is certainly more difficult to think the relation between God and man when we leave the luminous horizon of Greece and it has become the relation of the Word with a flesh from a poor birth and destined for a certain death!

It is true that Tertullian, as the majority of the Fathers, in no way limits the reality of man to the reality of his flesh. If in the beginning of *De carne Christi* he claims to speak only of the latter, it is, he says, only because, "everyone is in agreement regarding his spiritual substance" (CC I, III, 211). Tertullian still thinks "Greek." Thus Christ has a soul as well as a body, and we do not begin to see any critique of the classical definition of man as composed of these two substances. This definition remains, on the contrary, implicit in the treatise *De carne*, but it will come up explicitly and repeatedly even more so thereafter.

But there is nothing of the sort in John. The profound declaration that posits God's becoming-man as the Word's "becoming flesh" adds nothing to the definition of man it advances, namely man's definition as flesh. The proposition that follows, far from making allusion to a "spiritual substance," to a "soul" of Christ, merely repeats this definition: "He dwelt among us." It is thus truly in being made flesh that the Word is made man, and it is thus, by assuming our carnal condition, that he established in this way his being-in-common with men, his "dwelling" among them. But with the Word's carnal existence, then, is not the opposition between the two series of properties (divine and human, which must be united in the person of Christ) brought to the point of unbearable tension?

Nevertheless, the possibility of this union of divine and human properties is by no means merely a theoretical problem: It is the possibility of salvation itself. So it is necessary to say more on this point and recall the schema that it will assume for each of the Fathers and across the various councils: God's becoming-man is the basis for man's becoming-God. Christian salvation does not consist in the dispensation of particular and completely pre-eminent graces: It consists in the *deification* of man. It is only when man will bear within himself divine life, which is eternal life, when he will identify himself with this life, that he will escape death. But, according to Christianity, God's becoming-man resides in the Incarnation of the Word. Thus it is by identifying himself with the Word's flesh (with the body of Christ, *corpus Christi*) that the Christian man may identify himself with God. But this possibility of salvation, which will no longer be affirmed speculatively on the intellectual plane, but, in reality, as the unity of our flesh with the flesh of Christ, presupposes another possibility: *That the unity of the Word and flesh be possible and be realized first where the Word was made flesh, that is, in Christ.*

The problem of the existence of the Christ means nothing else. It is not the problem of his historical existence. That still concerns only Jesus. It is then a question of whether Jesus really existed, if he really said what he said, that he was the Christ, the Messiah, the expected savior, and not simply a prophet. No one today, with the exception of the ignorant or sectarians, doubts this existence. The problem of Christ's existence is one of knowing if this man named Jesus, who indeed existed and who was said to be the Christ—it is for this reason alone that he was condemned—really was him. From the philosophical point of view, to which we will restrict ourselves in this book, the question is thus formulated as follows: Is someone like the Christ possible, *is the becoming-man of God* qua *the becoming-flesh of the Word conceivable, at the very least?*

It is only with a second step that, placing ourselves still on a philosophical plane, we will wonder whether the existence of Christ, thus understood as the possibility of the Incarnation of the Word, is something other than a simple possibility—is precisely an existence. A mere possibility arises from thought, but an existence never does. I can indeed imagine, suppose, claim, or affirm that I have a Thaler coin in my pocket, but the existence of the coin will never follow from an act of my thought. The existence of the Christ as the incarnate Word surpasses infinitely the conception that I can make of it, supposing that I can make one at all. Where does it come from then? How is the existence of He who is one and the same as Word and as flesh capable of reaching us, of really being given, and *of showing itself to us?*

The ultimate motive of Incarnation, which contains the possibility of salvation, is uncovered for us: *The Incarnation of the Word is its revelation, its coming among us.* If we can thus enter into relation with God and be saved in this contact with him, it is because his Word was made flesh in Christ. The revelation of God to men is thus here the fact of flesh. The flesh itself as such is revelation. If this is so, two entirely new and equally surprising questions are imposed upon us: *What must flesh be, therefore, in order to be in itself and by itself revelation? But what must revelation be in order to be accomplished as flesh, to accomplish its revealing work in the flesh and by it?*

But here is a new line of questioning, which is no less baffling. The Word of God—according to theology but perhaps also in the eyes of a sufficiently perspicacious philosophical reflection—is nothing other than the revelation of God or, strictly speaking, his self-revelation. In this case, the essence of the Word would be nothing so opposed to the flesh, *which is itself, and in itself, perceived as revelation.* On the contrary, a secret affinity would reunite them, to the extent that a single power, the power of making manifest, would inhabit them both. The crucial affirmation enunciated in John's discourse would be less paradoxical than it seems. The work of the Word, which is to accomplish the revelation of God, would go on in some way inside the flesh, rather than running up against it as an opaque and foreign term.

Reflecting upon this last line of questioning, we see that it is capable of bearing two different meanings. Either the Word has taken on flesh *in order to reveal itself to man*, in which case revelation is indeed the work of flesh, and is entrusted to it. Or the revelation of God in his Word is the doing of the Word itself. Why does this Word then need to ask the flesh for a power that would belong specifically to the Word, for a revelation that the Word has already accomplished in and by itself?

A third hypothesis remains. Flesh would be its revelation thanks to the Word, to the Word it bears within it. This is because it would be the Word that, having taken flesh in it, would accomplish its own work of revelation in it, and it would owe to the Word its power of revelation.

The first hypothesis comes up more than once in the Fathers. Whether in Tertullian, Athanasius, Origen, or even, admittedly on rare occasions, Irenaeus, the coming of the Word in human flesh is interpreted as the way in which the invisible Word of God shows itself to men and women by making itself visible to them in the form of an objective body like their own. Becoming-visible in a visible-body would be the principle of the Word's revelation. We will point out in a moment the strange construction to which the same conception will lead Athanasius, and how he is forced to base the intuition of the invisible Word upon the external appearance of its body and its machinations.

But how can we not notice that the thesis that the Word becomes-visible in the visible body, which it has taken on and assumed (a self-evident thesis and one that is supposedly definitive of Christianity), comes up against two massive difficulties? The first is that, if the Word of God took on a body apparently like their own in order to show itself to men, what would show itself to them in this appearance would really still be only a body like theirs, about which nothing would allow them to know that it is precisely not the body of an ordinary man but of the Word. Thus if the Word comes among men looking like a body of this sort, his journey on earth will unfold with insurmountable incognito. From the theological point of view, the difficulty is formulated differently, but is related to the same aporia that arose from the beginning of our approach, that of a salvation consisting in the union with a mortal body. How would this union with a perishable body contain a promise of immortality? How would the resurrection of bodies come from a union of this kind, analogous in the end to a union established between two human bodies, in the amorous fusion of man and woman, for example? It is precisely this banalization of Christ as having come in the appearance of some kind of man that Athanasius will seek to overcome by using it as a counterpoint to highlight the extraordinary character of his every action. The more modest, the more humble, and the more anonymous the man Jesus appears, the more this appearance will really be that of a human being without social or honorary distinction of any sort, foreign to all "human glory," and the more his words, which no man has ever pronounced, the more his acts, which no man has ever accomplished, will show clearly that he is not a man like others, but the Messiah sent by God to save all.

The second difficulty, which is even more radical, arises from John's discourse itself. For John does not say that the Word took on a body, or assumed the appearance of one. He says that it "was made flesh." On the one hand, it is a question of flesh and not of the body; and if the difference between flesh and body appeared essential to us from the outset, it is because flesh and not the body must serve as the central theme for understanding Incarnation in the Christian sense (or any incarnate being, undoubtedly). On the other hand, neither does John claim that the word took on the "appearance" of this flesh, but precisely that it "was made flesh." It may well also be true that one can take on the form or appearance only of a body, whereas, with regard to flesh, or to put it more rigorously, with regard to *the coming in flesh that is incarnation* (every incarnation), only the "was made" in the Johannine sense of "was made flesh" would be appropriate. For then it is no longer a question of "form," or "appearance," or "semblance," but of reality. It is in itself, in its verbal essence and reality, as Word, that the Word was made flesh.

If that is a question of the secret hidden from the beginning in the heart of things, would we now be able to glimpse a fragment of it? For as long as the Incarnation of the Word, as taking custody of the body of a man and thus of our humanity, is put forward as the addition of a heterogeneous element (this material body which is destined for decomposition) to its invisible and eternal being, we are truly dealing with obscurities, impossibilities, and even absurdities. From the first propositions of *De carne Christi*, Tertullian asked what sort of flesh Christ's flesh could be, and in particular, "Where does it come from?" In his view, if this is a flesh like our own, then it is *a flesh formed from the silt of the earth*. When this is added in a mysterious way to the Word of God, which is itself misunderstood, then this truly leads to a series of enigmas.

Here again, John says nothing of the sort. According to him, the Word's flesh does not originate from the silt of the earth, but from the

Word itself. It is of itself, in itself, and by itself that it was made flesh. Now we will make John's thesis our own, before proceeding to elucidate it. *In the silt of the earth, there are only bodies, but no flesh. Something like flesh can happen and come to us only from the Word. All the characteristics of flesh come from the Word, and are explained by it and it alone: First of all, the fact, the little fact, that flesh is always the flesh of someone, my own for example, so that it bears a "self," which is immersed within it, and from which it does not have the leisure to separate itself any more than it can be separated from itself; that this flesh is not divisible or breakable, since it is composed neither of particles nor atoms, but of pleasures and sufferings, hunger and thirst, desire and fatigue, strength and joy—a wealth of lived impressions, none of which have ever been found by rummaging through the soil of the earth or by digging through its layers of clay.* We will show that each of them draws its substance from the Word alone, and was made only of the Word. They are not made in the Greek Logos, by which only significations or concepts are formed, representations or images, which speak and reason like men do, and think like them. But they are made in an older Word that, before any conceivable world and where there still is no world, speaks to everyone, in the flesh that is their own, in its sufferings and in the intoxication of existing—in the Word as John understands it, the "Word of Life" (I John 1).

In addition, at no point does the reader of John have the impression of crossing an obstacle course, or straddling an abyss of absurdities, or being crushed against a wall of aporias—even though John lets fascinating propositions flow and joins them together, each of which, *despite the fact that it is formulated here for the first time in the history of human thought,* truly seems to be one with all the others. It is not here a question of intelligibility in the ordinary sense, admittedly, or of a "chain of reasons," and even less is it a question of our habitual manner of perceiving the world or ourselves. An intelligibility of that sort pertains to thought, and to its capacity to make visible everything that, in some way spread out before its gaze, constitutes the visible universe—a collection of things that we can really see and that we call "true," "rational," and "evident," to the extent that we can actually see them.

From the Prologue of John another type of intelligibility emerges, an Arch-intelligibility that properly overturns these ways of thinking. "Arch-intelligibility" means that a mode of revelation comes into play that is different from the one by which the world becomes visible; and that, for this reason, what it reveals is made up of realities that are invisible in this world, and unnoticed by thought. The Prologue lists them: Life, in which Arch-intelligibility consists; the Word of Life, in which this Arch-intelligibility of Life is fulfilled; and, finally, the flesh, in which the Word of Life becomes identical with each of the living beings that we are, we men and women. So an entirely new definition of humanity is formulated, which is as unknown to Greece as it is to modernity: *The definition of an invisible, and at the same time carnal, human being—and invisible in so far as carnal.*

Johannine Arch-intelligibility also has another meaning. Far from being reducible to a list, or to a succession of mental objects that are connected by necessary relations, this Arch-intelligibility concerns reality, and, even more importantly, absolute reality, as philosophy calls it, and what religion names God—the God that according to John is life.

"To live" means to undergo experiencing oneself. The essence of life consists in the pure fact of undergoing experiencing oneself, and, on the contrary, everything pertaining to matter, or more generally to the "world," is devoid of this. This very simple definition of God starting from the definition, which is itself very simple, of Life as a pure "trial of oneself" (the most difficult is often the most simple, which also means that the most simple is often the most difficult) now gives us possession of the insight that will guide our investigation, which is precisely the Arch-intelligibility we are talking about.

Arch-intelligibility belongs to the internal movement of absolute Life, which generates itself, and is nothing other than the way in which the process of self-generation takes place. Life generates itself by coming in itself, into its own condition, which is to undergo experiencing itself. Yet no trial of oneself is possible if an Ipseity does not also happen within this trial, at the same time as it does and as its condition—thus, as consubstantial with it. "Ipseity" denotes the fact of being oneself, the fact of being a Self. To the extent that a real life is produced (and not the simple "idea" or the simple "concept" of life), and thus to the extent that Life's trial of itself is itself a real trial, actually experienced and lived, and as such is inevitably singular, the Ipseity in which it occurs is itself, *qua* an actually lived Ipseity, a singular Ipseity. It is a singular and real Self, the First Living Self that Life generates, as how it is experienced and has revealed itself in this Self, which is thus its self-revelation, its Word. This is Johannine Arch-intelligibility: The very essence of absolute Life, the movement of its self-generation as its self-revelation in its Word—a Word within this movement, as the very mode whereby this movement comes about, and as old as it is. "In the beginning was the Word."

From Johannine Arch-intelligibility the first law of Life follows: No Life is possible that does not bear within it a first living Self, in which it undergoes experiencing itself and becomes life. No life without a living being, but, likewise, no living being apart from the movement whereby Life comes in itself, in undergoing experiencing itself in the Self of this living being; no living being without life.

This law, decrypted from the essence of absolute Life, concerns every possible life, and thus our own. We have also encountered it in connection with one of the most ordinary modalities of the most ordinary life: Suffering. Did we not recognize from this first contact that all suffering undergoes its own suffering and at the same time bears a "self" within it, the self who suffers, without which no suffering would be possible (if it is true that no suffering could be the suffering of no one)? Thus life is anything but the impersonal and blind universal of modern thought, whether it's a question of Schopenhauer's will-to-live or Freud's drive.

The question that motivated our investigation is now before us: Would the word that suddenly appears in verse 14 of the famous Prologue, and which pronounces the Incarnation, also come within the competency of Johannine Arch-intelligibility? Far from being absurd in this case, as it was in the eyes of the Greeks, or at least very strange, as it remains for us, this Arch-intelligibility could gesture to Life, as familiar for living beings as their own life, and returning, as every conceivable life, to the spoken word of verse one, speaking absolute Life's self-revelation in its Word. Without being necessary in the same way or in the same sense, it would nevertheless belong to the same essence of revelation, to the Arch-intelligibility that is none other, in the end, than that of absolute Life.

Now, if flesh—and, first of all, coming in flesh, Incarnation—were grasped by the first Christian thinkers as a mode of manifestation of the Word of God, and if we suspect that the flesh's mode of manifestation and the Word's mode of manifestation could indeed be the same, as modes of Life's manifestation and revelation, then a systematic elucidation, a science of this revelation as such, is needed.

Yet this science exists; it is phenomenology. So it is from phenomenology that we will seek the best way to approach the subject of our investigation. The phenomenology invented by Husserl at the beginning of the twentieth century has given rise to one of the most important intellectual movements of this era, and perhaps of all time. The brief remarks in this introduction allow us at least to know on what condition philosophy could serve as a way of access for understanding the realities of flesh, on the one hand, and coming in flesh, or incarnation—and especially Incarnation in the Christian sense—on the other. It is on the condition that it is not a Greek idea. But does phenomenology meet this first condition? In no case. This is why it now seems that a recourse to phenomenology will not prove fruitful unless it can carry out the reversal of phenomenology itself, and challenge its most habitual presupposition—unless it can substitute a phenomenology of Life for a phenomenology of the world or Being.

Why then make an appeal to phenomenology? What good does it do to begin with an antithesis? Because behind the Greek presupposition of contemporary phenomenology* a much more general difficulty is hidden, which in the end affects all possible philosophy. If invisible life evades thought's grasp, how could we even come into relation with it and speak of it in some way, as we claim to do? Don't the preceding considerations and those that will follow belong to the domain of thinking? How can this escape from itself in some way in order to make itself adequate to what is "wholly other" than it? The reversal of phenomenology will respond to this question, and at the same time will lead us to the heart of Christianity's intuitions.

So the order of analysis will be the following:

1. The Reversal of Phenomenology
2. A Phenomenology of Flesh
3. Phenomenology of Incarnation: Salvation in the Christian Sense

A doubt slips into the spirit of the reader. What exactly is this book about: philosophy and phenomenology—or theology? We will make a distinction in each case in the course of our analysis between what arises from one or another of these disciplines, before posing in our conclusion the problem of their relation, and perhaps also the problem of knowing whether that which speaks to us first and foremost would not be another Speech that, though no more heard in our lost world, still continues to call us by making living beings of us.

---

*Leaving aside its recent developments in the fundamental problematic of Emmanuel Levinas, and of those researchers participating today in the renewal of phenomenology.

1

The Reversal of Phenomenology

§1. Object of Phenomenology: The Question of "Appearance."

What is titled "phenomeno-logy" is understood in terms of its two Greek constituents—*phainomenon* and *Logos*—so that taken literally the word denotes a knowledge about the phenomenon, a science of it. Reflecting on this very simple definition, we can propose that the first term, the *phenomenon*, qualifies the object of this science, while the second, *Logos*, indicates the mode of treatment that should be applied to this object, or the method to follow in order to acquire an adequate knowledge of it. In the very title it assumes, phenomenology advances its *object* and *method*.

Since all this is in Greek, some clarifications are necessary. Heidegger provides them for us in the famous §7 of *Sein und Zeit*.* Derived from the verb *phainesthai*, which means *to show itself*, phenomenon denotes "that which shows itself, the self-showing, the manifest" (*"das was sich zeigt, das Sichzeigende, das Offenbare"*). However, this apparently trivial shift from the verb to the substantive brings about a decisive though hidden substitution. Only by taking it into account are we confronted with the true object of phenomenology. This is precisely not the phenomenon, or that which appears (*"das was sich zeigt"*), but the act of appearing (*phainesthai*). This object proper to phenomenology is what differentiates it immediately from all other sciences. The latter actually deal with numerous phenomena, which are always considered in terms of their specific content, as chemical, biological, historical, or juridical phenomena, and so on, phenomena to which the appropriate sciences—chemistry, biology, history, etc.—correspond. Phenomenology, on the contrary, makes its task the study of what these various sciences never take explicitly into consideration. Not the particular content of these various phenomena, but their essence, what makes each of them a phenomenon: the appearing in which they show themselves to us—this appearing as such.

In the phenomenon, certainly, the content, on the one hand, and the fact that it appears, on the other, go together and seem to be one. That is why ordinary or scientific thinking does not worry about disassoci-

---

*Heidegger, SZ, §7, 28 / 25.

ating them. The cup placed on the table shows itself to me. Nevertheless, neither the table nor the cup have by themselves the capacity to bring themselves into their condition as "phenomena," and this ensures that within the phenomenon, its content, on the one hand, and the fact that it appears, on the other, differ in principle.

It is Husserl who introduced this essential distinction on which phenomenology will be based. Studying the stream of lived moments of consciousness that flow temporally in us, he considers them not as mere objects but as "objects in their How" (*"Gegenstände im Wie"*).* "Objects in their How" means: Objects considered not in their particular content but in the manner in which they give themselves to us and appear to us—in the "How" of their givenness.

We can understand Husserl's proposition better within the larger context of his analysis. In hearing a musical symphony, a sound or a sono-rous phase of this sound is given to me as an expected, and thus future, phase, or as a present phase, or again as a past phase. In fact, the same sonorous phase is given to me successively in these three ways: as future, as present, and as past. So the distinction introduced by Husserl between the content that remains identical (the same *A* of a violin) and its modes of appearing, which are modified through the temporal flowing, is per-fectly established.

The distinction between the content of the phenomenon and the manner in which it appears allows us to grasp more clearly the true object of phenomenology. A new and infinite field of investigation is now open. If we want to measure its magnitude, it will suffice for us to go back over a series of equivalent terms we have been using since the beginning of this book, without yet noting their reference to an identical object, which is precisely the object of phenomenology. Here they are in verbal form: To give itself; to show itself; to occur as a phenomenon; to unveil itself; to uncover itself; to appear; to manifest itself; and to reveal itself. And in substantive form: Givenness; showing; phenomenalization; unveiling; uncovering; appearance; manifestation; and revelation.

Yet it cannot escape us that these key words for phenomenology are also, in large measure, key terms for religion, or theology. Another word (and not the least, since it has guided philosophical thinking since ancient Greece) also refers to the true object of phenomenology: the word "truth." There are actually two ways to understand truth; one of them is pre-philosophical, pre-phenomenological, and, honestly, naive: Here "truth" denotes what is true. It is true that the sky is clouded over

---

*Edmund Husserl, Hua X, App. VIII, 117 / 121.

and it might be about to rain. It is true that $2 + 3 = 5$. Except that what is true in this way (the state of the sky or a mathematical proposition) must first show itself to me. It is true only in a secondary sense and presupposes an original truth, a first and pure manifestation—an unveiling power without which no unveiling would be produced, and without which, consequently, nothing true in the second sense, nothing unveiled, would be possible. It is to Heidegger's credit that he restored an explicit phenomenological meaning to the traditional philosophical concept of truth. He distinguishes quite correctly the truth that is always more or less confused with something true, and what it is that allows this thing to be true precisely, that is, to show itself as a phenomenon: the pure act of appearing, which he calls "the most original phenomenon of truth" (*"das ursprünglichste Phänomen der Wahrheit,"* SZ, §44, 220–221 / 203; translation modified).

Decisive though it may be, the trajectory that leads phenomenology through the prestigious analyses of Husserl and Heidegger, to the most original phenomenon of truth, still only presents us with a problem. When pure appearing, pure manifestation, or pure phenomenality is the condition of every possible phenomenon (that in which it shows itself to us and outside which nothing can show itself, so that there would be no phenomenon of any kind), this undoubtedly places appearing at the heart of phenomenological reflection as its sole theme or true object, but it in no way says anything about *what this pure appearing involves.*

In §44, Heidegger's analysis brings us from truth in the secondary sense (what is true, what is unveiled) back to original truth (what unveils, unveiling). However, original truth is not presented except, in a way that is still speculative, as the condition of truth in the secondary sense, where unveiling is the condition of the unveiled and appearing is the condition of what appears. Original truth is explicitly designated as a phenomenon, "the most original phenomenon of truth." What is implied in a proposition of this sort is that original truth is itself a "phenomenon." More than this truth, it is ultimately its phenomenon that is "most original."

This means that appearing is in no way limited to making appear what appears in it; appearing must itself appear, as pure appearing. Indeed, nothing would ever appear if its appearing (the pure fact of appearing, pure appearing) did not itself, and in the first place, appear. We claimed that the table and the cup placed on it are incapable of appearing of their own doing, through their own force, or because of their nature or their own substance, *which is blind matter.* It is thus a power different from them that makes them appear. When they actually appear, offering themselves to us as "phenomena," nothing has changed with regard to this powerlessness, which is congenital to them. The appearing that shines in every phenomenon is the fact of appearing and that alone; this pure appearing is what appears, an appearing of appearing itself, and its self-appearing.

If we then question historical phenomenology about this point, about the phenomenality of the most original phenomenon of truth (about what makes pure appearing appear as such) and about what, in this pure appearing, constitutes precisely its appearance, its pure phenomenological substance, its incandescent matter, so to speak, its incandescence, then we can distinguish two moments in the texts offered for our analysis. In the first, we face a non-response. Appearance, truth (or its original phenomenon), manifestation, revelation, and phenomenality are affirmed without saying what they consist in, without even formulating the problem. The presuppositions of phenomenology remain totally indeterminate.

§2. The Initial Indeterminacy of the Phenomenological Presuppositions of Phenomenology. The "Principles of Phenomenology."

Like every investigation, phenomenology involves presuppositions. But the presuppositions proper to phenomenology present a distinctive feature. In ordinary research the presuppositions that govern reasoning are *chosen by thought and, as such, can be modified.* Thus the mathematician freely posits axioms, from which follow the series of implications that make up the theory. In the course of his work, he adds, subtracts, and changes certain propositions intended to enrich or weaken the axiomatic system, in such a way that the dependence of the theory, with respect to thought, is constantly manifest. In other sciences, such as the empirical sciences, the presuppositions are constituted by a set of properties that pertain to certain facts, and are considered as their characteristics. One wonders, for example, why a phenomenon can be designated juridical, sociological, or historical, etc.

The presuppositions of phenomenology are distinctive because they are phenomenological, and in a radical sense: It is a question of the appearing just mentioned, pure phenomenality. This is what must guide the analysis of phenomena in the phenomenological sense, considered in the manner in which they give themselves to us, in other words, in the "How" of their appearing. As long as this remains misunderstood or unquestioned with respect to what endows it with the power of appearing, the phenomenological presuppositions on which phenomenology is based remain phenomenologically undetermined. This phenomenological indetermination of phenomenology's presuppositions reflects on all the research that derives from it, to the point of rendering it uncertain or misleading.

How can we analyze the most banal (or most decisive) historical phenomenon if the mode of appearing of temporality, which determines *a priori* the mode of appearing of every historical phenomenon by conferring "historicity" upon it, has not been questioned in itself? How can we understand the coming of the Word in this world and thus its appearance in the world, if the world's mode of appearing has not first been recognized and rigorously described? And how do we know whether this coming in the world is a coming in a body, as the Greeks think, or in flesh, as John claims? How, if the modes of manifestation proper to a body and to flesh have not become the object of a systematic elucidation, one that is capable of going back to what it is, in the manifestation of a body, that makes it a manifestation (to the phenomenological material of this manifestation), so that we could know with an absolutely certain knowledge whether the phenomenological material of the body's manifestation is the material of the body itself (the silt of the earth), or not? And, posing the same question about the flesh, how do we know if the revelation of flesh is different from flesh itself? Or if, on the contrary, the revelation of flesh is identical to it, as its own substance, as its own flesh, and as the flesh of its flesh? In this case, manifestation of body and revelation of flesh differ completely, since they belong to two heterogeneous and irreducible orders of appearing. Is it not equally appropriate to pose to the Word itself the question about the phenomenality of the revelation it accomplishes? If it is the revelation of God, and if, on the other hand, it has taken on flesh like our own, would we not have cornered, in our own flesh, God himself? Revelation of God in his Word, revelation of the Word in its flesh—are these epiphanies, which are aligned in Johannine Arch-intelligibility, not in solidarity? Or, to put it more radically, *would they not take on flesh in us in the same way?*

Let us limit ourselves for the moment to the observation that the phenomenological presuppositions of historical phenomenology are indeterminate. This can be recognized in the "principles" that historical phenomenology has given itself. We shall focus on three of them.

The first principle, which Husserl borrows from the Marburg school, is stated as follows: "So much appearance, so much being." Now we are capable of recognizing the equivocal character of this proposition on account of the possible double meaning of the term "appearance." By appearance, either we understand the content that appears, or its apparition as such, the appearing itself. Following the logic of our previous analyses, we will formulate the principle in way that avoids all ambiguity, and will say, "so much appearing, so much being."

This principle is important because it establishes a correlation between two fundamental concepts, of which philosophy and common sense alike make constant use. In the eyes of common sense, admittedly, the correlation is read by going from the second to the first, from being to appearing. It is only because things first are that they can appear to me. If I go out to buy cigarettes at a tobacco shop on the next street over, I will perceive the tobacco shop when I get there, and I will go in and make my purchase. It is self-evident that the tobacco shop, the cigarettes and cigars, and the street, exist well before my errand. But in what did this prior existence of the world consist? Could it occur without a primordial appearing, apart from which no man, no animal, and no God would have the least contact with it—with the world?

Because it is first of all attentive to the power of this correlation, phenomenology will read it in another direction. When something, whatever it may be, appears to me, it at the same time is. To appear is, hence, to be. Whether it's a question of a mere image that crosses my mind, an empty signification like that of a word (the word "dog" in the absence of any real dog), or a pure hallucination, for as long as I hold myself to the effective appearing, to what appears such as it appears, I cannot be mistaken. The appearing of an image (whether something corresponds to it in reality or not) is absolutely certain. But the appearing of the image has this certainty not from the particular content of this image, but from the fact that it appears. Consequently, every existence and all possible being depends on appearing. It is in so far as appearing appears, and for this reason, that being "is," and because appearing unfurls its reign being unfurls its own, so that they seem to have only one and the same reign, one and the same essence. "So much appearing, so much being."

And yet, despite this supposed identity of essence, appearing and being in no way lie on the same plane; their dignity, so to speak, is not the same: Appearing is everything, being is nothing. Or rather, being is only because appearing appears and in so far as it does so. The identity of appearing and being is summed up in the fact that the first founds the second. Identity of essence indeed means here that there is only one and the same power at work, but this power is the power of appearing. Independently of this, and for as long as it does not appear, being is nothing—at least it is nothing for us. Being unfurls its essence (that which allows it to be) only in appearing, which has already unfurled its own essence in it, the essence of appearing that resides in its effective appearance, in its self-appearing.

If we question further the principle of phenomenology that we are examining, we will be able to discern more clearly its importance and limit. Its importance is to have placed phenomenology before ontology, subordinating the latter to the former. And this subordination is not with the intention of disqualifying ontology, and especially not traditional ontology, but on the contrary of setting it on a sure foundation. That which is, or concerning which we claim that it is, truly escapes every challenge as soon as it appears to us incontestably. And only the line of questioning concerning appearing and concerning its ways of appearing can decide, depending on whether this appearing is itself incontestable or not, whether *what appears in it*, in one way or another, in turn escapes doubt or not.

But the first principle in no way allows a response to this line of questioning. Its immense weakness is precisely its basic phenomenological indeterminancy. It assigns a name to appearing without saying what it consists in, or how it appears; without going back to the authority within it that allows it to appear; without recognizing the pure phenomenological material of which all appearance must be made, to the extent that one claims that it is what appears, in itself and first of all—without telling the nature of the brightness or how its light shines, whether it is a matter of "light" or anything else.

As long as appearing remains in itself indeterminate, however, its determination of being also remains indeterminate. One might think even more that this indeterminancy leaves us with a mere affirmation without any way of knowing what makes it legitimate. In place of a speculative ontology, the construction of which was mainly a conceptual game, phenomenology wanted to substitute a phenomenological ontology, each thesis of which would instead rest upon something indisputable, upon a real phenomenon. A "reduced" phenomenon, as the phenomenologists still say, which means excluding everything from it that is not given in a clear and distinct view, "in person," "in flesh and blood," in accordance with a complete presence where everything would be shown without withdrawal or reserve. But how do we know whether appearing responds to such a description when, content to indicate it from the outside rather than examine its incandescent substance, we still have only a formal concept of it at our disposal? To the formal concept of appearing a formal concept of being corresponds. The formal concept of being lets us know neither what being is (the power of being), nor what is (a being), nor the nature of their difference, if there is one. It does not let us know whether such a difference has a general ontological meaning or whether, on the contrary, it concerns only a domain of being, because it is dependent upon a particular mode of appearing, without any ambition to universality.

The same remarks will concern what we conventionally call the second principle of phenomenology, a principle so important, in fact, that it is put forward as a slogan: *"Zu den Sachen selbst!"* ("To the things themselves!"). The "things themselves" are the phenomena reduced to their effective phenomenological content, thus to what appears, and such as it appears. To go straight to the things themselves, taken in this sense, is to consider the immediate given in its immediacy, freed from interpretations and successive knowledge that risk covering it, and coming between it and us. However, according to what was claimed about the true object of phenomenology, one might think that phenomenology's "thing itself," which it must treat, is not first the content of the phenomenon, but rather what makes this content a phenomenon: the pure phenomenality of it, or appearing. If we then ask, with regard to appearing, what allows us to go straight to it, what way leads to appearing as such, then there is no other response than this: the appearing itself! It is pure appearing, as it appears, of itself, by itself, and in itself; it is the auto-appearing of it that takes us by the hand in some way and truly does lead us to it.

Some very serious implications are at stake here. In analyzing the Greek constituents of the word "phenomeno-logy," we had distinguished at the outset its object (the *phenomenon*) and its method (the *Logos*): the knowledge that had to be applied in order to grasp such an object correctly. The slogan of phenomenology returns us to this distinction: *"die Sache selbst,"* "the thing itself," that is, the true object of phenomenology, on the one hand, and on the other hand, the *zu*, the path that leads to it. But if it is appearing itself, as it appears of itself and in itself, in its auto-appearing, that leads us to it, does this not mean that it is phenomenology's thing itself that clears the way to itself, that *the object and method of phenomenology are one?* Not in the sense that they could be placed on the same plane, but in the very precise sense that *the object constitutes the method.* Like the lightning that rips through the night, it is its own light that makes it visible. Does the reabsorption of phenomenology's method into its object not imply in turn the elimination of it pure and simple? At the very least, does it not render the method quite useless? What need is there of a method for going to appearing and knowing it, if it is appearing that comes toward us and is made known of itself?

It is true that the objection goes against our habitual conceptions. We have the idea of a knowledge that is different from what it has to know and so is always separated from the object whose nature it strives to grasp. It now needs a number of procedures or methodologies, which it invents for this purpose, and these are the procedures and methodologies of thinking. In phenomenology, the method is a process of elucidation that aims to bring progressively to light, before thought's gaze and in the "clarity of evidence," what in this way will be known with certainty. This method, moreover, is implicitly that of all learning that strives to produce a "scientific," that is to say, well-founded, knowledge. It is founded upon evidence, in this case, and as such "rational." When it is a question of knowledge of an intelligible archetype or even the intellectual intuition of an ideal object (a geometric or mathematical object, a linguistic signification, a logical relation, etc.), do we not, as a condition of access to this intelligible, still and always insist upon a prior power of knowledge, or of intuition? And does the same not go equally for the sensible? Does not all knowledge, but more fundamentally every form of experience, refer necessarily to the *a priori* of a power of knowledge, to this *a priori* condition *of all possible experience* that Kant made the subject of his philosophy?

What about an Intelligible that escapes every prior condition, whose access, *intelligibility*, would not be subject to thought, and would not arise at the end of a process of elucidation—which would do without every process of this kind, and would precede it inexorably? A goal, if you will, but to which no path would ever lead—a goal like the one Kafka speaks of when he says, "There is a goal, but no way. But what we call the way is hesitation"? A goal to which no path would ever lead because it would be the path, the Way, and the precondition? Thus an Intelligibility placed at the beginning, and the condition of every other conceivable intelligibility? An Arch-intelligibility, which is still misunderstood, and perhaps analogous to the one John speaks of?

For the moment, it is impossible for us to respond to these questions. If we turn back to historical phenomenology, we understand why: Precisely because it left indeterminate the phenomenological presuppositions on which it rests; because the appearing toward which these presuppositions converge was not elucidated in a way that was pushed all the way to the end. What, in appearing, we have called its pure phenomenological material, or even its incandescent flesh, what shines or burns within it, must now be exposed. Or does this incandescent matter not lend itself to any "exposure" or any "evidence"—or the "sight" of any thought?

§3. The Prejudice Hidden in the Presuppositions of Phenomenology. The Ruinous Reduction of All "Appearance" to the World's Appearing.

So we should return to the presuppositions of historical phenomenology. Their indeterminacy can be noticed, we claimed, in the purely formal character of the principles in which they are expressed. "So much appearance, so much being." "Straight to the things themselves!": What Appearance? What being? Which "things"? What does "to go straight to" mean? Do we not notice here that in historical phenomenology this indeterminacy is only provisional or apparent? *Behind it, and in its favor, a certain conception of phenomenality slips in, the very conception that occurs first in ordinary thought and that at the same time constitutes the oldest and least critical prejudice of traditional philosophy. It is the conception of phenomenality that is borrowed from the perception of objects in the world, or ultimately from the appearance of the world itself.*

Certainly we cannot forget the contribution of phenomenology, its ability to distinguish within the world's phenomena between the power that makes them appear, the manner in which it does so, and, finally, this appearance itself. Still, since the phenomena which are spontaneously subjected to analysis belong to the world, the appearing drawn from them can only be the one in which such phenomena show themselves to us: the world's appearance and none other. The formal and still-indeterminate concept of appearing cedes place surreptitiously to an entirely different concept, which this time is perfectly determined. While the pertinence of the formal and empty concept of appearing extends, at least at first, to all possible phenomena, to every conceivable form of manifestation or revelation, and can serve as a guide for new questions, it is not the same when the appearing is reduced to the appearing of the world. A decisive limitation slipped fraudulently into the investigation. Modes of appearing that open onto forms of experience that are perhaps essential are excluded *a priori* by a philosophy that claims to be free of every presupposition.

Let us suppose for example that a body can be given to us only in the world, by which we mean properly the world's appearing, to the point that some of its essential properties follow from this mode of appearing and are determined by it. In this case, a phenomenology of the world will furnish a key of great fecundity for understanding corporeal phenomena. If it establishes that the *intuitions* of space and time are co-constitutive of the world's appearing, under the form of an original phenomenological spatiality and temporality, it will make use of the intelligible archetype of all possible bodies before finding in each one the properties that belong to it by virtue of its mode of appearing.

Let us now suppose that no flesh can show itself in the world (in the world's appearing) while this mode of appearing is nevertheless the only one thought knows. Everything suggests that, since the mode of revelation proper to flesh is obscured in principle, its nature would be inevitably falsified, and confused with that of the body. Since the essence of flesh would be reduced in an illusory way to the essence of the body, and since the body would be invested with a flesh that in itself is foreign to it, this flesh/body or body/flesh would be put forward as a kind of mix, a dual being, without being able to give the ultimate reason for this duplicity.

And what should we deduce from John's proposition at the center of our investigation? For the Word to have come in the flesh would equally mean that it has come in a body and thus, because a body belongs to the world, that this is the way it has come into world, by coming into a body. But to come into the world in a body also means to take on the human condition. This thus implies equally that men are beings of the world, and beings that must be understood on this basis. But here again John says nothing of the sort. According to him, men are Sons of God. Therefore they must be recognized on the basis of another intelligibility than that of the world; on the basis of an Arch-intelligibility whose Sons they are, and which belongs only to God. It shines on everything that is generated in it and by it, thus on its Word, on its coming in flesh, on this flesh itself in so far as it comes from God, and on ours finally, in as much as it is like his own. But all of this, once again, assumes a mode of appearing that is radically foreign to that of the world.

Confusing the world's appearance with all conceivable appearing does not only block access to Christianity. It corrupts the whole of western philosophy, before reaching phenomenology itself. In Husserl's phenomenology, it is his most famous principle, "the principle of principles," that exposes this confusion in all its magnitude.

In §24 of *Ideen I*, the principle of principles posits intuition, "all originary giving intuition as a source by right for consciousness.* "Intuition" is a phenomenological concept: It does not relate to an object but to its mode of appearing. This is why it is said to be "giving," because a mode of appearing is a mode of givenness. This is also why it is qualified as "originary." Because if we consider not things but the way in which they are given to us, it is evident that, for example, they can be given clearly or confusedly. If I presently perceive a table in the room where I am standing and if I concentrate my attention on it, at least on the side facing me, this is given to me originally. If it is a question of a table in the salon where my mother used to play the piano for me, I have only a vague memory of it. The perception is "an originary giving intuition," the memory is not: it is only a second re-presentation of a first perception and cannot be attained with the same degree of evidence and certitude.

Now, as we have unceasingly claimed, if intuition is a mode of ap-

---

*Edmund Husserl, Hua III, §24, 52 / 44.

pearing, we must say what this appearing consists in, how it appears, and thus how it makes appear within it everything to which it gives appearing. Under various formulations, the answer is highly illuminating, and always the same. What, in intuition, gives, and makes it a "giving" intuition, is the structure of consciousness such as Husserl understands it: this is intentionality. Intuition owes its phenomenological power to intentionality— its power to establish in the phenomenal condition, and to make phenomenality emerge in order to do this. *This bringing into phenomenality consists in the movement by which intentionality throws itself outside itself when it goes beyond itself toward what is now placed in front of its gaze,* and which Husserl calls its "intentional correlate" or even a "transcendent object." The distancing of this object in the primitive "outside," where intentionality goes beyond itself, is phenomenality in its purity. The phenomenalization of pure phenomenality (or, to speak like Heidegger, the "most original phenomenon of truth") consists in this "outside," in the "outside itself" of the very movement by which intentionality goes beyond itself.

So in this conception of phenomenality one can easily detect the way the principles of phenomenology formulated by Husserl emerge from their initial indeterminacy. It is not just the principle of principles, since intuition draws its phenomenological power (its role as a "source by right" for all consciousness) from intentionality. The slogan of phenomenology is illuminated in the same way. The *zu* of the *"zu den Sachen selbst,"* the movement that leads "straight to the things themselves," is equally intentionality. The latter is described in a rigorous way as a "relating-to the transcendent object," so that "relating-to" belongs to the reality of consciousness, is "an internal character of the phenomenon," while the object is thrown back outside it.* In this way a very clean break is traced between the substantial reality of consciousness and what is placed outside it, what is not part of it—that is what the word "transcendent" means in phenomenology.

A misunderstanding of extreme importance must then be rejected. If intentionality belongs to the reality of consciousness while the object to which it is related is situated outside it, should the power that reveals, namely, revelation itself, not be placed "within" consciousness? Would there not be in this case an "interiority" of consciousness opposed to the exteriority of the object? But in what does this supposed interiority consist? As soon as it is understood as intentionality, it is no longer anything but the movement by which it throws outside its "reality" and its "substance," drifts away, and exhausts itself in this coming outside, in the

---

*Edmund Husserl, Hua II, 46 / 35.

process of externalization in which exteriority externalizes itself as such. Because it is this coming outside that produces phenomenality, the revelation that intentionality carries out is rigorously defined: It is accomplished in this coming outside and is identical to it. To reveal in a coming outside, in a distancing, is to make visible. The possibility of vision lies in the distancing of what is placed in front of sight and then is seen by it. This is precisely the definition of the ob-ject. Ob-ject means: Placed in front and made visible in this way. Intentionality is the act of making visible that reveals an object. *Revelation is here the revelation of the object, and appearance is the appearance of the object, and in a two-fold sense: In the sense that what appears is the object, and also in the sense that, since what appears is the object, the mode of appearing involved in this appearing of the object is the object's own mode of appearing, and makes it possible—the distancing in which the visibility of everything that can become visible for us arises.*

We cannot minimize the scope of the intentional analysis inaugurated by Husserl. It consists first in a systematic description of various types of intentionalities or intuitions, of all the manners of making visible available to consciousness and with which it coincides: perception; imagination; signifying intentionalities like those that form meanings conveyed by words in language; the intuition of "essences"; categorial intuition, which makes ideal objects such as logical relations evident, etc. The great forms of experience that are ours and that we denote under a global heading as "experience of the world," "experience of the other," "aesthetic experience," in reality involve a plurality of intentionalities of different types. For example, the perception of the sensible objects that surround us implies in reality the perception of subjective appearances of them that continually flow away in us, and thus the intentionalities constitutive of the internal consciousness of time, which we have already encountered. In the analysis of the very simple phenomenon of hearing a sound, each sound, as we have seen, or each sonorous phrase of the same sound, gives us the future, the present, and finally the past. Each of these modes of appearing is the work of a specific intentionality, the "protension" that gives the sonorous phrase as to come, but first of all the future itself, the consciousness of the present that gives the present, and the retention that gives the past. One sees without difficulty that each of these types of intentionality brought to light by Husserl is indispensible for the most elementary perception of a worldly object.

So with the discovery and analysis of these multiple types of intentionalities at work in the infinite diversity of human experiences, an extraordinary extension of the field of vision takes place. Because each type of intentionality is properly a way of making visible what would never be seen without it, this extension of the reign of seeing is also an extension of the domain of what is seen, and thus, to a large degree, is the discovery of a new domain of objects. It is a question of an enlarged and deepened understanding of all types of objects to which it is possible for us to relate.

The intentional definition of experience confers a new characteristic on it that also deserves to be mentioned briefly. Intentionality is indeed never limited to the vision of what is seen through it. The nature of what is seen, on the contrary, is such that one must discern in it what is really seen, given in itself, "in person," and what is only an "empty intention." Thus, in the perception of a cube, only one of its sides is perceived by me with incontestable evidence, while the others are only intended without being actually given. The same goes for the successive appearances of the house, where only the current phase contains a proper given. And yet intentionality never limits itself to the intuition of the visible side, but always projects itself toward the sides or phases that are not given. Every "fulfilled" intuition is surrounded by a horizon of potential appearances, every effective presence by a horizon of non-presence or virtual presence. Because intentionality aims, beyond the given, at the non-given, it is never an isolated act, but is inscribed within a process of knowledge whose immanent teleology is to increase continuously the field of vision. In a process like this, all the significations potentially implied in the present evidence come to evidence in turn, so that they complete, confirm, invalidate ("strike it out," Husserl says), modify, or correct it in some way. It is therefore each time a new evidence, a *new seeing*, that enables the indefinite progress of consciousness.

Because the structure of consciousness is borrowed from that of intentionality, the making visible in which this consists governs all the relations that bind man to being. In this sense phenomenality is the precondition of being—by making it visible. This empire of the visible stands out vividly in the following text by one of Husserl's assistants: "We must see, only see." And it is claimed no less explicitly that this seeing is the principle, which no longer needs to be analyzed, but only deployed: "Vision must be put into operation, establishing the originary evidence so that it is the ultimate criterion [. . .], vision is legitimated only in its operation [. . .] we can not go behind vision [. . .]. Vision can be imprecise or incomplete, but only a new vision that is more precise and more complete can rectify this. Vision can 'deceive', or can mis-see: The possibility of deception contradicts vision so little that only a better vision can rectify deception."*

Intentionality is the "relating to" that relates to everything we can

---

*Eugen Fink, "Le problème de la phénoménologie," in *De la phénoménologie*, French trans. Didier Franck (Paris: Editions de Minuit, 1974), respectively pp. 212 and 225. Again Fink writes: "The hypothesis of Husserlian phenomenology rests upon the supposition that originary consciousness understood as intentional is the true access to being."

access as something held in front of us. Thus we discover the immense empire of being. But how is this "relating to" related not to every possible ob-ject, to every "transcendent" being, but to itself? *How is the intentionality that reveals all things revealed to itself?* Is it by directing a new intentionality onto itself? Doesn't the question rely on intentionality? Can phenomenology escape the bitter destiny of classical philosophy of consciousness, pulled into an unending regression, obligated to place a second consciousness behind the one that knows—in this case a second intentionality behind the one that is supposed to be snatched from the night? Or is there a mode of revelation other than the way intentionality makes visible, a revelation whose phenomenality would no longer be that of the "outside," or of this foreground of light that the world is?

There is no response to this question in Husserl's phenomenology. So an extremely serious crisis arises in it. This crisis stems first from the reductive character of the concept of phenomenality it employs. Is our destiny truly limited to the experience of the world, whether it is an issue of a sensible or intelligible world? Does to know mean anything other than to see? And if knowledge consists in such a vision, what will we say about vision itself? *Who has ever seen his own vision?* Can all our experiences, especially those that provoke the "great hunt" Nietzsche discusses, be shut up within consciousness in the sense of a relation between seeing and what is seen? Are they only ever *theoretical* experiences?

More serious than the reduction, which remains implicit when it is not undertaken as a deliberate decision, is the aporia that follows from it. The very possibility of phenomenology in general becomes problematic if intentionality is incapable of securing its own promotion into its condition as a phenomenon, if the principle of phenomenality escapes it. *Can what is seen still be seen if vision itself sinks into the night and is no more?*

§4. The Crisis of Phenomenality in Heidegger. The Ontological Destitution of the World's Appearing.

But the crisis of phenomenality that will shake the foundation of Husserl's phenomenology is not proper to it. It comes from the very concept of "phenomenon" that he uses, but which, as we know, originates in Greece. It runs through the entire development of western philosophy before determining that of phenomenology itself. Let us therefore return to §7 of *Sein und Zeit*, which provided our initial approach to this concept. Whereas the derivation of *phainomenon* from the verb *phainesthai* merely suggests the idea of "something that shows itself," which appears in general and in a still undetermined way, the mode of appearing implied in the phenomenon in question is, on the contrary, perfectly defined. As Heidegger recalls, *phainesthai* is the middle form of *phaino*, which means "to bring into daylight," "to place in brightness" (*an den Tag bringen, in die Helle stellen*). Its root *pha, phos* denotes light, clarity, or, as Heidegger continues in this decisive text, "that within which something can become manifest, visible in itself" (*d. h. das, worin etwas offenbar, and ihm selbst sightbar werden kann*, SZ §7, 28 / 25). Appearing thus signifies "coming to light" or "taking place in the light," in the horizon of visibility within which all things can become visible for us. However, before this appearing can take place within the horizon of light and be uncovered for us, the horizon itself must be opened and show itself; the horizon must become visible. The horizon becoming visible is the world's appearing. So appearing cannot mean simply coming into the light (the world's light) and becoming visible in this. Appearing denotes the coming of the world itself, the emergence of light, and the horizon becoming visible.

The second part of *Sein und Zeit* confirms brilliantly that this coming of the world consists in a coming outside and thus, as we said, in an externalization of exteriority as such. The phenomenology of the world that it constructs is a pure phenomenology. The world is no longer confused, in a naive way, with the sum of things that show themselves in it, with the totality of what is, and that Heidegger, in his Greek language, names "being" [*l'etant*]. The account of what appears has given way to that of appearing. Then this appearing is thought as time. Though it was received as if it were absolutely new, Heidegger's conception of time in fact stems from that of Husserl, to which we have already alluded. In this relationship (which will also work in the opposite direction), it will be easier for us to grasp one and then the other.

We have seen how, in hearing a sound, consciousness is projected toward the expected (future) phase of the sound, through an intentionality called protension. This expected phase comes in the present; it is perceived in a consciousness of the now, before sliding just as soon into the past, which is *retained* in an intentional consciousness of the immediate past, called "retention." These three intentionalities function at the same time when a continuous sound is heard, and they constitute the temporal grasp of it. But the grasp of this temporal object, which is the continuous sound, is first a grasp of time itself, an "internal consciousness of time," if it is true that the intentional grasp of the sound's future phase presupposes *a grasp of the future as such*, the grasp of the current phase, a grasp of the now as such, the grasp of the sliding into the past of the phase just present, a grasp of the past as such. While the intentionally constituted sounding phases never stop sliding from the future to the past, the intentionalities that give them do the same: They each pass continually in the flow that, according to Husserl, makes up our original subjectivity.

This continuous sliding of phases of an original temporal flow leads Heidegger to substitute for the traditional concept of time what he calls, in a way that is very significant, a *temporalization of temporality* (*die Zeitigung der Zeitlichkeit*). Time "is" not in the manner of some thing, but occurs in the form of a pro-jection of a horizon in front of us, which is the horizon of the future. This horizon in fact never stops widening before us as something that comes towards us, which comes into the present before sliding in to the past. Husserl's three intentionalities that are constitutive of internal time consciousness (protension of the future, consciousness of the now, retention of the past) have become three "Ek-stases," which are of the future, the present and the past. In the continuous passage of these three ekstases into one another (of the future into the present and into the past) the horizon of visibility is formed, of which the world's ap-pearing is composed. The world's appearing comes about in this way in the form of the temporalization of temporality—its appearing, its pres-ence for us, or, as Heidegger says, its "being-there," its *Da-sein*.

Of what does this appearing consist, and what makes it appear? Precisely the coming outside as such, the "outside itself" we have men-tioned. If temporality makes appearing happen, therefore, it is because it is nothing other than the way externalization originally becomes ex-ternal in the triple form of the three Ek-stases, each of which denotes a fundamental mode in which this coming outside is completed. Hence Heidegger's thesis avoids all equivocation. "Temporality is the original 'outside itself' in and for itself" (*Zeitlichkeit is das ursprüngliche 'Außer-sich' an und für sich selbst*). No less explicitly, he states that the appearing that appears in this way in the Ek-stases in which temporality is temporalized is precisely the world's appearing, its way of "being-there," and of being present. "The world [. . .] is temporalized in temporality. It is with the 'outside itself' of the Ek-stases that it 'is' 'there'" (*Die Welt [. . .] zeitigt sich in der Zeitlichkeit. Sie 'ist' mit dem Außer-sich der Ekstases 'da'*, SZ, §65, 329 / 302; §80, 365 / 334; translation modified). So with force and exemplary clarity, Heidegger reaffirms that the most original phenomenon of truth is identified with the appearing of the world, and he does so with a very precise description of the way this appearing appears: As the Ek-stasis of the "outside itself" that the world and time identically "are."

The various forms of critique that Heidegger aimed at Husserl's in-tentionality amount to a reproach for passing over in silence the "being" of intentionality, or for having placed it inside a consciousness as if it were in a "box." But if, in a phenomenology, being is always second in relation to the appearing that founds it; and if, on the other hand, the consciousness in which one places intentionality is "always consciousness of something," precisely this bursting outside itself that is intentionality, then it is only the appearing of this intentionality that can and must be called into question. As long as this appearing is understood, based on the *phainomenon* and the Greek *phainesthai*, as a coming to light, and as long as the latter lights up when the "outside itself" is externalized, or in the clearing of an "Ek-stasis," then a critique of this sort, from a phenomenological point of view, has no content.

Three decisive characteristics pertain to the world's appearing. A brief enumeration of them will serve as an introduction to the phenomenology of flesh, whose first thesis will be, as we have suggested, that no flesh can appear in the world's appearing.

1) Provided that the world's appearing consists of the "outside itself," in the coming outside of an Outside, then everything that shows itself in this shows itself on the outside—as exterior, as other, and as different. Exterior, because the structure of the Ek-stasis in which it shows itself is exteriority; other, because this ek-static structure is the structure of a primordial alterity (everything outside me is other than me, everything outside itself is other than itself); different, because this Ek-stasis is equally a Difference; it is the operation that, hollowing out the gap of a distance, makes different everything to which appearance is given with the help of this distancing—in the horizon of the world.

What differs is thus two-fold. On the one hand, it is a question of the horizon, which is formed in the gap of this Difference and becomes visible in it. On the other hand, it is a question of that which is different, of what appears in the appearing constituted in this way by this horizon. Difference is here the difference between that which appears and the horizon in which it shows itself, the difference between what appears and the appearing itself. How can we not recognize the distinction with which phenomenological analysis begins, in order to dissociate its own subject from those of the sciences, the distinction between things and the way in which they show themselves, between the "phenomena" and pure phenomenality? We are beginning to suspect that such an opposition does not have the absolutely general meaning that we were trying grant it initially. We are certainly permitted to isolate the "thing itself" of phenomenology, whose task is to elucidate it. We cannot forget one of our previous remarks, however: The fact that, since the phenomena, which are brought under consideration with the aim of extricating from them the essence of pure phenomenality, are phenomena of the world, this phenomenality is, by the same token, the world's phenomenality. It would not be the case for the essence of every conceivable phenomenality that appearing differs from everything that appears in it, but only for the nature of this particular mode of appearing, which consists in the Difference of the "outside itself."

An appearing of this sort turns away from itself with such violence, it casts outside with such force (since it is nothing other than this original expulsion of an Outside), that everything to which it gives appearing can indeed never be anything but exterior in the terrible sense of that which, put outside, chased in some way from its true Dwelling, from its Homeland, and deprived of the goods most proper to it, is henceforth abandoned, without support, and lost—prey to the abandonment to which Heidegger would deliver man by making him, as "being in the world," a being of this world and nothing more.

2) The appearing that unveils in the world's Difference does not only make different everything that is unveiled in this way; this appearing is totally indifferent to it in principle. It neither loves it nor desires it, nor protects it in any way, since it has no affinity with it. Whether it is a question of the sky that is clouded over, or of the equality of a circle's radii, of a goat or a seaplane, of an image or a real thing, or even of the formula that would contain the secret of the universe, hardly matters to it. Like the light Scripture speaks of and that shines on both the just and the unjust, the world's appearing illumines everything it illuminates without making a distinction between things or persons, in terrifying neutrality. *There are* victims and executioners, charitable acts and genocides, rules and exceptions, abuses of power, wind, water, and earth; and all this stands before us in the same way, in the ultimate way of being that we express by saying: "it is," "there is."

3) Except that the indifference of the appearing of the world to what it unveils in Difference makes it anything but a Father for his Sons, a brother for his brothers, a friend for his friends (a friend that knows everything his friend knows, a brother that knows everything his brothers know and especially the first among them, the Firstborn Son)—a difference of this sort, we claim, cannot hide a more radical destitution. *The appearing of the world is not only indifferent to everything it unveils, it is incapable of conferring existence on this.* Undoubtedly, the incapacity of the world's appearing to account for what is unveiled in it explains its indifference toward what is unveiled. Indifference, neutrality, etc., here mean powerlessness, and that is where they originate. Heidegger, who was the first to think the concept of the world in its original phenomenological meaning as pure appearing, was mistaken neither about this indifference (the anxiety in which everything becomes indifferent) nor this powerlessness. Unveiling unveils, uncovers, and "opens," but does not create (*macht nicht, öffnet*). A being, what is, gives itself in its very unveiling as indepen-

dent of the power that unveils it, as anterior to that power. The "there is," the "it is," cannot say *what* "is" or *what* "there is," and this is because it has never been able to bring it into existence.

How is it possible not to notice that this situation calls seriously into question the fundamental principle of phenomenology? According to this principle, phenomenality does deliver being. Only from appearing and only in so far as appearing appears can anything at all be capable of being. The precedence of phenomenology over ontology is just that. Yet this precedence is broken in the case of the world's appearing, if it is true that it is powerless to bring into being that to which it gives appearing. In this case, what appears in the world, even though actually appearing in it, still does not exist. And there is more: It does not exist precisely because it appears in the world. The principle "so much appearing, so much being" is here not only called into question, it is properly reversed. We must confront this extraordinary paradox. But let us first ask: Can we cite a single case, or a single example, that presents us with a situation as incredible as *this reciprocal exclusion of being and appearing?*

§5. The Criterion of Language. The Breakthrough and Limits of the Phenomenological Interpretation of Language.

There is one such case, and not a minor one: the case of language. Language is not only one of the recurring themes of twentieth century thought; it also concerns the highest point of our investigation. We will find it repeatedly, and where we would least expect it, in connection with the body and the flesh—and even more so with Incarnation. Can we forget that, for Christianity, Incarnation is the fact of the Word, and that the Word is an Utterance?

Another particular reason that the question of language is decisive for us is that phenomenology has given it an entirely new clarity. From now on, language cannot be the exclusive privilege of "philosophy of language" any more than it can the various disciplines, which are always more numerous, that have directly or indirectly made it the object of their reflection, such as linguistics, literary criticism, psychoanalysis, etc.—but we could also cite the human sciences in their entirety.

Phenomenology's great discovery concerning language is to have subordinated the analysis of language to a foundation without which it is no longer able to function. Yet a subordination of this sort is consistent with phenomenology's presupposition: It is the subordination of the phe-

nomena of language to pure phenomenality. Far from obliterating the
specificity of linguistic phenomena, this alone presents us with their most
original possibility. It is called *Logos.*

We recognize one of the two terms from which what is called
"phenomeno-logy" is constructed. In the analysis of §7 of *Sein und Zeit,*
phainomenon, the phenomenon, at first denotes the object of phenomenology, and Logos its method. When pure phenomenality (coming to
light in the world's light) is then substituted for simple phenomena (what
is shown in this light) in order to define the true object of phenomenology (its "thing itself"), then the identity of the object and the method of
phenomenology is shown to us. The phenomenality of the phenomenon,
the light in which it shows itself, leads to it and thus defines the method
to be followed in order to reach it.

But this reduction of the method to the real object of phenomenology also concerns language, if it is true that *we cannot speak of any thing
unless it first shows itself to us. Just as everything we say about it and can say
about it, every predication that we could formulate about it, obeys this inescapable
condition.* That is the decisive intuition that emerges in §7: The Logos is
the final possibility of all language; it is the original Speech that speaks
in every word. It does so to the extent that it is identified with the pure
phenomenality on which it is based, which is one with it. Phenomenality
and Logos ultimately mean the same thing.

Yet how can we forget the presupposition that governs Heidegger's
entire analysis, and precisely at the moment when language, defined as
Logos, first receives the possibility of phenomenality, to the point of being
identical with it? Phenomenality and Logos are interpreted in the Greek
sense: They both denote the world's appearing. But it is this very appearing whose principal features we are examining. After having established
how this appearing differs from everything that shows itself in it, we have
noticed its basic ontological powerlessness—its incapacity to bring into
being that to which it gives appearing. It uncovers the being, Heidegger
said, but does not create it. Yet "being" [*l'etant*] denotes the totality of
what is, the whole collection of things whose infinite diversity makes up
the content of the world: What is in question is this content, and the
reality of it, which has always been a human concern. What would the
world's pure appearing be, independent of this content, and what would
the Ek-stasis of time's pure horizon of becoming visible be if nothing ever
became visible in it? A pure time cannot be perceived, Kant claimed. In
any event, a formidable difficulty remains: *if the world's appearing is in principle incapable of laying down the reality of that whose appearance it gives, then
where does that appearance come from?*

The destitution of the world's appearing, which is incapable of bringing any ordinary reality into existence, highlights language—*this* language, which finds its possibility in the Greek *Logos* and *phainesthai*, in the world's appearing! If every conceivable language (or this one, in any case) must make visible what it speaks of, together with what it says about it, is it any surprise that it would reproduce the deficiency of the appearing that makes any showing possible?

Language also repeats the structure of this appearing. The property of language indeed (a language of this kind) is that it is related to a referent external to it whose reality it cannot establish. A similar deficit is masked in the case of everyday language, which is content most often to accompany the perception of objects that we have before our eyes. "Take out that dog that won't stop barking!" The way ordinary language has of standing alongside reality, and of going at the same pace, is what hides the abyss that separates them.

Poetic language unveils this abyss, because unlike everyday language, what it speaks of is never there. When I read Trakl's poem, now famous from the commentary that Heidegger offered on several occasions*—"When snow falls against the window, / Long sounds the evening bell . . . / For so many has the table / Been prepared, the house set in order."—I "see," in a certain way, the snow and the window, I hear, so to speak, the ringing of the bell, I represent to myself the table prepared for the sacred meal. And nevertheless, in the room in which I read and meditate on this poem, there is nothing at all of what it mentions. The window does not open out to the snow, no bell rings, and the table is not set. Snow, window, sound of the bell, a meal, all these strange, discolored, fantastical apparitions float on the void. When the poet calls them by name, they become present without finding a place among the objects that surround me, in a kind of absence, like visions in a dream, or death blossoming over. They are present in the sense that, born from the speech of the poet, they appear, but they are absent in the sense that, *though appearing, they are deprived of reality.* The principle of phenomenology now reads: "So much appearing, so much unreality."

But poetic language is not responsible for the destitution to which we are referring. It is the property of every language that relates to an external referent to be incapable of conferring any reality on it but an illusory one. But neither is it language as such that manifests this powerlessness; *it is the appearing from which it borrows its capacity to make visible that de-realizes in principle every reality shown in it.* Because it is thrown outside

---

*Cf. the lectures gathered in *Unterwegs zur Sprache*, GA 12 (Frankfurt a. M.: Vittorio Klostermann, 1985) / *Acheminement vers la parole* (Paris: Gallimard, 1976) / *On the Way to Language* (New York: Harper & Row, 1971).

itself in the very process by which it becomes visible, and is put outside itself in this way, it is properly emptied of its substance, reduced to a film with no thickness, no depth, and no consistency—reduced to these phantom apparitions over which the gaze can only slide, going from one to another, without ever penetrating the interior of any content. Language is thus here only a revealer. There is no need for it to detect a deficiency that is rooted in the phenomenological structure of the world itself.

§6. The Paradox of the "World" as a Power to Derealize.

It is a great paradox indeed that the world (its appearing) derealizes in principle everything shown in it. Isn't what we see around us in the world, isn't that, on the contrary, the real, the only thing for which there is immediate evidence, and which thus makes it the object of universal belief? Nonetheless, a quick examination of the greatest philosophies that have thought the *phenomenon* of the world suffices to shake this self-evident conviction. When at the dawn of modern thought, whose essential themes he would determine, the cobbler Jakob Böhme formulated the immense and apparently theological question* *Why did God create the world?*, the extraordinary response he put forward belongs to phenomenology. God created the world *in order to manifest himself.* The phenomenological structure of this sort of manifestation is clearly indicated. It consists in an objectivation, specifically the objectivation of the world, in such a way that (here at the end of the Renaissance as well as in Greece) placing the self outside itself gives rise to manifestation. Since the issue is actually the manifestation of God—a manifestation that Böhme calls his *Wisdom* (another name for the Word)—the manifestation is thus produced as an objectivation of an initial Outside.

But this is what matters for us now, and this is what at once founds and condemns modern thought, which in broad terms follows from Böhme's unknowing repetition of the Greek presupposition.† For as long

---

*A theological question, but of which it is permissible to give a purely philosophical formulation: "Why is there something like a world?"

†We say "unknowing" because this repetition occurs under the authority of a concept of subjectivity that is foreign to Greek thought, which is centered on the question of Being, or Nature. But when a more radical reflection seeks what they obscure under the diversity of conceptual systems, when subjectivity is grasped as intentional, Being as "ecstatic Truth," and Nature as coming outside, we must indeed recognize that a single phenomenological basis secretly determines this thinking, whose different formulations lose all decisive character.

as God does objectify himself in order to be known, opposing himself to himself in his own Wisdom, which is this self-knowledge, the phenomenological milieu deployed by this initial opposition is still, according to Böhme, only virtual: a mere diffuse clarity that is unable to transform itself into an actual manifestation, whether of forms or of singular objects. The appearance of the latter requires that an element foreign to light and to pure appearing be posited—thus an opaque element, "material" in the sense of a material thing, in short, a "being." Only by coming up against this opaque being, by reflecting itself upon it like the tain of a mirror, can light be illuminated and become light. In his conception of a nature within the Absolute, Böhme maintains this requirement that an element opaque to light is the condition for its own illumination. So Böhme's God bears within himself an eternal body because he wants to manifest himself by objectifying himself in a world, and because a pure objectivation is still powerless to produce from itself the concrete content that must be shown in it. This content is then posed metaphysically—purely and simply affirmed—and this signifies once again that its reality does not depend upon the phenomenological milieu in which it unveils itself.

This situation, which we have described as the ontological destitution of the world's appearing (the incapacity of this appearing to account for what appears in it), is at once unmasked and disguised in Jakob Böhme's philosophy. Two totally different powers, the objectivation of a horizon of becoming visible, on the one hand, and the creation of a concrete content called to become visible in it, on the other, are attributed to a single theologico-metaphysical moment and are thereby confused. Nonetheless, by showing that a "nature" or "body" (a being) must be added to the appearing of the world in order for it to be something other than an undifferentiated and empty milieu, Böhme denounces at the same time the deficiency of such an appearing left to itself. The power of God here serves only to conceal the powerlessness of objectivation as such.*

It is this very powerlessness of the world's appearing, veiled and unveiled in Böhme, that the *Critique of Pure Reason* exposes plainly. Kant understands the question of the world as a phenomenological question. That is why the *Critique* consists—in its essential positive sections, which are the

---

*Through German Idealism runs the sophism that consists in attributing to objectivation the power of creating the content objectivated in it, which in reality it only "uncovers." Against this sophism Marx unleashes a brilliant critique directed at Hegel in the third of the *1844 Manuscripts*. On this topic, cf. Michel Henry, *Marx I, Une philosophie de la réalité,* and *II, Une philosophie de l'économie* (Paris: Gallimard, 1976), vol I., pp. 297–314 / *Marx: A Philosophy of Human Reality,* trans. Kathleen McLaughlin (Bloomington: Indiana University Press, 1983), pp. 135–38.

"Transcendental Aesthetic" and the "Transcendental Analytic"—of an extremely rigorous description of the phenomenological structure of the world. It is co-constituted by the *a priori* forms of the pure intuitions of space and time, as well as by the categories of the understanding. "Forms of pure intuition" means pure ways of making visible, or making appear, considered in themselves, independent of the particular and contingent content (denoted as "empirical") of that which they make visible each time. *A priori* means that these pure ways of making visible precede every actual experience, that appearing precedes and makes possible everything that appears in it. Beyond their specificity (substance, causality, reciprocal action), the categories of the understanding have the same fundamental phenomenological meaning, as pertaining to this "making-visible" and making it possible by ensuring its unity. And yet the phenomenological structure of this unifying power is the same as that of the pure intuitions; it is a making-visible and (like Böhme's objectivation, or the Greek *phainesthai*) consists in posing outside what thereby becomes visible. According to Kant's decisive affirmation, the forms of intuition and the categories of the understanding are both representations. This way of representing is called *vor-stellen* in German, which means very precisely "to pose in front." Yet what is important for us in all this, the repeated thesis of the *Critique*, is that the phenomenological formation of the world in the conjoint and coherent action of these various instances of making visible is forever incapable of positing by itself the reality that constitutes the concrete content of this world—a reality that Kant had to demand from *sensation.*

We find the same situation in Husserl. Consciousness is *always* consciousness of something. The intentionality that defines its phenomenological structure projects us immediately outside onto the things that it attains "in person." When considered more closely, however, these first achievements of phenomenology strangely decompose. Intentionality does not produce the immediate givenness of the thing; rather, it produces the signification that the thing has of being given immediately. But every signification is an unreality, an object-of-thought—a "noematic unreality." So the object of the most immediate perception is precisely not, for Husserl, a reality, but an "ideal pole," a rule of presentation for the series of sensible appearances through which it shows itself to us and which are related to it—through precisely the intentionality that aims at them as moments or qualities of this object-pole. This is the case for the "cube" object, the "house" object, and for the series of concrete appearances I experience successively if I "turn around" them.

Is reality thus seated in the appearances themselves, in "sensory *data*"? But these in turn decompose. If we examine the sensible, colored appearances of some object, we should make a distinction between the colored area spread over the surface of the object, and on the other hand the pure subjective impression of color, whose color spread in front of the gaze is only an intentional projection. In Husserl's terms: the noematic color apprehended on the object, visible on it (*noematische Farbe*), on the one hand, the impression of color, lived, and invisible (*Empfindungsfarbe*), on the other. *And yet the reality of the color is only where it is felt in us, in the impressional or sensual color, in the* Empfindungsfarbe. In a way that is as paradoxical as in Kant, but equally explicit, *the real content of the sensible world does not arise from its phenomenological structure—re-presentation for one, intentionality for the other—but from the impression alone.*

§7. The Now Crucial Question of the Impression, Understood as Founding Reality. The Problem of Its Phenomenological Status. Intentionality and Impression.

The impression thus calls for further analysis. It is a question of knowing what the exact situation of the impression is relative to consciousness, or, to ask it in more phenomenological terms, what its phenomenological status is. Husserl has responded to the first question with precision. While the color that is spread over the object, which has thereby become visible (the noematic color), is exterior to consciousness, the impressional (material, hyletic, and invisible) color belongs to the reality of consciousness just like intentionality does. The reality of consciousness is thus divided between two distinct elements. Admittedly, these elements are not only different, but also heterogeneous, if it is true that *the originary impression, the pure sensual element, is in itself foreign to intentionality*: "The *sensuous, which in itself has nothing pertaining to intentionality*" (Hua III §85, 172 / 203, Husserl's emphasis).

Given that appearing in Husserl's phenomenology is entrusted to intentionality in the form of a making visible that throws outside that which becomes visible by being posited in this outside, a crucial question cannot be avoided: *What about the appearing of the impression itself?* Since it lacks all intentionality, is the impression then handed over to the night, unconscious? Does it not also owe its appearing to an intentionality that takes it in view?

But as we have seen, this last question strikes at intentionality itself. It was necessary to ask: How is the intentionality that makes all things visible revealed—to itself? To hand this task over to a second intentionality that would aim at the first is to enter into an infinite regression. Several texts that are as rare as they are laconic seem to ward off the menacing aporia. They give a glimpse of a consciousness, and thus an intentional consciousness (since all consciousness is intentional), that is in itself an impression, an impressional consciousness. Consciousness would seem to impress upon itself in such a way that this original self-impression would reveal it to itself, making possible its own revelation. In this case, the distinction Husserl inscribes in the very reality of consciousness between a non-intentional impressional element and the intentional element would be overcome, and in favor of the impression. Not only would the "hyletic," material layer of consciousness be composed of impressions; the "noetic," intentional element would be ultimately of the same nature. In it, too, an impression, in its impressional material, would accomplish the ultimate revelation. As the *phenomenological material of the intentional act*, it would allow the revelation of that act. Is it an accident if this revolutionary philosophical thesis (revolutionary even if one can relate it historically to Hume) is formulated with regard to the specifically intellectual modes of intentionality, where the "noetic" character of consciousness is evident? "The consciousness that judges a mathematical state of affairs is *an impression*." But the same goes for all modes of consciousness, of belief for example. "Belief is actually present belief; it is an *impression*." It is also claimed that the impression reveals belief itself without this belief having any need to be apprehended objectively by a subsequent intentionality, which by aiming at it would make it into a "psychic state." "We must distinguish *belief in itself or the belief-sensation*, from the believing in the apprehension, understood as my state or condition, my judging" (Hua X, §45, 96 / 101; App. II, 103 / 109, our emphasis).

These indications, though liable to challenge the primacy of the Greek *phainomenon*, remain unfortunately scarce. Quite quickly a slippage occurs: The *hyle*, or matter of consciousness (the impression) ceases to be understood as phenomenological in itself. It no longer brings about the original revelation in and through its very material—in its impressional matter thus grasped as pure phenomenological material. On the unquestioned concept of matter that is in itself phenomenological, the schema from afar is superimposed, which means that matter is only ever matter for a form that in-forms it and which, through this informing, gives appearing to it and turns it into an actual reality, into a "phenomenon." The form that makes visible a matter that is in itself undetermined and blind is for Husserl precisely intentionality. Because an intentional gaze comes across matter, which is composed of impressions and obscure sensations, and which the intentional gaze illuminates by throwing in front of itself, matter becomes a sensible given, or "sense *datum*." A given that no longer owes its givenness to its very material, to the impressions and sensations of which it is made, but to this gaze. So the circle is closed and Husserlian phenomenology will never escape it. To answer the aporetic question of knowing how intentionality is revealed to itself before it makes the totality of being visible for us, a few illuminating texts appealed to the impression. But now, permeated by its gaze and thrown into the world by it, the impression owes to intentionality the power to show itself to us.

"Not only the hyletic moments (the sensed colors, sounds), but also the animating construals—thus *both together*: the *appearing* of the color, the sound, and and thus of any quality whatever of the object—belong to the 'really inherent' composition of the mental process" (Hua III, §97, 203–4 / 238, Husserl's emphasis). It was already very difficult to understand how two heterogeneous elements (the non-intentional hyletic moment, and the intentional apprehension that animates it) can be united in a single reality (of consciousness), which is a unitary reality here designated as "the real composition of the mental process." But finally, by taking the two together as Husserl wants to do, we obtain the totality that is the "appearance of color." But we do so in such a way that this totality is immediately decomposed into two elements: that which possesses the power to appear and that which lacks it. Then the aporetical circle is clear, where each element making up the reality of consciousness requires the other to make it appear (intentionality the impression, and the impression intentionality). We are now considering the global experience, which is the "appearance of color" taken as a whole. In this whole, the appearance of color is not the fact of color; the experience of the sound is not the sound itself (its sound); the impression's revelation is not the work of the impression. The material (whether visual or sonorous or otherwise), the pure impressional material, is now only matter for a form that is responsible for making it manifest—the ek-static form of the "outside itself." The classical opposition between form and matter is secretly based upon the Greek concept of *phainomenon*, and expresses that concept in its own way.

When the power of appearing abandons the impression in favor of intentionality, another displacement is produced, one that is equally decisive because it is the immediate consequence: Unveiled by intentionality, permeated by its gaze, the impression is no longer revealed in itself, where it impresses upon itself. It is torn from its original site in order to be thrown onto the object; it then shows itself as one of the moments of that object, as one of its qualities, an *objective* quality which is explicable by it in the end, and visible *qua* part of its objectivity—"a sensible *objective* quality." When, in the text just cited, the hyletic moment and the intentional apprehension are taken together to constitute the "appearance of color, sound, etc.," the color, the sound indeed, offer themselves like "any other quality of the object."

With the impression now placed outside itself, the great illusion of the "sensible world" is born. This illusion is two-fold. Its first facet consists in believing that the impressional, sensual, and thus "sensible" truth actually takes place in the world, where it is shown to us as an objective quality of the object. The second form of the illusion, on which the first is based, is to attribute the impression's original revelation to the intentionality that throws outside itself, and ultimately to the "outside itself" which is the world's appearing. So even though it has been established that the world's appearing is unable to create the reality of its content (the impressional content, which then becomes "sensible" content), the world's appearing is surreptitiously invested with a power that it does not have, while, unduly attributed to the world's appearing, the revelation proper to the impression is obscured. At the same time as its power of revelation, the reality of the impression itself is denatured, in so far as its essence is to give itself to feeling, in itself, of itself, and by itself. Properly speaking, there is no longer any impressional color, impressional sound, or impressional odor. The distinction Husserl himself established between *Empfindungsfarbe* and *noematische Farbe* tends to fade away.

And yet how can we conceive a color spread over the object, without an impression of the original color, or sounds related to the instruments of an orchestra, which would not be first pure "internal sounds," not re-sounding anywhere but in the grand silence where each is given to itself? This is not about poetry. *The worldly object, to which we relate these impressions under the form of sensible qualities, is forever incapable of bearing them, because it is incapable of feeling anything at all, or of feeling itself.* The beige or gray wall of the building from the Third Republic, or the yellow or turquoise of the English antique dealer's gallery, is no more beige, gray, yellow, or turquoise than it is "hot," or "painful." Does one imagine a wall after long exposure to the sun, suddenly having a "hot flash" and begging for a drink?

It is the principle of this absurdity that must be made the subject of a radical investigation. Here it is: Abandoned to the world's appearing in order to show itself in it as an objective quality, the impression is not only torn from its original site, it is quite simply destroyed. For there is no possible impression (and thus no possible objectivation subsequent to this impression) unless it touches itself at each point of its being, in such a way that, in this original self-embrace, it auto-impresses itself, and its impressional character consists in nothing other than this basic impressionality, which is unceasing. In the outside itself of the world's appearing, in its pure exteriority in which everything is dis-posed and is dis-posed as exterior to itself, no impressionality of this kind, and consequently no impression, ever occurs.

§8. When the Impression Comes outside Itself and Is Destroyed in the Temporal Flow.

Husserl's extraordinary *Lectures* on time delivered in Göttingen in the winter semester of 1904–1905 show again that every conceivable impression is destroyed in the "outside itself" of pure exteriority, where everything is always external to itself and where every auto-impression is banished in principle. To place the impression outside itself does not here mean to project it intentionally in the form of a sensible objective quality—the first moment in the construction of the objective and spatial universe, which is the one of perception of ordinary objects and which in everyone's eyes defines the real universe. The way of placing the impression outside itself that is in question here is much more original, and also much less obvious; it is produced in some way within us, where we feel all of our impressions and sensations, at the level of what Husserl calls the hyletic (material, sensual, and impressional) layer of consciousness. Let us look again at the stratum that is in principle non-intentional, at an impressional sound, for example, which is felt in its pure sonority and reduced to this.

It decomposes, as we have seen, into different sonorous phases, so that as soon as it is felt, each current phase slides into the "immediate past," to the "just now past," (*soeben gewesen*), and the immediately-past phase now slides in turn into a more and more distant past. *Because this sliding into the past is given to an intentionality (retention), it is the primitive form of coming outside,* the original emergence of Ek-stasis, and the Difference that one can indeed write as "Differance" because it is nothing but the pure fact of dif-fering, diverging, or separating—the first distance. The impression sliding out of itself is the very flow of temporality, the original way temporality becomes temporal; it is the "stream" of consciousness. When the impression comes out of itself in retention, this signifies the destruction of it, and we can see this in so far as the "immediately past," or "just now past," *is nevertheless entirely past*—not being, but nothingness: It is not an impression lived in the moment, and present; no fragment of reality subsists in it. This is Husserl's explicit declaration: "The retentional tone is not a present tone [. . .] it is not really there in retentional consciousness" (Hua X, §12, 31 / 33; translation modified).

It is true that retentional consciousness is not isolated; it is constantly tied to a consciousness of the now, which is itself connected to a protention, such that the unbroken synthesis of these three intentionalities constitutes the internal consciousness of time, which gives us the *continuous sound* through its successive phases, and in its concrete flow. To put this in other terms, rather than considering the consciousness that constitutes the temporally-extended sound, or the continuous sound if we consider instead the flowing away, no phase of this sound is separated from the others; no "immediately past" phase is possible without the current phase, whose immediate sliding into the past it is; and no current phase is given without the "immediately-past" phase, into which it immediately changes. The same goes for the future phases, which are constantly modified into current and then past phases. Therefore, if retentional consciousness always gives us only an "immediately-past," and yet entirely-past, phase, can we not say in the same way that consciousness of the now gives the current phase of the sound, and thus the reality of the impression, the present impression in its effective presence?

Two insurmountable difficulties arise here, and they are correlated. In the same way as retention and protention, consciousness of the now is an intentionality; it makes visible outside itself, and if no impression occurs in a milieu of pure exteriority (because the reality of the impression and thus all impressional reality touches itself at every point of its being and never differs from itself), then consciousness of the now turns out to be just as incapable of giving the impression's reality, its presence, or its actuality as retention or protention are. This is what the correlate of this intentional consciousness of the now shows, or what it gives, to be precise: the temporal flow, which flows in its entirety, in which there is no fixed point and no "now" properly speaking. "*In the flow and in principle, no fragment of the non-flow can appear*" (Hua X, App. VI, 114 / 118, Husserl's emphasis; translation modified).

The idea of continual synthesis, by which a retentional consciousness ties itself to this consciousness of the now, tends to camouflage the paradoxical incapacity of consciousness of the now to give in the present what is precisely never present in itself, but always flow, passage, and constant sliding, such that the current phase is given only sliding into the past, so that what is given in the end is this sliding into the past as such. It is indeed true that the "immediately past" phase is conceivable only as the past phase of a phase that was just current. But what is this current phase other than a logical exigency, in so far as consciousness of the now is in reality incapable of giving it? If we do consider the flow in its entirety as this continuous sliding of impressional phases into the past (sonorous phases, for example), then we must agree with Husserl: The present, "the now, is only an ideal limit" (Hua X, §16, 40 / 42). Caught between future phases and past phases that are both unrealities, in which no real sonor-ity makes a sound, the present phase, in which there is nothing present and that constantly collapses into the non-being of the past, is nothing more than the place of annihilation: Reduced to an ideal limit between unrealities, and itself doubly unreal, it proves to be unable to insert the reality of an actual, sonorous impression into the hearing of the continu-ous sound, however brief it may be; and without this no hearing of any kind seems possible.

Finally, what about intentionality, which gives the present with this sense of being present—consciousness of the now? Is it not itself an im-pression (in so far as it escapes the night of unconsciousness where no givenness happens)? Grasped as a whole and just like the sonorous im-pression, through the flow, how would this intentionality escape the uni-versal blackout any more than the flow does?

Husserl asked what, within the flow, might escape the flow. "The form of the flow," he says (Hua X, App. VI, 114 / 118). The form of the flow is the synthesis of the three intentionalities (protention, conscious-ness of the now, and retention) that together constitute the *a priori* struc-ture of any possible "flow." The emergence of exteriority, the externaliza-tion of it, occurs in this form; and this "outside itself" is identically the tri-dimensional horizon of time and of the world, its appearing. But like the world's appearing (for which it is only another name), the form of the flow is empty, and for the same reason. It is unable to produce the content of it, the tide of impressions that parade through it (through future, present, and past) without obtaining their reality from it. Quite the contrary, in so far as they owe their appearing to the intentionalities that make up the formal structure of the flow, all these impressions are equally unreal: The future or past phases, which are still or already only phases of non-being; the phase called "present," which is only an ideal limit between two abysses of nothingness.

Where does the impression come from, the real impression, if it is neither from the future nor the past, and even less from a present that is reduced to an ideal point? Husserl was not unaware of this unavoid-able difficulty; it gives rise to an extraordinary reversal in the text of the *Lectures: It is no longer consciousness of the now that gives the real impression; it is the real impression that gives the now.* That is the massive and unexpected declaration: "*a now becomes constituted by means of an impression*" (Hua X, App. VI, 114 / 118, our emphasis). Here are two further formulations, which are just as clear: "Properly speaking, the now-point itself must be defined by original sensation"; "The content of the originary impression is what the word 'now' signifies, taken in the most original sense" (Hua X, §31, 67 / 69–70; translation modified). It is no longer intentionality, consciousness of the now, that defines the present instant—it is the "origi-nary impression" that contains the reality of the now, or "what the word 'now' signifies, taken in its most original sense."

Far from being thought all the way through, however, this singular exchange of roles between the consciousness of the now and the impres-sion becomes an immediate travesty. Intentional consciousness of the now produces, as we have seen, only the *idea* of the now, the *signification* of being there now, being present, the empty form of the now and the present, without there being anything yet present, any real content in the flow. Husserl suddenly adds to this empty consciousness the real and concrete content that it lacks: the impression. Where does this come from? What does its coming consist in? *What is its appearing?* Because this continues to be thought as the "outside itself" of the form of the flow, he demands from this form precisely what it cannot furnish, the real impres-sion that never shows itself in the flow. Then a series of slippages occurs in Husserl's text: from the empty form of the flow, to the observation of a content that is supposed to show itself in it; from this observation (in itself fallacious), to the idea that this content, foreign to form, is external to it, nevertheless is not external to it, but connected to it, and is in some way the result of it and determined by it, even if this determination does not suffice fully to give an account of it. Notice this series of equivocations: "What abides, above all, is the formal structure of the flow, the form of the flow [. . .] but [. . .] the constant form is unceasingly filled anew by 'content,' *but the content is certainly not something introduced into the form from without. On the contrary, it is determined through the form of regularity—only in such a way that this regularity does not alone determine the concretum.* The form consists in this: that a now becomes constituted by means of an impres-sion [. . .]" (Hua X, App. VI, 114 / 118, our emphasis). The empty form, foreign to every content and as incapable of creating it as of manifesting it in its reality, by the wave of a magic wand becomes its own content, the impression itself: The empty form bears the impression inside it, and the impression belongs to it. There is no need to question the impression on the basis of anything but the form of the flow—starting with it and its coming, its own mode of revelation. The Greek prejudice closes on the radical event that came to break it.

But when the impression that was supposed to belong to the form of the flow then comes into that form, it does so in an intentional con-sciousness of the now, whose peculiarity is to destroy the impression by throwing it outside itself. It is no use tying the consciousness of the now to a retention that turns all reality into the non-being of the past; conscious-ness of the now is already responsible for doing that. For indeed that is all it means for the impression to come into the flow of consciousness: It is to insert a gap into the impression whereby, separated from itself, and cut in two—like the infant over whom the two women fought before King Solomon, who offered to cut him in two, and give half of him back to each of them—it thus comes un-done, deprived of the internal enjoyment that forever differentiates it from all inert things, from everything given to us in the world's appearing.

Husserl's description strains to avoid the ontological collapse of the impression, and with it, of all reality and every effective presence, by making the reality that it annihilates at each moment of the flow come back to life without any difficulty. Right where the impression was just put to death, torn apart in the "outside itself" of time's Ek-stasis, a new impression from elsewhere arises but is immediately destroyed. This is what gives Husserl's flow its hallucinating character, the continuous outpouring of being over the abyss of a nothingness that constantly opens under it to swallow it—the supposed continuum of this flow is constantly broken, the so-called homogenous reality of it left in splinters, in pieces of being and non-being that swap places in a scarcely thinkable discontinuity. The text just cited continues as follows: "The form consists in this, that a now becomes constituted by means of an impression, and that a trail of retentions and a horizon of protentions are attached to the impression. But this abiding form [the form of the flow] supports the consciousness of a constant change, which is an original fact: The consciousness of the mutation of the impression in retention, while *an impression continuously makes its appearance*" (Hua X, App. VI, 114 / 118, our emphasis; translation modified). The incoherent text that pretends to impute to the empty form of the flow the content it so cruelly lacks (the real impression that it puts immediately in its tomb) can offer to our admiration only the resurrection, as miraculous as permanent, of an impression that is always new and always and at every moment comes to save us from nothingness.

Where does it actually come from? How? How would it take hold of us? Would it bring us to life by pressing up against us?

§9. The Origin of the "Originary Impression." The Inevitable Reference of the Phenomenology of the Impression to the Phenomenology of Life.

"I am not of the world." Words that will resound through the centuries and beyond, which will not pass away when the world passes away, whether the poorest impression (provided that it is one, and even though we pay it no attention), the humblest desire, the first fear, a naive admission of hunger or thirst, minute pleasures and unbearable pains—*each of the most ordinary modalities of our life can claim to be the definition of its being.* Indeed none of them is of the world, and none is embraced where the "outside itself" has already undone every embrace. Husserl calls an "originary impression" (*Ur-impression*) each of these impressions that are "always there anew," summoned to fill in each moment of the empty void to which the ek-static form of the flow had already reduced each one of them.

"Originary" must then be understood in several senses. "Originary," as a qualifying term that Husserl attributes to the impression, denotes the impression before it is subjected to the modification in retention, which shifts it from its present or current condition to that of "immediately past" or "just now passed." Before it is modified in retention, however, the impression has already been subjected to intentionality, and been dislocated from its reality: It has already lost its "originary" status, if this must signify *an impressional reality in the phenomenological effectuation of its auto-impressionality.* Because, as we have shown at length, consciousness of the present—like all consciousness according to Husserl—as intentional and as what makes visible, bears primitive distance within it, where, separated from itself, every conceivable impression is already destroyed.

So "originary" can no longer denote anything but this: What comes in itself before every intentionality and independently of it, before the space of a gaze, and before the "outside itself" for which intentionality is itself only a name. What truly comes in the beginning, before the world, and apart from the world; what is foreign to every conceivable "world," and *a-cosmic.* The "originary" is not "before" in the sense of an initial yet provisional situation, the beginning of a process, or something that, occurring before the distance of the "outside itself" widens, would still be destined to slip into and become lost in it. The originary is "before" in the sense that it marks a permanent condition, an internal condition of possibility, an essence. And so what comes before the world will never come in it. It will never come in it for a truly essential reason—in principle, as phenomenologists say. It will never come in the world because it can never show itself in the world, but can only disappear there. So this "disappearance" is still only a way of speaking, a kind of metaphor that assumes we know in some way what it is that we say disappears in the world's appearing. Otherwise, knowing nothing about what disappears, we have no idea of its "disappearance" either, and no means of knowing that a "disappearance" has taken place.

Therefore we cannot follow Husserl in taking the "originary" impression as a self-evident existence, a simple presupposition whose inner possibility remains unquestioned. And this is because we have nothing else at our disposal to conceive the reality of the impression except the process of its destruction. So the problem is no longer for us to understand how the new impression is endlessly destroyed in the Ek-stasis of the flow, which by separating it from itself makes it incapable of feeling itself. It is a question of knowing how, apart from the world and independently of its appearing, before it and "in the beginning," a truly originary impression builds itself up within, so as to come in itself, experiencing undergoing itself and impressing upon itself in its own impressional flesh—so as to be an impression.

But the impression, however original it may be, is precisely not what possesses this power. *No impression brings itself about as such* [*s'apport d'elle-même en soi*], no impression is self-grounding. In that case, does it not have the capacity to determine the kind of impression that it would like to be? And also to remain in such a state, if that suits it? Don't all our impressions pass, on the contrary, and are they not indeed constantly modified, *not into the non-being of the immediately past where they vanish,* but into another and always "new" impression—sickness into well-being, desire into satisfaction, worry into rest, suffering into joy, and despair into beatitude?

No impression, whatever it may be, has chosen *to be an impression* (what it experiences in its own flesh, or in an impressional material that Husserl in a very equivocal way gave the Greek name *hyle*) any more than it has chosen the kind of impression it is; nor, consequently, has it chosen to remain in its own state or to change it—to be this impression no longer, or to be no impression at all.

What is the origin of the impression, if it is not itself, and if no impression has the power to bring itself into its own condition, a fragment of impressional flesh that is endlessly modified and changed—not into nothingness, but into a new and ever-present modality of the same flesh? Origin, in phenomenology, refers to the origin of being, its principle, what makes it to be and to be what it is. The origin of being is appearing. The origin of the impression is its appearing—an appearing such that everything that reveals itself in it occurs as an ever-present and always real fragment or moment of the impressional flesh we are discussing. It is not the world's appearing, whose "outside itself" excludes *a priori* the very possibility of every conceivable impression, but Life's appearing, which is Life itself in its originary phenomenalization.

Of the phenomenology of life, to which the phenomenology of the impression refers, we will note here only a few essential characteristics, specifically those for which the impression's originary appearing turns out to be nothing other than life's own. Let us consider the most elementary impression. Let us not consider it the way Husserl does, as an entity drifting by in the flow according to the modalities of its threefold ek-static structuration and showing itself in this, but in itself, in its originality, as it immediately undergoes experiencing itself before any dehiscence, before it differs from itself when the future or the past slips out of it—or even the present, which gives it in an intentional givenness of meaning that confers on it the meaning of being present.

Because in ordinary apprehension a pain is first taken to be a "physical" pain connected to the body, let us practice the reduction on it and retain only its painful character, the "painful as such," pure pain without reference to whatever else it might be. Pure pain precisely does not refer to anything other than itself; it is given over to itself, immersed in itself, submerged by itself, and crushed under its own weight. Pure pain is pure suffering, it is this suffering's immanence to itself—a suffering without horizon, without hope, entirely occupied with itself because it fills the entire place, so that there is no other place for it but the one it occupies. It is impossible for it to leave itself, or to escape itself, or to get ahead of itself—by throwing itself outside like one subjected to torture throws himself through the window to escape his persecutors—in order to escape its torture, and its suffering. So this impossibility is not due to the circumstances, or the layout of the surroundings, or the torturers; *in the end it stems from the internal structure of suffering.*

As soon as suffering is there, it is entirely there indeed, as a sort of absolute. For the one who suffers, nothing infringes upon his suffering. Suffering has neither doors nor windows, and no space outside it or within it that would allow it to escape. That is why it cannot flee behind itself in some way, sparing a place in back of it where it might be at liberty to withdraw, and to shrink back from its own being and from what oppresses it. There is no possible way out. Between suffering and suffering, there is nothing. For the one who suffers, for as long as he suffers, time does not exist. To slip out of itself into the salutary separation that would unburden it from itself, into a noematic unreality that would only be the representation or thought of a suffering, is something that suffering, in its suffering reality, can never do.

Suffering is driven back against itself. It is not driven back against itself as one is against a wall, from which a kind of limit (our skin) still separates us, while the wall's pressure against it turns it into a burning partition. In such a representation of things, the affection that suffering suffers must be called, in all rigor, *a hetero-affection,* the affection by something which, however close it may be, is still other, so the hope still remains that it can step aside and the painful pressure will stop. Suffering is not affected by something else, but by itself; it is *a self-affection* in the radical sense that suffering is what is affected, but it is by suffering that it is so. It is at once affecting and affected, what makes it hurt and what hurts, without distinction. It is suffering that suffers. It does not cling to the surface of a skin that it does not have. Suffering feels nothing if feeling is always opening up to something else. Suffering feels nothing other than itself. "Feeling its suffering" is an improper expression. It implies a relation to suffering, a way of "living" it that would be carried out in different ways, by giving it excessive attention, and thus with a sort of hypersensitivity about it, with what Nietzsche calls "sensitive nerves," or again with indifference, with a proud courage that stoicism holds up for our admiration. In all these cases, as the condition for all the attitudes toward suffering that are described in moral treatises, an exteriority is required, and this exteriority presupposes feeling as the medium through which it reaches everything it reaches, and feels everything it feels. It is a medium of exteriority in which, in the same way as every impression, a suffering deprived of its suffering no longer suffers; it is reduced to an inoffensive intentional correlate, to an object-of-thought.

§10. The Originary Passivity of the Impression, and Its "Passion" in Life's Transcendental Affectivity. The Living Present.

For this reason the passivity of suffering must be radically distinguished from what we habitually understand by this term, *a passivity with respect to something other than it, toward which it then shows itself passive*, and which it experiences as a foreign presence or as prior to it. We know that, as it advanced, phenomenology stopped considering as active syntheses of the transcendental ego the set of intentionalities that constitute the world by conferring on it the meaning it has for us. Other syntheses have been exposed that underlie these, are presupposed by them, and are not, properly speaking, acts of the ego. They take place in it independently of it, without being a product of its intervention as an ego: These are passive syntheses, which will become one of the major themes in the last section of this book.

In truth, because these passive syntheses are always at work, Husserl's extraordinary vision had recognized them very early, in the admirable Göttingen *Lectures*, which we have dwelt upon at length. Protention, consciousness of the present, and retention are the originary passive syntheses that constitute the internal consciousness of time. "Originally passive" does not mean only that, because they are always already at work; the phenomenologist discovers them only *a posteriori*. The transcendental ego itself only discovers them, and that is why it finds itself fundamentally passive with respect to them. The future does not come from what the ego throws toward it in an attitude of expectation or fear. On the contrary, only because a future never stops growing wider before its gaze in the manner of a horizon can this ego turn toward it in expectation or fear, expecting or fearing at the same time everything that will show itself in it, as what is to come. The same goes for the past and the present. Only a retention that always precedes it allows the ego to keep an eye on the past phase and to recognize it (as an unreal noematic correlate), and first of all the "just now past" phase of the impressional phase it just experienced. Finally, only a passive, intentional, pre-comprehension of the "now," the "current," or the "present" allows it to confer on the so-called current impressional phase the signification or pre-signification of being there now, of being "present." *But it is all these passive syntheses taking place originally in the ego and independently of it that have beaten the impression to death.* As originary, passive, and even prior to the ego as they may be (in so far as the ego itself would be constituted by them), these syntheses are no less intentional; their phenomenological structure is incompatible with that of the impression.

Husserl misjudged the most original essence of passivity. There is no relation between a passivity that obtains its ultimate condition from intentionality and another whose internal phenomenological possibility excludes it insuperably. It is even an important philosophical problem to understand how two essences (and, moreover, two pure phenomenological essences, irreducible to one another) can have the same name. But this paradox leads us deeper. The originally passive syntheses constituting the pure forms of future, past, and present, which are co-implicated in the ek-static structure of the flow, are themselves given to themselves in a much more original, invisible, and in-ecstatic passivity; only for this reason can the event that opens us to the world borrow its force from it, and pass its own passivity off as one that founds it. The foundation of every ek-static passivity upon an older, non-ecstatic passivity explains the ruinous confusion of two different phenomenological realities, or rather *two modes of* becoming phenomenal, whose dissociation is the first task of every radical phenomenology. This confusion reaches its apex in the Husserlian concept of "passive synthesis."*

The absence of every passive synthesis allows the passivity proper to every impression to be recognized. We recognized its first decisive characteristic: The powerlessness of every originary impression to rid itself of itself, to escape itself in any way whatsoever. The pure impressional element of an impression, the pure suffering of a pain, as we put it, suffers

---

* On this decisive point, the important work of Rolf Kühn has corroborated the fundamental thesis of a phenomenology of life. Cf. R. Kühn, *Husserls Begriff der Passivität, zur Kritik der passiven Synthesis in der Genetischen Phänomenologie* (Freiburg/Munich: Alber, 1998).

in such a way that it is nothing other than this pure suffering, undergoing its suffering in and through its own suffering—in its identity with itself. Pure suffering is its passion. Its coming in itself is its suffering. So the impossibility of suffering escaping itself (or relating to itself by setting itself apart in an observation or syn-thesis, however passive it may be, that would hold it together) is only the opposite of an absolute positivity: coming in itself in suffering in its passion, in this identity with itself that is its very substance. Suffering's passion is thus not only what prohibits it from ever escaping itself and running away from itself; it signifies this prohibition only because it is suffering's coming in itself that first loads it with its own content and connects it to this content in an indissoluble way. The passion of suffering is its gushing forth in itself, its being-grasped-by-itself, the adherence of it to itself, the force in which it coheres with itself and in the invincible force of this coherence, of this absolute identity with itself in which it afflicts itself and is revealed to itself, its revelation—its Parousia. The passivity of pain and the suffering of it is thus not the property of a particular impression, or a modality of existence occurring in adverse circumstances, when it suddenly afflicts itself like a burden; it is an essential property, and the unavoidable phenomenological presupposition of every conceivable impression.

We said that no impression brings itself about as such. This is the first meaning of the radical passivity we are talking about. The impression, the pain in its suffering, feels itself passive in the depth of itself in as much as it is not for nothing that it has come in itself, in the powerlessness that brands every impression, like a seal stamped on an envelope that receives, in a singular way, its content. What is at issue here is a very strange precondition indeed: a precondition immanent to that for which it is the precondition, which does not take place before the impression, and never goes away, but remains within it—*which remains in it as that in which it remains itself in itself.* Of what does this coming in itself consist, which every conceivable impression in it precedes?

It is life's coming in itself. For life is nothing other than what undergoes experiencing itself without differing from itself, in such a way that this trial is a trial of itself and not of something else, a self-revelation in a radical sense. How does the revelation operating within this self-revelation come about and make it possible as such, as a radically immanent self-affection, exclusive of any hetero-affection? Life undergoes experiencing itself in pathos; it is an originary and pure Affectivity, an Affectivity that we call transcendental because it is indeed what makes possible experiencing undergoing itself without distance, in the inexorable submission and the insurmountable passivity of a passion. Life's self-revelation takes place in Affectivity and as Affectivity. *Originary Affec-*

tivity is the phenomenological material of the self-revelation that constitutes life's essence. It makes this material an impressional material, which is never inert matter or the dead identity of a thing. It is an impressional material undergoing experiencing impressionally and doing so unceasingly, a living auto-impressionality. This living auto-impressionality is flesh. Every conceivable impression can be what it is (an "impression," a suffering and enjoying impressional material in which it impresses its impression on itself) only because it belongs to flesh, because it bears within it this pathos-laden and living auto-impressionality.

The affective, "impressional" character of the impression is thus nothing whose facticity we would have to be content merely to notice, coming who knows how, from who knows where, in who knows what. This refers to its most internal possibility, the fact that it belongs to a flesh, to the pathos-laden self-revelation of flesh in life. And that is why, considered in its material, the impression is nothing blind either, why it doesn't need to ask intentionality to make it visible, or the ek-static structure of the flow to show it to us, when this can only destroy it. Because in its very impressionality, in the pure phenomenological material of its self-affection, and as affective material, it is itself, all the way through, revelation.

In support of Husserl's thesis, we asked whether it was not true that every impression, as soon as it arrives, disappears. Each of our impressions, the strongest as well as the weakest, those we did not notice, so to speak, and on the contrary those whose memory we keep forever—each of the "moments" to which, like Goethe's Faust, we wanted to say: "Stay a while, you are so beautiful!"—did not all these ephemeral epiphanies in fact slide into a past that is further and further away, and ultimately sink into the unconscious? If life is short, it is not because of the limits of objective time, but because it is in fact a flow, in which no impression remains, whether happy or unhappy, and at every step nothingness eats away at it.

In the apologue entitled "The Next Village," Kafka tells the story of an old man whose house is the last in the hamlet and who sits on his doorstep, watching those who are going to the neighboring village pass by. If they suspected, he reckons, how short life is, they would not even leave for the next village, knowing that they wouldn't have time to get there. This systematic unreality of time, the fact that no reality is ever built up in it, is expressed in Eckhart's intuition, where what happened yesterday is as far from me as what occurred thousands of years ago.

And yet *do we not live in a perpetual present?* Have we ever left it? How could we if we are living beings, invincibly joined to themselves in a Life that never ceases being joined to itself—undergoing experiencing itself in the enjoyment of its life, and in the untearable flesh of its originary Affectivity—inexorably weaving the flawless thread of its eternal present? Life's eternal living present, the Dwelling it has assigned itself (the Dwelling of Life in which everything is life, outside of which no life is possible) is thus also our own, and that of all the living. That is why there are so many places in this Dwelling. That we always remain in Life's eternal present, that this is the condition of every conceivable living being and every fragment of life, the flesh of the least of our impressions, which makes up the "now" and the "reality" of it, one can also recognize in the fact that *we do not stand in any future and we never will*—"the future," Jean Nabert says, "is always future." We will never stand in the past either, not even the most immediate, because the distance of unreality has already made every life impossible there, and because no living being, no particle of life, can embrace itself anywhere other than where life embraces itself in living, arriving in itself, endlessly becoming and never coming undone. That is why what has passed, however slight it may be, is entirely past, as removed from us as the origin of the world, as far as the next village that we will never reach. Proximity and remoteness are categories of distance, categories of the world, and if the essence of Life is identically the essence of reality, they determine the world *a priori* as a milieu of absolute unreality—the empty place into which, in the carnal and impressional reality of its life, no living being will ever venture.

According to Husserl, in the flow, no fragment of the non-flow exists. That is why amid the universal flow only the form of the flow is fixed. It is a form that is unfortunately as empty as the appearing of the world whose phenomenological structure it constitutes. With all reality then situated in the impression, but the revelation of it entrusted to the form of the flow, it was through its very appearing that the impression was hurled into nothingness. Is it not so, we ask? Do all our impressions leave anything in us but the bitter taste of their regret?

The problem is that we speak rather badly about our impressions, applying the language of the world to them, and confusing them with these "states" or "lived moments" that are only the objectivation of them in the first Outside, tirelessly crossed by the ek-static form of the flow. So they are already confused with the "sensory *data*," or "sensible givens" that according to Husserl make up the material content of the flow. They are an evanescent content, admittedly, emptied of substance, reduced to phantasmatic apparitions that are as separated from themselves as from all the others, pieces of the nothingness into which they sink inexorably, and from which they resurface inexplicably.

No discrete and separated impressions of this sort have ever existed in us. Because the internal possibility of each impression is its coming to life, which gives it to impress upon itself, to be alive, real and present only in life, in and by life's pathos-filled self-affection; this is what remains, *one and the same self-trial continuing through the continual modification of what it feels, and that indeed does not stop undergoing itself feeling—being absolutely the same, one and the same life.* That is what subsists in the "impression's" incessant changing: what is always already there before it and thus remains in it, what is required for its coming and in which this coming takes place— not the empty form of the flow but life's unfailing embrace in the pathos-filled self-affection of its living—in its living Present.

The impression's reference to life's living Present, from which it draws the auto-impressionality constitutive of carnal reality—of which the various "impressions" are only modalities, whose real continuity it ensures (the continuity of living flesh and not an unreal flow)—refers us to a phenomenology of Flesh, which we will explain in the second section of this book. But all of this assumes that the originary appearing on which this phenomenology will be built is recognized in its opposition to the traditional intellectual horizon, in which thought strives to grasp the being of our "sensations."

Two tasks are thus imposed on us for the moment. We must clarify the nature of originary appearing, and ask in particular whether the essential phenomenological determinations implied by it have ever been foreseen in the history of philosophy. We must also respond to the inevitable objection of knowing how it would be possible for thought, for a phenomenological investigation, for example, to know what escapes it by nature, not some mysterious "metaphysical" principle, but quite simply the flesh that is ours in so far as it never appears anywhere but in life.

§11. The Question of Originary Appearing and Descartes's Cogito. Three Fundamental Questions It Involves.

Thought's inability to know life is an aporia whose power we will first recognize in a paradoxical way: by seeing it at work in Husserl's phenomenology. For Husserl was in no way unaware of life. Does he not call it by name, exactly where Descartes situated the unshakable foundation of all reality: in the cogito? This comes out again in the formulation of it offered in §46 of *Ideen I*: "I am, this life is, I am living: *cogito*" (Hua III, §46, 85 / 100). This life, which is my life, which is my I, and which is the essence of this I, defines ultimate reality in Husserl's eyes as well, the originary region (*Ur-region*) to which every other region, every specific domain of being, must be related (sensible, intelligible, imaginary, signifying, cultural, aesthetic, ethical, etc.). In a completely remarkable way, this life is at once both a universal life and also my own, and because it defines the condition of possibility of every other conceivable reality, it is constantly and rightly called "transcendental life."

Yet we cannot forget the radical phenomenological meaning that the cogito takes on when formulated in the first two "Meditations"—a meaning that was immediately lost in the work of the great Cartesians (Malebranche, Spinoza, and Leibniz)—as well as in the subsequent development of modern philosophy, and in Husserl himself.

Descartes never says, as a premise, "I am." He says, "I think." It is only because I think, and as long as I think, that I am. We can identify easily the priority of the "I think" over the "I am." It is the priority of appearing over being. "I think" means I appear, I appear to myself, and it is only by the effect of this self-appearing for me that I can then say in human language, which is also the language of thinking, "I am." But if cogito means "I appear," in the sense of this primordial self-appearing that is my own, then it is a question of knowing how this appearing appears, what its phenomenological material is, and how it is that this appearing is mine—precisely, that it inescapably bears an "I" and a "me" within it—that it has this relation to the ipseity of a Self, a relation that seems as original as it does essential.

The responses Descartes provides to these three fundamental questions demand our attention. With regard to the third, Descartes is content with a simple observation, as insufficient as it is improperly formulated: "The fact that it is I who am doubting and understanding and willing is so evident that I see no way of making it any clearer."* Whatever the importance of such an affirmation may be, the absence of any problem aiming to legitimate it, to ground the fact that an "I" co-belongs to the primordial self-appearing, co-appears in it and is connected to it by some essential reason, reveals a lacuna whose consequences will prove catastrophic for modern thought. We will see for ourselves how the phenomenology of Incarnation gives us possession of what should be added to the mere observation of this singular fact, the presence of an "ego" in primordial appearing. What makes this intelligible, or arch-intelligible, but Johannine Arch-intelligibility? The immanence of the Ipseity of the First Self to the trying process of Life's self-generation, in whose Ipseity it undergoes feeling itself, so that no life is possible that does not enclose the ipseity of an ego within it, and no *cogitatio* that must not say cogito.

As for Descartes's second question, of knowing whether something

---

*Descartes, AT, IX, 29 / PW, II, 19.

exists like what we call pure phenomenological material, some "thing" whose substance is nothing but appearing itself in the effectuation of its appearing, the all too brief response is no less categorical. That it occurs the moment Descartes shows us who he is and what he is—and that what he is, what man is, is precisely appearing in the effectiveness of its self-appearing—does not only advance, for the first time in the history of philosophy, a phenomenological definition of the essence of man that is as radical as it is explicit. Radical, because man is no longer some thing, some thing that appears, but appearing itself. The material man is made of is no longer the silt of the earth or some other material of this kind, but phenomenality itself, pure phenomenological matter, as we put it: "Nothing else belongs to my nature or essence except that I am a thinking thing" (AT VII, p. 78 / PW II, p. 54). Now if the material man is made of is pure phenomenality, appearing as such, then we must say what this phenomenality consists in, how it becomes phenomenal, and how appearing appears.

The first and most decisive question potentially implicates the other two and motivates Descartes's entire set of problems surrounding the cogito. Unlike contemporary phenomenology, this is not limited to referring what appears to us to its appearing, as if it were an inescapable condition. It is immediately situated on the plane of appearing. At the heart of appearing, considered in and for itself, a line of separation is traced, between the appearing of the world—everywhere challenged in its ambition for autonomy and universality—and a more original appearing of another sort, whose appearing is different, whose phenomenality becomes phenomenal otherwise—and *that* appearing alone is the ultimate and unshakable foundation.

The grandiose move is striking in its simplicity. The disqualification of the world's appearing takes place in the form of a doubt that strikes down the totality of sensible and intelligible, rational, and "eternal" truths, such as $2 + 3 = 5$. But the doubt can reach all these truths without sparing any of them only because it first reaches the appearing in which they show themselves to me—in this case, the "seeing" in which I see them, the evidence in which this "seeing" achieves perfection. Because this seeing is reputedly deceptive in itself, everything that it makes visible in turn collapses under the stroke of doubt.

The prior and global disqualification of "seeing" is featured in the dream, where everything that shows itself in this seeing is false and does not exist, so that the entire visible universe and every possible "world" is destroyed at once. And here (in §26 of *Passions of the Soul*), in the absence of "world," in this radical a-cosmism, when the visible universe has disappeared because visibility has been nullified, the ultimate foundation Descartes was looking for is discovered: sadness, any sentiment at all, the most modest impression. This is indeed the extraordinary and unshakable affirmation. If I dream, everything that I see in this dream is only illusion. But if in this dream I feel sadness, or any other sentiment, or "some other passion," the text says, then even though it happens in a dream, this sadness is true; it exists absolutely and *as I experience it.**

But sadness, any other sentiment, or the most modest impression, cannot appear as absolutely true—*experiencing undergoing itself as an absolute existence*—when the world and its appearing have been disqualified, except on one condition: on the condition that its appearing not be the appearing of the world and not owe anything to it. This appearing is a self-appearing whose phenomenological structure excludes the "outside itself," whose essence is experiencing undergoing itself, where sadness, every sentiment, every passion, and every impression do become possible, and whose phenomenological material is a transcendental Affectivity— the pathos in which all life, and every modality of life, arrives in itself and embraces itself in this living Self. This is what a radical phenomenology recognized as its object and proper theme: precisely Life—the Life of which John speaks and that, grasping it immediately as the only life possible, a life that provides itself life in itself [*s'apporte soi-même en soi*], he calls God.

Descartes calls this life *cogitatio*. When the term we translate as "thought" denotes the appearing from which all thought, all seeing, and all evidence is excluded in principle, and which for this reason no thought, no seeing, and no evidence can give us to see, or make known to us in some way however slight it may be, this is a textual difficulty that philosophy must resolve. The incredible burden of contradiction concerning Descartes's cogito, of which the famous circle of evidence is only the most obvious, can be avoided only at this price. Having subjected evidence to radical doubt in the hypothesis of the *malicious genie*, how could Descartes entrust the ultimate foundation to this doubt in this instance? By making us see in a clear, distinct, and, as such, indubitable vision that if I doubt and if I think, then I must indeed be? The analysis of the *cogitatio* pushes the objection aside, as do the majority of commentaries that struggle to overcome it. The *cogitatio* itself (in which neither distance,

---

* "Thus often when we sleep, and even sometimes when awake, we imagine certain things so strongly that we believe we see them in front of us . . . even though nothing is there; but, even when we sleep or dream, we would not feel sad or moved from another passion, unless it where very true that the soul had this passion within it."

nor vision, nor evidence is possible) brings itself about in itself, and does so on account of its own essence, in so far as it resides in self-revelation.* The second definition of "Arguments Proving the Existence of God" calls the essence of every *cogitatio*, as self-revelation, an *Idea*: "By the term *Idea*, I understand this form of any given thought, immediate perception of which makes me aware of the thought" (AT VII, 160 / PW II, 113, our emphasis). This "form," which the *Idea* is, in which each *cogitatio* reveals itself to itself immediately, what is it other than life? Section 26 of the *Passions* recognizes this internal structure of the *cogitatio* in its own phenomenological essence, its self-givenness in life, here designated under the heading *Idea* (in a way that is as strange as the *cogitatio* itself, admittedly): its irreducibility to the world's appearing, which is disqualified by falling under the same category as a dream, on the one hand; on the other, its phenomenological material, which is identified with that of a sadness, or of "some other passion"—with Life's pathos.

The internal structure of the *cogitatio* is unveiled for the first time in the "Second Meditation," in an analysis of demanding subtlety. At the crucial point in his approach, constrained by its very progress, Descartes takes the unheard of risk of establishing, with regard to seeing itself, that the *cogitatio* is irreducible to seeing, and therefore to all possible evidence. Seeing is made responsible for providing the proof of its own incompetence, and it is in seeing that its bankruptcy must be deciphered.

One will observe that it is with the help of a hypothesis that Descartes begins to signal that he is taking leave of the world's appearing. If an evil genie deceives me when I believe I see that all the radii in a circle are equal, then this vision is fallacious in itself; and all the supposedly rational, evident, and eternal realities that give themselves in the e-vidence of a vision like this are uncertain at the same time. The hypothesis hardly seems likely, moreover, so the blow it strikes at seeing seems superficial. What is decisive about the hypothesis of the evil genie, however (in spite of its extravagant character or because of it), is that it holds before us *the idea of a possibility— the possibility that a vision, and consequently all vision, and thus vision as such, may be fallacious*. Once a possibility of this sort has been posed, no vision by itself can exclude it. For it could indeed be false, and distort what it makes visible to the point of making us believe in an existence where there is nothing. There are so many visions of this sort (hallucinations, sensible or

---

*In numerous ways that are not possible to analyze here, Descartes recognized or presupposed this essence of the *cogitatio* as auto-revelation. We refer readers interested in this question to the first three chapters of our *Généalogie de la psychanalyse* (Paris: Presses Universitaires de France, 1985, 2nd ed., 1990) / *Genealogy of Psychoanalysis* (Stanford: Stanford University Press, 1993) where the *cogito* is the subject of a systematic analysis.

ideological illusions, beliefs without foundation or allegedly founded) and for every kind the problem will in fact be to circumscribe a single one of them that escapes the suspicion that it is deceitful, a suspicion that it now carries in its very seeing, as an indelible possibility that is inscribed in it. One thing seems certain: If we had to assure ourselves about a seeing of this sort, despite this possibility of deception that is inherent in it, it would certainly not be by appealing to another seeing that is inevitably marked with the same suspicion. Fink's affirmation that a deceptive vision can only be corrected by a new vision has lost all credibility.

Yet Descartes's approach rests upon seeing and its evidence, and at the height of radical doubt he has nothing else at his disposal. Before the abyss of nothingness that engulfs the world, all that now remains in his hands, and which depends upon him to become the ultimate and unshakable foundation, is the seeing that has been decimated by doubt, by the possibility of being fallacious that inhabits his very vision.

If the seeing now remains when the manifestation that it accomplishes and that consists in seeing has been disqualified in principle, then this can only be on one condition: that the seeing be given to itself, that it appear to itself *somewhere other than in seeing, and through another means*— where "seeing" does not intervene, and where vision (and then it hardly matters that it is deemed fallacious) has nothing more to do, quite precisely nothing more to see; and when the entire universe of the visible has been hurled into nothingness. By disqualifying the world's appearing, the devastating doubt frees the space where originary revelation fulgurates, absolute Life's self-revelation in which every life and every modality of life is revealed to itself—including, notably, the modality of life that seeing is.

If seeing is certain, it is thus not in the operation of its seeing, in the intentional surpassing through which it throws itself outside itself toward what is shown to it in the light of this outside. The light of the world can no longer define truth. On the contrary, the world's light has been disqualified so that a truth of higher origin might be recognized, which we also call certitude: the Truth of Life. Seeing is certain as *cogitatio*.

But the disassociation between a seeing whose seeing is doubtful (when considered only in its seeing, in the intentional surpassing of it toward what it sees) and the seeing that is certain in its *cogitatio* presupposes a prior and essential dissociation between the appearing of the world and the appearing of Life. In seeing's *cogitatio*, Life's originary self-revelation is substituted for intentional vision in the world's "outside," and for this reason alone the wild unleashing of nihilism suddenly gives way to an absolute of truth. This substitution presupposes in turn the duality of appearing, and outside this duplicity, the set of problems surrounding Descartes's cogito is no longer possible.

This duplicity can be read in Descartes's text at the moment of its greatest tension, at doubt's limit. What does it rest upon? A deceptive seeing. But how can this seeing subsist, positing itself as the ultimate foundation of all certainty, if it is deceptive, if it is in itself only illusion? *At certe videre videor.* At least, Descartes says, it is certain that I seem to see. In this decisive proposition (because it is in fact here that nihilism changes into an absolute truth that grounds and legitimates itself) all the terms are phenomenological. Everything signifies appearing, making appear; and everything refers to phenomenality. Only a radical phenomenology that has established the duplicity of appearing can give a meaning to this. *Videre* means seeing in the sense that we habitually understand it, as perceiving outside, in front of oneself, what becomes visible in this outside and by it. *Videre* denotes the appearing of the world. *Videor* designates the semblance, the appearing in which seeing is revealed to itself. *Only because the appearing in which seeing is revealed to itself differs in principle from the appearing in which seeing sees all that it sees can the former be certain when the latter is doubtful.*

Thus the phenomenological content of this group of problems concerning the cogito is such that, at bottom, the passage from ek-static seeing to the immanent self-revelation of Life rests on the duality of appearing. One can finally understand very well that ek-static seeing would be deemed problematic, since it is possible to imagine truths other than those one sees—and also the possibility of seeing them differently, of no longer intuiting things in space or time, for example. God, according to the unfathomed affirmation of Descartes, could have created other eternal truths, other rational systems, another reason, and thus, as in Liebniz, other possible worlds. Worlds might be different not only in their content but also in their way of becoming world, becoming visible, and "worlding"—the other worlds, and the series of "little worlds" that Kandinsky simply began to paint. Other visible universes, other ways of seeing, other "seeing," other evidences. Before it will be led astray by nihilism, these great themes will become the best modernity has to offer.

Seeing can be made problematic. But it no longer has any assignable phenomenological meaning to say that the one who experiences a sadness, an anguish, or any kind of passion does not experience it, or does not experience it just as he experiences it. The fact that Descartes recoiled before an explicit definition of the *cogitatio* as pathos follows from the connection he established between affectivity and the body. Because, following Galileo, he understood the body as a material extended thing—as *res extensa*—the connection between affectivity and the body, which would confer on the former a doubtful origin, or at least an equivocal status, made it difficult for this to belong to the *cogitatio* in principle.

A fortiori, the decisive interpretation of Affectivity as the *cogitatio*'s own internal condition of possibility, as the phenomenological material of its self-revelation, seemed definitively ruled out. And yet how is it possible to be unaware of the paradigmatic role played by passion in §26 of *Passions of the Soul*, when the *cogitatio* alone emerges from the void? How can one forget, in any event, the central theme of the first two *Meditations*? Grasped in its originary self-revelation and thus in its self-legitimation, the *cogitatio* sets evidence aside and does so in the very process through which it becomes an ultimate foundation.

§12. Husserl's Misinterpretation of Descartes's Cogito and Its Consequences: Denigrating Singular Life and Replacing It with Life's "Essence" in the Phenomenological Method's Thematic Turn.

That evidence for Descartes defines the *cogitatio*'s mode of originary givenness, and that vision (clear and distinct vision in particular) opens us to this givenness and allows us to know it with a certain knowledge that in itself can play the role of a foundation—this is Husserl's massive misinterpretation. We find the error formulated as early as 1907 in the five lectures devoted to a systematic presentation of the phenomenological project and its method. "Descartes, you recall, after having established the evidence of the *cogitatio* [. . .] wondered: what will assure me of these fundamental givens? Well, precisely *clara et distincta perceptio*." When this foundation of the *cogitatio* (of its reality and existence) takes place in clear and distinct evidence, it means that this clear and distinct vision makes me certain of every existence and every reality. And when this clear and distinct vision plays this role of foundation with regard to the *cogitatio*, this implies that it can and must play it with regard to every other reality and every existence. "With Descartes, we can now take [. . .] the additional step: whatever is given by a *clara et distincta perceptio*, as it is in any singular *cogitatio*, we are entitled to accept." So this is the meaning of the cogito. "In essence, this is to say: seeing, grasping what is self-given [. . .] in so far as it is an actual seeing [. . .], that is something ultimate" (Hua II, 49, 50 / 37, 38). Thus an extraordinary reversal occurs, the complete denaturing of the Cartesian cogito. Whereas the *cogitatio* arises as the arch-revelation of a self-revelation, which is as such a self-legitimation and thus the only conceivable foundation (a self-revelation that one can reach only in and through it, in the phenomenality proper to it, and at the end of the process by which every other form of manifestation, in this case the *clara et distincta perceptio* of evidence, has been disqualified), here, on the contrary, this very evidence, by making it see clearly, is now responsible for revealing the *cogitatio* to us. By an unprecedented *coup d'état*, that which has been separated from the self-founding of the foundation, and through it, now simply takes its place.

This error runs through Husserl's entire published work, and he offers numerous formulations of it, which are all the more significant when the capacity of the gaze to unveil the *cogitatio* intentionally in its originary and real presence is affirmed at the same time this *cogitatio* is identified with life. "The kind of being proper to any mental process is such that the gaze of an intuitive perception can be directed quite immediately to any mental process as an originary living present." "As soon as I look at the flowing life in its actual presence and, while doing so, apprehend myself as the pure subject of this life [. . .] I say unqualifiedly and necessarily: I am, this life is, I am alive: cogito" (Hua III, §45, 83 / 98; §46, 86 / 100).

Within originary givenness, the reversal of roles between evidence and the *cogitatio* is certainly not innocent. Intentional vision, whose final form is evidence, belongs to thought and defines it. To entrust to thought the unveiling of the *cogitatio* in its reality (and thus the unveiling of all reality) is to identify thought as the way to access this reality, as the method to be followed by every consciousness that is assured of itself and capable of attaining reality in itself and as it is. In this way the marvelous identity of the method and its object implied in the Greek title of phenomenology is reconstituted. The method is intentional thought, and the object is this same thought, the *cogitatio*, whose revelation is entrusted to the *clara et distincta perceptio* and reduced to it. *Adequatio rei et intellectus*: The adequation of consciousness and its object regains its pre-Socratic depth. "Thought and being are the same."

Now, if life slips away from intentionality's vision in principle, then the phenomenological method will amount to a complete failure, to the extent that it claims to be founded on such a vision, taken as an "an ultimate." The method and object of phenomenology have become heterogeneous again, irreducible to one another, because their phenomenality differs to the point of being mutually exclusive, because life comes in itself, sheltered from every gaze, and in the absence of "world." From now on, in reflection (whether it's a matter of transcendental, phenomenological reflection, or of simple natural reflection), whenever thought turns to life, in an attempt to grasp it and know it in its vision (in the *sehen und fassen* that belongs to it in principle), thought does not uncover the reality of life in its "originary presence," but only the empty place of its absence—its blackout, its disappearance.

We have already encountered life's blackout under the gaze of intentionality. According to Husserl's thesis, every reflection assumes a retention. A gaze can look back upon life in an attempt to see it and grasp it only if the phase of this life that has just sunken into the immediate past is held back by retention, in order to be offered to the view of this gaze and furnish it with the given, without which it sees nothing, without which no reflection is possible. This first vision of retention, the one that slides into the first gap hollowed out by temporality (by what Husserl calls the internal consciousness of time or even the form of the flow) carried out life's killing: In this separation from itself, the impression is destroyed. In fact, in consciousness of the now, because this is itself an intentionality, the impression is already torn apart, and the dispersed, dead shards are projected everywhere. The temporal flow of the 1905 *Lectures* was nothing other than the random collection of this unreal debris, inexorably doomed to nothingness.

This is what Husserl himself notices, and with extreme displeasure. In the temporal flow of subjective impressions, whose appearing was entrusted to the intentional vision of the form of the flow, life self-destructs instead of revealing itself; after 1907, Husserl calls this by the more appropriate name of "Heraclitean flux," a parade of evanescent apparitions where nothing remains, where all goes to naught—which forever mourns reality. Not that this ever disappeared, properly speaking, but because it never arrived. Speaking of these "pure phenomena," which are sensations reduced to their temporal subjective givenness, Husserl denies that they constitute a specific dimension of being, what he calls a "region" or "field." "We move in the field of pure phenomena. But why do I say 'field'—is it not rather an eternal *Heraclitean flux* of phenomena" (Hua II, 47 / 36).

This designation is repeated across all the work, notably in the major texts. In a surprising way, §20 of the *Cartesian Meditations* claims that "the possibility of a phenomenology of pure consciousness seems *highly* questionable," and this is because subjective phenomena are presented to us as a "Heraclitean flux" where there can be no "final elements," so one cannot grasp them in fixed concepts, as the objective sciences, for example, do for their own objects.[*] Section 52 of the *Krisis* affirms that, even for his own account, a philosopher cannot make any true observation concerning "this elusively flowing life, cannot repeat it with always the same content, and become so certain of its *quid* and *quod* that he could describe it [. . .] in definitive statements."[†]

The massive failure of the phenomenological method, the impossibility of reaching real life, its originary presence, with the vision of in-

---

[*] Edmund Husserl, Hua I, §20, 86 / 49.
[†] Edmund Husserl, Hua VI, §52, 181 / 178; translation modified.

tentionality, explains two major events that will mark Husserl's philosophy. The first is the discredit it casts upon life's reality, which it proves incapable of grasping. We have recognized the decisive traits that belong to life: the fact that every life, undergoing experiencing itself in an effective and thus singular self-trial, necessarily bears a singular Self within it, so that it is a singular life of some particular ego. Consequently, the same goes for every modality of life, for the most humble impression, of which none, we said, could belong to no one. Its reality (or existence, as one can still call it) resides precisely in this particularity of life, in the singular ipseity of the ego in which it feels itself.

And here Husserl tells us that *the singularity of this life (of the* cogitatio *and its real existence) have no importance.* For in the end phenomenology is not a novel wanting to tell us the story of Pierre or Yvette. Whether he is hungry or she is filled with anxiety upon learning she has a serious illness is of no interest for the phenomenologist. Phenomenology is a science. Singular facts, however subjective and "reduced," can have no meaning for it. On singularities of this kind, on what Pierre or Yvette or experience, one can establish only singular propositions. Yet science does not deal with singular judgments, but only with universal propositions that alone are capable of expressing laws—universal, and as such "scientific," truths. As soon as he notices the dissolution of subjective phenomena in the Heraclitean flux, Husserl claims: "What statements can I make about it? While I am seeing it, I can say: this here!—it exists, indubitably [. . .]" But he adds: "Thus we will not attribute any particular value to such judgments as 'This is here," and the like, which we make on the basis of pure seeing." And again: "Phenomenal judgments, as singular judgments, are not terribly instructive" (Hua II, 47, 48 / 36, 37).

When singular judgments are disqualified by a science whose objective validity implies universality, this cannot suppress an unavoidable philosophical question—*about the possibility of such judgments.* That Pierre's hunger or Yvette's anxiety does not mean much for science (even when, from another view, under the regard of the Christ, for example, these singular lives may well be essential: "I was hungry and you gave me nothing to eat," "I was thirsty," etc.) does not exempt us from asking how it happens that the modalities of one's own life are revealed each time to the one who experiences them, why and how they are precisely one's own, in their sometimes overwhelming original presence, in their real and indeed singular existence. On their own, once their phenomenological possibility as self-revelation has been established, these "singular *cogitationes*" can result, it seems, in "singular judgments," however uninteresting they may be. The same goes for the subject of the *cogitatio*'s real existence: No more than its singularity, the reality of it cannot be set aside as lacking interest. In the aforementioned texts, which entrust to the pure sight of a gaze the "this one" of the singular *cogitatio*, its existence at least seems maintained: "this exists." But now it is no more than a groundless presupposition, an impossibility perhaps. Doesn't the pure sight of the *cogitatio*, the intentional grasp of the impression in the internal consciousness of time, always reduce this to a simple noematic correlate whose unreality Husserl everywhere affirms—in this case to the evanescent apparitions that the flux, in its inexorable flow, brings to nothingness?

Here the second major event we mentioned is produced, and it will modify little by little, though in a concealed way, the meaning of the phenomenological method. After the denigration of what we cannot grasp, this singular and real life that eludes vision (as if one has to behave toward it like the fox declaring before the grapes that he cannot catch them: "They are too green"), we now witness the outright disqualification of this singular life, which lacks any scientific interest. In its place a new object arises, not this variable event of life, but its essence, the essence of universal transcendental life. This is the thematic turn.

The substitution of life's essence for its singular existence displays three characteristics. The first, already noted, is that it appears *as a way to cope*, intervening in Husserl's problematic at the very moment it notices the *cogitatio* vanishing in the *clara et distincta perceptio* of evidence. In the 1905 *Lectures*, it is a matter of substituting the form of the flow for the flow itself and its evanescent content. The permanence of this form, the only fixed point in the flow, is the permanence of an essence, where the tridimensional ek-static structure of the flow's form is opposed to the sensible content that flows by and whose destiny it prescribes *a priori*.

In the 1907 *Lectures*, where the question of temporality is absent, the passage from the singular *cogitatio* to its essence becomes the explicit subject of the analysis. If the profound motivation for this persists, the reason invoked is the necessity for phenomenology to be constructed like a science that is capable of explicating facts by formulating their laws instead of limiting itself simply to noticing them. In the domain of transcendental life, these laws have lost all inductive character; they are laws of essences, which presuppose that those essences are brought to light. From a gnosiological point of view, the contribution of a new object of the method seems undeniable. To take in view the *essence* of the *cogitatio*, the core of intelligibility and being that in each *cogitatio* always makes it what it is, determining the set of properties that belong to it in principle, and to institute in this way a rational apodictic discourse that is capable of pronouncing *a priori* the validity of such properties—this is what is advantageously substituted for an uncertain reading of them that is based upon elusive facticities.

These two characteristics of the method's thematic turn go together in the great texts: the phenomenological and ontological collapse of the singular *cogitatio* in the vision of evidence, whose existence it had to ensure, and the replacement of this existence by its essence, by life's essence, on the basis of which all the essential properties of this life will be able to be determined with certainty. Immediately after having doubted "the possibility of a phenomenology of pure consciousness," in other words, of subjective phenomena carried away in the Heraclitean flux, §21 of the *Cartesian Meditations* proposes the solution. The evanescence of the subjective modes according to which objects are given can be overcome, because "these modes, no matter how fluid these may be, and no matter how inapprehensible as having ultimate elements, still they are by no means variable without restriction. They are always restricted to a set of *structural types*, which is 'invariable', inviolably the same: as long as the objectivity remains intended as *this* one and of this kind" (Hua I, §21, 88 / 51). This is the case, as we have seen, for the form of the flow when it is a question of subjective, temporal phenomena.

Similarly, after having noticed that the "particular philosopher" is incapable of acquiring any kind of certainty about the existence and the nature of his own experiences, §52 of the *Krisis* adds: "But the full concrete facticity of universal transcendental subjectivity can nevertheless be scientifically grasped in another sense, precisely because, truly through an eidetic method, the great task can and must be undertaken of investigating the *essential form* of the transcendental accomplishments [. . .] that is, the total essential form of transcendental subjectivity" (Hua VI, §52, 181, 182 / 178, our emphasis). Thus the transcendental performances, in other words, the various operations of a particular subjectivity, can be known and analyzed only on the basis of their essence—their "essential form." In all the "regions" of being and even more in the originary region (*Ur-region*) of transcendental life, the properties of singular phenomena—here the properties of singular *cogitationes* considered in their conscious operations—cannot be deciphered except upon the arch-type of essences, the "essential forms" of the structural types these phenomena always obey. The phenomenon, the "fact," is knowable only by its essence, and on that basis. "The *factum* is determinable here only as *factum* of its own essence and by its essence" (*ibid.*). Thus we see the concrete modes of subjective individual life sliding into the type that regulates them even within their fleeting becoming. The thematic turn consists in this substitution of eidetism for the singular *cogitationes*, and it will allow the phenomenological method to acquire a positive knowledge of life despite its invisibility—in its absence.

§13. Analysis of the Thematic Turn. The Aporia of the Phenomenological Method.

This turn should be examined more closely. At first glance, it consists in replacing one object—the concrete modalities of transcendental life, which are real and singular *cogitationes*—with another—the set of essences and essential forms that determine their properties *a priori*. But, as we know, the object of phenomenology is precisely not objects, but their mode of givenness, their appearing. Considered from the phenomenological point of view, the meaning of the thematic turn changes completely. It is no longer a matter of replacing one object with another, *cogitationes* with their essential types. It is the mode of revelation of these objects that is at stake; the phenomenological method has replaced one mode of appearing with another. This is the third characteristic of the substitution of life's essence for its singular existence: It substitutes absolute life's originary mode of revelation, in which every life, every modality of life, and every *cogitatio* is revealed to itself (a mode of revelation that phenomenology ignores), with the only mode of manifestation it knows, the appearing of the world where vision unfurls. The substitution of objects is only the consequence of the prior substitution of modes of appearing. Because it failed to recognize life's originary mode of revelation, the phenomenological method did not entrust this life (which it is forever incapable of seeing) to vision, but to a new object that is appropriate to it, and can be seen by it.

For this is what is proper to an essence in general. As a noematic correlate of the intentionality that aims at it, it is the object of a possible vision, not like a sensible object that is constructed on the basis of sensible appearances, whose perception is complex, but in a higher degree of vision—an intellectual vision, whose object is not a contingent existence, but a rational structure. We know the effort Husserl took to understand the sphere of vision, well beyond sensible experience: Everywhere a *clara et distincta perceptio* is possible, it discovers new domains of objects (the immense domain of essences, categories, meanings, kinds, ideal objects, etc.), whose existence and structural types are established in and through the evidence of this *clara et distincta perceptio*.

With respect to transcendental life, in place of its existence, now the essence of it is presented for analysis, its "essential forms" and fundamental structures, which are intentionality, the form of the flow, the essential forms of each type of intentionality (perception, imagination, ideation, signifying intentionality, intuition of genera, and of essences, etc.). If the *clara et distincta perceptio* proves to be inadequate precisely where one had thought to recognize its power for the first time with respect to the singular *cogitatio*, how can this power be underestimated when it presents us with rigorously rational contents, which cannot be other than they are, as in the exemplary case of geometrical essences? Try, Malebranche says, to make the radii of a circle unequal . . .

Still, phenomenology is a transcendental philosophy, and is concerned to go back to a phenomenon's final possibility, rather than limiting itself to the mere observation of it. The set of problems pertaining to the intuition of essences cannot escape this exigency. How can one be content with the factual existence of an intuition of life's essence and characteristic structures—an intuition that after all must unveil for us what we are in reality and truth, behind the appearances and deep within ourselves—without asking how such an intuition is possible? For the essence of life, the essence of its temporal or intentional structure, the essence of each type of intentionality, etc., cannot come to occupy our mind if some prior order had not lead from the latter to the former. How can someone who has never seen a color intuit its essence? How can an instance that is in itself foreign to life, which would be anything but a living being, become aware of life's essence, or catch hold of its most internal possibility?

In addition, as soon as he proposes to produce a theory of essences, as one of the centerpieces of the new method he has in view, Husserl knows that the mere factual vision of a particular essence does not suffice: One must show how such a vision of an ideal generality is formed—so that it could occur in our experience. And one must also show why and how it happens that this vision is of this essence rather than another one, of life, rather than of a circle or a horse. For the fact of "seeing," considered in its intentional phenomenological structure, does not allow the particular content of what is seen to be determined. The appearance of the world, the "outside itself" in which seeing is deployed, we claimed, can never account for what is unveiled in it.

The theory of the intuition of essences treats this problem. The intuition of an essence is always constructed from singular givens. Let it be the essence of red—the genus, the species, and *the red*. The process that will end up in the intuition of "red" as such does depend on a series of particular perceptions which are always of particular objects: the red of the blotting paper on my desk, the red of this dress, etc. Leaving to the side the particular objects of these various perceptions so as not to consider *what there is in common between them*, I fix my attention on this *identical universal* that vision can draw from all of these perceptions, and I then see it, in a very clear view. "We see it—there it is; there is what we mean, this species red" (Hua II, 57 / 42). This is the process of idealizing abstraction that on the basis of singular givens reaches the clear and distinct vision of an identical element that is common to them, which is a new object, of another order, an ideal object that is itself given in an intuition of another order, the intuition of an ideal generality perceived as such: the intuition of the essence.

Let us now apply this theory of the formation of the intuition of essences to the intuition of life (and, in the same way, to all the essences or "essential forms" that are connected to it). For the essence (species, genus, and generality) to be seen in a clear vision, and as such to be certain of itself, thus implies the process of idealizing abstraction that necessarily takes its point of departure from singular and real givens. In the case of life's essence (and all the essences that concern it), these givens are real, singular *cogitationes*. From a multiplicity of *cogitationes* of this kind, what they have in common can and must be read—the identical universal that properly defines their essence.

And yet when vision looks to catch hold of them, the singular and real *cogitationes* vanish under its gaze, along with all the actual modalities of life (its hyletic as well as its noetic content, in Husserl's language— impressions as well as intentional operations). That was the hidden motif of the thematic turn whereby the phenomenological method sought to substitute in place of these elusive *cogitationes* their "essences," which are ideal objectivities, external to the reality of consciousness, "transcendent," offered to the gaze of intentionality, and both visible and capable of being intuited in it. But the possibility that these essences are capable of being intuited in a clear and distinct vision collapses if it is the result of a process of ideation that rests on singular and real *cogitationes* that are inaccessible to vision. This is the aporia that breaks the phenomenological method.

§14. A Final Attempt to Overcome the Aporia. The Question of Invisible Life "Given in Imagination."

Husserl strives to overcome the aporia with admirable patience. How can one have a clear vision of the *cogitatio*'s essence when the reality of it is invisible? Upon which of life's singular givens can the process of ideation still rest *if they are no longer those of its reality*? Upon the givens that at least play the role of representing these real invisible *cogitationes*: upon their images. For this is what an image is, the representation of a reality in its absence. By forming images of multiple perceptions, for example, I would be able to recognize, on their images, the common structure of all of these perceptions: the essence of perception. And the same goes for the essence of imagination, memory, signifying thought, etc. Not only is the free imagination of all possible *cogitationes* (for each type of *cogitatio*) capable of supplying an indefinite multiplicity of singular givens for the work of the act of idealizing abstraction, but this free fiction is constitutive of such an act and its operation. For it is by forming as many singular givens as one likes (as many singular perceptions, singular imaginations, and singular memories)—by conferring on them all possible, *imaginable* characteristics—that fiction traces the dividing line between those that are necessary for the internal constitution of the reality in question (the reality of an act of perception, an act of imagination, etc.) and those without which it is still possible—between the characteristics necessary for its existence and the accidental or contingent characteristics; only the former constitute its essence. "Fiction," Husserl claims in a famous proposition, "is an essential element for phenomenology as for every eidetic science in general." Fiction in this case means the substitution for the givens of life's reality, which elude us, their imaginary representatives—the singular givens "in imagination," of which the imagination can supply as many and as varied copies as the analysis can wish. The theory of eidetic analysis rests upon the free fiction of properties and their variation; this is the ingenious palliative Husserl put forward in order to make possible, by basing itself exclusively on the evidence of pure vision, a rigorous and precisely eidetic science of transcendental life, even when the reality of it is hidden to every grasp of this sort.

But the difficulty is only displaced. Two crucial questions cannot be avoided. The first concerns the phenomenological value that one can attribute to the *image-data [données-en-image]* of the singular *cogitationes*, which the fiction has substituted for their *real-givens*. Indeed, a fundamental prescription of the phenomenological method is in question. This method posited clear and distinct evidence as the absolute criterion of validity: Only what is seen in this evidence is given in itself as it is, "in person," in its reality, so that it merits the title "absolute given." Is the image of a *cogitatio* an absolute given of it, the given of a *cogitatio in its reality*?

In the fifth of the 1907 *Lectures*, where this problem emerges in all its acuity, Husserl seems constrained to give vision such an extension (suddenly holding as nothing the criteria of clear and distinct evidence) that it threatens at the same time all the phenomenological distinctions that are based on it, the distinction between the real and the imagined, between the given in itself and the "simply aimed at" or "empty intention," etc. It is enough for something to be seen—however it may be seen, and provided that one takes it as it is seen—for it to be able to function as an indisputable given. So what is "aimed at" without being given in person (the signification "dog" when no dog is there), even a fictive or absurd object (a chimera or a round square), still appears to me in some way, such that this appearance (provided that one limits oneself to it) is something indisputable. In all of these situations, vision, here taken in its fading and crepuscular modes, remains the final criterion. As soon as something is seen, "an intentional object is nevertheless obviously there" (Hua II, 73 / 53).

This is notably the case for the image, the only case that interests us here in that the given in imagination must supply its substrate to the vision of essences. In every image something is indeed present to the mind. "When I call forth a fiction in my imagination, so that, say, before me St. George the knight is killing a dragon, is it not evident that this imagined phenomenon represents precisely St. George [. . .]?" (Hua II, 72 / 53). A demonstration that the given in imagination can be used to support the intuition of an essence is made with respect to color. If I consider an imagined color, and not a sensed one, it is still something before my gaze. It suffices then to "reduce" it, not to consider it as the "imagined color" of a blotting paper or a dress, but in itself, in order to be in the presence of the phenomenon "imagined color," and to take this just as it appears to me. "It appears," Husserl says, "and it appears in itself [*"sie erscheint und erscheint selbst"*] [. . .]; in an act of seeing it in its re-presentation, I can make judgments about it and about the moments that constitute it, and their interconnections" (Hua II, 70 / 51). But to perceive the moments and their relations that constitute an imagined color is to perceive the essence of the color, which is nothing other than this necessary relation of these moments. So the intuition of the essence of the color takes place in the absence of any real color and of every consideration having to do with its existence.

The same goes for the intuition of the essences of the *cogitationes*, of life and of all its modalities. On the basis of the image-data of singular *cogitationes*, in the absence of their real existence, it is possible to read the properties of these *cogitationes* as well as the set of necessary relations that unite them and which constitute their typical structure (their essences). For life, as for all other sorts of "objects" or "phenomena," the intuition of its essence is still possible in the absence of its reality. The possibility of a phenomenology of transcendental life based on vision seems guaranteed.

A difficulty remains, under which the aporia is now hidden—the entire aporia! We will willingly concede that the image has a content, and that this constitutes an incontestable given for as long as one holds to what actually appears in it (even while we retain some doubt about the capacity of the image to supply a clear and distinct content on which one could perceive clearly and distinctly the properties or structures that will be those of the essence). For it is rather a certain "haziness" that characterizes every given in imagination, on account of its unreality in principle, because everything that it gives, it gives in the absence of the reality of what it gives. As we know, it is impossible to decipher how many columns a temple has from the image of its façade.

But in the end, let us suppose that despite this "haziness" the multiplication of the givens in imagination in the free fiction makes it possible to obtain constant, invariable properties from them, which will define the essence sought. It is the content of this given in imagination that should be investigated further. It is there, we see it in a certain way, and we can concede its existence—its imaginary existence. But the question is whether it is possible for such a content in imagination to represent, not anything at all, but precisely a *cogitatio*. For as long as we refer to a factual possibility, this seems to exist: I can indeed represent fright or sadness in an image. With an observation like this, however, one no longer remains within the domain of philosophy, any more than one remains within the domain of philosophy if one is satisfied to allege that I have the power to move my hand and to grasp an object. It must be repeated: Philosophy is essentially transcendental. Its task is to understand *a priori* how a particular thing is possible, precisely its transcendental possibility. So before the most simple and self-evident "phenomenon," phenomenology asks how such a phenomenon—every conceivable phenomenon—is possible in general. By virtue of its appearing. But in what does this appearing itself consist, what is it in it that allows it to appear, and of what is its phenomenological material made? In short, this is the set of questions whose numerous implications the phenomenology of life endeavors to explore.

If we look back at Husserl's theory of the intuition of essences, we see that it breaks down into two distinct moments, one of which is philosophical and the other of which is not. The first consists in inquiring about the internal possibility of an intuition of "essence" in general, and the response consists in the analysis of a process of idealizing abstraction that takes its point of departure from singular givens—with it being understood that these initial givens have no need to deliver a real existence to us; the image-data of this existence can suffice. In this way, for the vision of life's essence, the image-data of the real *cogitationes* make it possible to read upon them the characters that are common to every *cogitatio*.

But how are the image-data of the real *cogitationes* themselves possible? How could one in fact see from an image the specific content that one calls a *cogitatio* and whose property is to shy away from every possible vision and thus from every image that one would form of it—and do this in some sense where one takes the word image (since it's a matter in each case of what offers itself to the sight of a vision) from its objective or noematic correlate? Husserl here abandons the transcendental inquiry into the *a priori* possibility (capable of being grasped and comprehended in itself) of the formation of an image of the invisible *cogitatio*, in order to hold to the naive, pre-critical, and also highly problematic affirmation that such an image exists. That is how the transcendental phenomenology (which claims to be and wants to be transcendental) of subjectivity (in other words, of life and its *cogitationes*) moves in a vast circle—the circle of the phenomenological method: Wanting to grasp these *cogitationes* in a vision and being unable to see them, it substitutes their own essence for them—a transcendent, noematic essence that one can in fact see in clear and distinct evidence. But the construction of this essence must rest upon these real *cogitationes* being given in person, givens that do not exist. One then substitutes, so to speak, image-data for these inexistent givens of real *cogitationes*. This is the second substitution in which the aporia occurs: For how and on what basis can one form an image of what one knows nothing about?

Let us consider givenness-in-image, in itself and as such. It is an imaging, putting outside what constitutes as such the pure dimension of the imaginary—a milieu of universal and empty exteriority, which still contains no image, but sketches *a priori* the form of every conceivable image, the possibility of it coming to appearance, in which it will give itself to vision as an image and in the form of an image. This appearing, which gives in an image, which effectuates this imaging, this milieu of pure exteriority where every visible takes form and becomes visible in the form of an image, and *qua* image, this is the appearing of the world. For the world, grasped in the nudity of its pure appearing, independently of every content, is an *Imago*, the originary and pure Image, the pure Imaginary— *ens imaginarium*—in which everything that will show itself in it will take the form of an image.

We have recognized three decisive characteristics of the world's appearing:

1) The fact that it is impossible, on the basis of it, to give an account of what appears in it, of the particular content that it unveils.

2) The fact that since this unveiling occurs as an auto-externalization of exteriority that places everything outside itself, stripping it of its own reality, everything that is unveiled in it is marked in principle with the seal of unreality. The interpretation of the world as *Imago*, as a pure imaginary dimension in which everything that shows itself bears *a priori* the form of an image, in its own way names the process of unrealization that makes up every ek-static appearance.

3) The fact that, in this appearing which unfurls as auto-externalization, something like a transcendental life that nothing ever separates from itself is impossible in principle. That is also why the reality of life, its invisible pathos-filled flesh, never shows itself in it.

These are the characteristics inherent to the world's appearing in which vision is deployed, and with which the phenomenological method colludes in its aporetic attempt to see what one never sees. Thus the inability of the *clara et distincta perceptio* to grasp the *cogitatio* in its reality is explained. And at the same time, its inability to explain the set of properties that the *cogitatio* takes from this reality, from its self-revelation in life (in particular its ipseity); and finally also its inability to produce, for lack of the *cogitatio*'s reality, at least its given in imagination—if it is true that from the *Imago* of the world, in which every image takes form, the fact that this has this particular content (that it is, for example, the image of a *cogitatio*) is never legible.

In Eugen Fink's *Sixth Cartesian Meditation*, dedicated to a transcendental theory of the phenomenological method, which he thought should be added to Husserl's five *Cartesian Meditations*, the aporia is fully exposed. The goal of the method is indeed to see transcendental life, and this vision is accomplished by putting this life outside itself, in its division from itself, in its cleavage. When it does come outside itself and in this division with itself, life gives itself to be seen by a possible spectator, in this case the phenomenologist himself. "In the achievement of the reduction, transcendental life is put *outside itself,* by producing the Onlooker, it cleaves itself, and divides itself. But this division is transcendental subjectivity's *condition of possibility for reaching itself.*"* Thus by lending to life a mode of appearing incompatible with its essence, phenomenology claims to ground this life's very self-achievement, the access to itself that constitutes precisely the essence of it.

§15. The Originary Self-Revelation of Life as the Foundation of the Phenomenological Method. A Response to the General Philosophical Problem Concerning the Possibility of Thinking Life.

But what do we ourselves say about this aporia? How does the radical phenomenology of life claim to overcome it? Is not phenomenology a philosophy, and philosophy a thought, a thought that comes about through vision? According to one of our previous observations, a work of philos-

---

*Eugen Fink, *VI. Cartesianische Meditation. Teil 1. Die Idee Einer Transzendentalen Methodenlehre* (The Hague: Kluwer, 1998) / *Sixième Méditation cartésienne. L'idée d'une théorie ranscendantale de la méthode,* French trans. N. Depraz (Paris: Ed. Jérôme Millon, 1994), p. 76 / *Sixth Cartesian Meditation: The Idea of a Transcendental Theory of Method,* trans. Ronald Bruzina (Bloomington & Indianapolis: Indiana University Press, 1995) (Fink's emphasis).

ophy is nothing other than a series of intuitions or evidences needing to be connected according to a chain of necessary reasons and to be formulated in propositions whose givenness (reading or writing) itself looks to vision, to the Greek Logos, for its possibility. If life is invisible, then, how is it possible to have access to it in thought, and how is a philosophy of life still possible?

There is no access to life that would take its point of departure outside life, in the "outside itself," or that would owe to this outside of self its power to find its way toward life and to encounter it. No access to life comes by taking it in view in some way, whether directly as an absolute given (perceived in clear and distinct evidence); or indirectly (on this life's image-data); or again on its essence (offered to the apodictic vision of the *intueri* of a pure understanding, or *intuitus*); or in a superior intelligibility; or on some ideal archetype (seen by it and eluding fate). There is no access to life resting on any object, or any noematic correlates, from which it would be possible to recover the intentionalities that "constituted" them; or on intentional objects that serve as a guide for describing and analyzing the performances of transcendental life that confer on them the meaning they have for this life (of being of real objects, imaginary, of essences, of sense, of nonsense, etc.). There is no access to life resting outside it, and thus resting on that which is outside it, on what is other, external, and different. It is impossible to seek, in the world, among the dead, what comes from life—a single living being.

There is no access to life except in it, by it, and from it. It is only because already, before us, always, in the beginning and as this very Beginning, an absolute Life (the unique and absolute Life of God, which is none other than this unique and absolute Life) has come in itself by undergoing experiencing itself in the pathos-laden trial of the First living Self (which is its Word); that in absolute Life's arrival in itself, and in the test that it makes of itself in its Word, we arrived in ourselves in us, in such a way that we are living beings. How do we have access to life? By having access to ourselves, in this relation to oneself in which every conceivable Self, and each time a singular Self, is edified. But this relation to oneself (this access to ourselves) precedes us; we are the result of it. It is the trial of our generation, since we have arrived in ourselves, becoming the Self that we are, only in the eternal proceeding in which absolute Life comes in itself. In and through *that* trial alone, the living come to Life.

Living, we are beings of the invisible. We are intelligible only in the invisible, and on the basis of it. Thus we cannot understand our true nature in the world on the basis of its phenomenological structures, from which life is concealed. All the worldly explanations of the human being, which proliferate today, confer on the human being properties taken from things, forgetting its living reality. In the world, the human being puts up its fragile and precarious silhouette, and one naively identifies oneself with this silhouette, which one believes to be that of one's body, whose posture one imagines explaining on the basis of the posture of other bipeds, even quadrupeds, or from aquatic precursors. So the force that runs through this body, which makes this silhouette stand erect, is that of the physico-chemical processes that constitute the material of this body, its true substance—a body born from the silt of the earth, decidedly. *As if something like a force could exist somewhere other than where it undergoes feeling itself as a force*—where, given to itself in pathos, in Life's absolute self-givenness, it feels the pathos. As if a human body could be something other than a living flesh, an invisible flesh, intelligible in the invisible of life and only on that basis.

Abandoned to its vision, thought cannot see any of this: Its knowledge has become a science of objects, which knows nothing about man. The intelligibility at its disposal is thought's vision, the visibility of the horizon where its vision is deployed. It is an intelligibility that allows us truly to understand things—not just because these things simply show themselves in it in their opaque and incomprehensible facticity. Their archetypes also give themselves to seeing, in this vision of a higher degree, in the supreme Intelligibility, which confronts us with Intelligibility itself, opening us to its resplendent light. The salvation of man, in other words his true reality, does not only reside in this higher Intelligibility (as all the Platonic gnoses will repeat). Because these Archetypes are also those of things, and because the contemplation of them served as the model for the creation of this world (which is our own, it seems), it contains precisely the intelligibility of this world. Not its mere observation, but precisely the seat of intelligibility that presided over its formation, and because it is this possibility which is intelligible (because we read the Archetypes in the light that illuminates them), the possibility of *a priori* knowledge of the world and of everything that exists. The theories of knowledge that will characterize modern philosophy will preserve the trace of this ambition, even if, centered on this world and having become prosaic, they will have abandoned every soteriological pretension.

Arch-intelligibility denotes an Intelligibility of another order, fundamentally foreign to the one that has just been in question, and which does indeed come about before it: before the vision of things, before the vision of Archetypes according to which things are constructed, before every vision, before the transcendental event from which every vision gains its possibility, before the coming outside of the "outside itself" of the horizon of visibility of every conceivable visible, before the appearance of the world—before its creation. The Arch-intelligibility is that of Life—of the Invisible. In Life's Arch-intelligibility life itself becomes intelligible—the trial of its self-generation as the generation within it of the First Living Self in which it undergoes experiencing itself and is thus revealed to itself—the generation of its Word, which indeed comes in the beginning, since life arrives in that generation and undergoes experiencing itself only in its Word, which arrives in it and undergoes experiencing itself only in life. It is this trial of life's self-generation as its self-revelation in the Word that constitutes the Arch-intelligibility of which John speaks. Not a gnosis, but (because it owes nothing to the contemplation of Intelligibility, or to any kind of contemplation) an Arch-gnosis.

And this means in particular that in its Arch-intelligibility, Life comes into it before every thought; it gains access to itself without thought. And that is why no thought can reach into it. No thought can live. So Arch-intelligibility really means an Intelligibility that precedes everything we have understood by this term since the Greeks—precedes all contemplation, and every opening of a "space" to which a vision can be open. An Intelligibility that, as it reveals itself to itself before thought and independently of it, owes it nothing, but owes revealing itself to itself only to itself. An Arch-intelligibility that is an Auto-intelligibility, a self-revelation in this radical sense: Life.

In this book, however, are we not trying to "think" life? And yet it is never life, it seems, that carries out the unveiling of what is said, in this series of evidences and propositions that make up its content. Propositions, intuitions, or evidences can be given only to the view of a vision, and if possible in a clear and distinct view. Thus we claim against Husserl that it is never life's reality that is shown in this way, in any kind of vision, and that, for example, the *clara et distincta perceptio* of a *cogitatio* is simply impossible. Is Husserl's aporia not our own?

But if no thought enables us to reach life, our life, should we not turn the question around, and ask: How does thought, just one thought, reach itself? This was precisely the extraordinary intuition of Descartes: It is precisely not by thought, or in thought, that thought attains itself. It is not in a vision that vision is given to itself. The appearing in which vision is revealed to itself (the semblance in which it seems that I see) is not the appearance in which vision sees what it sees. The *cogitatio* is not attained in the evidence of a *clara et distincta perceptio*, but in the absence of it, after doubt has disqualified all evidence. The *cogitatio* reveals itself in itself. Its essence consists in that: in the fact of being revealed to itself in the absence of the world and of everything that one sees in it. The *cogitatio* is a self-revelation.

It is true that Descartes thought self-revelation only in a speculative way, negatively through the immense process of doubt, and positively under the heading *Idea*, which is the form every *cogitatio* takes in the immediate perception of which we are conscious of this same *cogitatio*. It was only a first step, quickly forgotten, toward calling Greek presuppositions radically into question. The task of a phenomenology of life is to think self-revelation phenomenologically, not to grasp it as a higher degree of factuality, but in it most internal, transcendental possibility, in what makes it effective, in the phenomenological material of which every self-revelation consists, in which it takes place and can take place—in life's pathos-filled flesh.

As soon as life replaces the *cogitatio* as the site and theme of the meditation, as soon as the Johannine Arch-intelligibility stands out behind a Latin word, the equivocations and terrible limitations of a problem that is still supposedly rational (as to its outcome in the *intuitus* of an *intueri*) are swept aside. First, the equivocations: The same term—thought, *cogitatio*—cannot denote both the intentional vision that is thrown outside itself toward a transcendent object and the first self-revelation of this thought in the absence of every vision. Consciousness cannot be "always consciousness of something," "*having consciousness of something*, something that I experience, or that I think, or sense, or see," in short, always possessing "its *cogitatum*" (Hua VI, §20, 84 / 82; translation modified) and, at the same time, be pure *hyle*, non-intentional material, pure, "originary" impression. In this latter case, one must actually say what makes up the revelation—the revelation of the impression when it is no longer the work of intentionality—and whether there is still one.

Next, the dreadful limitations surrounding this set of problems: Even when taken in its authentic Cartesian sense, as a self-revelation independent of all evidence, the *cogitatio* cannot be left to itself. That it reveals itself to itself is not its own doing. It is not what brings itself into its own condition: It is a *cogitatio* only in absolute Life's self-revelation. And, in the same way, if we detect an *ego* in every *cogitatio*, it is only because, having arrived in itself in absolute Life's arrival in itself in the Ipseity of its Word, it is marked at its birth with this indelible Ipseity, which belongs to every arrival in oneself, as its condition, every phenomenological accomplishment of which is a singular Self. Far from the cogito being a point of departure and the *cogitatio* a self-sufficient order on its own, they are both only the result of a generation. On this side of the cogito (and of its *cogitatio* and its ego), before it, well before it as within it, Life accomplishes the eternal work in which, engendering itself on its own, it engenders everyone alive. The most ordinary *cogitatio*, the most humble impression, is intelligible only in Johannine Arch-intelligibility.

But is all this not something we see? Is it not in a vision, in its clear view, that we have recognized the trial of our birth, what arrives before us and that John places in the beginning? What then is this trial of absolute Life's self-generation in the first Self in which it is undergone, self-revealed, and becomes life, the implication of this trial in every life and every living Self, in every *cogitatio*—what is this in our philosophical reflection if not *the intuition of the essence* of an absolute Life that brings itself about in itself, *the intuition of the essence* of immanence, its immanence in everyone living, *the intuition in evidence of the essence* of ipseity, of the *essence* of an ego like ours, which is possible only in this ipseity that precedes it, which unceasingly says "I," "me," yet without being brought by itself into this condition of being the ego it is, and without being able to do so? But how is all this knowledge, the intuition of all these "essences," possible if no vision and no thought ever sees life?

And yet this vision is a *cogitatio*. It is revealed to itself, not in a vision and as the object of this vision, but like every *cogitatio*: in absolute life's self-revelation in which every modality of life is given to itself, revealed to itself, undergoes experiencing itself, feels itself, and enjoys itself—in the pathos-laden immediacy and certitude of this enjoyment of itself. As *cogitatio*—revealed to itself in life's self-revelation and being nothing other than this pure trial of itself in its pathos-filled immediacy—the vision is at every point like a sadness, or like some other passion, as Descartes said—this sadness or passion that emerged alone from nothing when seeing and its evidence had been disqualified, the world and its appearance rendered void.

And certitude, which emerges as the ultimate foundation at the very moment evidence is disqualified, and in favor of its disqualification, must be clearly understood. It is precisely not a phenomenon of thought, some judgment brought by thought with respect to sadness or any other passion, or to vision, itself understood as a *cogitatio*. The certainty of a sadness is the experience it has of itself; it consists in the experience in which the sadness consists, in such a way that it begins and ends with it and the material this certainty is made of is none other than the one sadness is made of, its pathos. Certainty is life's certainty, the certainty it has of being alive, the triumphal Parousia of its pathos-filled self-revelation enjoying itself.

So we are now in the presence of phenomenology's reversal, thanks to which these numerous aporias fall apart. This reversal has a prior condition, the enlargement of the concept of phenomenality on which the entire phenomenological enterprise rests. By opposing a more originary mode of manifestation (the immanent self-revelation of life in its invisible pathos) to the ek-static appearance of the world, which governs the development of western thought from Greece, the phenomenology of life offers entirely new tasks for investigation. Not only the systematic exploration of the invisible, which determines the depth of our being and apart from which it becomes impossible to understand anything of man, or the set of problems that concern his true reality. One of these problems, in particular, arises with urgency, because it follows immediately from the duality of appearing, or, as we put it, its duplicity. It is a question of making intelligible the relation that obtains between these two decisive modes whereby phenomenality becomes phenomenal: the visible and the invisible. This is precisely where Husserl's aporia stands, which we must in turn resolve. How is the phenomenological method still possible if it is a question of thought following the analysis of something that escapes it in principle, of grasping it in adequate concepts, or forming various "essences" that this mysterious invisible obeys?

The reversal of phenomenology is written as follows: *It is not thought that gives us access to life; it is life that allows thought to access itself,* to undergo experiencing itself and at last to be what it always is, the self-revelation of a *"cogitatio."* Precisely because it is always and necessarily a *cogitatio,* thought has come to denote indistinctly, under the same fallacious concept, two appearances as different as intentional vision and that which allows this vision to occur to itself in the absence of every vision: its pathos-filled self-givenness in absolute Life.

Thus Arch-intelligibility does not only come before every conceivable intelligibility, it founds intelligibility and makes it possible: What is intelligible, comprehensible, and capable of being grasped by us is what we can see, in a clear view. Intelligible: that which is given to thought's sight, things, and first of all essences, the archetypes without which we would only see without knowing what we see. Before *that* Intelligibility, to which modernity limits its knowledge, comes the Arch-intelligibility in which absolute Life is revealed to itself, and in this way, every life, every modality of life and every conceivable living. According to Marx's too-seldom pondered words, *thought is a mode of life.* There is no thought, therefore, that is not given to itself in absolute life's self-givenness. Only because, given to itself in life, vision has been placed in itself, coinciding with self in its immanence to itself and in its pathos-filled embrace with itself, is it a vision that is certain of itself, certain of seeing and of seeing everything that it sees. It is only in vision's certainty of being a vision, and thus of seeing what it sees, that evidence is possible. The certainty that owes nothing to evidence and that is foreign to it is the one that establishes it. The one who says, "I do not believe what I'm seeing" formulates an absurd proposition if there is no vision that does not owe being vision (and thus seeing and seeing everything it sees) to the invisible certainty that life, in its pathos-filled self-givenness, has of being life—if there is no vision, and no fragment of the visible, that doesn't require the invisible. If there is no Intelligibility, which men and women have always demanded of their knowledge and their science, that carries the omnipotent secret one cannot see within it, the Arch-intelligibility of absolute Life in which every power is given to them.

Now, if thought is possible as a mode of life, because the certainty of its vision is in reality life's own certainty, a question remains, which is our own: How can we gain in thought a knowledge of this life that gives this vision to itself, yet without showing itself to it? In one sense, we have set the aporia aside. We know that we can never attain life in a vision, but only where it attains itself (where we have always already arrived in ourselves) in absolute Life, according to the Arch-intelligibility of the trial of its self-generation as its self-revelation. Never again will we appeal to vision, to any knowledge, for our living condition.

Nevertheless, we look to see this invisible life, which inhabits our vision and makes it possible, and we look for it in a thought that marks all knowledge, every philosophy, and notably phenomenology, with its decisive characteristic. It was the ingenious characteristic of Husserl's phenomenological method in the grips of the aporia (and despite the presupposition always maintained about evidence as originary givenness), to understand that this vision would still be effective only on one condition, which we have expounded at length: to substitute for life's invisible reality an objective equivalent that one can see, a "noematic" correlate that is life's "essence," a "transcendent" essence, offered to the gaze of eidetic intuition—objective indeed. And to understand that this objective equivalent would not be life's own, except by sacrificing its invisible reality, by renouncing the pretension of bearing it in itself, of offering its "existence" to us—by giving itself explicitly as an unreality, a noematic unreality, in this case an "ideality," an ideal essence.

It is only at the end of this extraordinary trajectory, colliding again with the aporia he thought he had gotten rid of, that Husserl cannot face up to the final difficulty. How can this ideal essence, or how can these image-data from which such an essence must be constructed, really be those *of life* precisely and not something else or nothing at all; how could the visible let the shadow of the invisible stand out against it, even in an indigent form, in an imaginary or ideal form?

The response is there for us. Because in the Arch-intelligibility in which absolute life arrives in itself, we arrived in ourselves in our living condition, *in possession of the life that has put us in possession of ourselves, thus knowing it in the way it knows itself* (in the Arch-intelligibility of its pathos) we can then form a re-presentation of it, throwing the image or "essence" outside us, in such a way that in them real life in the reality of its pathos is never given to us, but only its double, a copy, or an image—some objective equivalent indeed, but empty, fragile, and *as incapable of living as of subsisting by itself.* And this is in fact why we call it an image. For what is proper to every image is that it cannot exist unless supported by a performance of life, the act of imagination that forms it and keeps it in front of its gaze, without which it would immediately collapse into nothingness.

There is no Archetype of life, no visible basis on which we would have the leisure to contemplate in an adequate vision what it "is," its true essence. Fink's thesis, whereby life's occurrence to itself consists in putting life outside itself, in the gaze of a spectator, is nonsense. The invisible comes before every conceivable visible. In its invincible certainty, in the pathos of its suffering flesh or its Joy, it owes nothing to the visible. If in him it is a question of Life, God is far more certain than the world. So are we. A phenomenology of flesh is now possible.

2

Phenomenology of Flesh

§16. Appearing and Content of the World: The Question of the "Sensible World."

The reversal of phenomenology overcame the aporia that thought constantly comes up against in its effort to see and grasp our invisible life. By opposing absolute Life's self-revelation to the world's ek-static appearance, where vision only ever sees the visible, the phenomenology of Life has recognized in Life the originary essence of all revelation. Because life originally reveals itself to itself in its pathos-filled trial that owes nothing to the world, every living being knows with an absolute knowledge (with the knowledge of life that engenders it by giving it to undergo experiencing itself and to live) what of this comes from life and what from itself. But in relation to life, thought turns out to be in the same situation as this living being. It does not first think, in order then to live. It is never thought, based on itself in some way, that advances toward life in order to discover and know it. *Thought does not know life by thinking it.* Knowing life is life's own doing, and life's alone. It is only because life comes in itself, in its pathos-filled arrival in itself (which always takes precedence) that something like vision coming to oneself, for example, can occur—that vision is possible, consequently, along with everything it sees. The reversal of phenomenology is the recognition of this prerequisite, which prohibits us from relating life to a thought that would be capable of making it manifest, but on the contrary refers thought to the trial of life's self-givenness, outside of which there is nothing.

The reversal of phenomenology is the movement of thought that understands what comes before it: the self-givenness of absolute Life in which it occurs to itself in itself. The reversal of phenomenology thinks Life's precedence over thought. The thought of life's precedence over thought can indeed be the work of a thought (the one we are developing now), yet this is possible only because, in the order of reality and consequently also of philosophical reflection itself, life is already revealed to itself. So in thinking the precedence of life over thought, it is life, in its actual phenomenological accomplishment, life always already accomplished, in which this thought is given to itself, which allows thought: 1) to be thought, a *cogitatio*, and 2) to be, possibly, this particular thought, however essential, which ensues from this reversal, which shows itself capable of thinking life's precedence over thought, and as the inner condition of this precedence. Because given to itself in life's self-givenness, thought bears life within it as its very substance and thus as an essential gain, it can then represent this life by producing its image or essence. The entire phenomenological method that endeavors to think life rests upon this prior givenness, which is the work neither of phenomenology nor of thought. It is always life that makes its self-objectification possible in thought, as the internal condition of this thought as well of as its object.

This radical phenomenological precedence of life is what thought constantly forgets when it takes itself as the principle of all knowledge, of everything that we can know, of everything that can exist for us. This forgetting is particularly catastrophic when it's a question of thinking the body, or what is connected to it according to an invisible relation, the flesh—our flesh. The phenomenology of life alone, whose possibility we have just recalled, allows us to approach the question of the body and the flesh in light of entirely new phenomenological presuppositions. Only these presuppositions can clarify a domain where the most extreme confusion has always prevailed.

According to the phenomenology of life, there exist two fundamental and irreducible modes of appearing: that of the world, and that of life. So if it is a matter of treating the question of the body and the flesh in a phenomenological perspective, it becomes evident that two ways are open for the investigation—two ways that are essentially phenomenological since they are nothing but the two modes of appearing we are discussing.

The body's appearance in the world is confused with the ordinary experience of this body, to the point of becoming identical with it and defining it. This *worldly* experience of the body is what the traditional knowledge of humanity expresses about it. In the eyes of what we call "common sense," which is, moreover, only another way of naming the habitual representation that human beings make of themselves and their environment, the body is indeed that: an object of the world that more or less resembles other objects, and is accessible in the world as they are because it shows itself in it. The ordinary experience of the body can seem vague, approximate, and without value, if one relates it to the exigencies of a true knowledge. In as much as such a body shows itself in the appearing of the world, it receives by virtue of that reality *a phenomenological and ontological determination that is as radical as it is rigorous.* So the banality of the properties it manifests cannot hide their decisive character. If, *qua* "synopsis," *qua* unifying modes of showing, the pure phenomenological intuitions of time and space are, as we have noted, modes of the world's appearing that are inherent to its phenomenological structure, then all bodies that are shown to us because of this structure take on the determinations (which are indeed essential) of being spatial and temporal bodies. If the categories of the understanding, in so far as they are representations, are themselves modes of presentation (precisely modes of "presenting-in-front," "positing-in-front") that co-belong to the world's phenomenological structure, then everything submitted to these categories is connected according to the interplay of the correlations and rules they prescribe, and notably causality.

The appearing of the world determines *a priori* the phenomenological structure of the worldly body, *yet in such a manner that still no real body is posited that way*. The existence of the real body, and of the collection of bodies that form the concrete content of this world, demands the intervention of sensation. Kant's thesis, as we have seen, is only one illustration among others of what we have recognized to be a general and decisive characteristic of the appearing of the world: its ontological indigence, its inability to posit on its own the content that it makes appear without being able, for all that, to confer existence on it (without being able to "create" it). When this indigence in principle is now manifest to us with regard to the body, it leads us to this paradoxical observation: It is precisely not the appearance of the world that can account for the body (a body of any sort, our own as well as any other body), the body that by all accounts has its site in the world and has always seemed to belong to it. This is the paradox: At first glance, the phenomenological elucidation of the worldly body tears its existence away from the world, calling seriously into question the approach chosen for circumscribing its nature and carrying out the analysis of it.

The real body, the worldly body considered in its concrete existence—the collection of bodies that "populate" the universe, our own, as well as the bodies of other men and women, animals, or even the inert bodies of "things"—all these bodies are sensible bodies. They have colors, odors, and tastes, they are sonorous, or can be if we knock on them, they present numerous tactile properties—soft to the touch, smooth or rough, sharp, solid like a stone, languid like mud, dry or humid, or even vanishing like water between our fingers. It is by this whole set of sensible properties that bodies in the universe have always been defined in the eyes of men and women (in their eyes, but also their ears, their nose, their palate, their hands), since each of these bodies is nothing but a certain grouping of sensible qualities that entirely determine our behavior with respect to them, making them objects that are agreeable or dangerous, useful or not, within our grasp or escaping it.

Yet none of these sensible qualities, which constitute the objects that make up our environment, derives in any manner whatsoever from the appearing of the world. This is not to say that the world is not determining with respect to them in so far as it makes them spatial or temporal objects, or even (which is no less important) coherent sets of sensible properties and objects each linked according to necessary connections, whose correlative variations make our action on them possible. Thus the world is not only an ordered collection, but also a practical totality. The world we are now speaking about is nothing more than this, however: the world reduced to its appearance, to the empty form of Ek-stasis; it is the world considered in its concrete content, the world of real objects where men and women live and act, the *sensible world.* And the world owes this sensible content to sensation—to life. Thus taking into account the sensible character of the world and its objects refers the phenomenology of the world to a phenomenology of life.

§17. The Radical Critique of the Sensible World. The Impact and Limits of Galileo's Reduction.

Before applying the phenomenology of life and understanding the world itself as life-world (*Lebenswelt,* to use Husserl's expression, in which we will recognize a more radical meaning than the one he gives it) it is worth our while to open an important historical parenthesis. At the beginning of the seventeenth century, the sensible world is the object of a radical critique. In parallel with this, the traditional conception of the body is overturned. For it is nothing less than the sensible nature of the world as well as of the bodies that compose it that suddenly is called into question and rejected. Unlike the changes that affect great civilizations and extend over long periods, which are the result of multiple and various causes, the decisive event that in the history of human thought is the disintegration of the ancestral conception of the body is the result of an intellectual decision. Taken by Galileo at the dawn of the modern era, we can regard it as the proto-founding act of modern science, and to the extent that it will then guide the world, of modernity as a whole.

Galileo's categorical assertion is that the sensible body that we take to be the real body—the body that we can see, touch, feel, hear, which has colors, odors, tactile and sonorous qualities, etc.—is only an illusion, and that the real universe is not made up of bodies of this kind. That is also why the knowledge of this real universe can be a sensible knowledge, which was always considered, even by the scholastics, as the ground of all human knowledge. In truth, the real universe is made up of extended material bodies, and this extended matter constitutes precisely the reality of these bodies, and, at the same time, of the universe. The property of a material extended substance is that it is potentially delimited by figures displaying certain forms. It is a question of knowing this material, extended body that is endowed with forms and figures. Yet a science of pure forms and figures exists—a science consequently adapted to the knowledge of the material extended bodies that make up the real universe; it is geometry. Geometry is a pure science, giving rise to a rational knowledge of figures and forms, because instead of describing them in their facticity, it proceeds to construct them ideally, so that their properties become plainly comprehensible, and necessary with an *a priori* necessity, on the basis of this construction that in each case plays the role of a seat of intelligibility. Thus the rational knowledge in geometry of the figures and forms of the real extended bodies of the material universe comes into conflict with the sensible knowledge of sensible bodies, which is to say, of their sensible qualities. While the latter gives rise only to singular propositions, analogous to those Husserl denounces as of little interest with respect to the intuitive (and for that matter impossible) knowledge of singular *cogitationes*, the former constructs necessary propositions of universal and, as such, scientific validity.

The Galilean decision to establish a geometric knowledge of the material universe does not merely precede the founding of modern science. On the plane of reality, and not of knowledge, it substitutes for the sensible body a body unknown until then—*the scientific body*. For the extended, material body, whose figures and forms are graspable geometrically, is not only the inert body of "things," but also of men and women. That is what is new, and it opens a new era founded on an unprecedented conception of the human body, and consequently of the human itself. Thus is born the pretension that a geometric science of material nature can now constitute the true knowledge of humanity. And, correlatively, the pretension that a new technology that itself is scientific and material, and in itself foreign to the human, can furnish the true approach to humanity, and find man in the depth of his being, even in his pleasure, in the heart of his suffering or distress—of his life or death. But these remarks are premature.

One man alone of course does not have the power to accomplish the extraordinary revolution, of which we are all the children, whether consciously or not. The presuppositions put into effect by Galileo had long been present. On the one hand, Democritus's atomism had resurfaced in certain circles of the late Renaissance; on the other hand, geometry had a long history. Galileo's genius, it has been said, was to apply the latter to the former, to use geometry as the mode of knowledge of matter instead of limiting its field to ideal figures.

But it is not only on the plane of knowledge that Galileo's invention shows its extraordinary fecundity. The analysis of reality is even more surprising. In imagining the free variation of properties of things that must be determined essentially, it is in every way like what Husserl's phenomenology calls an "eidetic analysis." It is a question of knowing "what" the body is while contending with the ordinary experience of a sensible body, and on the other hand interpreting it as a material extended substance, which Galileo wants to make the theme of the new physics. Even though the imagination proves capable of making the diverse sensible qualities vary to the point of being able to conceive a material, extended substance deprived of all these qualities, it is on the contrary incapable of conceiving this same substance without representing at the same time its size, location, figure, and movement. Sensible qualities do not belong to the essence of material substance, which can exist without them; they are inessential. Limit, place, figure, size, and movement, on the contrary, are properties that are necessarily connected to it, and cannot be separated from it: They constitute the invariant that properly defines its essence.

This is the essential analysis on which rests at once both scientific modernity and the radical modification of our conception of the body that is connected to it. "I feel constrained by necessity," Galileo writes in the *Saggiatore*, "When I think of a physical material or substance, I immediately have to conceive of it as bounded, and as having this or that shape, as being large or small in relation to other things, and in some specific place and at any given time, as moving or at rest [. . .] *I cannot separate it from these conditions by any stretch of the imagination.* But whether it is white or red, bitter or sweet, noisy or silent, and of a pleasing or unpleasant colour, my mind does not feel compelled to bring this in order to apprehend it [. . .]." Thus it is possible to know the being-true of Nature or, as Galileo even says, of reading in the great Book of the Universe—on the condition of knowing its language, whose characters are "triangles, circles, and other geometric figures, without which it is humanly impossible to understand a word of what is says."*

The new intelligibility promised by Galileo and consisting in a geometric reading of the universe rests as we have seen upon the eidetic analysis of the body. By substituting for the sensible body a material extended

---

*Galileo, *Opere*, ed. Nazionale, respectively vol. VI, p. 347, and Vol. VII, p. 129 / *Selected Writings*, trans. William R. Shea and Mark Davie (Oxford: Oxford University Press, 2012), pp. 119, 115 (our emphasis).

object that can then be assimilated to the geometric object, a reduction is carried out. It is true that every science is constituted in a reduction by which it delimits its proper field and defines its objects. At the same time, it disqualifies everything with which it is not preoccupied, and which, because of these initial decisions, it will never thematize. In this way the history that purports to be, for example, a "history of living individuals" is hardly preoccupied with the chemical molecules that compose their bodies, which are instead the theme of chemistry. This determination of a domain of competence, together with a determination of a domain of incompetence as its correlate (which is also infinitely broader), is inherent in the constitution of any science.

Nevertheless, in Galileo's epoch, it is not a particular science that emerges, and one that would be the effect of a specific reduction. It is a science that will reject all traditional knowledges of humanity and will take their place, understanding itself as the single form of all possible knowledge. This science claiming universality is also constituted by a reduction, but this reduction does not cast itself as the delimitation of a specific domain of objects, but as the condition of all truth. For this reason, it is important to assess the magnitude of it.

The reduction disqualifies nothing less than all sensible qualities, and at the same time sensible bodies in so far as these are always only an assembly of such qualities, a synthesis of them. Yet to the extent that these show themselves to us under the heading "sensible apparitions," or "phenomena," they are not nothing. What does Galileo say about them? Immediately after having declared that the imagination can very well conceive real extended bodies independently of the sensible qualities that they bear, he adds: "Whereby I am led to think that these flavors, colors, odors, etc., as far as it concerns the subject in which it seems to us that they reside, are nothing other than pure names and only reside in the sensory body, so that if one takes away the animal, all these qualities are taken away or annihilated."[*] These sensible apparitions, which are sensible qualities, are thus only "apparent." "Appearance" is opposed to reality: In so far as these apparitions are appearances, they do not belong to real bodies as real properties. And this is what the variational method has just shown, by allowing us to conceive the existence of the former independently of the latter.

The Galilean reduction does not, however, limit itself to excluding sensible qualities; it offers to explain them. They are attached to the bio-

---

[*] *Ibid.*, vol. VI, p. 347. Federigo Enriquez remarks that the term "names" applied by Galileo to sensible qualities takes over the term "conventions" by which Democritus denotes them. Cf. "Descartes et Galilée," in *Revue de métaphysique et de morale*, 1937.

logical structure of the particular animals we are. It is the contingency of this structure that determines the contingency of these qualities. Other species hear other sounds, see other colors, and smell other odors. Some of them probably see nothing, or see very poorly, and hear nothing, or are deprived of other senses. The decisive character of the determination of sensible qualities by the biological structure of organisms is formulated in a radical way when it is claimed that the suppression of the latter leads to the disappearance of the former. Except that the determination of sensible qualities by the organisms is nothing other than their determination by real bodies of which these organisms are composed. The new geometrical science of the material universe does not only place off limits sensible qualities, sensible bodies, and the sensible world; it takes them back up and treats them as effects whose causes it displays. Thus forming a system, giving account of material things, but also of *the manner in which we sense them*, it offers itself in its proto-founding act as a universal knowledge (the only real one) from which nothing escapes.

We will take the full measure of this reduction of every form of knowledge to the geometric science of material nature if we add the following remarks. As the set of problems surrounding the impression has established, the sensible qualities of bodies, the colors spread over their "noematic" surface, and in the same way their sonorous, tactile qualities—all the properties related to them, perceived and "sensed" on them, which have the signification of being their properties and belonging to them, belonging to the material of which these bodies are made, so that we believe these bodies possess such qualities in themselves, are red or yellow, sweet or bitter, cold or hot, of agreeable or disagreeable odor—all these qualities attributed to bodies are only the projection in them of sensations and impressions, which never exist anywhere but in the place they sense themselves and undergo experiencing themselves, given to themselves in the pathos-filled self-givenness of life. That is the reason why these qualities possess this so poorly understood character of being "sensible," which ultimately means affective, because their matter is not the matter of material bodies, which in reality sense nothing and have never sensed anything, but precisely the pure phenomenological material of life, this affective flesh of which they are only modalities.

Yet if the reality of sensible qualities does not reside in things but in life, if their material is not what the universe is made of but the impressionable, phenomenological material of life, the meaning of the Galilean reduction intensifies vertiginously. It does not merely initiate a sort of universal cleansing, tearing away from the universe its "sensible layer," paradoxically attributed to insensible bodies, and discovering it in its nudity as an external material substance finally opened to calculations and measures, to objective parameters whose infinite determination is the task of the new science. Precisely because these sensible qualities are, at bottom, modalities of our phenomenological life, the reduction disqualifies them. At first, the impressional modalities of our life are classed as mere "appearances," to which nothing in reality corresponds. All at once our entire life, as we experience it, turns into an illusion—our sensations, our emotions, our feelings, our desires, our hopes, our renunciations, and our loves.

But we have just seen that the Galilean reduction is not confined to dismissing from the true science's new field of interest the qualities and sensible impressions that at once make up the texture of the world and of our lives—the living flesh with which we identify ourselves, which determines our elementary behaviors, and through them our representations and our culture. It does not take them merely for illusory appearances. By seeking their origin in the biological structure of organisms, which ultimately means in the movements and processes that constitute the reality of the universe, it gives an account of them. Two consequences follow, which we must now confront directly.

On the one hand, our life can no longer cope; it is no longer something autonomous that has its foundation, reasons, and laws in itself. They are the laws of a foreign reality—a blind reality that feels nothing and cannot feel itself, that does not "think," and that has no relation with the reality of our life. And which nevertheless determines it, submitting it to regulations it knows nothing about. And thus the principle of its action, its modalities, and the meaning it confers on them, escape it, as do the meanings of its pleasures, its anguish, or its sorrows. The kiss lovers exchange is only a bombardment of microphysical particles.

On the other hand, it is this world life withdraws from, the world divested of every sensible quality, foreign to every impression, which we must try to conceive since now this is what defines both our actual reality and destiny. Conceiving this seems at first glance difficult. How can we imagine this place that totally escapes our senses, and about which they have nothing more to learn—vortices of particles, charges and discharges of energy that know neither cold nor heat, neither light nor shadow, neither distance nor proximity, nor design of any sort, nor good nor evil, which has none of our bearings, with no contact between them, nor attraction nor repulsion in the sense we give to these words, so that everything that we can say about it will never amount to anything but a web of naive and uncalled-for metaphors. Which has, for example, no "weight," no "mass," no "speed"—despite all the parameters by which we seek to determine these "primary qualities," if it is true, as has been said, that something like a weight has never come into the hands that try to lift it.

"The eternal silence of these infinite spaces [. . .]." We must therefore understand that this "silence" has no relation to what we denote by the term, the blessed state that takes hold of us when, having arrived in a place set apart, and crossed the entrance of a cloister, we escape for a moment the tumult of the world. *That* silence supports an essential reference to the universe of sounds, of which it is only a privileged variation— this silence is *audible*. In the universe of the new science, *no sound is possible*. It never had one and it never will. Prescribed by the phenomenological reduction, the absence of every conceivable noise is a structural condition of this "universe," it pertains to its definition, its status. That is why one can say this silence is eternal.

Pascal himself attested to the terror it brings. And rightly so. This "eternal" silence is terrifying not because the author of the *Pensées* had his sensibility tormented; but because it is inhuman. That is, in the end, a simple name to designate what no longer has a name in any language, that which, divested of every human quality, every amiability, and every affinity with us, as a skeleton for its flesh, is no longer there for anyone. It is the inhuman that is frightening. As frightening as it may be, the inhuman, it is true, is never quite that. It is for us, for human beings, that it is so. In itself, having passed through the Galilean sieve and turned into this collection of insensible material bodies that are nothing more than the correlate of geometric propositions, the "real" universe of modernity is as foreign to terror as to sound, to light as to "silence": it is so far from us that the problem is to know how we can still form the inconceivable concept of it.

How can we rejoin it, recover it, and open ourselves to it? Reestablish a relation to that with which we apparently no longer have one? The Galilean reduction holds the response to the question it raises. These extended material bodies foreign to our sensibility, to our needs, which are indifferent to our desires, substrata to our gaze as well as to our grasp, literally inaudible, enclosed forever in their monstrous silence, a knowledge that is itself foreign to all of these human determinations leads us straight to them: geometrical knowledge, in perfect conformity and adequation to their forms and figures. And it does this in the clear and distinct evidence of the theorems that introduce us to the heart of what remains hidden in the great Book until an ingenious discoverer deciphers its language. More terror indeed: the assurance of rationality, the happy pathos of a truth that cannot be other than what it shows us of itself in the light of its evidence.

§18. Descartes's Counter-Reduction.

And yet geometry is itself a problem. Let us follow for a moment the extraordinary ideational sequence that follows Galileo's invention. Galileo's
ideas spread rapidly in the first half of the seventeenth century. Descartes
took them up and perceived immediately what immense possibilities they
unlock for human knowledge. He was fascinated by the decisive intuition
to make geometry the principle for knowledge of the material universe,
and we find the proof of this in the famous analysis of the piece of wax in
the "Second Meditation." How can we not recognize what we have called
the eidetic analysis of the body, which the *Saggiatore* carried out? The
variations of the sensible qualities of a body, in this case the piece of wax
Descartes imagines that he heats, manifest the inessential character of
its properties, which can change and disappear, while the invariant that
constitutes the essence of this body, namely its extension, subsists. "But
even as I speak, I put the wax by the fire, and look: The residual taste is
eliminated, the smell goes away, the color changes, the shape is lost, the
size increases; it becomes liquid and hot; you can hardly touch it, and if
you strike it, it no longer makes a sound. But does the same wax remain?
It must be admited that it does; no one denies it [. . .]" (AT VII, 30, 14–9 /
PW II, 20). Descartes, however, is not content to take over the founding
intuition of Galilean physics; he proposes, by means of the system of
abscissas and ordinates, a mathematical formulation of the geometrical
determinations of bodies. The proto-founding act of modern science, the
objective, geometrico-mathematical knowledge of the material universe
qua correlate of such knowledge, is accomplished.

What is striking in this sequence of ideas, which will determine
modern science and, through it, will shape modernity, is that in a certain manner Descartes immediately takes the opposite view. Galileo has
reduced the real content of the world to these extended material bodies,
which physico-mathematical science makes its new object, and which it
knows in the evidence of its rational and universalizable propositions. As
for sensible appearances, bodies of the sensible universe, sensibility, and
subjectivity in general, he places them beyond the field of investigation
of the new science, entrusting it all the more with the task of producing
a causal explanation.

Descartes carries out a counter-reduction. Even though he follows
Galileo in his work of founding the new science and perfects it with his
project of generalized mathematization, still he does not consider subjective appearances, impressions, volitions, and affectivity as illusions. What
would it mean to take sadness for an illusion anyway? In so far as I feel

it and such as I feel it—more precisely, in so far as it feels itself and as it feels it—an original and incontestable revelation happens in it, one of sadness, infinitely more certain than the appearance of the world. Has §26 of the *Passions of the Soul* not shown that this self-revelation of sadness is produced in the absence of the world and its supposedly misleading evidence? This is the radical meaning of Descartes's counter-reduction: *Everything Galileo's reduction had taken away from the rational knowledge of the real universe, as "apparent" or "illusory," as a "name" or "convention," the counter-reduction gathers up, in order to make it more certain and more essential than the reality of the universe:* cogitationes, crystals of absolute certainty. Far more than this, these *cogitationes*, which the Galilean reduction claims to exclude from the knowledge of the real universe, become through a decisive reversal the incontrovertible condition and foundation of this knowledge.

The eidetic analysis of the body that is offered to us in the "Second Meditation," when Descartes heats his piece of wax, doesn't simply repeat the Galilean reduction; it differs from it through a nuance that modifies its meaning to the point of inverting it. Galileo, a physicist, works to determine the object of his science, detaching it from the appearance that conceals its true nature. Because this nature, exposed by the elimination of sensible qualities, is an extended, material substance, geometry is necessarily the adequate mode for knowing it. Galileo's analysis is an ontological analysis of the body. Conversely, according to a pertinent observation by Ferdinand Alquié,[*] when the analysis of the piece of wax occurs in the "Second Meditation," the set of bodies that make up the world's content was deemed doubtful, and so was everything I see. Thus it is not the nature of these bodies (which may not exist) that is in question, it is the possibility of knowing them, the mode of knowing them—in case they do exist.

Descartes's analysis is a phenomenological analysis. It can be understood only back in its place amid the set of problems concerning the cogito to which it belongs. Leaving things aside, wondering about the mode of their appearing, and presupposing the duplicity of it, Descartes's analysis is situated immediately in the dimension of *cogitationes*; it works within this. On the one hand (and this is where Descartes follows Galileo) sensible qualities do not have their seat in the body; they reside in the soul, they are *cogitationes*. When, separated for this reason from knowledge of the piece of wax, they are replaced by the geometric intuition of extension and its figures, this intuition refers of course to an exteriority, it is

---

[*] Descartes, *Oeuvres philosphique*, ed. F. Alquié, vol. II (Paris: Gallimard, 1967), p. 425, notes 2 and 3.

precisely the intuition of it, of a *res extensa*. But on the other hand, how can one forget the most radical theory of the cogito on which we have insisted at length? The *intueri*—the vision of the understanding that knows the *res extensa* and its properties, such as the property of receiving figures *ad infinitum*—is in itself a *cogitatio*; it is given to itself not in a vision but in the same way a sensation, a sadness, or any other passion is, in the self-givenness of absolute life. Sensation, sentiment, and the understanding's intuitive vision establish only a hierarchy among the *cogitationes*, which anyway are all relative since it is a question only of evaluating their aptitude with respect to knowing this simple, particular nature that is the *res extensa*.

In Descartes we see that the certainty of the body—the body understood, following Galileo, as *res extensa*—does not come from its worldliness, but from the knowledge I have of it. It is only because my perception of the body—in other words, the intellectual intuition of its extension—is certain, that this body can itself be posited as certain. But the intellectual intuition of extension is itself certain only because it is a *cogitatio*. This is the meaning of the counter-reduction carried out by Descartes, even though it takes over Galileo's invention: Far from it being the case that the truth of the body eliminates the truth of the impression and of subjectivity in general, on the contrary, it is the absolute certainty of the subjective perception of the body, as a *cogitatio* that is certain, that will be capable of founding the certainty of the universe and its knowledge. The conditions for reversing the perspective opened by Galileo, which will be that of modern science and modernity in its entirety, are already set.

§19. Husserl's Critique of Galileo's Reduction in the *Krisis*.

Husserl will take it upon himself to develop them fully, in his last major published work, the *Krisis*. Husserl could still observe Galileo's impressive results three centuries later, and so did not doubt the fecundity of his presupposition any more than Descartes did. Like Descartes, and following him in fact, he perceived that this presupposition implied others, which would limit its scope radically. Yet the latter presuppositions, without which Galileo's construction of modern science would have been impossible, are nevertheless never taken into account by it. The phenomenological critique of the Galilean reduction consists in this: not in contesting the breadth or value of the knowledge that science continues to produce, but in denouncing the forgetfulness of its ultimate foundation. If we take this into account, we are led ineluctably to what Galileo had thought he could avoid: Sensible qualities, sensibility, and subjectivity in general.

Thus Husserl's reproach of the Galilean universe of modern science is that it posits itself as an absolute—a universe which would be true in itself in some way, and would draw its truth only from itself. Yet one has only to reflect upon the analysis of the universe from which the reduction proceeds to recognize immediately why this claim to autonomy is futile. The universe, Galileo tells us, is a Book written in a language whose characters are geometric figures. However, none of these characters exist in the real world. In the real world, there are neither lines, nor circles, nor triangles, nor squares, but only what is round, vague traces like the bank of a path or a stream, the section of a plank, the edge of a table, and other approximate characteristics, *which are all sensible appearances, moreover, with "forms" that are themselves sensible.* Something like a line or a circle, in the geometric sense, is an ideal entity whose existence, which is never encountered in the material universe, is always preceded by a mental operation—an operation that one rightly calls transcendental in so far as it is nothing other than the condition of possibility for the formation of this line or this circle, of any ideal entity in general. The set of these geometrical figures, and, similarly, the mathematical formulations for them, presuppose as many "performances" of transcendental consciousness, without which they would not be. But these performances are seated in the subjectivity of transcendental life, of which they are only various modalities. The reduction that leads to modern science, to the delineation of its domain and the definition of its procedures, far from being able make an abstraction of subjectivity, still hangs on this and constantly presupposes it.

The idealities that form the content of scientific theories not only proceed from operations constitutive of transcendental consciousness, they cannot dispense with the sensible world that Galileo wanted to do without—seeing in it at most a fabric of appearances of which science would give account. Scientific idealities certainly do not belong to this world, they arise from an intellectual activity of the mind from which they consequently draw their nature as well as their existence. In what does this activity consist? It is a process of ideation that we have already seen at work in the theory of the constitution of essences and of the eidetic intuition to whose aporia the phenomenological method falls prey, seeking its ultimate possibility. Let us limit ourselves to recalling that the point of departure for the activity of ideation is singular givens, which are actually the sensible forms of ordinary perception. On the basis of these, the process of ideation produces geometry's pure and ideal figures, and leaves aside their sensible, singular, vague, and approximate character (for example, the thickness, color, or irregularities of a "straight line" traced on the chalkboard by the professor during a demonstration), retaining only the intellectual principle that presided over the construction of such a line—its geometric definition. Though they do not belong to the world of sensibility, geometrical idealities still bear an essential relation to it as the place of their origin.

Precisely because geometric idealities intrinsically bear this reference to the sensible world from which they come, Galileo's intuition of their power of intelligibility with respect to this world was made possible. That is also how this intuition is ultimately founded. Not only do the idealities of Galilean science refer to the sensible world on whose basis they are constructed, they have meaning only in relation to it. It is their reference to this world as the explanatory principles of its reality, and also of its sensible appearances, that justifies the whole of Galileo's scientific theories.

Take for example the theory of light. Does the physico-mathematical substructure that it deploys have any other goal than to give account of luminous phenomena as sensible phenomena? And this is not at all because the mastery or manipulation of them would present an obvious utility for humanity, but by reason of its properly theoretical finality—of the desire immanent to every mind to explain and to know. On the theoretical plane itself, however, is the consideration of these luminous phenomena actually limited to a general interest of knowledge? Isn't their intervention already implicated in the very construction of the theory, as the ever-present moment of a *verification* apart from which the theory is only a dream, however mathematical it may be? When the theory is presented as a coherent, abstract whole, does its claim to truth draw from anything other than a sensible phenomenon, to the apparition or not of a luminous flash on a screen? Thus the entire physico-mathematical substructure of the theory seems to depend on a sensible order and finally on the whole set of sensible phenomena that science claims to explain. As if these phenomena were not only the point of departure of science but its insurmountable reference, its meaning and its final legitimation.

So this is the twofold limit of Galileo's reduction. On the one hand, transcendental subjectivity, which cannot be eliminated, to the extent that the new science draws its properly theoretical content from it. On the other hand, the sensible world, to which this content inevitably refers. We have hinted at the inhuman character of a world deprived of every sensible quality, the frightening character of it. A world where the most tender and most ordinary human gestures are reduced to inert material processes homogeneous with those that physics studies—to bombardments of particles. We now see that such a world of *insensible* particles, where there would be neither coolness, nor odor, nor light, nor shadow, nor sound, nor color, nor sweetness, nor pleasure, nor charm, would not be only an unlivable world—it is an *impossible* world, if it is true that a world cannot exist for us unless it entertains a final relation with us, even though it would be reduced to a sensible efflorescence, to a sensation. We must therefore return from the scientific world, which is only an abstract world incapable of subsisting by itself, or, if one prefers, existing for us, to the sensible world that the world-of-science presupposes and to which it refers in all respects. The ontological analysis of the body in which the Galilean reduction consists, which opened the space of modern science, is inseparable from a phenomenological analysis, for which the appearance that had been taken for an illusion remains the alpha and omega, an inescapable foundation.

A final remark will underscore the limits of Galileo's reduction. Let us place ourselves one last time within its perspective, seeing only what it sees, and suppose we have acquired, conversely, the totality of knowledge that it makes possible. Galileo's omniscient God, who knows the whole material universe and consequently the structure (that we still today call, in an obsolete way, "biological") of diverse species of animals—a structure that according to Galileo follows from every series of sensation that can be felt by it—this God would know none of this, would have no idea of red, black, yellow, or any color, no idea of sound or music, of odor, or perfumes, or what is agreeable or disagreeable, lovable or detestable. He wouldn't have the least idea, nor could he. A foreign God, truthfully, and that also means a foreign Science, which is what we are offered today in school as the one real knowledge, which in fact, at the end of its prodigious development, still knows far less than the most undeveloped child or the most primitive primitive. To put it as Descartes does, there is a creation of sensible truths of which a science limited to the field of material nature can know nothing.

§20. A Return to the Analysis of the Worldly, Sensible Body. The Reference of the Sensed Body to the Transcendental Body that Senses It. The Ambivalence of the Concept "Sensible."

Let us therefore close the Galilean parenthesis, the fallacious identification of the body in general (the "essence" of the body) with the material extended body, the *res extensa*, and come back to the sensible world where men and women live. In the sensible world there is the sensible body. This point of departure for our reflection is not as simple as it seems. The reversal of phenomenology we have just advanced in the first part of this book compels us now to de-compose the sensible body, which is immediately involved when the "sensible world" is decomposed. "World" signifies an appearing, the coming outside of the Outside, the "outside itself" of the temporal horizon in which everything that shows itself to us in this way becomes visible. The content of the world, in this case the sensible body, is opposed to the pure appearing of the world, which has been shown to be incapable of positing its content by itself. It is precisely no longer to the appearing of the world that this content owes its existence, but to sensibility. This sensible body does offer itself at first as a sensed body, a body that is seen, that can be touched, makes a sound if one strikes it, that has an odor, the sweet smell of honey that the piece of wax has, that is smooth or rough, cold or hot, dry or damp, hard or soft. Common sense and in turn the majority of theories of the body hang on this sensed body, which is also an object of the world. It is precisely in the world that we see this body, it is in the world that we strike it, so we can see for example whether it is made of glass or crystal; it is in the world that we hear the dull or faint sound it makes, just as it is in the world that the surface of a body appears smooth or rough, and around it, also in the world, that its odor drifts.

As long as the sensible body is considered as a sensed body, its worldliness is not clearly challenged. Just as it is in the world that the real substance of this body extends—in fact, this is the case for ordinary perception as well as for the ancients or moderns—it is also in the world, in a sort of extension, that these "sensible qualities" are dis-posed, extend, or radiate. Doesn't the world—and by this we always mean its appearing, the Ek-stasis of its exteriority—take back within it and precisely "contain" this "sensible content," which is spread over the objects and ex-poses itself in them, unfolding itself like them, with them, in the unfolding of the horizon in which the world is externalized and appears to us?

The illusion that the sensible world would constitute an autonomous reality—because in it the sensible quality finds the phenomenological condition of its appearing *qua* exterior sensible quality, and thus has this appearance of exteriority—*that* is the paralogism of what should indeed be called a crude realism. But this is not proper to common sense; it inhabits every thought, which, whether explicitly or not, considers the body as a *sensible worldly object*. Or, to put it differently, considers the world's sensible content as an in-itself. There is thus a pure Sensible, something that at once possesses an impressional texture—which is red, gloomy, sonorous, painful, or nauseating—but whose appearing is nevertheless the "outside" of the world. Galileo's essential analysis (to the extent that it is true and unalterable, and as Descartes takes it up in the set of problems surrounding the cogito) has denounced this illusion.

A worldly body reduced to what it owes to the world, an external body reduced to its exteriority, an extended body as such possesses no impressional matter, indeed no sensible quality; it is no more red than painful, nauseating, or irate. The sensible, axiological, affective stratum of the world does not come from its ek-static structure any more than the impressional content of the Husserlian flow comes from its form as a flow.

It is no longer possible to avoid this obvious fact. Every sensed body presupposes another body that senses it; every body that is seen presupposes a power of vision and the implementation, operation, or, as we would say, performance of this power; every sonorous body, a power of hearing, and the operation and performance of such a power; every body touched, felt, and scanned by the hand that touches it, the power to touch, the application of it, *and also the power to move this power to touch—presupposes the hand that touches, and consequently the application, operation, and performance of this second power as well as the first.* The same holds true for odor, for everything that is capable of being sensed, whose being-sensed always implies a power of sensing without which it would not be.

So we are inevitably referred from a sensible, worldly body, which is an object of the world, to a body of another order entirely: a transcendental body endowed with the fundamental powers of seeing, sensing, touching, hearing, moving, and being moved—and defined by these powers. A "transcendental" body, because it is a condition of possibility for the worldly, sensed body. A sensing body, and no longer sensed; giving, and no longer given; a body that gives the world and all the bodies sensed in it—and our own body, therefore, as a body that is also sensed in the world, among other worldly bodies. A subject-body, as opposed to an object-body, whose condition it is. An *a priori* "subjective body" that is different from the objective body, in the sense that it appears as its foundation. A subjective, transcendental body, giving and sensing the body given and sensed by it—every worldly, objective body. It is above all the theory of this originary and founding body that is required.

We are thus confronted with difficult problems, each of which must be clearly perceived and treated for itself. The difficulty, however, does not only stem from the multiplicity of questions raised, such as those pertaining to the essence of the originary body, its relation to the worldly body, and the principle of the difference that is established among the worldly bodies between natural bodies and a body like ours—our transcendental body, in particular, in so far as it too appears, it seems, under the aspect of a worldly body; or even the relation between our own body and that of the other, whether it's a question of the relation between our transcendental bodies or our worldly bodies, etc. And to this we must add the question of the relation between sensible qualities and impressions, between these and fundamental powers (vision, hearing, etc.), which co-constitute the originary body to which the objective body owes its nature and properties. The list goes on.

The difficulty is first one of deciding the order in which these numerous questions should be approached. With regard to this issue, it is true that we already have decisive indications at our disposal. The order of an investigation is also the method it must follow if it is to arrive at its object. According to the presuppositions of phenomenology, its own object is what founds its method; pure appearing is what constitutes, as we said, the way of access that leads to it. These general presuppositions of phenomenology take on a rigorous meaning when the analysis of phenomenality has shattered the illusory unity of this concept. Thus we have disassociated two fundamental modes according to which pure phenomenality becomes phenomenal: Against the monotonous interpretation of the Greek *phainomenon* we have opposed the fundamental duality of appearing, its "duplicity." This is what must guide our approach, working out the order of questions whose elaboration is now its task. Have we not indeed recognized that two ways are offered *a priori* for the analysis of the body, according to whether it entrusts the appearing of the body to the world's Ek-stasis or to life's pathos?

Following the first path, naturally, we have found the worldly body, the body that shows itself to us in the world and at the same time seems to constitute the content of it. The sensible character of the body (which Galileo's reduction does not manage to eliminate) has given rise to a first difficulty: The sensible character of the body is inexplicable on the basis of the world and its appearing. So we found ourselves unavoidably referred from the sensible body, in so far as it is a sensed body, to a body that senses it: *a body that is no longer an object of experience, but its principle.* This body-principle of experience, a condition of its possibility—the transcendental body—is composed, as we said, of a set of fundamental powers. These are nothing other than the *traditional senses. Yet the structure of each of these senses is an ek-static structure.* Each sense is a "sense at a distance." Sight, for example, looks in the distance, beyond the first houses along the river, across the field, to the top of the hill, to the trees that cover it, and even further, to the sky and to the furthest star. The closest objects, those that surround us, are held in the same distance. The distance that separates us from them is not first a spatial distance, which can indeed be greater or less: it is the transcendental exteriority of the world whose structure is the tri-dimensional horizon of time that precedes (by making it possible) the intuition of space, and cannot depend on it. This originary exteriority cannot be abolished without the very possibility of vision being abolished at the same time. The same is true for all of our senses:

They all throw us outside, in such a way that everything sensed by us is already outside us, different from the power that senses in as much as this power is one of distancing, the Ek-stasis of the world. Thus every sound resonates in the world, the odor floats around the flower, the perfume around the face, and around us. Can we not, however, touch an object in an immediate contact, run our finger along its surface? It is true, what we touch in the case of this contact, what is against us, wholly against, is the exterior itself—the wood of this table, this wall, my own body in as much as I make it the object of one of my senses, but which, at the same time, becomes for me something external.

But if all our senses are senses "at a distance," if the structure of each of the powers that make up our transcendental body is an ek-static structure, such that everything we sense is external to us, the following paradoxical consequence cannot escape us: Far from being incapable of founding the body's sensible character and thus the content it makes appear, the appearance of the world would on the contrary be its condition. We would like to examine the subjectivity of this transcendental body, which is no longer an object of experience, but its principle. We recognize without difficulty the true name of this subjectivity, which borrows its phenomenality from the world's, with which it is identical: It is intentionality, pushing one's limits outside oneself, seen in the light of the "outside oneself," which is the world. At the same time the sophism is unmasked that consists in attributing to the senses of the transcendental body the sensible character of what they give us to sense as exterior to us. What they explain in their transcendence is this external character, and in no way the sensible character of what is sensed: the felt material of red, of cold or heat, the affective reverberation of a sound or an odor—and we do not even know whether these are in us or in things.

What is here required is an *eidetic analysis not of the material body, but of sensibility*, whose concept traditionally remains submerged in almost total obscurity. Let us thus consider again the performances of the transcendental body which do indeed open us to things by giving them to us in this very particular way, which consists in sensing them—which are the performances of our senses, of sight, hearing, or touch. In an incontestable way, these performances are intentional; they are drawn toward the world. In the movement of passing outside, they make visible that which the "outside" ensures in its visibility. When this is accomplished as vision properly speaking, as hearing, as the act of smelling an odor, tasting a dish, or touching an object, it is always in arriving outside that the experience of sensing becomes possible. Seeing, in the phenomenological sense of the term, as a synonym of grasping—*sehen und fassen*—refers to this transcendental clearing which is neither the light of the sun nor that of electricity, and in which, nevertheless, independently of every natural or artificial lighting, things already appear to us. In the dark of my room, I still "see" this darkness, I touch my bedside table, and I hear the silence *that surrounds me*.

If seeing, touching, and hearing always bear an intentionality in them, it is no longer possible to explain them by structures and inert processes that in themselves lack any intentionality—the first by the eye, the second by touch, the third by the ear. The set of transcendental performances of our senses, our sensations, and the sensible qualities that they allow us to know, cannot result from the biological structure of the kind of animal that we are. Galileo's explanation is dismissed, and with it every form of materialism, whether it be that of common sense or of scientism. From the philosophical point of view, it is always absurd to explain a condition of possibility by what it makes possible—in this case, the body that senses, on the basis of what is sensed.

§21. The Attempt to Overcome the Opposition between the Sensing Body and the Sensed Body: The Issue Facing the Later Merleau-Ponty and the Absolutization of the Sensible.

This insurmountable duality between the two bodies, one a principle of experience, the other its object, confronts us for the first time with the extreme ambiguity of the concept of sensibility. It actually assumes two totally different meanings, when we speak, as we habitually do, of the "sensible body." It is a question of the sensed body, on the one hand, and the body that senses it on the other; it is the former body, the inert body of material nature—which is in itself opaque, blind, and deprived precisely of the power of sensing that defines the essence of the latter—that constitutes the condition of possibility of the former and makes it what it is. "Sensible" thus denotes at once the capacity of sensing and that which is forever deprived of this capacity. *The extraordinary fact that our own body can be considered and described from these two originally different and incompatible points of view—and that it seems, moreover, to unite them within it, to the point of being understood on the basis of this duality*—has in no small way contributed to this confusion.

By taking our own body into consideration instead of some natural body, it is true that the difficulty becomes less obvious. Isn't our own body just this, a body that senses at the same time as it is sensed, and sensed by itself? It would thus be "sensible" by virtue of the two acceptations that we wanted to dissociate. Wouldn't the "confusion" of the sensible in this case refer us to its true nature, allowing us finally to perceive it? "Sensible" would then mean sensing/sensed as a pair, the two taken together, indissolubly. "Visible," in a sense as radical as it is unexpected, would mean bearing within it the Seeing that sees it, the Seeing overwhelmed by what it sees, taken up by it, illuminating what becomes visible only by having absorbed the Seeing within it, and with which it is now one: the fluorescent matter that forms the texture of the world, appearances in seamless continuity; the Sensible and pure Visible, confused, so that they are finally recognized in themselves—the flesh of the world, the luminous flesh whose light is the world's appearing.

And all of this—the absurdity of a flesh that is always already like one who has been skinned alive, like Marsyas the faun or St. Bartholomew—this ek-static flesh, torn from itself, separated from itself, placed outside itself, fleeing to the horizon, this flesh forever at a distance, worldly, that does not know the burden of being itself and being a Self inexorably tied to itself, under house arrest in itself, crushed against itself in the untearable suffering of its infrangible pathos—that knows no suffering and joy—the translucent, transparent flesh, reduced to a film with no thickness, which would not belong to anyone but the world—all of this, the entire bundle of paradoxes that strip our flesh of everything that makes it flesh, would not be so absurd if we could discover its principle and place in our body.

We can, as long as we reduce it to the touching/touched (touching/tangible) relation, which can also be written as seeing/visible, since behind these designations, which in turn are referred to our different senses, it is a question of the general relation between the power of sensing and what it senses, of the transcendental body to the sensed body, and of the structure of sensibility that has not yet been understood. To reduce our own body to such a relation is to make it into an absolute, to give an account of the body that is ours, of its relation to the sensible world, and of the world itself, without any need for recourse to another authority.

Let us make use of one such relation, as the later Merleau-Ponty does in *The Visible and the Invisible*. My right hand (the touching) touches my left hand (the touched). In an incontestable way, the structure of this relation is an oppositional structure, between a transcendental body capable of sensing (a constituting body), and that which is sensed only by it (constituted as such). But this relation is reversible. It is the left hand now that touches the right. At once its condition totally changes, it is raised to the kind of self-control that pertains to constituting—it has become the touching, the power of sensing—while the right hand is subjected to an opposite destiny: Abandoning the self-control that constituting requires, it has taken a place among what is constituted, in other words, among things. In this inversion of roles between the two hands, the (touching/touched) structure it is produced within is not abolished, but maintained. Against all logic, however, Merleau-Ponty reads this as disqualifying the oppositional structure of constituting and constituted. And this is because, in a surreptitious but also illegitimate way, he *extended to the entire world the touching/touched relation that characterizes one's own body and occurs nowhere but in it.*

When the right hand that touched loses its command of touching, this now means not simply that it has become part of one's own body that is touched, but part of the world in general, and is consequently homogeneous with it. Thus it is the transcendental power of sensing that, by being inserted into the world, testifies to the permanent possibility that it might become a thing among others, and like them. Conversely, when the right hand that is touched (situated in the world) is in turn made into the hand that touches, it is then the entire world (whose condition it shared up to that point) that it installs in the new register now its own, that of a transcendental, constituting, and touching body. This two-fold possibility is inherent to the transcendental body and to the world: The former becomes world by turning the touching that it was into the touched, while the latter becomes the transcendental body by turning the touched it was into the touching. And from this two-fold possibility Merleau-Ponty's Sensible follows: Sensing/sensed, Touching/tangible, Seeing/visible, all at once and combined and interlaced, an entity as eclectic as it is inconceivable, that purports to define one single reality, the world's, appearing and content confused, the sensible world, and the flesh of the world.

And these are not two homogeneous moments, where the Seeing somehow "incarnates itself" in the visible, which "unwinds itself around the Seeing," but a single moment, which is reality, where from the start, the being seeing the visible and the being-visible of the Seeing are one and the same. "He who sees cannot possess the visible unless he is possessed by it, unless it *is it*, unless, in principle [. . .] he is one of the visible, and capable, by a singular reversal, of seeing them, he who is one of them." "The body unites us directly to things by its own ontogenesis, by welding one to another [. . .] the sensible mass that it is and the mass of the sensible where it is born by segregation, and onto which, as seeing, it remains open." "Such that when the seeing is grasped in what it sees, it is still itself that it sees: There is a fundamental narcissism in every vision." The body, finally, "is Visibility sometimes wandering, sometimes gathering,"*—in other words, together, the parade of visible bodies, the *visibilia,* and the transcendental power that sees them. The transcendental power of constitution, whose systematic elucidation Husserl's phenomenology pursued and whose fundamental structures it had so much

---

* Maurice Merleau-Ponty, *Le visible et l'Invisible* (Paris: Gallimard, 1964), pp. 177–8, 179, 183, 181, respectively / *The Visible and the Invisible,* trans. Alphonso Lingis (Evanston: Northwestern University Press, 1968), pp. 133, 135, 136, 139, 137–38; translation modified.

trouble attaining, is in this way flattened into the constituted, reduced to it, confused with it, and identified with it—lost and evaded. And this is not by accident, but for essential reasons: because the phenomenological status of the power of constitution remains unthought. Absorbed in the constituted, the theory of constitution cedes place to a literary description that in a dangerous way returns to naive realism. As with Bergson before him, was Merleau-Ponty not duped by his prestigious writing to the point of replacing philosophical analysis with a system of metaphors?

§22. Splitting the Transcendental Body. Finding in Life the Essence of Originary, Immanent Corporeity.

Before showing why it is impossible to extend to the universe the oppositional Touching/touched structure—understood as reversible in principle, a characteristic of our own body, which emerges and is exercised in this body and in it alone (we have still never seen a stone that is touched by my hand begin to touch it, feel it, and caress it in turn . . .)—we must reflect further upon a structure of this sort. How can we accept it naively, simply by seeing it at work in the most ordinary experience, when one of our hands really does touch the other or is touched by it? Here as elsewhere, just because we do something like this does not mean we have given an account philosophically for the transcendental and *a priori* possibility of such an act. Yet this possibility is not just about touching, but also vision, hearing, taste, and smell—it is the possibility of all our senses as a whole, of our transcendental body itself.

Here the question of this transcendental possibility of our own body, which we ourselves have called a transcendental, originary, and constituting body, splits strangely in two. Defined by the whole of our senses, where its activity cashes out in the multiple performances of seeing, touching, hearing, and feeling under all these forms, our own body is transcendental, in the sense that it makes possible everything that is seen, heard, and touched by it, the set of sensible qualities and objects that make up the reality of our world—a sensible world indeed. If this sensible reality is precisely that of a world, it is because these senses are senses at a distance: *In the mode of intentionality they are led to feeling in various ways, by making-it-appear in the light of the ek-static horizon where things become visible, toward which intentionality always throws itself.*

And yet the reversal of phenomenology has taught us that intentionality—the intentionality of the transcendental body that makes the sensible body possible, and as a result the sensible universe in general—

never constitutes by itself its own condition of possibility: Opening us to the world, making it manifest, it is incapable of securing the work of manifestation with regard to itself, of revealing itself to itself. Thus we are referred invincibly from the transcendental possibility of the sensible world (which resides in the intentional, transcendental body that leads it to feeling) to the transcendental possibility of this intentional body itself—*to the self-revelation of intentionality in life.*

This reference from one transcendental possibility to the other is decisive because it is the second that founds the first. Each of these intentional, transcendental performances of our various senses can take place, can give us what it gives (vision what is seen, hearing what is heard, touching what it touches, taste what it tastes, odor what it smells) only *if it is revealed originally to itself in the phenomenological completion of the givenness that it accomplishes,* qua *giving.* In this way, we would say following Descartes, a vision that did not feel itself seeing*—in a self-revelation that is different in nature from the appearing in which it discovers what it sees—would be forever incapable of seeing what it sees. This is true for each of the intentionalities that are constitutive of our various senses. The transcendental body, which opens us to the sensed body (whether it is a question of our own or of things), rests upon a corporeity far more originary, which is transcendental in a final, non-intentional, non-sensible sense, the essence of which is life.

The new way opens here, a royal road, even if it was only rarely taken by philosophy: to understand the body starting not from the world, but from life. It is a question, first, of preserving the radical character of this new approach. The analyses of the body that we have conducted to this point (most notably, the critique of the Galilean reduction, and the reference of the sensed body to the transcendental body that senses it) belong to the first way, since both remain under the light of the world. This is evident for the Galilean reduction, which in its own way substitutes the intelligible for the sensible without questioning the mode of appearing that makes up the intelligibility of the intelligible—and of the sensible itself, for that matter. The question that goes from the sensed body back to the transcendental body that senses it asks instead about the relation that arises between them—such that this relation is intentionality. If taken as self-evident, this does not, as we know, introduce any new mode of ap-

---

* *"Sentimus nos videre"* says the famous letter to Plempius from October 3, 1637, which places our own vision, as effective phenomenological vision, in opposition to that of animals, who precisely do not see—which implies that an older feeling of another order is immanent in vision itself, a self-feeling that seeing would not see without. AT, I, 413–36 / PW III, 61 ff. Cf. Descartes, AT, IX, 28 / PW II, 19.

pearing other than that of the world. Quite the contrary: In the Ek-stasis of the world, everything that occurs in our experience, it makes visible and felt *as an object sensed outside us,* vibrant and resonating in a world. Thus the sensible is split between a subject-body—*a subjective body*—and an object-body.

Rather than holding to the traditional account of the body as a mere object, modern phenomenology contributed to the discovery of this subjective body. It is certainly not nothing to place at the origin of our experience, not Kant's empty and formal "I think," but a subject that is a body, an incarnate subject, as the "first" Merleau-Ponty of the *Phenomenology of Perception* does. The world to which we have access is indeed different depending on whether it is known by an ideal geometry (as Galileo believed), by the intellectual intuition of a pure understanding (as after him Descartes and classical philosophy thought), or if it is on the contrary a question of an originally sensible world at every moment resulting from the concrete performances of our various senses.

The renewal of the question of the body, and thereby of the world, in as much as it is the former that now fashions the latter, nevertheless remains very relative: Far from escaping from the presuppositions that determine the Greek concept of the phenomenon, the supposed renewal remains within the horizon they outline and remains subject to them. This happens in such a restrictive way that, far from being weakened, the interpretation of the body based on the visibility of the world is on the contrary reinforced, extended to the new transcendental body—to the incarnate subject that is responsible for our experience. This is indeed an intentional body, *subjected to the world in the originary sense that it opens us to it.* Precisely because the transcendental body that senses with all its senses opens us to the world, everything it makes sensible—and thus itself as a sensing body, but capable equally of being sensed, by itself—takes place in this world as a sensed object. *The "outside itself" determines both the body as a new subject of the sensible world, and the traditional body situated in this world as an object and sensed in it.* The new transcendental body is thus only the condition of the old one, to the point of being able to slide itself into this old position, as one sees occur in the later Merleau-Ponty. With the identification of the two bodies, old and new, with the myth of the Sensible as Sensing/sensed, Seeing/visible, we are not only confronted with an aberration; more accurately, this is a result of taking the presuppositions of phenomenological monism to their limit, and it must be understood as their ultimate consequence.

In a rigorous phenomenological analysis, the opposition between a "subject-body" and an "object-body" thus comes down to an opposition encountered by this analysis at its first step: the opposition between appearing and what appears in it. Such an opposition is not properly phenomenological in the sense that it does not arise between two modes of appearing that are different and thus "opposed" to each other. On the contrary, in the phenomenological structure that opposes appearing and what appears in it, one and the same appearing is at work and carries out its power of manifestation. Precisely because this single appearing is "outside itself," it places outside, in a world, everything it makes appear, and an opposition arises between this appearing and what appears in it. That is why the subject-body, the transcendental body that makes sensible outside itself what is in this way sensed by it on the outside, reigns unchallenged over the sensed (but equally over itself as soon as it becomes for it a question of appearing). It can only do so by bringing itself outside itself, so as to be sensed by it. The reversibility of the touching and the touched means nothing other than this reign of a single appearing, which in turn busies itself with what it gives outside itself (with the sensed) and then with itself, which gives this sensed but is not given to itself except in this outside itself, as also sensed. Such that there is always only the sensed, and the power of sensing, in order to always be displaced from one moment to the next, from one hand to the other, *is always presupposed anywhere but in what comes to appear only under the form of what is sensed.* Like the "subject" of classical philosophy, this elsewhere remains "an eternal absentee." Stripped of every phenomenological effectiveness, the performance of each of its now-mysterious powers, the transcendental body that is supposed to open us to the sensible world—to the sensed-body, whether our own or any other—is no more than a useless hypothesis. These are the presuppositions of phenomenology that collapse when the condition of all phenomena must itself renounce every claim to phenomenality. The object-body of the tradition and common sense remains in fact what it always was, truly an object-body, owing its manifestation only to its status as an ob-ject—*to the fact of being thrown-there-in-front-in-a-world,* in the absence of every other legitimation, without any philosophical question about its legitimacy even needing to be posed.

§23. The Generation of Flesh in Absolute Life. The Originary Phenomenological Characteristics of Flesh that Arise from This Generation.

The conception of the body is completely changed only when its mode of appearing is called explicitly into question, when the way of access to the body (to our own, first of all) is no longer the world's Ek-stasis, but life. Then all the phenomenological properties that the traditional body gets from the world must be crossed out. Not only does our body no longer present itself in the guise of an external body that is sensed by us—a thing among things, and an object among objects. If it is a question of thinking our body no longer as an object of experience but as a principle of experience, as a power of givenness that makes manifest, then the intentional transcendental body, which senses all things (and itself outside itself as a sensed body), must also be disqualified. Neither the sensing nor the sensed nor their oppositional structure is involved in what must now be thought. Nor is the Touching/touched, Seeing/visible chiasma—whether it is still understood as a chiasma, as an oppositional structure, or, on the contrary, as interlaced, as the inconceivable identification of constituting and constituted, and as their confusion. For if life is responsible for the revelation of the body, then there is precisely within it neither oppositional structure nor intentionality, nor Ek-stasis of any sort—nothing visible at all. And the originary power of becoming visible, the arrival of the world "outside oneself," the first externalization of exteriority, is no longer at work here either, in the revelation of our originary corporeity, in so far as this is entrusted to life. It is *an invisible, originary corporeity*, therefore, stripped of every worldly characteristic as well as of the power of givenness in a world—and endowed, on the contrary, with all the phenomenological properties that it inherits when it becomes phenomenal in life.

What properties does our originary corporeity inherit from life? This amounts to asking: How does life reveal, and what does it reveal, such that what is revealed by it is in this case the entire set of properties constitutive of this originary corporeity we're talking about and which is our own? Our question thus refers to what we know. Life reveals in such a way that what it reveals never takes place outside it—since it is never anything external to it, other, or different, but precisely itself. So that the revelation of life is a self-revelation, the originary and pure "experiencing undergoing itself" in which what feels and what is felt are one and the same. But this is possible only because the phenomenological mode of revelation in which life consists is a pathos, an embrace without distance and without regard to a suffering and an enjoyment whose phenomenological material is indeed pure affectivity, a pure impressionality, the radically immanent self-affection that is nothing other than our flesh.

The complete upheaval of the traditional conception of the body, as soon as its appearing is entrusted to life and not to the world, does not only consist in the substitution of one mode of appearing for another; it equally affects the content of what is revealed each time: This is not the body that we always understand as an external body, but something totally different—precisely a flesh, a flesh like ours, which never occurs anywhere but in life.

But this is the difference that must be thought through to the end. As soon as the body shows itself to us in the world, it owes to that mode of appearing certain phenomenological characteristics, all of which derive from exteriority—but *never its existence*. So one must recognize that all the bodies that are uncovered in the world (whether it is an issue of our own body or any body at all) *exist before this uncovering and independently of it.* When life reveals flesh, on the contrary, it is not confined to reveal it as if we were still there in the presence of two terms, the one that reveals and the other that is revealed. And that is why we say the first is not confined to revealing the second, in the way the world unveils a body it does not create. *Life reveals flesh by generating it, as what takes birth in it, being formed and edified in it, and drawing its substance (its pure phenomenological substance) from the very substance of life. An impressional and affective flesh, whose impressional character and affectivity never result from anything other than the impressional character and affectivity of life itself.*

At first glance, in fact, as soon as we encountered flesh in terms of the "impression," it could be described as an affective flesh—since that's all it was, a living flesh, feeling itself and undergoing experiencing itself in an impressionality and an affectivity that are consubstantial with its essence. But this impressionality and affectivity are not its own. The flesh is impressional and affective only because it arrives as such in an original arrival by itself, which is not a characteristic of flesh, but of Life. Where every arrival as such and every conceivable life is accomplished by the power of absolute Life, which brings itself about in itself, *this original arrival in itself is accomplished in the original pathos of its pure enjoyment of itself—in the Arch-Pathos of an Arch-Flesh. Only for this reason, everywhere and necessarily, everywhere a life will arrive as such, this arrival will be identically the arrival of a flesh—the arrival of this flesh as such in the Arch-Flesh of Life.* The flesh is precisely the manner in which life is made Life. No Life without a flesh, but no flesh without Life. But this originary connection and this reciprocity (this reciprocal interiority of Flesh and Life) concerns a life like ours only because, before time, before every conceivable world, it is established in absolute Life as the phenomenological mode according to which this Life arrives eternally in itself in the Arch-Pathos of its Arch-Flesh.

Following the teaching of Christ, John understands God as Life. The Old Testament already said of the God of Abraham, Isaac, and Jacob that he is the God of the Living. With this Life, it is a question of absolute Life, which brings itself about in itself. As Cyril of Alexandria recognized in turn: "Of God alone can it be said that he is Life by nature." In what does this nature consist? We call Arch-passibility the *a priori* possibility of experiencing undergoing itself in the Arch-Pathos of an Arch-Flesh:

So we see quite clearly that this Arch-passibility belongs to absolute Life as its very "nature," as the phenomenological material in which its originary coming in itself is accomplished. It is not that God obeys some prior determination, or some Reason that he himself could not escape, but because he is Life and thus the God of the living. No living without Life, but no Life without the Arch-passibility of its Arch-revelation. Because all this must be understood dynamically, the *a priori* possibility of Life is never a "pure possibility": Always already life has come in itself, it is the eternal coming in itself in the Arch-passibility in which it undergoes experiencing itself unceasingly, and enjoys itself in the infinite love in which it loves itself eternally.

The Christian God is thus not the Greek god. The Fathers of the Church, despite how difficult it was for them to think otherwise than Greek, were not mistaken. They never imagined that the god they adored could be an "impassible" god, a stranger to the affairs of humanity, indifferent to their lot—indifferent to the adoration they brought him, and who would not have, in return, or first of all, loved them himself. And they thought this not out of some naive anthropomorphism, but for an opposite reason. *Phenomenologically they experienced themselves as living, they experienced their own life passively as a life that arrived in them without their contribution or consent, which was not their own and which nevertheless became theirs. A life in which they suffered, and from which they drew the immense joy of living. Given to themselves in this life, loving themselves in it, they experienced that it loved them necessarily, and that this is what its love was: giving them to themselves in the exhilaration of its own joy, making itself known to them in this way—to those who experienced themselves in the exhilaration of its joy in them. So they prayed with Tertullian, asking God not for them to love themselves in him, but for them to love him in them—and him alone.* With furor the master Tertullian denounces the Greek god as a distant, uninhabited god, reduced to an empty concept, deprived of all meaning. A god who would not come to our knowledge where we come to his—separated from our life and its destiny. Dupes of this bloodless God, a stranger to mankind and human affairs, the heretics imagined above the "true God [. . .] who has breathed into us a breath of life [. . .] a great God that no one can know, who does not communicate with the human race and does not look over earthly affairs: It is certainly the God of Epicurus that they found, a God of no use either to himself or to anyone else."*

What in Christianity should be understood by the term *Transcendence* is now in view. It is not, as in contemporary phenomenology, the world's

---

*Irenaeus of Lyon, *Contre les hérésies* (Paris: Le Cerf, 1991), p. 396.

coming outside, or the arrival of what is shown in the world—the objective correlate in the direction of which intentionality "surpasses itself." Nor is it the God of the philosophical tradition or the Architect of the universe. Nor is it even the Creator, who would have thrown his creation outside himself, and us with it, in as much as we would be part of it, which would leave us all the more the task of deciphering the trace he would have wanted to inscribe on his work. In a radical sense—and the only acceptable one, if it is indeed a question of the absolute—*Transcendence denotes the immanence of Life in each living being.* Because this immanence concerns the self-revelation of each living being in so far as it is accomplished in the self-revelation of absolute life, the phenomenological possibility of it and thus the concrete effectuation of it lies in the Arch-possibility in which absolute Life reveals itself originally to itself. "Transcendence" is only a still-undetermined word for this essence.

In so far as it undergoes experiencing itself only in absolute Life's passibility, in the Arch-Pathos of its Arch-Flesh, every living being has a flesh, or, to be more precise, is flesh. This is why the dualism between the soul and the body does not in any way concern it—does not in any way concern man, understood originally as living: because in living, there is no dualism of this sort, but only Life and itself, as given to itself in that very Life. The givenness of the living in Life is the work of Life alone—the givenness in which the appearing of the world has no part, such that there is no outside within it, nor is there body in the sense that we assign to this word. The givenness of the living in Life refers to Life's eternal proceeding, which arrives in itself by undergoing experiencing itself in the Ipseity of the First living Self in which it originally reveals itself to itself. Because Arch-possibility is the phenomenological mode according to which the Arch-revelation of Life in its Arch-Self takes place, it bears within it the Arch-Flesh in which every flesh from then on will be possible. The generation of a flesh like our own becomes possible only in its relation to the eternal generation of the Arch-Flesh of the Arch-Self, in the self-generation of Absolute life as its self-revelation in Arch-Passibility, which belongs to every conceivable living and first of all to absolute Life's own living. And at the same time it becomes intelligible too, in the Arch-intelligibility of Life and in it alone.

This new evidence then strikes our eyes. The generation of the flesh that is ours is strictly parallel to that of our transcendental Self, which in each case makes us the "me" or "ego" that we are. Or rather, it is here a question of one and the same generation. The generation of the living in Life is that of our transcendental Self in the Arch-Self of absolute Life (in its Word) and, identically, of our own flesh in the Arch-Flesh of this Word.

The evidence, then, is this: Because it denotes the phenomenological effectuation of Life's self-revelation in the Ipseity from which each transcendental Self inherits its possibility, because it is nothing other than the *phenomenological material of the self-revelation that makes every Self a Self,* flesh is connected to it as its most interior phenomenological condition of possibility, to the point of identifying with it. There is no Self (no me, no ego, and no "man") without a flesh—but there is no flesh that does not bear a Self within it. There is no Self that in the passibility of its carnal, phenomenological effectuation would not be this one or that one, yours or mine. No flesh, consequently, that would not be that of a particular Self (the flesh of no one, of the world), an anonymous and impersonal flesh, unconscious, feeling nothing and not feeling itself, an impassible flesh! As if, by skinning Marsyas or Bartholomew, one would still not hurt anyone, but arouse only a mundane event, one modification of the Visible among all the *visibilia* that together compose this uninhabited spectacle we call the world—an empty world, which is only the echo of silence.

The flesh is thus not added to the self as a contingent and incomprehensible attribute, a sort of synthetic adjunct to our being, coming to split it into two opposed and irreconcilable moments. Because the flesh is nothing other than the most interior possibility of our Self, it is a unitary Self. Man does not know dualism. The Self thinks where it acts, where it desires, where it suffers, where it is a Self: in its flesh. As was the case in Judeo-Christianity, I and Flesh are one. If I and Flesh are one, it is because they both come from Life, and because they are nothing other than the originary and essential phenomenological modalities according to which life arrives in itself and happens to be life.

To arrive in life as a transcendental living Self that undergoes experiencing itself in its flesh in the way every flesh experiences itself is to be born. Being born thus does not mean, as one imagines naively, to come into the world in the form of an object-body, because then there would be no *living individual,* at the most the apparition of a thing, a worldly body subject to the laws of the world, inheriting its phenomenological properties (its spatiality, temporality, and relations of causality with the collection of other bodies) from the appearing of the world. It would, however, be deprived in principle of what happens only in life: the originary and transcendental possibility of undergoing the pathos-filled experience of itself in a flesh. Such a possibility takes place in the Arch-passibility of absolute Life. To be born means to come in a flesh where every flesh comes in itself, in the Arch-Flesh of Life. In this way the phenomenology of flesh refers invincibly to a phenomenology of Incarnation.

Since something like a "flesh" is comprehensible only starting from its arrival in itself in absolute Life's arrival in itself—and this occurs as the phenomenological mode according to which this originary arrival in itself is produced—the phenomenology of Incarnation should logically precede that of the flesh. If we are following the reverse order, it is for two reasons. The first is that since the phenomenology of Incarnation is connected to the Christian conception of salvation, whose founding possibility it constitutes, we will treat these two questions together in our final section. The second reason is that the phenomenology of flesh does not only refer behind itself, so to speak, to the phenomenology of Incarnation as to its ultimate presupposition; it makes possible the intentional, transcendental body that opens us to the world through sensing and so to everything that is sensed—to the worldly bodies that serve as the exclusive model for the way common sense ordinarily understands the body. The relation of flesh to body is thus an unavoidable question. But it is easier to approach by starting from the phenomenology of flesh alone, and leaving provisionally to one side the more difficult themes of the phenomenology of Incarnation. The latter, *the relation of Arch-Flesh to flesh* recorded in John's word—"And the Word was made flesh"—indeed takes place in Life, far from the world, before it, and independently of its appearing, which thought has so much difficulty overcoming as long as the reversal of phenomenology has neither been carried out nor understood.

§24. From the Hellenic Conception of the Body to the Phenomenology of Flesh. The Fundamental Problems of Irenaeus and Tertullian.

The phenomenology of flesh has presented us with two essential correlations: that of flesh and Life, on the one hand, and that of flesh and birth on the other. We are going to follow the way this two-fold relation deepens the moment it emerges in the history of human thought with incredible singularity. Is it so extraordinary to establish a connection between flesh and Life or, in the same way, between flesh and birth? Certainly not, if one remains in a naive understanding of life, where it is identified with a particular being endowed with specific properties (motility, nutrition, reproduction, etc.) and *shown to us in the world*. But when life is no longer a being, some thing, or *what appears*, but *pure appearing* itself (and an appearing that is precisely not the world's, but excludes it in an invincible way), then the two-fold correlation of Life/flesh and flesh/birth becomes very original, and very difficult to think. Is it not necessary then to dissociate what always goes together, *to separate the flesh from the body and wrest from the grip of the world the idea of birth that we make for ourselves?* The time for such radical disruptions, such agonizing reassessments, was precisely when John's speech reverberated through the antique world and shook it to its foundations. These foundations support not only the theoretical universe of knowledge, but also the most trivial and ordinary matters of existence, which concern all the living, "the simple": Birth, flesh, and what they themselves call life—their life.

The violence of this confrontation between *the Greek conception of the body* and *the Christian conception of flesh* will thus explode on the scene from the first propagation in the antique world of the new religion, whose essential content is the affirmation of the coming of God in the human condition in the form of his incarnation. Are we not here again brought back to the point where the phenomenology of flesh is related to a theological problem and contaminated by it? In no way, if it is true that in the eyes of the Fathers the flesh of Christ is like the flesh of every man. Let us recall that this is the thesis defended relentlessly against the heretics. Thus when the Fathers struggle to grasp the nature of Christ's flesh, they do not have in view a flesh different from our own: It is a theory of flesh in general they construct. Amid extraordinary difficulties, admittedly, since for them it is a question of explaining the Judeo-Christian intuition of flesh in light of the Greek conception of the body. At least what must be thought as proper to man—and consequently to the Christ himself in taking the human condition—is already apprehended in a Hebrew and not a Greek way—as a flesh. Thus the double and essential correlation that flesh maintains with Life, on the one hand, and birth, on the other, comes to the foreground.

"There is no birth without flesh, and no flesh without birth," Tertullian says. From the philosophical point of view, we must recognize that the correlation that is categorically the principle of analysis in *De carne Christi*, remains totally undetermined as long as one knows neither what flesh nor birth are. At most one can think that the nature of the one depends upon the nature of the other. Or, more radically, that both are connected in so far as they are cut from the same horizon of understanding, in so far as one assigns the same foundation to them. Tertullian knows it well. What he reproaches precisely as heresy (in this case that of Valentinus and those who follow him), was "recognizing flesh and birth, but *giving them another meaning*" (CC I, 213, our emphasis).

Leaving here the debate with the Valentinians in order to go directly to the essential, we ask: *On the basis of what phenomenological, and in turn ontological, presupposition does Tertullian understand birth, flesh, and their necessary correlation?* This is not to forget that, in the historical horizon in which the problems of the Fathers of the Church unfold, the flesh/birth correlation awakens various subjects, on which the shadow of the Christ of course falls. However, all of them have a meaning and an undeniable philosophical validity, and we will examine them from this point of view. And they are all related to the central question of flesh.

The first presupposition claims the solidarity of birth and death: To the former, the latter is necessarily connected. "Birth has a debt with regard to death." If the Christ is born, it is because his mission was to die for the salvation of the world. It was thus necessary that the flesh that he took on at his birth was a mortal flesh. It is exactly in this way that it is a flesh like ours, "a flesh which is destined to death." Which flesh is destined to death? Which birth places us in this mortal flesh? It is a flesh that is made from the silt of the earth, from the matter of the world, an "earthly flesh" (CC I, V, 237; VI, 241; IX, 253). And to be born, if it is not a question of being born for death, can mean only to come in an earthly flesh, actually in the flesh of a woman, in her womb. Born in the womb of a woman, the Christ draws his flesh from her, an earthly and human flesh, and that is why he lived in the manner of human beings, needing to be nourished, feeling fatigue, sleeping, in short sharing the destiny of man—in order to be able to accomplish his own, which was to be crucified, to die, to be buried, and then—and then alone—to be resurrected.

By denoting its origin, the correlation between flesh and its birth thus unequivocally reveals the true nature of this flesh, an earthly flesh like the woman's from which every flesh issues, of which it is initially a part. The two characteristics that interest the Fathers follow from this: the mortal character of flesh (in so far as the Christ must die), and its human character (in so far as it is by taking on this flesh that the Christ assumes the human condition). Thus the heresy is rejected that claims to assign the birth of the Christ to a place other than the womb of a woman, a flesh of a "celestial," "astral," "psychic," "spiritual," or other origin—and thus to assign it a nature less unworthy of its divine condition.

The true motif of the rejection of heresy must now hold our attention. In the eyes of Tertullian and the Fathers the reality of the incarnation of Christ is in question, and consequently the reality of the flesh he has assumed. If the origin and nature of the flesh of Christ are not identical to the origin and nature of our own flesh, then by becoming incarnate he has not actually assumed our own condition, actually shared our existence, actually endured the weight of a finite flesh like ours (thus its needs, its thirst, its hunger, its precariousness, and the death inscribed in it from its birth); he has not actually died, nor been resurrected either—in brief, the entire Christian process where the real identification of the Word with man as the condition for the real identification of man with God is reduced to a series of outward appearances, and at the same time to a sort of hoax.

The fact of Christ and all of his teaching would be even more of a hoax—the one who invites us to accept injustice and the wrongs done to us (including our body's wounds), to endure them with patience and humility, with a sort of naivety, like the modest and simple of this world do. As he endured them himself, during his fast in the desert, amid his tribulations, and in the course of his passion, while the brutes struck him and whipped him, driving the crown of thorns into his bruised forehead, piercing his flesh with nails and the spear. But, in order to endure all this, one needs precisely a flesh, a real flesh that can be struck, whipped, pierced, and ridiculed, while it endured hunger, thirst, cold, and fatigue over the course of its earthly existence. And if this flesh is not real, none of that is either: It only looks like hunger—a hunger that isn't hungry, a thirst that isn't thirsty, a burning that burns nothing, a rupture in the flesh where there is neither rupture nor flesh. The Master of humility and gentleness, the one who never retaliated against his enemies, who bore everything in silence, and who "suffered his passion," has not suffered or borne anything if he had what only looks like flesh. The Master is an imposter. He grossly deceived his contemporaries, but also all those who were to believe in him through the centuries, practicing the *imitatio Christi*, giving themselves to asceticism, refusing pleasure, overcoming egoism, welcoming injustice or calumnies because of Christ and his name, entering in turn into their passion, in one of the many forms of passion of which the world is prodigious, and finally accepting sacrifice and martyrdom. The terrifying words of Irenaeus reverberate to this day. "As he deceived men by appearing to be what he was not, he deceives us too by exhorting us to bear what he himself did not. We will even be above the Master when we suffer and bear what this so-called Master neither suffered nor bore" (Irenaeus, *op. cit.*, p. 365).

Echoed throughout the thought of the Fathers, the argument advanced against Gnosticism is everywhere the same and very clearly formulated: *it is the categorical affirmation of the reality of the flesh of Christ.* Yet such an affirmation cannot remain in this state, as categorical as it may be. It refers immediately to a decisive line of questioning, which is precisely our own: *In what does the reality of the flesh consist, what allows us to speak of a real flesh?* How can one not see (even limiting ourselves provisionally to the texts of Irenaeus and Tertullian evoked on this point) *the modification that is inexorably produced in them and which is as radical as it is imperceptible?* When, in his relentless polemic against Marcion, Tertullian analyses this reality of flesh and describes it at the moment of its birth as bluntly as possible, adding up details liable to invoke disgust; when, in a general way, still interpreting the flesh starting from its birth, he assigns it an origin in the silt of the earth, the phenomenological and ontological horizon that presides over this conception of flesh, its birth, and its reality, is the appearing of the world. This is true in a two-fold sense: On the one hand, the flesh is grasped as the content of the world, as its matter; on the other hand, it is precisely in the outside itself of the world that such a content is shown to us, precisely as an exterior body, as a collection of objective, contingent determinations that are foreign to the nature of our mind, incomprehensible by it, and indeed more or less repulsive.

We will not fail to notice that the metaphors with whose help Tertullian endeavors to establish the reality of flesh against heresy are of Hebrew origin, referring to the text of Genesis rather than to any Greek treatise. But it is precisely not just a matter of metaphors. On the contrary, the far more precise and almost objective description of childbirth addressed to Marcion is based on Greek medicine, Greek knowledge, and the Greek heritage. A text of Tertullian—"the muscles similar to clods of glebe" (CC I, V, 253)—also indicates clearly the assimilation made in his mind between the Greek heritage, with its objective pre-scientific knowledges, and the biblical metaphors: Both refer to the content of this world, and this content refers to its appearance, to the primitive exteriority of nature and the creation in which the earth and its silt, and the disgusting processes that come about in the wombs of women, are shown to us, outside us. Thus the collection of bodies that make up the reality of the world unfold before the eyes of men, so that, by seeing that alone, they do perceive it as the site and source of all reality.

In the universe of objective material bodies (which make up its real content), there is earth (which is only another name for this content); clay and mud, and everything that can be fabricated with them; the entire set of processes and phenomena that we preoccupy ourselves with knowing better, and upon which we act (the processes of childbirth, notably)— *there is never the feeling they inspire for Tertullian or Marcion, and no feeling in general, for that matter; no impression either:* neither hunger, nor fatigue, nor pity, nor anguish, nor joy, nor suffering. No suffering, actually, *none of the suffering by which Irenaeus and Tertullian alike will define the reality of Christ's flesh, and the reality of our own flesh too.*

Here the decisive turn occurs in the thought of the Fathers, whereby the objective determinations of the material body that are shown to us in the world give way to impressional and affective determinations revealing themselves in the pathos of life. Yet these are the impressional and affective determinations that constitute the phenomenological material flesh is made of, the flesh of this flesh, its true substance, and its reality. It is indeed true that the nature of the flesh depends on its birth. But what does birth signify? To be born, we have seen, means to come into appearing. Because appearance is double, there are two ways of coming into it: In the "outside itself" of the world, and in the pathos of life. In the outside itself of pure exteriority, nothing touches itself, feels itself, or experiences itself in any way. To come into the world means to be shown in the manner of an external *insensible* body. In the world, there is no flesh and no birth, if being born means coming into a flesh. It is only in life that a flesh is possible, a real flesh whose reality is the phenomenological, impressional, and pathos-filled materiality of life itself. *When impressional determinations are substituted for objective ones, the Christian problematic insurmountably dissociates body and flesh (and thus makes it impossible to confuse them)—the former are given back to the world in such a way that it is never a flesh, the latter restored to life in such a way that, in itself, it is never a body.*

In Tertullian, the dissociation is so brutal that it leads to no explicit awareness. It is a question, in the enumeration of the properties of the flesh, of a spontaneous passage from the objective determinations of the material body to the pathos-filled subjective properties of flesh, and to the most significant among them, suffering. For, let it now be said, suffering is not a given that one must limit oneself to noticing without understanding, a contingent, "empirical" content, according to the language of classical philosophy. Inheriting its primitive possibility from the suffering that marks the pure trial of living, where pathos and Ipseity happen jointly as its originary phenomenological effectuation, suffering defines one of the fundamental affective tonalities by which life touches its own Depth. It is not an accident that in the affirmation of the reality of flesh, its suffering is ranked first. In its suffering, the flesh does not express some kind of affective modality of our life; its truth is not psychological; and it does not depend only on what is incontestable in such a modality, on the fact that suffering is a *cogitatio*. It refers to absolute truth, to the hidden trial in which life occurs immediately in itself in its primitive suffering, in the Arch-Flesh and the Arch-Pathos of its Arch-revelation.

And thus it is no longer an accident if the reality of flesh is established starting from suffering's own reality. Because this, we claim, is not an ordinary reality, a sort of facticity affecting the human condition for who knows what reason. Because it belongs to the interior edification of every reality, to the absolute reality from which it proceeds and in which it is inscribed for some essential reason. Because flesh and pathos, the Arch-flesh and Arch-pathos they imply in every case are consubstantial with the trying process in which absolute life comes in itself as the originary phenomenological material in which this Arch-revelation takes place.

It is no accident, finally, if the connection between reality, flesh, and suffering refers immediately, in Tertullian and the other Fathers, to the passion of the Christ. In a sense, of course, it is the event of the

Passion that leads them who await salvation to reflect indefinitely on this inconceivable paradox, and on the abyssal questions that it raises. Can an impassible God suffer? Can an intelligible God have a sensible flesh? If he does, can this flesh be like ours? Can an eternal God die—and die precisely because he has taken on an earthly body destined for corruption?

Since this line of questioning is unintelligible in a Greek horizon, this horizon is condemned to death. At first, Tertullian—who attempts desperately to demonstrate the reality of the flesh, a reality without which the incarnation and passion of Christ have no meaning—must dispose of a flesh whose reality is evident, of a body whose concept he borrows from the ordinary experience that underlies Greek thought as well as our own. In addition, the flesh is assimilated to the material bodies that are shown in the world, whose properties and objective structures presented in evidence are indubitable—"A flesh like ours, *irrigated by blood, constructed by bones, traversed by veins*" (CC I, V, 229, our emphasis). It is without philosophical transition and without any conceptual justification that to this conception of the objective body (whose reality is the world's matter) the presupposition of a radically different flesh (of another order) is juxtaposed—*a suffering flesh that draws the reality of its suffering from its pathos-filled phenomenalization in life.* The incarnation of Christ, and in an exemplary way his passion, now have their reality and truth from a flesh that is defined by its suffering.

This decisive modification of the conception of the body (of an objective material body that has become a suffering flesh) explodes in the polemic against Marcion. By denying the true reality of the body of Christ, Marcion attacks this flesh: It is the reality of suffering, and of the passion, that he takes for an outward appearance. It is the being of Christ, defined by this suffering flesh, that he empties of its reality, reducing it to a phantom. This is what the context indicates with incredible violence: "Would you not have precisely neglected to eliminate the sufferings of Christ because *his phantom was too hollow to feel them* [. . .] Has God not really been crucified? Oh most heinous of men [. . .] you who exonerate the murderers of God. For the Christ suffered nothing at their hands *if none of these sufferings were real*" (CC I, V, 229, our emphasis).

§25. The Radical Interpretation of Flesh as the Phenomenological Material of Life and as Its Self-Revelation. Irenaeus's Christian Cogito.

The explicit theme of the fundamental problematic Irenaeus addresses is the definition of the reality of flesh, not through the material of the world but through suffering and thus through life's phenomenological material. What makes so decisive this substitution of life for the world as the site of the flesh's revelation (understood from now on starting from this revelation) is that the life here in question is no longer the one known to the Greeks, the *bios* of their biology: It is transcendental phenomenological life, the pathos-filled self-revelation from which the flesh draws its pathos, its reality *qua* pure phenomenological reality, as a pathos-filled reality.

This is what the context of Irenaeus's thought and that of the other Fathers demonstrates. What must be thought, according to them, is the Incarnation of the Word in its Johannine formulation. It is thus *the original correlation between flesh, the coming into flesh, and the self-revelation of absolute life in its Word.* And that *this* flesh, this flesh that comes in the pathos of life, is not the flesh of heresy (for example the astral flesh of Apelles, which comes straight from stoicism), but precisely our own flesh, the real flesh indeed that undergoes experiencing itself in each of our most humble or most elementary impressions, this is what we already know. What then has the problematic of the impression shown if not that, thrown into the world in the Ek-stasis of time, having become "just now past," that is, entirely past, reduced to the noematic correlate of an intentionality, every impression falls into unreality, and at the same time loses its impressional phenomenological completion, its real flesh, and its condition as an Impression?

We are now witnesses to the true reversal of the Gnostic positions. Gnosticism did not want a real flesh like ours for the Christ, an earthly, material flesh, which was too trivial to its liking. It preferred it to be less opaque, lighter, and transparent to the mind: intelligible. But it is precisely in the world that every flesh is an unreality (an ideality) that merely looks like flesh. If it is a disincarnate flesh that responds to these wishes, Gnosticism would indeed have been able to leave it in the world. That is where, thrown outside itself, relieved of itself in some way, discharged from its own weight, from the weight of suffering or fatigue, deprived finally of the phenomenological possibility of suffering and enjoying that are constitutive of its true substance, it has indeed lost this substance. We must thus ask in all phenomenological rigor: Where is the flesh only apparent? In the world. The world's appearing strips every flesh of its reality. And this concerns our flesh as well as that of Christ, as well as that of the Word.

Irenaeus deepens in an extraordinary way the unconditional assignation of flesh to Life, from which it draws its pathos-filled effectiveness. The entire context of the problematic proves in the first place that the life in question is indeed absolute phenomenological Life. It is *that* life, the Life of God self-revealed in its Word, that was made flesh. To the gnostic question of knowing whence Christ's flesh proceeds—a question to which, having grasped its principle in the phenomenological essence of Life itself, they respond in an aleatory way by giving free course to their imagination which is nourished from the culture of Greek concepts—Irenaeus knows the response inscribed in the Word that fascinates him more than any other. The flesh in which the Word comes comes from the Word itself, in other words, from Life.

If flesh thus comes from Life, it is a question of understanding how this coming is made. As we know, Life comes in a flesh by coming in itself—in "undergoing experiencing itself" whose pure phenomenological materiality is a pathos. Irenaeus approaches the question differently. He asks if flesh is capable of receiving life—the only Life that exists. Why examine the possibility of flesh receiving Life rather than that of Life being made flesh? Because the horizon of his thought is dependent in part upon the Greeks. "We are a body pulled from the earth." Thus the Christ had a body of this sort, "if not he would not have taken nutrients drawn from the earth to nourish his body drawn from the earth." We have suggested that it is easier to maintain these theses because of their at least apparent agreement with the texts of Genesis. The material and worldly body of the Greeks is like this piece of earth that becomes flesh under the divine breath, which is the breath of Life. But when the body is transformed into flesh by the operation of Life, it draws its fleshly condition only from Life, which gives it to undergo experiencing itself in it and to become flesh in this way—which is in no way like a material body that in itself has no power to feel or experience anything at all, that is forever incapable of being flesh.

The reversal of Gnosticism maintains two fundamental propositions that we will express as follows: *far from being incapable of taking on flesh, life is its condition of possibility. Far from being incapable of receiving life, the flesh is its phenomenological effectuation.* In Irenaeus's language, "God can vivify the flesh" (God *alone*, we will add). "The flesh can be vivified by God" (and can be vivified *only by him*, we will add). "If he did not vivify what is dead, God would cease to be powerful." What is dead is the inert body, which God makes into flesh by communicating Life in it (his Life, the only one that exists). And this is why the givenness of the first flesh to the first man prefigures his salvation. "If he wants, the one who made in the beginning [. . .] what was not, will reestablish in life what existed"—will resurrect the flesh that never gets its carnal condition unless from its own life, his.

Derived from the first, the second proposition is more than intelligible—it is arch-intelligible. Precisely because Life is the condition of possibility of flesh, flesh (every flesh) is possible in it, and is possible only in it. The flesh can receive Life as exactly what makes it flesh, and without this it would not be—as just what it is. "The flesh," Irenaeus says, in a fundamental proposition, "can receive and contain the power of God" (Irenaeus, *op. cit.*, pp. 383, 384, 576, 577, 577).

Life's immanence in the flesh does not only make up the phenomenological substance of every conceivable flesh and thus its reality; it makes possible at the same time that of each of the fundamental phenomenological structures of what we have called our originary corporeity. Thus we pick up again the critique of contemporary phenomenology at the point we had left it. The reference of the sensed body to the transcendental body that senses it had unfolded in that body the structures we are speaking of and which were still perceived only in their intentionality: vision related to what it sees, hearing to what it hears, etc. In this way the problem of the phenomenological status of these intentional performances of our various senses arises, in so far as, given to themselves in the self-givenness of life, the phenomenality of their immanent accomplishment is foreign to the phenomenality of Ek-stasis.

It is remarkable that Irenaeus recognizes immediately in each of these transcendental structures the immanence of absolute life as constitutive of its phenomenological reality, and, at the same time, of the possibility for it to exercise its power. Because the capacity of flesh to receive life appears as the definition of its reality, it extends at the same time to the various elements that compose it. Rendered in its entirety, the proposition previously cited reads: "The flesh is capable of receiving and containing the power of God since in the beginning it received the art of God and thus a part of itself became the eye that sees, another the ear which hears, another the hand which palpates and works [. . .]. Yet that which participates in the art and the wisdom of God also participates in his power. The flesh is thus not exclusive of the art, the wisdom, and the power of God, but the power of God, which procures life, deploying itself in the weakness of the flesh" (*ibid.*, p. 577). That the power of flesh is also called weakness means: The life where our flesh draws its reality, in which it is given to itself and made able to act—this life is nothing by itself. It does not take from itself the reality of its own flesh—since it is given to itself only in the self-givenness of absolute Life, in the Arch-Flesh of the Arch-Self.

With the immanence in flesh of Life, which constitutes its reality, the Arch-intelligibility of Life is communicated to it. Here one of the most astonishing theses formulated by human thought is offered, *the interpretation of flesh as ineluctably bearing an Arch-intelligibility within itself,* Life's own, in which it is given to itself, and in which it is made flesh. There is no flesh that is not self-affirming and self-legitimating as to its existence through exactly what makes it flesh (or rather living flesh)—no flesh that does not bear Life within it and the Arch-intelligibility that makes it an unshakable foundation. Irenaeus's astonishing affirmation—implied elsewhere in John's Word—is the cogito of flesh or, if one prefers, the Christian cogito.

Naturally, an affirmation like this must be understood appropriately, since it is different in principle from the propositions found in philosophical texts: *it is not thought that formulates it but precisely flesh; it formulates it in its flesh, in a Speech that is the Speech of flesh, more precisely of Life.* If the flesh never lies, it is because it is given to itself in the Parousia of the absolute, because the Parousia of the absolute takes place in an Arch-Flesh from which no flesh is separated.

In Irenaeus's text (as in every philosophical text), the speech of flesh cedes place to the speech of thought, which takes everything it says, however, only from the speech of Life, in this case from the speech of flesh, which is here the original *cogitatio.* This is what furnishes the premises that Irenaeus will develop: *Nothing that is living fails to attest in its life that it is living. Nothing that is flesh fails to attest in its flesh that it is flesh.* The thesis of Gnosticism is reversed in the light of the carnal *cogitatio.* That thesis claims that *the flesh is incapable of receiving life*—the only Life that exists, absolute Life. From now on those who claim that flesh is incapable of receiving the life immanent in every flesh, that gives it to itself and makes it flesh, must say that they are not living, that they do not have flesh—and do this while they live and accomplish all the activities of flesh. The living must say that they are not living, the flesh that it is not a flesh.

"What they are saying to us, those who claim that the flesh is incapable of receiving the life that God gives, either they affirm all of this while actually living and having part in life, or they admit to having absolutely nothing of life, to be presently dead. But if they are dead, how can they move themselves, speak and accomplish all the other actions, which are the accomplishment not of the dead but of the living? And if they are living presently, if *their entire body has part in life,* how do they dare say that the flesh is incapable of having part in life while they admit to having life right now?" (*ibid.,* p. 578, our emphasis).

We would be wrong to think that these sequences of absurdities that Irenaeus denounces are proper to Gnosticism and to its specific theses. We recognize them everywhere the revelation of the flesh is not attributed to the revelation of life, and where the revelation of life is not attributed to life itself, understood as its self-revelation. Thus everywhere the appearing of flesh and life is reduced to the world's appearing, confused and identified with it. This affirmation of Heidegger, for example, is absurd: "Life is a particular kind of being, but essentially it is accessible only in Dasein" (SZ, §10, 50 / 46; translation modified). We can see that the horizon of phenomenological monism, within which almost all philosophies of the body and the flesh are constructed, must here be dismissed.

In Irenaeus, the polemical denunciation of the contradictions proper to the gnostic theses that he has in view—"[. . .] these people guarantee that they live, boasting of bearing life in their members; then, contradicting themselves, they claim that their members are incapable of receiving life"—is only the inverse of a positive phenomenology. That Life is present in every flesh as what reveals it to itself, makes it a flesh and gives it Life—in every flesh, Life attests to this in the radical self-attestation of its absolute self-revelation. This is the extraordinary content of the cogito of flesh proper to Christianity, which Irenaeus formulates in a too-dense proposition: "That the flesh is capable of receiving Life, *this is proved by this very Life from which it* [the flesh] *already lives right now*" (Irenaeus, *op. cit.*, our emphasis).

§26. Analytic of the "I Can." The Power-to-Move as Condition of the Power-to-Touch, and of Every Power Attributed to the Body. Condillac and Maine de Biran.

It is now a question of perceiving all that this phenomenology of flesh, as an essential piece of a phenomenology of Life, still allows us to understand, on the one hand, concerning flesh itself, and, on the other, its relation to the body. We find that precisely this *relation of flesh to the body is intelligible only starting from flesh and not starting from the body*. It is here that the second way (the interpretation of flesh starting from the appearing of Life) affirms its primacy over the first, which is limited only to the appearing of the world. This primacy is decisive not only because it is impossible to understand flesh starting from the worldly body. Contrary to traditional interpretations, which here include those of contemporary phenomenology, it is here established that *the worldly body is possible only once we have presupposed a flesh already revealed to itself as living flesh in the pathos-filled self-revelation of life*. Thus it is indeed another mode of givenness than the world's that here must be thought, if something like a flesh, like our flesh, is not to remain an unwarranted presupposition.

Let us look again at the transcendental body that opens us to the world, which senses the sensed body by relating itself intentionally to it so as to be able to see it, hear it, touch it . . . —where sensing in general is identified with this intentional relation, with these ek-static senses as "senses at a distance." Let us examine with closer attention the touching/

touched chiasma on which it seemed one could read the structure of our originary flesh. Instead of positing this structure as a self-sufficient totality, let us question further each of the terms that it puts in play. We know that the possibility of touching is in no way exhausted in its intentional relation to the touched. It is precisely the radical phenomenological possibility of intentionality that is in question—this possibility for which intentionality itself never gives account because it resides in an essence that is fundamentally foreign to its own: its pathos-filled self-affection in life. This originary and fundamental possibility is sidestepped when touching is now considered only in its relation to what it touches, when the chiasma is raised to the level of an absolute.

There is more. To behave like a "touching," "to touch" in the sense of an act that touches, has precisely nothing to do with a "behavior," or some kind of facticity, even if it is active rather than passive. To touch in the sense of an effective action necessarily comes within the competence of a power, a power-to-touch of which the "touching" (the fact of touching) is only the operation, or actualization. But this power-to-touch is not in turn a simple facticity, or in some way the quality of a being that is endowed with such a property. *Power-to-touch means finding oneself in possession of this power, being placed in it beforehand, coinciding with it, being identified with it, and in this way and this way alone being able to do what it can.* Every power pertains to an essential immanence; in this immanence it deploys its force and is an effective power, not simply the concept of a power.

Where and how is every power's immanence to itself accomplished? In Life, in the way Life comes with pathos in itself. The possibility of every power is its arrival in itself in the form of flesh. If corporeity is the entire set of our powers, it is in flesh and as flesh that this corporeity is possible. The flesh is not the result of the touching/touched chiasma and cannot be correctly described by it. The flesh comes before the chiasma as the condition of the power-to-touch and thus of touching as such. It comes before the power-to-touch itself as that which installs this power in itself, making an effective power of it. But as we have seen (and we will come back to this), flesh arrives in itself only in absolute Life's arrival in itself, in the Arch-Flesh of an Arch-Power.

Life's immanence in every power, which makes a carnal corporeity of the originary corporeity in which these powers are gathered, stands out more obviously if, among each of these powers, we retain one to which only a brief allusion has been made. For touching doesn't just bear within it a power-to-touch whose phenomenological possibility resides in its flesh; another power inhabits it that must be analyzed in its distinctiveness. It is a question of the power to move in which the power-to-touch is self-moved so that it can touch all that it is capable of touching. For as long as the power-to-touch was considered only in its relation to what it allows one to touch, the fleshly immanence that puts it in possession of itself beforehand is easily obscured. It is no longer possible to evade the condition of every power if the power-to-move is not related originally and in itself to any intentional correlate, if it remains within the power-to-touch, and belongs as it does to the carnal immanence from which it draws its force. Separated from this originary power to move itself, in the sense of what moves and is moved indissolubly, incapable of moving itself, the power-to-touch would touch almost nothing—like lofty characters invited out on some official hunt who, while seated on their armchair, shoot only the prey thrust out before them by diligent touters.

The demonstration that the *power-to-move* is immanent to the *power-to-touch* (without which it would be dislocated from every power) was the quickly forgotten achievement of a sequence of modern thought that was as brief as it was decisive. It is a question of the critique Maine de Biran addressed to Condillac. He was one of the first to pose explicitly the question of the knowledge of one's one body. To resolve it, he proceeded in a series of the most remarkable phenomenological reductions. First, he reduced our subjectivity to itself and to its pure impressions. Condillac calls this reduced impressional subjectivity a statue. The impressions it experiences come to us from these senses, from the world, but (this is the first reduction) it knows nothing about it, and is limited to experiencing them as it experiences them, since it is nothing else. "If we present it with a rose, to us it will be a statue that smells a rose: but to itself, it will only be the very smell of this flower. It will thus be the smell of a rose, a carnation, a jasmine, or a violet [. . .]. In short, the smells are for it only its own modifications or states; and it cannot think of itself as anything else, since these are the only sensations of which it is capable."*

We have nevertheless left the sense of smell (though it knows nothing about it) to the pure, impressional subjectivity reduced to its olfactory impressions. Condillac then proceeds to a new series of intersecting phenomenological reductions that in turn envisage the statue as "limited" to the impressions that correspond to each of these senses taken in isolation—to the associations of several senses, in accordance with the various conceivable combinations (taste joined to sight, to smell, seeing joined to smell . . .). In each of these phenomenological situations, which are freely imagined through the operation of a genuine "eidetic analysis," an impressional subjectivity that is reduced to its pure impressions cannot (despite their diversity) be made into the least idea of an external

* *Traité des sensations* (Paris: Fayard, 1984), p. 15 / *Philosophical Writings of Etienne Bonnot Abbé de Condillac* (Hillsdale, NJ: Lawrence Erlbaum Associates, 1982), p. 175.

body. Hence Condillac's question: How do we go from our sensations to the knowledge of bodies, whether it is a question of an external body or our own?

A man of the eighteenth century, Condillac entrusted the task of resolving the problem to "nature," which is here only another name for life.[*] As the impressions are not indifferent (some are pleasant, others disagreeable), movements spontaneously arise in the statue, whereby it engages in the sensation it enjoys and refuses the one that hurts it. In the course of these more or less disorderly and "mechanical" movements (still in the eighteenth century sense of movements accomplished spontaneously in the absence of reflective thought), the statue happens to put its hand on its own body: It then feels a sensation of solidity. But it is different from other sensations that the statue perceives as its own modifications and where "it finds only itself," because the sensation of solidity gives it the idea that the body it touches is impenetrable, so it perceives this as a different body. Thus a first distinction arises between the pure subjectivity of the statue and the reality of the bodies external to it.

Yet, while the experience unfolds when a body situated beyond pure sensation is touched, a second decisive split will take place according to whether the touched body belongs to the statue or not. When the statue's hand encounters its own body, when it touches its chest for example, the sensation of solidity that the hand and the chest "refer mutually to each other [. . .] puts them necessarily outside one another." At the very moment the statue distinguishes its chest from its hand, however, it "rediscovers itself in one and in the other, because it feels itself equally in both." A similar relation, where the statue's hand is distinguished from its chest all the while it still identifies with it, holds obviously for each part of its own body on which it is brought to bear.

Let us now suppose the hand encounters a foreign body, the self [*moi*] that inhabits the hand, and feels itself modified in the sensation of solidity it experiences in contact with this body, does not experience itself and does not identify itself in the latter, it "does not feel itself modified in it." Or, as Condillac again says, "the self that answered to it, ceases to answer." Thus the second differentiation we are discussing takes place, where one's own body is decisively separated from the foreign body. Condillac expresses this in a text of rare density: "When several distinct and co-existing sensations are circumscribed by touching within the limits where the self answers to itself, it [the statue] is aware of its body; when several distinct and coexisting sensations are circumscribed by the touch-

---

[*] As Paul Audi has profoundly shown with respect to Rousseau. Cf. *Rousseau, Éthique et Passion* (Paris: Presses Universitaires de France, 1997).

ing within limits in which the self does not answer, it has the idea of a body different from its own. In the first case, these sensations continue to be its own qualities; in the second, they become the qualities of a wholly different object."

As remarkable as Condillac's problematic may be here in the *Treatise*, from the phenomenological point of view it presents several uncertainties that should be noted. Is it not strange to call pure subjectivity a statue, and thus identify it with a foreign objective body, whose knowledge it is precisely a question of establishing? The image of the statue was undoubtedly chosen in order to signify the absence of every relation to any exteriority. "We supposed [. . .] that exterior entirely of marble would prohibit the usage of any of these senses" (*Treatise*, respectively, pp. 104, 105, 106, 11). The isolated statue of the world is a figure of the phenomenological reduction, it delimits a sphere of absolute immanence where one restricts oneself to the impressions as they undergo experiencing themselves, independently of any idea or any interpretation from elsewhere. Nevertheless an initial and serious difficulty arises: When the pleasure or the disagreeability of the sensations felt arouses spontaneous movements destined to make the former arrive and to reject the latter, *where does the ability to accomplish such movements reside?* In the impressions themselves? This must be demonstrated, which hardly seems possible as long as the sensations are viewed as psychological givens, as passive modalities of our soul whose arrival it has nothing to do with.

Yet it proves decisive that the passive sphere of subjective impressions is weakened by the emergence of spontaneous movements within it. On the one hand, these movements ensure the interior equilibrium and the entire affective economy of the statue, guaranteeing its pleasure, and sparing it the weight of intolerable pains. But, on the other hand, these are what must explain the passage from the subjective sensations to the awareness of exterior bodies—resolving the issue of awareness in the problematic of the *Treatise*. How then can one not notice these aporias or gaping lacunae in it?

The statue was only a figure for pure subjectivity. But this is what is in question. Its movements have become those of its hand, of an objective organ that bears on other external, objective bodies, touches them, and feels in this contact a series of sensations. The movement born in the sphere of sensations, in some way produced by them, is now what produces them, and awakens them as and when the hand thus moved touches the body that it meets and runs along its forms. Since it appeared in the sphere of pure, reduced subjectivity, the movement should be equally subjective, in a radical sense. Since it has become the movement of an objective organ, the hand for its part should be objective too. For that matter, this is the only way it would it be able to fulfill the role Condillac entrusts to it: To put the hand in contact with external bodies, to arouse sensations of solidity through this contact—the sensations he expects will give the statue the idea of an impenetrable body that is external to it. The sensation of solidity that must produce the idea of exteriority depends on this, on the prior exteriority of an objective hand in objective contact with objective bodies.

How is the subjective movement that is born in reduced, impressional subjectivity related to the objective displacement of the hand? How are we in a position to implement them both? And, above all, the first: Who displaces the subjective movement, since *this is what moves the statue's hand?* The unthought presupposition of Condillac's entire analysis is here uncovered. The displacement of the hand over the different parts of the body reveals the reality of this body and its forms to us through the sensation of solidity. But *our originary corporeity is not this body whose parts are circumscribed when the hand shifts over it. It is this hand itself as it shifts itself over our own body in order to touch it and mark out its contours.* Here Condillac's problematic shatters against two unfathomed questions. The hand is the instrument for our knowledge of the body, "But," Maine de Biran asks, *"how is this instrument known in the first place?"* So that it can be moved and directed as it needs to be: *"How has any kind of movable organ been constantly directed without being known?"**

As a radical elucidation of this two-fold presupposition, the phenomenology of Life allows us to offer a systematic critique that, beyond the thought of Condillac, concerns every worldly theory of the body. The following remarks thus have a general scope.

Considered as an objective organ, as part of the worldly body, the hand is incapable of touching and sensing anything at all, no more the "other hand" than another part of the body or any other kind of body. To touch and to sense—the subjective power of touching alone can do this. On the one hand, this power is related intentionally to what it touches. On the other hand, this intentional relation is possible only because it is given to itself in Life's pathos-filled self-givenness. This is the only way that, having been placed in itself beforehand and thus in possession of itself, it is able (in Life and *qua* living power) to deploy itself and to act, to touch what is never touched except by it, by a power like this.

But we claimed that, in this intentional relation to what it touches, the power-to-touch is only ever perceived, so to speak, in what makes it a power, in this pathos-filled immanence to itself outside of which no power

---

*Maine de Biran, *Mémoire sur la décomposition de la pensée*, ed., Tisserand (Paris: Alcan, 1932), vol. IV, pp. 6, 7.

is possible. From this radical immanence of Life, put in possession of itself by it, the power-to-touch not only draws the possibility of its own power; the power of moving also and first of all resides in it—apart from which, incapable of moving itself, the power-to-touch would be powerless. Because it remains in Life, the "moving" of the power-to-touch is an immanent movement—*it is the movement that remains in itself in its very movement, and it carries itself with itself, which moves itself in itself—the self-movement that does not separate itself from itself and never leaves itself, letting no part of itself be detached from it or lost outside it in some exteriority, in the exteriority of the world.* Thus in going beyond touching intentionally toward what it touches, the intentionality of this beyond never takes place anywhere but where it is given to itself in life's self-givenness.

Let us affirm this on a very general level. What philosophy calls the process of objectification, which plays so great a role in many of its developments, is never possible in the sense that philosophy understands it. Whether it is a question of "Mind," "Reason," subjectivity, consciousness, or any other fundamental moment, this process of objectification is interpreted as if the power that operates the objectification objectifies itself in the process, posits itself before it, and thus itself becomes the other, the external, the different—the "in front" or the "ob-ject." The analysis of the most simple and most concrete corporeal activity suffices to establish that nothing like this happens, that objectification is never a self-objectification. The "objectification" completed in each of our senses when sights falls at a distance, when touching touches an object, when smell breathes in the scent of a flower, when hearing perceives a sound that resonates in the world, this objectification always signifies the coming outside of an outside, an intentionality that goes beyond toward these horizons of transcendence. But this movement of going beyond remains in itself and is moved in itself; it is Life's self-movement that carries it with itself in the pathos-filled self-affection of its untearable flesh.

Here we are presented with a decisive connection between Affectivity and Power. If there is no power except that which is given to itself in Life's pathos-filled self-givenness, then every power is affective, not as the effect of circumstances that would be foreign to its own essence, but because it resides in this pathos-filled self-affection that, by installing it in itself, gives it the ability to exert itself—to be the power that it is. Thus, the prior power of a transcendental Affectivity reigns in every power of our body, the power of Affectivity to be given to itself and thus to give to itself everything that is given to itself only in it—in that which is the essence of Life. It is therefore not possible to refer to the power of Affectivity that places every corporeal performance in itself unless based on this foundation; every force in itself is full of pathos, and at bottom that is what the concept of drive expresses without knowing it.

Yet in the pathos-filled immanence of every power, it is not only given to itself and thus capable of acting. Because in such an immanence nothing goes out of itself or differs from itself, the power situated in it is not only given to itself, but constantly given, without any discontinuity. Moreover, it is not only continuously given, but also it cannot be made not to be, or not to be any longer. From this follows one of the most remarkable traits of our originary corporeity, in which all the powers that compose it are gathered and unified. As a self-givenness of each of them in pathos, it is properly the flesh of each one. And this is how it can implement it when it wants to, since it is placed in it as its innermost possibility. This possibility is not abstract, however. Because it is a flesh, and thus always determined in pathos, what brings it into play is this very determination in pathos in each of our powers. Here the unfounded presupposition of each of Condillac's analyses is easily recognized and becomes intelligible: *All the movements of the statue originate in its pure impressional subjectivity according to the play of these impressions.*

At the same time, the second unfounded presupposition of Condillac's analysis also becomes transparent. Maine de Biran asks Condillac how a movable organ can be constantly directed without being known. By itself the phenomenological presupposition initially assumed by Condillac, but quickly lost (the reduction to a radically immanent, impressional subjectivity), allows the problem to be posed in a way that avoids the aporia. The "movable organ" that must constantly be directed and known is precisely not the hand *qua* objective part of our objective body—any more than its movement is an objective displacement in space. Described in its pure subjectivity and reduced to this, the "hand" is nothing but the subjective power of touching and grasping, where this power is given to itself and put in possession of itself in the pathos-filled self-givenness of which we are speaking. For each of its powers, the flesh encloses within it both the ability to act and its revelation; the phenomenological completion of each of these powers takes place in flesh. This is also the case for the movement of this "movable organ" that is the "hand" of the "statue": the "moving" of this subjective power of grasping is the movement moving in itself and remaining in possession of itself in the immanence of our originary corporeity—Life's self-movement in its carnal self-revelation.

"I can" does not signify that now I am in a position to make this movement. The reality of a movement is not exhausted in its singular phenomenological effectuation: It resides in the power to accomplish it. This power in turn is not reduced to the sum of its potential actualizations. It is an in principle and *a priori* possibility that prevails over each of its "actualizations," which controls past, present, and future, and that cannot be removed by me; it is the possibility of deploying each power of my body. All of these powers are infinitely repeatable. All of them are, because there is not one of them that does not remain in possession of itself in Life's self-givenness. There is not one that does not belong to me, because, in the self-givenness that gives it to itself, the ipseity of this singular Self that I am is already edified in such a way that it is given only in me, as a power that is my own. In such a way that all these powers are in me as a single body, that is to say, a single flesh—in me who has the power to exercise them all in so far as it is in me, revealed to self in my own flesh, that each of them are disposed to act. Thus I know them before all thought and independently of it, before every conceivable world, where I occur to myself and in the same way that I occur to myself. This is how I act: in the pathos-filled immanence of my flesh.

§27. Flesh: Immemorial Memory of the World.

Because all of its powers are immanent in my flesh, it is the site of an original memory. In classical thought, for man to be a memory means that memory is a thought, the ability of consciousness to represent to itself events or feelings that have disappeared. Thus it is representation, an intentionality, which gives these to us by conferring on them the meaning of having passed. If I once put on my desk a statuette that had been offered as a gift, and if sometimes I take it in my hands in order to experience its beauty again, I am able to represent to myself each of these acts, or at least some of them if they stand out against the uniformity of time. Each memory, with its clarity and its lacunae, hides another one that is deeper. *It is the memory of a body that always remembers how to take the statuette and move toward it to grasp it.* This movement is not the displacement of an objective organ; it is given neither to any "memory" properly speaking, nor to any representation, nor to any thought: It is the self-movement of a power of grasping revealed to itself in the pathos-filled self-givenness of my original corporeity. Thus it bears it and guards it in its flesh as a first possibility from which it is never separated, and whose memory it never loses, since it is nothing other than this memory.

When memory shifts from the field of thought to that of flesh (the corporeal memory of which Maine de Biran had the astonishing intuition), it doubles depending on whether we consider it at work in the performances of our senses or in its immanence, before every intervention of intentionality. In the first case, that of touching, for example, each movement that had joined me with a particular body, whose contours it followed and to whose forms it molded (and thus in and through movement alone, it allows me to know it); when this same movement is repeated, and applies itself to the same solid, to its forms and various qualities, it allows me to know it, where this recognition has no other condition than this very movement, of which it will nevertheless be the "sign." "Thus there will be a true memory of tangible forms."[*]

This memory is inscribed in my original corporeity as the ability in principle to deploy each of these powers, and from this follows a decisive feature of the world of things, to which these powers lead us. Because, as constantly given to itself in my flesh, each of these powers is infinitely re-producible; the access to the sensible world that it prepares is an *a priori.* The things of the world are never presented to our body in an experience that has the character of needing to be unique; they are always offered to us as what we will see twice, as the solid whose forms we will always be able to follow, and will be able to find again as they are, and whose memory we retain—the memory that is nothing other than the ability, consub-stantial with my flesh, to move up to them. If the world does not give way anywhere, if the weft of the sensible is continuous, with neither defect nor lacuna nor tear at any point, if each fiber or grain that composes it is indefinitely evocable, it is because each of the powers that brings me to them is a power of a flesh that nothing separates from itself, that is always present to itself in its memory, without any distance, without thought, without past, and without memory—in its immemorial memory. My flesh is what cannot be torn.

The unity of the world is thus an immanent unity, and it is held in the Parousia of my flesh. The ultimate possibility of the experience of the world, perceived in accordance with the decisive characteristic that it can be infinitely iterated, requires a consciousness without world, an a-cosmic flesh; this ageless truth stands out in a passage from Maine de Biran's *Essay,* which takes Condillac's analysis back to its initial un-thought phe-nomenological presupposition: "Each of the movements executed by the hand, each of the positions that it has taken in traveling along the solid, *can be repeated voluntarily in the absence of this solid"* (*ibid.,* our emphasis).

From this immemorial memory of a flesh that keeps all of its powers within it, we should distinguish memory in the ordinary sense, which con-sists in the capacity to form representations both of these powers and of the things to which they unite us. Because there is a relation of depen-dence between the latter and the former, the recall of things is invincibly connected for us to the recall of the pathways that led us to them, to the recall of our efforts to take them or avoid them, or raise them up, to mod-

[*] *Essai sur les fondments de la psychologie et sur ses rapports avec l'étude de la nature,* ed. Tisserand, *op. cit.,* vol. VIII, p. 408.

ify their forms, or to work with them in some manner. And this recollection is itself only what happens when the possibilities we say lie dormant within it are freely awakened to thought, though they are of an entirely different order, that is actually foreign to thought, to all representation, and to all recollection—they are immemorial powers of my pathos-filled flesh. "The recollection of an act," says Maine de Biran in a text of infinite depth, "contains the feeling of the power to repeat it" (*ibid.*, p. 605, note).

§28. Flesh: Site of Givenness of an Unknown Body, Given before Sensation and before World. Structuration and Properties of the "Organic Body."

If the unity of the world refers to the fundamental ability inscribed in my flesh, to accomplish all the movements I can, then upon what do these movements act? Our first response is that these movements act upon themselves. They are not movements whose progress it would only be a matter of naively noticing, but each of them is a self-movement, placed in itself in our flesh and able in this way to be exercised at every moment. When this movement is no longer considered in the immanence of its final possibility, when, as a memory of the tangible forms of things, for example, it gives them to us, how does it give them? In its movement and by it, of course. But doesn't this movement now deliver us something other than itself? How does it do so, how does it act upon what (other than itself) it gives to us?

The urgency and acuity of the question appears if we recognize here the aporia on which the majority of theories of human action have run aground: How could a subjective authority that as such is un-extended ("soul," "consciousness," "psyche" or any other name one would like to give it) act upon an extended body and put it into motion? Once they recognized the massive contradiction of Descartes's "pineal gland," the great Cartesians could only avoid the aporia by entrusting the possibility of the soul's action on the body to wanton speculative constructions—Malebranche's occasionalism, Spinoza's parallelism, Leibniz's pre-established harmony—without being able to found that possibility in any way—without asking whether the supposed correspondence between the subjective series of volitions and desires, on the one hand, and extended, material processes, on the other, has only one meaning.

Maine de Biran's genius was to radicalize Condillac's initial phenomenological reduction, to never place himself outside the statue in order to describe from the outside the movements of its hand, that have become the objective displacements of a movable organ upon bodies situated in the space of a world. He understood that the Cartesian way of posing the question makes it unsolvable, that this question is a false question, and that the soul does not act upon the extended body. An experience that happens only to it must be circumscribed within the movement undergoing experiencing itself and moving in itself: the experience of something it will come up against, a term that resists its effort, which Maine de Biran calls the "resisting continuum." It is a question of "some thing" being given only in movement, and thus in the absence of every representative intentionality, in the absence of each of the traditional senses as well (sight, hearing, touch, smell, or taste).

In the absence of touch? Here the distinction established between the specificity of each of our senses and the self-movement in which its exercise consists allows its decisive character to show through. When one entrusts to touch the task of making us know the reality of exterior bodies, one confuses the two, the sensations owed to touching—an impression of coarseness, hardness, suppleness, softness, or warmth—and, on the other hand, entirely different, the feeling of resistance experienced through the succession of these tactile impressions. The former do pertain to the sense of touch, but the term that resists, resists only movement. Condillac's "feeling of solidity" describes in full clarity this confusion, which is also characteristic of nearly all theories that place touch at the heart of our experience of the world.

The importance of this sort of confusion (between the sensations proper to each sense and the movement that allows them to unfold) must be measured at its consequences. Tactile sensations are apprehended as belonging to exterior bodies, visual sensations to a thing that one sees, sonorous sensations to what one hears (and that one can possibly perceive at the same time). Similarly, sensations of odor are identified with the scent of a flower, or with the bad odor of a pig farm. And the body, the external body to which these sensations relate, is a body of the world, of this world that common sense spontaneously identifies as reality. The same is true if it is a question of our own body, its odor, the smoothness of a skin, or the coloration in a face. Thus our own body (or that of another man or woman) takes place immediately in the world where all the objects, whatever they may be, appear to us. Our different senses, through their various sensations, do indeed open us to this world of bodies. And this happens, we should not forget, in so far as an intentionality inhabits them, and always makes their specific sensations "representative" sensations, and in the final account, "sensible qualities," that belong to objects (to our object-body as well as to others). The subject-body that is the principle of this experience—the seat of sensations that we experience as well as the intentional acts that "animate" them—is related directly to the object-body, to the content of the universe.

On the contrary, if within our original corporeity and its immanent accomplishment self-movement comes up against a term that continuously resists it, *then reality has changed.* This resisting continuum is what manifests it, what defines the first opposition, the first exteriority we encountered in the internal deployment of our powers—*a new body discovered in this way and only in this way.* So it is *this* body, until now unexplored, that Maine de Biran called an "organic body." Its analysis is precisely what we have just carried out. It consists in the rigorous phenomenological description of its mode of givenness. Because such a mode excludes the traditional senses—the sensations they procure for us as well as the representative intentionality that permeates them—the body it reveals to us owes nothing either to the former nor to the latter: *It is a body before sensation, and before the world. An invisible body just like our originary corporeity, whose movement comes crashing into it,* into this continuum that constantly resists our effort even while this effort, resting and, so to speak, buttressed against itself, seeks and finds its greatest force.

Singular properties can thus already be recognized in the organic body. Because it escapes our senses, it can neither be touched nor seen nor heard, it has neither odor nor taste—in so far as it is indeed a question of the organic body. For it is truly nothing other than that: That which resists the "I can" of my originary corporeity, which reveals itself to it and to it alone, and whose manner of doing this is just to resist it. The entire being of what resists is then in the force it resists. The way it resists is the way this force is tested. The way it reveals itself is the way it reveals itself to itself as hindered, inhibited, unable to deploy itself freely according to its own wishes. The resisting continuum is to the force what the spatial figure is to space. Just as the spatial figure stands out in space and never exists anywhere else, the resisting continuum remains within the "I can" whose power it measures. If one still wants to speak here of exteriority, it is an exteriority fundamentally foreign to that of the world in so far as the experience in which it occurs excludes from itself every representative element, every *theoria*, every *a priori* intuition of space in the sense of Kant's "Transcendental Aesthetic," or even of time, or every ek-static horizon that makes possible something like a "seeing." It is a problem of knowing whether the relation of the "I can" to the term that continuously resists it can still be described in terms of intentionality, a motor intentionality, for example. And this is because all intentionality in the phenomenological sense is a *Sinngebung*, a givenness of sense, while in this pure experience of the resisting continuum in the immanent self-movement of the "I can," no signification, no ideality, intervenes.

We should therefore analyze this experience in a more precise way. While it takes place, a differentiation appears, which is as decisive as it is incontestable. Sometimes the resisting continuum puts up an absolute resistance to the operation of our powers, not giving in to them anywhere at any point—in such a way that no rift or passage opens up in the wall the movement breaks against. Sometimes on the contrary the resisting continuum gives in to the effort of our movement. This way of giving in cannot be signified except in these terms, so all our experience is reducible to a force under whose drive something folds, bends, and indeed gives way, relinquishing to the power of this drive a sort of "internal extension," of which there is, we would claim, no intuition, sensible or otherwise— which is nothing other than *that which folds under the effect of that force, and is driven back by it.*

Thus the decisive differentiation we are speaking of is established: When the resisting continuum puts up an absolute resistance to the original powers of our original corporeity, this continuum defines the reality of the bodies that make up the "real" universe. When on the contrary it gives in to these powers, the reality of our organic body is revealed in it. The organic body is designated as our own, as belonging to us, when it submits to the powers that together make up our carnal "I can," in contrast to bodies that are absolutely resistant to us and are foreign bodies. In each case, however, whether it is a question of a real body of the universe or of our own organic body—*the reality of the body* has nothing to do with what we habitually represent to ourselves by this term. We indeed call real the body that appears to us in the exteriority of the world—of this world, whose appearing is exteriority as such. Because, at the same time as our own organic body, the bodies of the universe are given originally only to the immanent powers of our corporeity, and are experienced by them according to the modalities of the resistance they oppose to them, so we must say, as strange as it seems: The reality of these bodies (ours as well as foreign bodies) is a reality foreign to the world and its appearing, an invisible reality, just as the reality of our flesh is.

Let us consider more closely the reality of our organic body—the body before sensation, and before the world, which is different from bodies of the universe, in the sense that it puts up only a relative resistance to the "I can." This phenomenological condition (which is its own) defines a homogeneous milieu whose homogeneity nevertheless allows new differentiations to appear within it, and these will prove to be essential. *They express the different ways it yields to my effort.* Let us suppose, for example, that under the direction of a physiotherapist, I voluntarily inhale: Something swells up in me that I call my chest but which originally has nothing to do with a part of the objective body. For if we limit ourselves to what is really given, it is a question only of something that gives way within my effort, that arises within me up to a sort of limit that I struggle in vain to overcome; it falls back when this effort stops and I am then asked to exhale. In this way an "organic expanse" opens out, which makes up the continuity of the resisting continuum. And one can see that this expanse is not the space of the world, or of the perception of exterior objects, in the sense that *these limits are precisely not spatial limits, but limits of our effort, practical limits*, defying every representation, and notably that of an intuitive space.

Yet what is said of our "respiration" also applies for all of the powers that constitute of our original corporeity. A kind of internal deployment corresponds to the implementation of each one; it will go as far as it can and once it attains the limits of its power and its effort stops, it comes back to what we will call, in a still-metaphorical way, its "point of departure." This is no point in space, and no point of the organic expanse, which is itself foreign to space. *The point of departure is our flesh, the primitive self-givenness from which each of these powers draws its ability to act.*

Because these powers are different, a particular way of being deployed between its fleshly "point of departure" and the moving term of its effort corresponds to each of them. Thus *pure phenomenological systems* are constructed, spans of resistance that immediately obey our movements and of which each of them is an organ. Our organic body is the whole of our organs *thus extended.* And such organs are different from the anatomical structures that science takes for its object. They are neither dis-posed nor ex-posed *partes extra partes*, but are held together and are as though held up out of nothing by the "I can" of our original corporeity. This is also why the unity of all these organs, the unity of our organic body, is not a unity situated outside us: It is the unity of powers to which these organs are submitted and whose limits they mark each time. This unity of all the powers resides in their self-givenness in pathos. This means they are nothing other than our flesh.

§29. The Original Possibility of Action as a Carnal Drive of the Organic Body. The Invisible Practical Reality of the World's Content. Constitution and Status of One's Own Objective Body.

The aporia in which the classical theories of human action end up—which uniformly understand it as an action of the soul upon the body, as going from the "inside" to the "outside," as "objectification," and as a process at the end of which our transcendental life would turn itself into a thing—this aporia is indeed removed. If our action never operates upon a worldly body, the result of this action would not be a modification of a worldly body, or some objective phenomenon or displacement. *Our action is the action of our original corporeity and its powers; it is the drive moving in itself and bending the "organs" that give way to its power.* Our action upon the world is produced at the end of this organic deployment, where, directly attained by it as its own depth, the world puts up an absolute resistance against it. For that is where the reality of its content is drawn, not in its appearance but at this limit of my effort, given in this way to my life's movement. Because, in my flesh, I am the life of my organic body, I am also that of the world. In this original, radical sense, the world is the world-of-life, a *Lebenswelt.*

But does our hand not cross an objective space to grasp the book resting on the desk, and open the pages with its fingers? Do our feet, solidly planted on the earth, or moving along the path, not collide with the stones—the stones *situated next to each other, in this res extensa* Galileo and Descartes speak of? Far from restraining phenomenology's domain of competence, these remarks help us to explore its expanse. If it is true, according to the presuppositions of a phenomenology of life, that there are for things two original and fundamental modes of manifestation, then a single reality, our body in this case, must be able to appear to us in two different ways. *Our body offers us the crucial experience in which the duality of appearing is decisively confirmed.* This alone allows us to understand how the body truly is a double reality, manifesting itself on the outside, in the outside itself of the world, on the one hand, and lived internally by us, on the other, in Life's pathos-filled self-revelation. Thus our own body, in its duplicity, is at once the effect of the duplicity of appearing, and its irrefutable proof. This paradoxical situation, which has nevertheless become clearly intelligible—arch-intelligible—legitimates the method-ological choice of the two ways followed by the problematic, the world, and life. Its result is that the existence of two bodies is demonstrated, one pertaining to the reign of the visible, the other to the invisible. Is such a distinction enough to account for the relation necessarily established between them?

Let us consider the final difficulty evoked, *where our hand shifts over the objective body in the space of the world:* One can ask whether the difficulty is truly removed. Conforming to the duplicity of appearing, there are in-deed two bodies, the one living, the other worldly, but how does the first join the second in such a way that it grasps it, moves along it, and possibly modifies its forms, position, or qualities—in brief "acts" upon it? Where, in all rigor, is such a shift situated? Is this not always the classical aporia? No, not if action is taken for what it is, entirely subjective: this living force bending the organic body under its effort and deploying it up to the limit where it no longer gives way, which resists it absolutely, which is the real content of the world. *Yet it is this entire process—where our radically immanent action holds within it both our organic body and the real body of the universe—*

that is perceived from the outside in the world's appearing. There are thus not two processes, but only one, the problem of our carnal corporeity. This is the one and only process that appears to us otherwise, in another appearing, and is then discovered by us in the "outside" of the world in the form of an objective process. Our action thus does not take place first in us in order to then arise suddenly outside us. Because it is living, it has always belonged to life and never leaves it. It has also always been objective, from the angle of the objective displacement of our hand, for example—a hand that is itself objective like the objective body of which it is a part. Living corporeity and objective worldly bodies are *a priori*. They are two *a priori* of the experience of our body that are themselves only the expression of the duplicity of appearing, which is an Arch-fact, and which nothing explains but is to be understood on its own basis, according to the rule imposed by the phenomenology of life.

This question cannot be evaded however. If conforming to the duplicity of appearing our body duplicates itself, is it truly the reality of this body that appears to us under a double appearance? *Does our worldly body carry this reality within it just like our pathos-filled flesh does?* Have we not seen that the appearing of the world strips all reality of its own substance? Is this decisive phenomenological situation not discovered precisely with respect to life? Yet all of the characteristics of our own body refer to life: None of them owe being what they are to the appearing of the world. Constituted by the entirety of our senses, our own body offers us specific sensations. But all of these sensations, including those that connect us to objects, are, as we have seen, only subjective impressions projected upon them. The furthest away as well as the closest, all of them are in actual fact experienced only in life. The impressional material of such impressions and sensations is life's pure phenomenological material; they are modalities of its flesh. And intentionality itself, which throws them outside, and allows each of our senses to open us to the world, is given possession of itself only in life. Thus in the depth of our corporeity, it is the original power to move oneself and everything that gives itself in it, the organic continuum with its internal differentiations, that elude the world's appearing. Is our objective body just an empty shell?

The most ordinary experience shows the contrary. Let us consider the objective body of the other. If in our opinion this is opposed to the inert bodies of the material universe, it is because *we perceive that a flesh inhabits it.* To be inhabited by flesh means to feel sensations other than those which, related to things, appear as their own objective qualities, such as the color of a fabric or the brightness of a lamp. Of course the objective body of the other is also adorned with such qualities: It has blue eyes, black hair, a pale complexion, etc. But it is equally *sensible* in an entirely different sense: Unlike foreign bodies, I apprehend it as feeling internally and in a continuous way a succession of sensations that form the substance of its own flesh and, in this way, I perceive it as unceasingly modified by such sensations.

Yet the other's body is not only inhabited by an impressional flesh that resembles my own, it is endowed with the same senses as me. That is how its body seems to be a body capable of sensing, and which through the exercise of its various senses is open to the world, and to the same world as mine. Its hand is never an object properly speaking, a "biological" organ described by the anatomist or examined by the doctor. Nor are its eyes or ears. These eyes, as Husserl says, are "eyes-that-see," these hands are "hands-that-touch." The other's body is thus run through by multiple intentionalities; it is the seat of endless movements that I apprehend not only, or even first, as objective displacements, but as movements lived by him, subjective just like my own. It is in this way that, according to Scheler's remarkable analyses,[*] when I look at the face of the other, I never see an eye, but its look, I see that he looks at me and possibly that he looks at me in a way that I do not see that he looks at me, I see that he diverts his look, or even that my own look bothers him, etc. Precisely because these movements are perceived as felt or wanted by him, their affective content, the affective tonalities in in which they are given to themselves and which thus preside over their accomplishment—effort, weariness, desire, pleasure, displeasure, discomfort—are there, in a certain way, for me. Far from being inert, insensible, and so identifiable with any material at all, the body of the other, despite its objectivity, offers itself to me as a living body, since all the characteristics that we have just mentioned (and that pertain to a flesh) are recognizable in him.

Would the *reality* of the flesh then be able to appear to us in the world? Has the set of problems surrounding the impression not shown that as soon as it is separated from itself in the first gap of time its reality disappears, giving way to a fundamental unreality? Is this irrevocable destiny of the impression not life's own, which never remains in itself except in the immanence of its invisible pathos, from which every exteriority is forever banished? *What is proper to every conceivable flesh is to be emptied of its substance in the exteriority of an "outside." Like my own, the other's objective body is just that: the derealization of a flesh in and by the appearing of the world.*

How the appearing of the world derealizes, that we know. The crucial experience of language has taught us this. Trakl's poem *gives things*

---

[*] Cf. particularly Max Scheler, *Wesen und Formen der Sympathie* (Bonn: F. Cohen, 1923) / *Nature et Formes de la sympathie* (Paris: Payot, 1971) / *The Nature of Sympathy*, trans. Peter Heath (New Brunswick, NJ: Transaction Publishers, 2008).

in their absence. It *signifies* the snow that we see fall across the windowpane when there is neither window nor snow, the sound of the bell when there is neither sound nor bell. This is the essence of a signification in general: Produced in an intentionality's givenness of sense, it gives a content-of-thought (a "noema"), but without giving the reality signified by it. Thus the signification "dog" is pronounced in the absence of any real dog. The objective body of the other, or my own, is constituted by the whole set of significations that aim at a flesh and define its reality—*in its absence, however, in the absence of any real flesh.*

If I look at my face in the mirror, for example, I do not see a nameless thing, of course, some mass of inert matter. I see precisely a face, my own; I see a look, a look that looks at me and perhaps says to me, "How sad this looks!" I try to smile and it is not the deformation of something deprived of sense—it is precisely a smile I see. Nevertheless, *where this look looks at me, where its sadness appears to me, where this smile smiles at me, on the smooth surface of the mirror, there is no real vision, no real sadness, no movement moving in itself, no flesh impressing upon itself in the effectuation of a singular life.* So if my own body that I observe in the mirror, or the other's own objective body, which I see just as well, are constituted of significations such as "to look," "to suffer," and "to move itself," it is only because these significations are borrowed from a living flesh. This alone makes possible the constitution in our experience of something like a body "inhabited by a flesh."

Here we discover in blinding clarity the paralogism that consists in giving an account of our own body, and first of all our living body, starting from a process of intentional constitution and as the product of it—when only an original and living corporeity that is originally revealed to itself in life can found this process. This paralogism claims to give account of our flesh through a phenomenology of constitution, which means in the end, through the appearing of the world. Descriptions of the constituted body have nothing original, they are even blind with respect to what is original. And they are so because they are blind to the original essence of revelation—in other words, to life.

The significations that constitute one's own objective body refer to a reality that never ex-poses itself in objectivity, and that is not localized. While I look at myself in the mirror and see the look that looks at me, its sadness, etc., this look, this sadness, never stops embracing in my night. And the intentionality that takes hold of them to produce from them the significations constitutive of the objective body is also embraced, otherwise this body would no longer be a human body, not even a cadaver. My flesh is thus not only the principle for the constitution of my own objective body—it hides its invisible substance in it. Such is the strange constitution of the object we call our body: In no way does it consist in the visible species to which we have always reduced it; in its reality, precisely, it is invisible. No one has ever seen a man, but no one has ever seen his body either, at least if by "body" we mean his real body.

The question thus arises of how one can know what comes from the constitution of the objective body of the other, to the extent that the life that supports it is no longer my own. Must I not first have access directly to his own life, to his own flesh, in the singular effectuation of its pathos-filled auto-impressionality, so as to understand the expressions of his body on which I struggle to read his joy, his pleasure, his boredom, or his shame?

We can recognize the general problem of the experience of the other, curiously neglected by classical thought. When in twentieth-century phenomenology it becomes the theme of an explicit investigation, it does not seem to have overcome all the difficulties it encounters (which are truly extraordinary), despite the admirable efforts of Husserl and Scheler. Before taking it up in light of the presuppositions of a phenomenology of life in our third section, in connection with the Christian problematic of salvation, some supplementary remarks are necessary.

§30. The Theory of the Constitution of One's Own Body in Chapter 3 of *Ideen II*. The Threefold Concealment of the Transcendental Possibility of the "I Can," of the Existence of the Organic Body, and of the Localization of Our Impressions upon It.

The first is that a theory of the constitution of one's own body must take into view not two elements (the constituting body and the constituted body), but in fact three; the third is the originary flesh on which our entire reflection is concentrated. Considered in its originality, actually, our flesh is neither constituting nor constituted; it is foreign to every intentional element, and pure *hyle* in the sense we understand it, not as a brute given, but as Life's arch-revelation. Hence the immense lacuna of a theory of the constitution of one's own body interpreted from the outset as the product of a constitution: The originally non-constituted flesh eludes it. This lacuna is completely concealed when the elucidation of the constituting body/constituted body correlation is reduced to a description of the latter. Before it determines the set of problems in the later Merleau-Ponty, we are faced with this situation in chapter 3 of *Ideen II*.[*]

---

[*] Edmund Husserl, Hua IV, §35–42, 143ff. / 151ff.

The meaning of the distinction, which phenomenology takes to be essential, between the body of a thing, the "thingly body," and the "fleshly body," very quickly appears limited: Just like the former, the latter is perceived from the outside. They are both worldly bodies. For this reason, our own body too presents visible parts and tangible parts. Some of these parts, it is true, escape my sight, but they remain accessible to touch. Stemming from a long tradition, the thingly body is differentiated from one's own body in the experience in which my hand touches either the body of a thing, or its own body.

In the first case, if I run my hand over a table, I feel sensations that are either related to the table and apprehended as its physical properties, such as smoothness, roughness, hardness, etc. Or I bring attention to the sensations felt by the hand while it slides over the table, sensations that are then related to the hand as its own, and that pertain to one's own body. The hand's sensations default to the physical (thingly) body and thus to one's own body considered as a physical thing. On the contrary, they are sensations of one's own body, of the "thing that is one's own body."

Quite correctly, Husserl remarks that the localization of these two types of sensations is different. The thingly sensations are extended over the spatial surface of the thing, of which they appear as material determinations. The hand's sensations are "propagated" on the hand, in virtue of which they are given as proper to the hand. There is still the fact that the sensation apprehended as a material quality of the thing, the color of the "hand-thing," changes if I turn the hand over, expose it to the light, etc., such that these luminous modifications announce an objective property of the thing, and thus function as so many "outlines" of this objective quality. Conversely, the hand's sensations are "nothing which would be given in sketches," they are impressions that arise from my soul.

Whether these sensations are referred to the body of the thing or to our own body (to our hand), it is an intentionality that confers on them this meaning, that perceives them as qualities of the thing or as qualities of one's own body, of our "fleshly body." The "soul" itself and the fleshly body (the flesh) are not grasped in themselves, but as constituted too, they are perceived as a soul, as the "psychic," as a flesh that belongs to an ego, to something that itself has the sense of being an ego and my own. Soul, flesh, and ego, as they are originally revealed in life's immanence, independently of every intentionality, and every signification, independently of our senses—this is not a problem.

The same situation is reproduced in the second case, when the hand no longer touches a thing but another part of one's own body— when the right hand, for example, touches the left hand. The sensations felt by the hand that touches are separated into two series, some related to the touched hand considered as a thing, and perceived consequently as objective qualities of this thing (the hand is smooth, cold, etc.), others are related to the hand that touches and apprehended as its own sensations (as sensations of movement, in particular). As for the touched hand, it too feels tactile sensations that are localized on it not as a material body, but on precisely what senses them, which it apprehends as its own, as sensations of its own body. Here again everything is constituted; a cluster of intentionalities governs all these apprehensions, and always confers a meaning on what is "perceived as," or "taken as" a property of the hand that touches, or of that which is touched, or of the hand considered as a thing.

Not only does the phenomenological status of the impression before its intentional grasp (before this strange "animation" that throws it outside life in unreality) remain in suspense (not just the intentionality always given over to its anonymity), but a final presupposition (the same one that supported Condillac's thesis) also remains unthought in all these analyses, even when it equally founds them all. It is a question of the ability of an originary flesh to move itself in itself, to move its organs from the inside, and where they do no longer cede, to have direct hold over a real body given to its practice, lifted, wrought, and worked by it—in the invisible. Here, on the contrary, as in classical thought, everything is entrusted to representation: The hand is treated as a visible thing bearing sensations whose final possibility is evaded—sensations that are derealized in the objectivity of the hand, but that (as an objective organ of its own body which is itself objective) allows itself to be acted upon by a transcendental ego, which attains it and moves it and no one knows how.

With respect to one's own body considered as a field where my sensations are localized, §38 declares that "it is *an organ of the will*, the *one and only object* which, for the will of my pure ego, is moveable immediately and spontaneously." And again, still regarding this body proper to a subject-ego, that it "has the 'faculty' (the 'I can') to freely move this body—that is, the organ in which it is articulated—and to perceive an exterior world by means of them" (Hua IV, §38, 152 / 159, 160). The immense problem of the transcendental, phenomenological possibility of the action of an "ego" on its own body and "consequently" on the external world becomes an objective designation that is itself external, where everything is self-evident, and reduced to a statement of common sense.

This denaturation of one's own body identified with a constituted body, mysteriously understood as an "organ of the will" and "support of free movement," leads to a series of consequences. It is first the reduction of the organ our originary flesh moves within (that is movable by its very condition, which is to surrender to this immanent movement) to an organ that is part of the extended body, which is equally represented or representable, and which no subjective motion can then encounter and move.

Yet this reduction not only conceals our own body in so far as it is an organic body, a sort of internal, practical continuum folding under the push of our invisible drive and never being given except in it; it also prohibits us from understanding the actual conditions the process of localizing sensations upon one's own body obeys. We should recall here the distinction made between the specific sensations that correspond to each of our senses (indeed, sensations that are visual, tactile, audible, etc.), and on the other hand the impressions relative to the movements of our original corporeity. This is not to forget the fact that the exercise of our senses always implies that these movements are implemented— movements that orient the senses, for example. Thus impressions of movements are connected in principle to the sensations of our various senses—the impressions of movements of our "ocular globes," for example—to visual sensations. This occurs in such a way that we can, it seems, give ourselves the latter on the basis of the former, on the basis of our "kinesthesis." But this is a two-fold illusion. On the one hand, these kinestheses are localized in the organic body and not in one's own objective body; on the other hand, these kinesthetic, constituted sensations are not what provoke our visual sensations (they accompany them at most)— the originary impressions do, in which the originary movements of our flesh impress upon themselves as they are carried out.

Viewed in themselves, these diverse impressions thus belong entirely to our originary flesh, prior to every intentional process of constitution or localization. Nor do they present differences stemming from their own phenomenological content, an impressional color, or a flavor being distinguished on its own from an "impression of movement." This is why, when these always different impressions are submitted to a constituting intentionality, the signification they have will be only the "empty" aim of the phenomenological content proper to each one: it will be a question of the signification "color," or "taste," or again of "movement." Thus a decisive thesis of the phenomenology of life is confirmed. It is not intentionality that is the principle of our experience, it is not an intentional field that confers meaning and status on the impressions of our flesh; they, in their original self-revelation, precede, regulate, and determine the process in which they are inserted and disposed in one's own body.

Is it not then evident that this process of constitution and localization is still necessarily submitted to what precedes it, to the nature of originary impressions on the one hand, and to the nature of one's own body, on the other? On the side of the impressions, we have distinguished the sensations of the senses and the impressions of our movements. On the side of one's own body, one's own objective body to which the tradition holds, on the one hand, the organic body, foreign to every objectivity and depending upon movement alone, on the other. The sensorial impressions are inserted in one's own objective body (with the exception of those related to the physical thing), the impressions of movements in the organic body. The "localization" of the impressions of movements is thus dependent on a moving organization, which is rigorously determined as it immediately submits to the powers of our flesh. Thus these impressions are originally nothing other than the phenomenological reality of our movements disposing themselves in our organic body as a function of their practical structuration. This is what their constitution consists of, the meaning attributed to them as the expression of their own pathos. And also of their dynamism, to the extent that the organic and non-spatial way these impressions (now apprehended as "kinesthetic sensations") are inserted conforms to the different modes according to which this dynamism unfolds—to the practical structuration of the resisting continuum.

§31. Return to the Chiasma. What "Being-Touched" Means. Phenomenology of Skin as Achievement of the Theory of the Constitution of One's Own Body.

Let us reflect again on the touching/touched chiasma. We have just elucidated everything that is implicated in the "touching" and that is passed over in silence when this is taken as self-evident. How can one not observe now that the superimposed strata that are implicated as essential conditions of possibility for "touching"—Life, originary flesh, affectivity, strength, movement, organic body, non-objective real body—are presupposed in the same way if something like "being-touched," in the phenomenological sense of an effective experience, must be able to happen to, and in, our flesh?

Our earlier analyses present us with this apparent paradox: The original "touched" ("being-touched") is not touched by the sense of touch, by the "touching" understood as the exercise of this sense. The "touched" is the resisting continuum at the moment when, in the effectuation of the power that moves it, it becomes suddenly impossible to move. *This is the moment in me when my own organic body becomes a thingly body*. In my own flesh and by it, the practical frontier that separates it from its own body as something in itself foreign to all flesh (from its own thingly body) is traced here. This is the point, in fact, in a way that is as un-representable as it is incontestable, where the flesh acts upon it and still moves it, no longer as a part of itself in which it inserts its own sensations (for example, sensations of its own movement), but as an opaque and inert mass in which there is no longer anything of itself, and nothing more living.

One then sees how *this interior practical relation of my flesh to its own thingly body defines its relation to any conceivable thingly body, to any kind of body in the universe as well as to the thingly body of the other.* If I would like to exert a pressure as strong as possible on the body of another man, for example, like a doctor does in the course of an examination, or a torturer in the midst of a torture session, this pressure, *within its own pushing*, would come up against what it no longer inhabits any more than its own sensations do, but precisely a "thing" that in itself is foreign to the drive as well as to these sensations. A "real" thing, a "thingly body," on which it can no longer act by remaining within it and deploying it from the inside, but can act on it only from the outside. "From the outside" does not then mean that this body remains within the exteriority of the world, where our flesh would never have any contact with it, and where no *lived phenomenological contact as such* is possible. The flesh acts "from the outside" upon its own thingly body *within the push that it exerts upon its own organic body*, when it no longer gives way to it, and it comes up against it as an insurmountable wall, blind and without cracks—against the impenetrable body *into which it will never penetrate because it has no inside and never will.* This is why the action of the flesh upon its own thingly body is the paradigm for all human action—for man's primordial relation to the universe. This is not an ek-static relation to the world but a practical relation to the content of this world (a relation shielded from the world's appearing); it takes place and is revealed to itself only in our invisible flesh. Because this action deals only with the impenetrable, even when it strives to build and to edify, it necessarily has the form of violence, and is limited to modifying, breaking, crushing, beating, and destroying, or at least altering, what no longer obeys it, is no longer submitted to it in any way, and remains for it, in a radical sense, foreign.

What is touched in me by me at the limit of my effort as a continuously resisting thingly body is so touched only as the powers of my flesh are deployed. Just as the "touching" does, the "touched" (the fact of being touched) pertains only to flesh. We see then very clearly that the possibility of "being-touched" reproduces that of being "touching" to the point of being identical with it. In the case of my own thingly body, it is precisely the same process that moves the resisting continuum, or that is touched by it, or, in other words, that immediately feels its resistance. Thus the resisting continuum is touched only by a flesh, as it moves it from within, or more precisely, as it can no longer move it. In itself, just as with a foreign thingly body or the other's thingly body, my own thingly body is no more touched than touching.

Let us now consider with greater attention the case in which I touch my own body. What is touched is not reduced to a thingly body that feels nothing. My objective thingly body, which feels nothing, is only the external apparition of the resisting continuum my flesh attains from within as the limit of its power. My flesh alone (by which we mean the auto-impressionality of its self-movement) is and can be touched. The same originary flesh is touching and touched at the same time. It is thus completely inexact to affirm with Merleau-Ponty that when my right hand that was touching my left hand lets itself on the contrary be touched it, it abandons its mastery at the same time, with its touching condition now absorbed in the touched (understood in the sense of something tangible, or of something sensible analogous with all the thingly bodies in the universe). Exactly the opposite is true: When the touching hand allows itself to be touched by the other hand and becomes a hand that is touched, *it keeps its condition as originary flesh within it*, the auto-impressionality that can alone be impressed upon, or "touched" by, whatever it may be. And the way it is touched or impressed upon has nothing to do with the naive representation of this phenomenon in the form of an objective contact with two thingly bodies that are as incapable of "touching" as of "being touched."

How then is a flesh "touched" and no longer "touching"? It is "touched" where it is "touching" and in the same way. With the following exception: Even though the resisting continuum cedes right up to the point it immobilizes as a thing under the push of the originary flesh, it is this organic, practical continuum that now stops me or now pushes back against the drive, thus changing into the pathos of a constraint that it suffers. From the *action* of the original powers of our "touching" flesh, a *passivity* follows, the "being-touched" whose pure phenomenological material is the same as that of action. Since activity and passivity are two different phenomenological modalities of a single flesh, their phenomenological status is the same, that of flesh precisely: of a flesh that experiences itself in the happiness of freely deploying its powers as well as in the constraint it feels when they stop. These affective tonalities proper to the dynamism of our originary flesh (active or passive) are thus equally those of our own organic body; they define the phenomenological modalities in which our own organic body is lived by us.

Numerous impressions are constituted on the organic body's resisting continuum. We should maintain here the essential distinction between originary impressions and constituted impressions. Only the first are real. When they are constituted, referred to our own objective body, and have for example the signification of being sensations of the face or the foot, it is only a noematic sensation that is actually reduced to this signification; it is an unreal, represented sensation, which is localized in a way, apprehended *as* a sensation of the foot, while in its impressional reality it does not stop auto-impressing itself in life.

But we want to speak about the constitution of our impressions on the organic body. This is where the duality of appearing should be invoked because it plays a decisive role in this constitution. The thingly body into which the organic continuum is changed when it assumes the role of an absolute obstacle to the force of the flesh is still only an invisible, practical determination in it. *It is this same insurmountable "wall" that appears to us in the appearance of the world as an objective thingly body, analogous to the other bodies of the universe.* The only difference is that it appears to us as being ours, as our own thingly body, in opposition to the thingly bodies that are foreign to us. This signification of being ours is not taken from its worldly apparition but from our originary flesh, which feels its own thingly body within it as the limit of its power. But this signification of having a flesh live within it is precisely what it receives and bears within it—it is constituted as such, *as a worldly, thingly body nevertheless endowed with an "inside."* This signification of having an inside, of being "inhabited" by a flesh, makes it what it is for us in the global experience we have of it, a body double indeed; this is demonstrated to me from the outside in the world, yet lived from the inside as my own fleshly body, opposed to all the others. We see then very clearly how the constitution of one's own body, which confers on it the signification of bearing a flesh within it, presupposes the reality of this flesh, its originary auto-impressionality in life's pathos-filled Ipseity; it is far from being able to explain it.

Let us continue the study of the constitution of our impressions in the organic body. The preceding analyses show that this is actually differentiated into three elements: 1) our own organic body submitted to the interior force of our originary flesh; 2) this organic body opposing itself to it, becoming a thingly body at the limit of this force; 3) this same thingly body *no longer felt as such in its fleshly force but shown to us from the outside, in the world.* This threefold differentiation, which conforms to the duplicity of appearing and is determined by it, is the principle for the constitution of the whole of our impressions.

It is thus a question of constituted sensations, even if we always presuppose a corresponding originary impression. Thus we are in the presence of a two-fold series of impressions, the one belonging to our flesh, and the other to our body—with the mode of this appearing differing fundamentally since it is a question of a real belonging in the first case, and an unreal one in the second. Thus, to the pathos-laden modalities of our originary flesh, so many sensations of our body respond, and signify them as empty. To these originary motions, "kinesthetic sensations" or "kinestheses" respond. The former are referred globally to the organic body, representing its dynamism according to the two active or passive modalities in which it occurs. The latter are related to the limit of this organic body when they are opposed to the fleshly force; they force it back, and it is transformed into our own thingly body. Yet we know that this is not only felt in us at the limit of our power; it also appears to us from the outside, in the world. On the outside face of our own thingly body another group of sensations comes to be grafted, which come from our senses. We call this frontier between the invisible universe of our flesh (to which our own thingly body belongs) and this same body perceived from the outside, our skin—this visible and invisible line on which our kinesthetic sensations and those that come from our senses are built up. Thus we are able to offer a rigorous phenomenological analysis of this.

Let us examine first the sensations of our senses. In themselves these are originary impressions. But they are constituted, related to our own thingly body as a thingly body appearing to us from the outside in the world. They are thus extended on its surface in the same way as upon any thingly body. It is a question of appearances that are sensible, visible, tactile, odorous, etc., serving as an outline for the constitution of the sensible objective qualities of the thing—of the "hand-thing" just as well as for the "table-thing." But as we have just recalled, and in conformity with the duplicity of appearing, our thingly body is two-faced. It does not only ex-pose on the outside this sur-face on which the sensible appearances are spread out as so many properties or sensible qualities of this thing, from which angle it very evidently appears—it also has an "inside," its dynamic revelation in our flesh. *This radical phenomenological duplicity of our own thingly body is the duplicity of our skin.* It is on account of this duplicity that the impressions of our senses are not only arranged on the visible surface of our thingly body (as tracks of colors, sensible tactile zones, or erogenous or even odorous zones, for example, giving way to the sensible qualities of the thing, like those of Descartes's wax). Because this duplicity is an *a priori*, and thus, by its effect, such impressions relate to this inside that belongs to our skin *as a practical limit of our organic body*. Thus, to the constitution of our sensible impressions over the external face of our thingly body, a second constitution is added, that of these same impressions inside the "organs," that this thingly body hides within it as its dynamic and living reality, as its flesh.

The sensible impressions inside the skin are then like so many replicas of thingly sensations. To the cold of the table, the cold of my hand corresponds; with the rugged character of its surface, an impression of ruggedness is felt in the hand. That these impressions felt by the hand are situated in it as its own means that instead of offering themselves on the skin in the light (changing along with it) they are referred to its invisible, internal side, at the limit of the organic body. This is the reason their organic disposition differs, as Husserl had noted, from their extension over the skin. Such a disposition would not be described as a propagation, however, or a "diffusion," *a difference in the way of being extended.* It refers to *an originary difference in the way of appearing,* to its duplicity. The constitution of our impressions "in the hand," or "under the skin," presupposes that, in a way that is as incontestable as it is enigmatic, its invisible revelation in our flesh is opposed to its ek-static ex-position.

"In" the hand, "under" the skin, another group of kinesthetic sensations are situated in the same way, and they mark the limits of our movements. Thus two series of sensations are united, no longer on both sides of the skin, but within it, inside our organs—the sensations of the senses constituted in us as the counterpart of sensible qualities of thingly bodies on the one hand, kinesthetic sensations on the other. Our skin is thus the site where multiple sensations interlace, are exchanged and constantly modified, and despite their multiplicity and their changes, always have a signification and a rigorous localization in the general process of constitution of our own body. In this way the pure phenomenological structures that we have recognized as belonging to our original corporeity—flesh, organic body, one's own thingly body in its opposition to the foreign thingly body—appear "filled" by a flux of diverse and changing sensations. Only the process of their constitution allows us to establish between them a rigorous order. This is not only a temporal order—it is the hierarchical order of pure phenomenological structures that is demonstrated in the phenomenology of flesh that we have just recalled. It is in their reference to these structures that our sensations occupy the place they do in our body and at the same time have the meaning they have for it. The theory of their constitution is nothing other than the theory of reference. We thus mark the point at which the constitution of one's own body proves to be dependent on the prior phenomenological analysis of our originary flesh, and even conceals or denatures it.

This last point calls for a final remark. In the process of their constitution, some of our impressions are referred to our originary flesh, others to the organic body, others to our own thingly body. As all these impressions are constituted, the terms to which they are related are as well. Our originary flesh doubles into a constituted flesh, our organic body into a constituted organic body, our own thingly body into our own constituted thingly body. We must be careful not to confound these different realities—for example, our constituted organic body with the originary organic body. When we speak of a "quasi-extension" of the organic body, of the "diffusion" or the "propagation" of our sensations in it, it is the constituted organic body that is aimed at. That is why we have been so careful to conceive the originary organic element in the primordial experience of our flesh. The constituted organic body is already a represented body. The same goes for the relation of our originary flesh to the flesh that we say "inhabits" our own body (as *Leibkörper*). And for our skin, and the "inside," whose limit it is.

When these originary realities are thought by phenomenological reflection, as we are doing now, we evidently have nothing to do with contents-of-thought, with significations essentially different from the originary realities they aim at, even if that is their provenance. The relation of these contents-of-thought to the originary reality of the flesh is only a particular case of the general relation of thought and life as we have elucidated it in the first part of this book. Here as everywhere it is not thought that allows us to attain life—it is life that attains itself in itself, and is nothing other than this originary movement of eternally attaining itself. As for thought, we have sufficiently demonstrated that it owes attaining itself and being a *cogitatio* only to life. The most decisive revelation of this phenomenological situation is in the flesh. Not only does no flesh—the entirety of its structures and originary modalities—attain itself except in life, but as pathos and in its effectuation, flesh defines the phenomenological mode according to which life's arrival in itself takes place. As if it were a thought that preceded *this primitive installation in ourselves, which is our flesh*, deciding in some way the existence of our Self as well as the phenomenological substance it is made of—the theory of an intentional constitution of our flesh is a form of insanity.

§32. A Return to Condillac's Thesis. The Statue's Auto-Eroticism: Flesh as the Site of Perdition. The Necessary Transition from a Phenomenology of Flesh to a Phenomenology of Incarnation.

We now have the means to return to Condillac's initial thesis for which the statue acts upon itself depending on the impressions that it feels, so as to avoid those that hurt it, and to welcome and favor those it enjoys.

We are aware of the importance of this analysis, and the breadth of the field opened by it. It is a question indeed of nothing less than human action in general. Whether this bears upon the world or directly upon the body proper to the individual, it is always in view of arousing certain sensations that this action is produced, starting from the sensations that it already feels, and doing so with a view to modifying them, increasing their intensity, or suppressing them. It is in order to satisfy his hunger, or his thirst, or to protect himself from the cold, etc., that for as long as he is on earth, man attacks another in order to take from him all the goods he needs, with the ultimate aim of arousing agreeable or satisfied sensations that must substitute everywhere for his initial or unbearable unease. All economic and social activity, the formation of civilizations and their cultures, have as motive the emotional phenomenological equilibrium of the statue and its inescapable demands.

As for the action of the statue upon its own body—when its hand shifts over the various parts in order to encounter their forms and feel their solidity—it takes a lot for it to obey a simple interest of knowledge. Precisely because these are specific sensible impressions of pleasure or displeasure at the origin of these movements, it remains inevitably subjected to a sensible, sensual teleology. If one of them, moving itself over the statue's own body, encounters pleasure, that is what it will fixate upon; it is in view of producing it or reproducing it that it will reproduce itself. Isn't the principle of erotic behavior (in this case of autoerotic man, and humanity in its entirety—its original sin, the sin of Onan) presupposed in Condillac's unconscious statue? Wouldn't this describe not only its initial autoerotic behavior, but hetero-erotic behavior as well, and all possible erotic behavior, if it seems that the eroticism that fills the landscape of contemporary "civilization," for example, is only an autoeroticism for two?

The more the fable of the statue proves to be significant for us (in so far as it covers the entire field of man's exploitation of nature as well as of the sensibility or erotic possibilities of his own body), the more serious its lacuna appear. Has the phenomenology of flesh succeeded in satisfying them?

In its effort to match the essence of an originary flesh, or in other words, its final possibility, the phenomenology of flesh has constantly borrowed what belongs to a phenomenology of Incarnation, whose systematic elaboration was put off only for propaedeutic reasons. An impressional flesh cannot indeed be made the object of a simple observation. From the beginning of our investigations, it was obvious that an arrival in the flesh precedes any conceivable flesh. It is not a question of a formal precedence, but of the generation of a substance. The phenomenology of the impression, a part of the reversal of phenomenology, had already persuaded us that the most humble impression bears within it a revelation of the Absolute. The entire critique of Maine de Biran against Condillac refers to an "inside" of sensation, of which sensualism never gives account. Regarding the Husserlian impression that is eternally reborn from its ashes, we have shown that this stupefying character is only the outer layer of an absolute presupposition, the self-generation of Life.

Our final allusion to Condillac's description of an impressional subjectivity striving to produce sensations of pleasure on its body meets with the first fact of autoeroticism, immediately interpreted in the Old Testament as idolatry and thus as sin. In the New Testament, flesh has this same signification of being sin, in a way that is so constant that the contempt of the flesh and the body will become a common site for the critique of Christianity and, beginning with Nietzsche, the most vehement reproach that will be addressed to it.

In being made flesh, however—according to John's Word, which fascinated the Fathers, and tore them from the horizon of thought surrounding the antique world—the Word brings salvation to men. Taking a flesh like theirs and being thus identified with them, it will allow them to be identified with him, to become God like him. How can the flesh be at once the site of perdition and of salvation? Since the phenomenology of flesh comes up against its limit here, only a phenomenology of Incarnation is capable of illuminating us.

3

Phenomenology of Incarnation: Salvation in the Christian Sense

§33. Recapitulation of Results Obtained from the Reversal of Phenomenology and the Phenomenological Analysis of Flesh.

The reversal of phenomenology has taken away from thought's intentionality (and, more fundamentally, from the world's Ek-stasis) the capacity to reveal the simplest modality of life: the impression. In the first gap of temporality, the impression's reality is abolished. The revelation of the impression can nevertheless be entrusted to the impression itself, the revelation of pain to pain, only if the impression bears life's self-revelation within it. Because this self-revelation takes place as a pathos, in the auto-impressionality of flesh, all life takes on an impressional form. Thus the phenomenology of the impression referred us to a phenomenology of flesh, which draws its possibility from life. This is the final meaning of the reversal: For the appearing of the world, where bodies are shown to us, it substitutes life's appearing, in the transcendental affectivity in which all flesh is possible.

Thus our own flesh cannot bring itself about as such any more than the impression can. If flesh is conceivable only in life's pathos-filled self-revelation, and as the pure phenomenological material of its auto-impressionality (since it is nothing but this), then it is now a question of continuing the analysis of life. Yet this analysis compels us to make a final reference. Even when interpreted in its radical phenomenological meaning, as the original mode whereby phenomenality becomes phenomenal, the life revealed in the auto-impressionality of its pathos-laden flesh still has a decisive characteristic. The life that arrives by itself in experiencing itself in its flesh is precisely not what brings about this arrival. If it streams through us and makes us living without our having anything to do with it, and independently of our power and will, then it is indeed a question of this life, which precedes us at the very heart of our being, and which is not solely our own—because always and already, before a single moment allowed us to turn toward it to welcome or reject it, or say yes or no to it, life is in us and we are in it, in the radical passivity that strikes the impression, but our entire life as well.

Thus all the characteristics we recognized in the impression—that its material is a phenomenological material endowed with the power to impress upon itself and thus to reveal itself in its very impressionality; that it can thus define reality in contrast to every worldly, noematic appearance; that it belongs to someone by right, and thus that an "I" is incontestably "present" in it—did not appeal to the simple existence of a factual life, even if this were understood in its pure and specific phenomenality. From the outset, the phenomenology of flesh borrowed each of its characteristics from an absolute life, and only on this basis did it struggle to understand them. Does the most significant of them, the fact that a new impression is unceasingly born in us, such that "an impression is continually there anew," express anything other than this Life's eternal arrival in itself?

And yet absolute Life's eternal arrival in itself, in the proceeding in which it generates itself by revealing itself in its Parousia without beginning or end, not only explains the enigmatic iteration and unending repetition of originary impressions in our flesh, it first gives an account of this flesh. It is *the way absolute Life arrives in itself*, in an Arch-possibility proper to the pathos-filled self-affection of every conceivable "living"; it is the Arch-pathos of this Arch-flesh that is presupposed in every phenomenalization of life, and thus in every living being—in so far as it precisely does not have the capacity to bring itself into life on its own. In spite of its finitude, or rather because of it, must not every living being go through life's conditions? The fact that it does not itself possess Arch-possibility—*the original capacity to bring itself about as such in the mode of a pathos-filled phenomenological effectuation*—keeps it from separating from this at any moment. In the Arch-possibility of absolute life all flesh is passible. And only there is it possible. Flesh in fact is nothing other than that: *The possibility of a finite life drawing its possibility from the Arch-possibility of infinite life*. If something like flesh is conceivable only on the basis of this original arrival in flesh, an arrival that flesh itself has nothing to do with, it is because the phenomenology of flesh does refer to a phenomenology of In-carnation.

In its reference to the Before of In-carnation, and thus to Life's Arch-possibility, flesh manifests a strange affinity with the other essential determinations of the living being. It stops being proposed as a contingent addition to its living condition, a sort of empirical appendix, in order to be integrated in a field of properties arising from an *a priori* more ancient than that of knowledge. How can we not notice that the situation of flesh as secondary in relation to Life's Arch-possibility is strictly parallel to that of the ego, and of the living being in general? In all cases, understanding what is in question—the living, its ipseity, and its flesh—implies that one places oneself in some way before them, in an original dimension. *It is precisely the same for each of the realities considered.* It removes from each of them the pretension it usually has of being a principle or beginning, or some autonomous or specific entity.

Thus there is a "Before-the-ego" that prohibits it from setting itself up as an ultimate foundation, an ultimate naturing, or the "absolute ego as the ultimately unique center of function" (Hua VI, §55, 190 / 186). Before the ego (seen as the source-point for the transcendental performances in which the world is constituted as well as the ego itself), what operates ultimately is precisely not the ego, but the absolutely originary Ipseity in which absolute Life comes in itself in the Self of its Word. Similarly, before the flesh, where it is joined to itself in Life's pathos, there is Arch-flesh, the Arch-passibility without which no "living" is conceivable. That is why the "Before-ego" and "Before-the-flesh" are really only one: It is a single pathos-filled embrace that makes the flesh a flesh and the ego an ego, *the auto-impressionality of the former and the Ipseity of the latter.*

Thus it becomes intelligible, arch-intelligible, that an ego belongs to every flesh, and flesh to every ego. Thus the decisive progress accomplished by the phenomenology of In-carnation asserts itself when the ipseity/flesh correlation is no longer deciphered from a feigned life, but within the trying process of life's self-generation. In this trying process, the "Before-ego" and "Before-flesh" together constitute the prerequisite of all living, and endow it *a priori* with the fundamental phenomenological determinations that make it the *carnal living Self* that defines our condition.

This reference from the phenomenological structures of the living Self to Life's original arrival leads us back to the question posed in our introduction about the compossibility of two Johannine utterances, which then determine the dogmatic content of Christianity. The first—"in the beginning was the Word"—relates precisely to this immanent proceeding of absolute Life. For John, it is a question of God's essence. Here we discover the originality of Christian monotheism, which cannot be reduced to the formal and conceptual affirmation of one God. It is a formal affirmation to the extent that the affirmation of this God is posited—a God of whom one knows nothing except that he exists. But if one knows nothing else about him, how can one even know that he exists? Does the affirmation of this existence not become totally arbitrary? Initiated by the Christ, on the contrary, John says what God is: Life. Yet Life is not a mere concept, *it is posited as an absolute existence in as much as a single living being lives, in as much as I myself live.*

Because I who live did not bring myself into life myself (nor into the Self I am, nor into my flesh, being given to myself only in flesh), this living being, this Self, and this flesh do not arrive in themselves except in the proceeding of absolute Life, which arrives in itself in its Word, and experiences itself in this Word, which experiences itself in it, in the reciprocal phenomenological interiority of their common Spirit. Thus in contrast to the formal God of monotheism, the Trinitarian God of Christianity is the real God who lives in each living Self, without which no living being would live, and to which every living being bears witness in its very condition as living.

Life's proceeding in its pathos-filled arch-revelation in the Word—so this is what John's first proposition pronounces. Because in the Arch-passibility of its Arch-flesh this proceeding holds the possibility of every flesh within it, the second Johannine proposition—"And the Word was made flesh"—is connected to the first. Both speak of the Word, the first by relating it to Life, the second by relating it to the flesh. Now if every flesh comes in life, then the second proposition, which treats explicitly the coming of the Word in flesh, seems to be a consequence of the first. What kind of implication is here in play the phenomenology of Incarnation proposes rigorously to establish.

The question of In-carnation is one of the heaviest if it calls into question at once the nature of the relation of man to God, the nature of Christ, and finally the possibility of salvation. But in addition, we claimed, the possibility of sin and perdition. The first Christian thinkers noted and explicitly formulated the ambiguity of a flesh that can mean salvation for man as well as perdition. With force and a singular clarity, Irenaeus affirms this double potentiality: "Thus in these members in which we were perishing and in which we accomplished the works of corruption, *in these very members* we are vivified as soon as we accomplish the works of the Spirit." What follows immediately in the text is no less categorical: "For, as the flesh is capable of corruption, it is also of incorruptibility, and as it is capable of death, it is also of life" (*op. cit.*, p. 599, our emphasis). Yet these are not isolated propositions related only to Irenaeus's meditations. On the contrary, they belong to what one can call a tradition, and to its initial source, which we can see from the fact that the *reason* for this ambivalence is presented in one of the first redactions that has come down to us, which was addressed precisely to those who were the least prepared to receive it—the Greeks! "Do you not know? Your body is the temple of the Holy Spirit [. . .]" (I Corinthians 6:19). It is in the Letter to the Romans that Paul explains, in terms taken up again by Irenaeus in his polemic against the Gnostics, life's immanence in every flesh, which also explains why each phenomenological structure of flesh, each of its powers—each "member of the body"—is capable of bearing within it idolatrous aims as well as the possibility of salvation. "No longer present your members to sin as instruments of wickedness, but present yourselves to God [. . .] and present your members to God as instruments of righteousness (Romans 6:13).

Thus we should go back to what comes in the beginning, before flesh—to the presence of this two-fold potentiality inscribed in each of the members of our body. If the destiny of flesh, which is also that of humanity, must be torn from an unbearable obscurity, it is a question of restoring to its arch-intelligibility the speech that proclaims the coming of the Word in flesh, its In-carnation.

The order of analysis in this third section will thus be the following: 1) the original possibility of sin; 2) the nature of the Christ understood as the Incarnation of the Word; and 3) salvation in the Christian sense.

§34. The Question of the "I Can" in a Phenomenology of Incarnation.

The phenomenology of flesh led us from our opening to the world through the transcendental performances of our various senses, back to their auto-impressionality in life's flesh. Our senses belong to a flesh only because of this pathos-filled self-givenness; and because of this alone everything given in our senses (the sensible content of our experience that we relate to things as their own qualities) is originally and in itself made of "impressions." Yet our senses' pathos-filled self-givenness in life has another decisive meaning: It makes each of them a power. This power is not limited to the production in us of a continuum of originary impressions ecstatically related to things, *it is first the power to be exerted*. I can open my eyes to the spectacle of the universe, give ear to a distant noise, put my hand onto a smooth surface or curved form—"I can" do all this and far more. But all these differentiated and specific powers, to whose immediate and continuous exercise our daily life gives voice, carry a more ancient power in them as an incontestable presupposition—the power to put themselves in play, to become an action, and to be able to do so constantly. Thus we must recognize in each of them (as implied by it, even though immaterial to its specificity) the reign of this original "I can," without which no power in general and none of the powers of our body would be possible.

On the one hand, this "I can" appears as an absolute "I can": It is power as such, the fact of power, and the ability of power to attest to itself and legitimate itself in its very exercise. Thus on the foundation of this original—and, one might say, unique—"I can," each power of our senses and our original corporeity in general is itself lived as an "I can," as the ability in principle to open one's eyes, feel, take, etc. And thus it is also lived as the possibility of bringing out these series of impressions, which make up the changing and seamless substance of our flesh.

On the other hand, the retro-reference of a phenomenology of flesh to a phenomenology of In-carnation leads back to a "Before-flesh," which precedes, by generating them, each of these essential phenomenological determinations of flesh: its auto-impressionality, its ipseity, and ultimately the power we are questioning ourselves about now. Only because it has possession of itself through this original "I can" does each specific corporeal power then become capable of being exerted, and become a power—in and through its flesh. But just as this flesh (which in itself is only an auto-impressional setting and is in possession of itself in this way) has nothing to do with this auto-impressionality (since it is only ever a natured, and not a naturing auto-impressionality), the same goes for the original "I can" we are discussing. Itself it is only an impression lived in its auto-impressionality; itself it is only a modality of a flesh. It does not have the power to bring itself about as such any more than flesh does. *Every power collides in itself with that about which and against which it can do nothing, with an absolute non-power.* Every power bears the stigmata of a radical powerlessness.

A phenomenology of In-carnation inexorably leads to this decisive intuition of a non-power more ancient than, and inherent in, every power. And yet a "phenomenology of In-carnation" is still only a way of denoting in the conceptual language of philosophy what is implied in every effective and real power: It is precisely not a concept, but Life's absolute self-givenness in the pathos-laden effectuation of its Ipseity in the Arch-Self of the First Living. It is thus no accident if the Christ takes it upon himself to say what human power comes from, and political power in particular, and does so at the very moment when in order to induce him to speak Pilate flaunts his power to ruin him or save him: "Do you not know that I have power to release you and power to crucify you?" Christ's brutal response—"You would have no power over me unless it had been given you from above" (John 19:10–11)—disqualifies in a radical way not only the idea we spontaneously have of "power," but also every real power, and our own in particular, emptying it of its substance, of the capacity that defines it, precisely its ability (whatever may be its specificity, its object, or its manner of exertion). "No power" . . . No power at all, for *it is only an actual power if it gets its power from itself, and it is a power only in this respect.*

"A fool who takes himself for a king is a fool," Lacan said. "A king who takes himself for a king is too." But the power of a king, an emperor, or a Roman prefect is not in question here; all power in general is, and first of all the elementary powers that the phenomenology of flesh recognized as constitutive of our original corporeity, and whose repeated exercise assures the maintenance and development of all human existence. To condemn a man to crucifixion presupposes other men, henchmen, soldiers, executioners, assassins, and in each of them the ability to take, to grasp an object or body, to strike it, to knock it down or pick it up—an ability without which no crucifixion would ever have taken place. It is all these powers without distinction, despite the hierarchy, contempt, or prestige that is attached to them in the eyes of men that have no actual power, to the extent that none of them has his power from himself, but only from a givenness with respect to which he has no power—not even, as we have seen, to accept or refuse it.

Where does this givenness come from? From above, the Christ says. And this means first that no man actually holds any kind of power since he never gets this power from himself. No power on earth, no kingdom of this world, and no actual reign, if what rules extends its rule on its own basis and owes its rule only to itself. But it is a question of grasping this decisive situation in its depth. *Why is no power possible in the world?* This is what the phenomenology of flesh, becoming in its very progress a phenomenology of In-carnation, has shown. Because the most elementary power of our original corporeity—whether it be intentional, like the power of a sense, or radically immanent, like the power of "moving itself," which belongs to it in principle—is given to itself only in absolute life's self-givenness; once it is placed in itself by this, it is in possession of itself and able to act. This is givenness from above, present in what is lowest, whether the act of clenching one's fist, driving a nail, or spitting.

No power is from the world: Because, placed outside itself in the "outside itself" of this world, and separated from itself like the soul is from its body when it is reduced to an object in traditional dualism, it would be unable to rejoin itself, to move itself in itself, and, thus, to exert itself. But this is the case first of all for the more original reason indicated by the Christ: because this immanent power, which alone is capable of acting, must first be placed within itself, and this occurs only in life.

What does the givenness from above consist in? Who gives it? And how? What does it give? And to whom? The phenomenology of In-carnation has responded to these questions. Every givenness in the sense of self-givenness, thus every givenness of a living Self, takes place in Life's original arrival in the Ipseity of the First Self; this is implied in every givenness, thus also in the givenness of any power. So it is not only "in Life," it is in the Ipseity of the First Self in which it is joined to itself, that every power in turn is possible, and given to itself in the Self whose power it becomes. This is what the Christ says to Pilate in a veiled way:

"Pilate asked him, 'So you are a king?' [. . .]—'You say that I am a king' [. . .]" And, directly, to his disciples: "apart from me you can do nothing [. . .]" (respectively, John 18:36–37, and 15:5). And this does not mean, "you can do nothing good," but "you can do nothing at all."

The reference Christ affirms from every power to "givenness from above" is thus not at all limited to the ethical field, even if it plays a decisive role there, as we will see in a moment. Even less would it aim at political power as such. If "every power comes from God," then political power can also rely on a metaphysical intuition, which nevertheless does not establish any hierarchy between the different possible types of power and confers on none of them any privilege. In this respect, the use that will be made of the thesis of the divine origin of all power by the theorists of the divine right of kings in the seventeenth century is not only an arbitrary salvage effort, it is the complete denaturing of foundational utterances that have no more to do with kings or emperors than constituent or legislative democratic assemblies. What they posit is *a universal definition of the human condition grasped in its original possibility, namely absolute Life.* The only power that exists, the hyper-power to bring oneself into Life and thus to live, belongs only to this unique Life, so every living being inherits from it all the powers it has received at the same time as life. The fact that the Royalty from which they proceed "does not come from the world" is highlighted by the immediate context affirming that these powers have nothing to do with a political authority. So it is not the powers of the powerful, the "great of this world," but the least, those who at the limit have nothing other than their own body and its most trivial powers, whose possibility nevertheless refers us back to abyssal questions.

Because the most ordinary of these powers are given in absolute Life, their gift is of a singular character. In a gift as we understand it habitually, there is the one who gives, the gift, and the one to whom it is given, so that a sort of exteriority is established at the outset between three terms. If it is a question of a present, the one who receives it becomes the possessor, and he can keep it for himself or make it a present again. Thus in Japan one finds "floating presents." Thanks to changes in packaging and labels they circulate indefinitely in such a way that an individual can come into possession of an object that he himself offered several months before. But the present that Life gives to the living—of its life, its Self, its flesh, and each of the powers that compose it—is nothing from which it could separate itself. This impossibility is two-fold. Inscribed in givenness, given to itself in absolute life's self-givenness, generated in its Self in its Arch-Ipseity, and possible in its Arch-passibility, where each of these powers is exerted in the heart of an Arch-power, the gift of life that is internally built up in the latter only subsists within it.

It is this original inability of the living to be separated from life that founds its own inability to be separated from itself. Thus the living cannot cut itself away from itself, from its Self, its pain, or its suffering. If in the "outside itself" of the world that is the site of separation our own body still cannot be placed outside itself, even when it is extended and its parts are external to each other, it is because that body, far from defining our actual body (our invisible and indivisible flesh) is only its external representation. In an analogous way, on the economic plane where "alienation" reigns, where the worker hires out and sells his work like the prostitute her body, turning it into "merchandise" that goes from hand to hand, it is himself he hires out and sells—not his objective body but its activity, its "real, subjective, individual, and living work." As Marx says, "the worker goes to the factory" just like the prostitute goes to bed.

The powerlessness of every power with respect to the absolute power that placed it in itself and against which it can do nothing, the resulting inability of it to get rid of itself, *this double impotence is extraordinary because it bestows on every power that which makes it a power.* Thus a singular reversal takes place, as a result of which the non-power, which carries every power within it and upon which every power dashes to pieces, is discovered to be its own condition of possibility. *"Cum impotens tunc potens sum,"* Paul says ("Whenever I am weak, then I am strong"). And again: "We boast in our sufferings" (2 Corinthians 12:10 and Romans 5:3, respectively).

This paradoxical relation between powerlessness and power means that the former is, if not the cause of the latter, then at least the opportunity for it to break forth; and most frequently Paul offers an ethical interpretation of it. The weakness of man that manifests itself in sin and of which he is acutely and painfully aware proves that since he is nothing by himself except this sinful man, his salvation can only come from the intervention of a superior and sovereign power. By a gratuitous gift it will bestow confidence on him, and first the strength of which by himself he is so deprived. Such a situation is open to various interpretations, one of which proves to be decisive for understanding the temporality of our existence: From his destitution and distress against which he is precisely powerless, man will escape only by an abrupt rupture—what Kierkegaard calls the "leap." It is a question of the leap of faith. Henceforth the leap cannot be understood as the simple transition from one psychological state to another; it is a condition always in play of a man lost in sin and determined by it, followed by an entirely new condition, which in a provisional and global way we will denote as salvation. So it is indeed a question of an ethical or more precisely religious problem or process.

And yet, ethical or religious, a leap must be possible. That it is inexplicable by psychology or by any other theoretical discipline, or that as Kierkegaard likes to repeat, it presupposes itself, makes no difference for the question of its final possibility. Foreign to theoretical knowledge and its domain, would this question not instead lead us back to reality, to the paradoxical relation whereby every power collides with a powerlessness in itself, from which it nevertheless receives at each moment what makes it a power? By showing him the nothingness of his own condition, sin at the same time shows the sinner that no living being could live from a life that is nothing; that, silently, always, this Life streams forth in him and makes him live, despite his nothingness; and that the possibility of salvation, for the sinner himself and for him more than anyone else, rests on this unique and absolute Life.

A life that is nothing, that by itself would not be alive, that is incapable of providing life to itself, deprived of this original power and of every actual power at the same time—this is a finite life. Life that brings itself about in itself in the First Living Self, in which it undergoes its own trial and joy—this is the infinite Life of God. No finite life exists as such. It is alive only because it is given to itself in the self-givenness of infinite Life. For the same reason, it has no power if it is forever unable to give it to itself. In sin, the one who commits it has the tragic experience of powerlessness which strikes at the root of his entire life to the extent that, deprived of all actual power, it is at the same time deprived of the power to do what it wants. It wants what is good and does what is evil.

When in the experience of its error a finite life discovers that it has neither the power to do what it wants, nor even the power to live, then it must be the case that, if it lives, a Life is in it which gives it to live even in its sin. The unlimited emotion of the prodigal son in his rags, it is the abrupt revelation that he is alive only in Life, and this revelation is infinite Life's self-revelation revealing itself to him in his emotion. All finitude is woven of the infinite, blended with it, inseparable from it, and draws from it all that it is, has been, and will be. The most elementary power, the most precarious gest, rests in the Arch-power. As Paul says, "In him we live, move, and have our being" (Acts 17:28).

Thus the one who had neither right nor power over it, and was begging for his part of the inheritance, has reclaimed as his own possession this Life in which everything is given. Only when he was stripped of everything did he experience it suddenly within him as what, in his very destitution, was unceasingly giving him the gift of life. It was then that, overwhelmed by it, he collapsed, and uttered the word of Christ: *"Abba!"* For the one that has none of them, where does the illusion of possessing life and exhausting all its powers come from? Before determining ethics, this line of questioning concerns the reality of our living condition. This is what Paul again says: "What do you have that you did not receive? And if you received it, why do you boast as if it were not a gift?" (I Corinthians 4:7).

§35. Illusion and Reality of the "I Can."

The ambivalence of the "I can" plunges us into uncertainty: It posits both its illusory character and its reality. If it is given to itself only in absolute Life's self-givenness, as the phenomenology of Incarnation has established and as Paul, following Christ, has just reminded us, it arises from this one and absolute Life and from this alone. But since each power of our flesh is capable of moving itself in itself, and acting, only to the extent that it bears this "I can" within it (which is itself given to itself only in Life), we must say that none of them in reality is a power. They tend to appear as the exclusive properties of the Life that runs through every living being, which is no more than a *mode* of it. In other words, it is something that has no consistency by itself, but only as a manifestation, modification, or peripeteia of a reality that is other than it, and without which it falls into nothingness. It is not just the capacity of each of its powers to be deployed and exerted that is unable to constitute itself, and through itself an effective and autonomous existence—it is the flesh itself in its singularity that is unable to do so.

But does this ruinous result not strike against every thought of immanence, since it calls into question every singular reality and takes away its capacity to subsist by itself (and allows this only *in alio*, in something else, which operates within it as a foundation that allows it both to be understood and to exist)? Is the phenomenology of Life not an interpretation of this kind? Is not the immanence of life in every living being its main argument? If a Life is in it that it would vanish without, is the living being not then bereft of what assigns a price to its living condition—the feeling of having one's own, free, and independent life—a life of one's own that does not belong to anyone else? The joy of life, of breathing, walking, going where seems good, thinking as you will, letting your imagination drift like a ship cruising at its own speed, or like Rousseau abandoning himself to his reverie, casting a vague glance through his myopia at the plants he makes out along the path—do all these epiphanies, which are resplendent in their irrefutable appearance, not lose their brilliance when the suspicious theory casts its sad glance their way, and denies them the right to be sufficient in themselves?

At the beginning of the nineteenth century, after it had been long suppressed, life invaded the fields of philosophy, literature, poetry, and art in general. Its presence within every living being led to pantheism and this introduced a new sensibility into European culture. Contesting the narrow vision of a rationalism that exhausted itself in the objective consciousness of material entities and enclosed man within their limited horizon, life opened man to the infinite. After the abstract and conceptual universality of science and its indifferent truths, a universe of concrete forces followed, and these forces are all one. Everything outside us and within us changed: Outside us, in place of a collection of discrete and inert objects, grand cosmic forces unfold. And within us, because the single drive that moves them, and that they express in various appearances, also runs through us, lifts us up, and carries us, a great tremor from which nothing distinguishes us, a river without banks, in whose torrent, like a rite of baptismal immersion, a boundless experience submerges us and merges into us.

The rigorous phenomenological status of such an experience must nevertheless be produced. In the romanticism of the nineteenth century as in that of other epochs, in pantheism but also in the various forms of experience that claimed to unite us with the absolute, the identifying fusion is accompanied by the dissolution of individuality. This is precisely what must be destroyed for the opening to the absolute to take place. It must be destroyed because individuality is thought starting from its "limits." Why do limits pertain to individuality in principle and thus to every individual? Because the principle that individuates—the *principium individuationis*—is the world itself, understood phenomenologically as constituted by its phenomenological structures, which are space, time, and the concept. Each thing is stamped with the seal of individuality to the extent that it is situated here or there in space, with every space of space around it—and now, or earlier, or later in time, always lost in the immensity of this time—whether it is finally this or that, a tree, an armchair, or a man—a particular thing to the exclusion of all others. In so far as the possibility of the individual takes place in the world (in the world's appearing), this individual is limited from the very way it becomes an individual—from this "way" that is its appearing in a world.

Where, when, and how will the apparent individual part with its limits if they are constitutive of her individuality? In life, one will say; in the river of life that is indifferent to the individuals it runs through, "to the nature of the wheels that it turns," according to Hegel's expression. "Indifferent" is saying too little or too much. If life is foreign to the world and to the phenomenological categories of the world from which every conceivable individuality follows, then life is not only indifferent to individuals—it is foreign to them, and radically so. In life, no individual is possible. So the very possibility for the individual to be open to Life, understood as the absolute, is a problem. What does the experience of the All mean if it must do without the individual? What moment is still there to test? Thus is not the experience of the absolute that of no one? If in the end it is a question of being annihilated in the All, *what is the phenomenological reality of this "annihilation"?* If it has none, is the proposition that formulates it anything but a *flatus vocis?* The fusion of the individual with the absolute in the sense of its dissolution and dissipation in it can indeed be affirmed speculatively, but from the phenomenological point of view it is meaningless.

But what about the phenomenality of Life itself then? How is it phenomenalized if it is irreducible to every possible individuation? Here one of the crucial events occurs that will mark the modern world and determine it entirely. With Schopenhauer and his grandiose rejection of classical thought at the beginning of the nineteenth century, life returns to the European scene, our culture is invaded by it, and it will furnish our culture with other bearings, or more precisely will remove from it all those it had laboriously acquired. On the one hand, Schopenhauer reactivates the *principium individuationis* of the tradition by referring it to the phenomenological structures of the world, grasped, following Kant, as "representation." On the other hand, he opposes to this, and perceives in its unitary phenomenological structure that is actually irreducible to it, what he calls the Will or the will-to-live, which is only another name for life. *To the extent that the will-to-live escapes the world, the principle of individuation is not in play in it; the new and essential metaphysical dimension opened by the Will is an anonymous and impersonal dimension.* Before defining (as in the Romanticism that is contemporary with it) a sort of ethical program, it is prescribed by its nature that the individual will dissolve in the unlimited stream of the will, to the extent that, because it is in itself foreign to the world, it is at the same time foreign to the principle that individualizes.

Contesting the conception of the experience of the absolute as a dissolution of the individual in life—because then, for the individual in any case, this dissolution is phenomenologically nothing, and thus is nothing—we would ask: But what about life and its phenomenality then? *Escaping individualizing representation, having become impersonal and anonymous, life is deprived of phenomenality at the same time; it takes place in the unconscious.* An impersonal, anonymous, unconscious, and blind life— blind and unconscious because impersonal, and separated from what makes up the individuality of the individual—this is Schopenhauer's devastating intuition, which will indeed flatten modern culture and give it a tragic destiny. For life is a movement; it is not first a movement ahead of consciousness, "which always goes from a now to another now ahead of it," as Husserl says, a life whose illumination would come from the intentionality of a protention, but the original life that owes its revelation only to itself. From then on, deprived of all phenomenality, life's movement is only a blind force, a "drive" about which one does not very well know, as in Freudianism, whether it is a question of a "psychic" notion or of a biological—or, in other words, material—and ultimately chemical, process. Still, this difference between what is properly psychical and purely biological tends to fade for modern thought, to the extent that, in overwriting the former by the latter, the psychic by the biological, it offers an explanation of human reality that will identify it (as in cognitivism) with its neuronal and genetic potential. The time of the Nazi doctors is not far away.

Schopenhauer's devastating intuition reintroduces life into Western thought, and as a foundation, but only by taking away its phenomenality at the same time as its individuality, and for this reason it is only a late effect of the Greek presupposition that saves the work of phenomenality, its "light," for the exteriority of the world. It is clear in this case that everything that does not owe its appearing to this world is already the prey of the unconscious. It is in contrast with this horizon that we must gauge the identity between Truth and Life in Christianity. When radically elucidated, this identity denotes Life's self-revelation (= the Revelation of God) in the Ipseity of an Original Self and as the phenomenological mode in which it is accomplished. Such an Ipseity happens in principle when Life comes in itself, and that is what dismisses the concept of an unconscious, blind, anonymous, and impersonal life—and makes it absurd *a priori*.*

Life's immanence in every living being thus does not mean that the reality of the human being is dissolved at the same time as its individuality, while (in a phenomenological interpretation that is as decisive as it is novel) the immanent process of absolute Life generates in itself the Ipseity of an original Self as the internal condition of its self-revelation—as the internal condition of its own life and thus of every conceivable life. Thus a Self belongs to every living being; every living being is built up in the manner of an "individual." It is nothing by itself—neither a living being nor an individual—and lives only in this process of Life's self-generation, and *that is what, far from taking the effectiveness of a singular reality away from it, on the contrary endows it with reality.* Given to itself in the Ipseity of abso-

---

*We must repeat that such an interpretation is not at all that of science: It arises from pseudo-philosophical analyses that constantly graft themselves onto science to the extent that they never arrive at the (Galilean) "origin" and thus at an actual understanding of this science itself. Turned over to philosophy, Galileo's intuition, which opens modern science, is in the end that of Descartes: That no "subjective" determination belongs to a material process as such, that the wall is no more "white" than "painful" or "perverse." Nothing more, nothing less: How much nonsense would we avoid if we were attuned to these basic propositions?

lute Life, joined to itself and undergoing experiencing itself in it, in this absolute life's trial of itself and in the Ipseity of its original Self, it is itself generated as a Self, as the singular Self it forever is.

To be a Self is indeed nothing other than this: to be given to oneself without this self-givenness being one's own doing. *To the extent that absolute Life's self-givenness (in which it is given to itself) takes place effectively within it, every Self is at the same time a real Self.* It undergoes the trying experience of itself in the certainty and irreducibility of this self-trial that joins it to itself and makes it the Self it is. Undergoing experiencing itself, it possesses itself, it has taken place within it, it rests in itself as upon a ground it can lean on; it has taken foundation in itself, so to speak. Have taken place in it, it inhabits an Abode that, though not built with human hands, is no less its own, and from now on no one can rob it of this.

But the problematic has shown that the generation of the transcendental Self in absolute Life is identically the generation of a flesh that belongs to it in principle. And this is because Life's self-givenness, in which the Self is given to itself, draws its phenomenological material from a pathos whose auto-impressionality is nothing other than the flesh that joins it to itself. In the flesh, however, every power is given—given impressionally to itself, placed in possession of itself, and thus able to be exerted and to act. Life's immanence in every living being does not only bestow it with the original and essential phenomenological determination of being a carnal Self, it makes it a real and effective "I can." The "I can" that can implement itself and move itself in itself, that inhabits every power of our flesh, and in turn makes it a real power capable of being exerted when and for as long as it wants: free. For freedom is not a "liberation," or who knows what subjective derivative of our thoughts, images, or fantasies at the mercy of unknown forces, our desires, or our unconscious drives—even less is it a liberation of the individual with respect to its own being, or a dissolution of every singular reality, which can lead only to nothingness. Freedom is a power, a power that always possesses itself and thus has access to itself—it is a permanent, incontestable, irreducible, and invincible power, to which our original corporeity bears witness in each of its acts or movements, from the most humble and elementary to the most complex and difficult.

Flesh does not lie. And this does not only mean that each of its impressions is "true," and experiences itself as it is. That flesh does not lie—*never lies to itself*—again means that with respect to each of its powers everything in it is real, actual, and truthful, which it exerts from itself, from an original Power that lives in it and gives it to itself constantly, such that it exerts it when it wants and as often as it wants, so it is free indeed.

It is thus not merely that it undergoes experiencing itself in its action as it unfolds, much as a pain is experienced in its pain, or as a *cogitatio*. At the same time as its action, it experiences this action *as being in its power—it undergoes experiencing itself as this radical, incontestable, and in a certain way absolute power, not only to accomplish it, but to be able to accomplish it and thus to be able to accomplish it again.*

Freedom is not a metaphysical, speculative affirmation, which is always contestable and always contested—today more than ever by science, it is said. Freedom has a phenomenological meaning; it is the feeling of an incumbent power undergoing experiencing itself in its exercise, and as such is irrefutable. From the phenomenological point of view, however, such a definition does not suffice. One can always claim that the subjective experience of freedom is only the objective unconsciousness of a determinism. But freedom is in no way reducible to the artificial order of an unfolding movement—even if it were understood in its pathos-filled givenness and thus as a sentiment. *Freedom is a feeling of the Self to be able to implement each of the powers that belongs to its flesh.* Yet this original power that inhabits and makes possible every concrete power is not adventitious, ideally separable from the Self itself: *It is part of the way the Self comes in its own flesh; and it is generated in this coming at the same time these powers are, and is consubstantial with them.* It is an "I can" consubstantial with the carnal and living Self, established in its own power and so free to deploy it from itself—as incontestable in this power and its freedom as the Self and its flesh to which it belongs.

"If you knew the gift of God": Life's givenness to the living as a givenness of its Self, its flesh and its power, is not a pseudo-givenness, nor it is the givenness of an alleged Self, an apparent flesh, or an illusory power. The reiterated utterance that determined Judaism and was fulfilled in Christianity—"God created man in his image"—finds a radical explanation in the phenomenology of life. For one indeed sees here, first, what it means "to create," when it is not a question of the world, but of man and his life. To create does not then mean to place an exterior entity outside oneself, enjoying a separated and thus autonomous existence. Freed of the ideas of exteriority, externalization, and objectification—of the world—the concept of creation now means generation, and the generation in absolute Life's self-generation of that which happens to oneself only by coming in that self-generation, and for as long as it keeps coming in it. Freedom, autonomy, movement, being, power, ipseity, singularity: Exteriority does not give these; Life's immanence to itself does. With the Christian concept of immanence as Life's immanence in each living being, every form of pantheism is struck dead.

§36. Forgetting Life and Recalling It in the Pathos of Everyday Praxis.

If, in the same way as our Self and its flesh, the "I can" is given to itself only in absolute life's self-givenness, then our question is suddenly revived: How can it forget this original givenness that by putting it in possession of itself gives it the capacity to be freely deployed from itself, and makes it an actual power drawing its own power from itself—a power to be able? Yet it is precisely because life's givenness is a real and effective one, because life is given totally and without division, *because its gift is the self-givenness in which every power receives itself and hence is self-empowered*, the "I can" has come to forget the most original gift of life. Here the inversion we have spoken about takes place *phenomenologically*, the inversion of powerlessness into power: the fact that the non-power of every power with respect to itself changes into the constant and irrefutable experience of its free exercise.

The most remarkable characteristic of our entire practical life is to act in every circumstance with such ease, in a freedom so great that it pays no attention to the transcendental condition of the numerous actions it constantly accomplishes spontaneously. And this is because these actions indeed pose no problem for it. Thus, I get up and walk, I take an object, and look in the direction of an unexpected noise; I breathe in the morning air, I go to work, and eat, and I execute a host of extremely precise gestures, each of them adapted and effective—without thinking of it. In the event that one represents the most banal and quotidian activity, and thus refers it to the objective body, one then attributes to that body all these varying movements and displacements, which are now grasped as its own. One identifies this sort of half-light in which they take place (even when they appear in the world's light) with the unconscious character of physiological, biological, and ultimately material processes that are produced in the organs. This multiform activity is now theirs, and its facility, its instinctive perfection, and the silence of its accomplishment, is what one calls health—"the silence of the organs." Health is forgetful, as forgetful as life.

When a concept as decisive as forgetting intervenes in this set of problems, one who wishes to offer a radical elucidation of it must bring it back to fundamental phenomenological categories.[*] *Forgetting must thus be understood starting from the duplicity of appearing.* On the plane of thought,

---

[*] Thus we have constantly proceeded—with respect to language, for example, and more generally with respect to the body and the flesh that are the theme of this work—with results that the reader will appreciate in accordance with the phenomenological imperative: in relating them *to the phenomena of his own life as they are given to him in and by this life.*

forgetting consists precisely in no longer thinking something, which in this way is "forgotten." This changes in the case of an unconscious memory. In principle, and despite numerous obstacles, what one no longer thinks can become the object of an actual thought again; then "recalling a memory" occurs. Every thought, every representation in the most general sense thus carries within it the two-fold possibility of forgetting and remembering. Yet what a contrast between these two possibilities! Whereas nearly all of the content of our representations remains in the so-called unconscious state, only a minute part of this virtually infinite content takes place under the gaze of consciousness, and most often in a marginal zone of it for that matter. In the most favorable but also the least frequent case, it becomes the object of a "clear and distinct vision," and thus shows itself "in itself and as it is," "in the plain light of evidence," according to the wish of Husserl's phenomenology, which is also, as we have seen, its methodological *telos*.

Yet this finitude—this extraordinary and indeed unlikely finitude that would reduce our existence to scraps of reality, to discontinuous and insignificant fragments of being, nearly all of which permanently escape us—this finitude pertains to thought only in a secondary way. What is finite is the phenomenological milieu in which thought moves, the transcendental horizon ecstatically hollowed-out, structured, and limited by time; it is this empty light that is finite. Only a finitude like this, which is phenomenological in principle, explains why the indeterminate totality of being overflows on all sides this circumscribed and closed site of the world's bright interval, the "clearing" lost in the obscurity of the forest. Thus the split occurs between the precariousness of an always-derisory presence and the immensity of a forgetting that strikes almost everything that is.

When it is related to life and not to the appearing of the world, the meaning of the concept of forgetting totally changes, to the point that new terminology is here necessary. It is only in terms of thought that life can be called "forgotten." It is "forgotten" to the extent that, since no space opens in its radical immanence, and no dehiscence breaks it, there is no place for any thought in it. Hence everything that pertains to thought has disappeared: No forgetting, which means precisely no thought turns away from its content in order to abandon it to the condition of an "unconscious memory." No calling this back to mind either, since recalling itself is an act of thought. No forgetting, no recalling, no memory in the sense of a representative faculty, and no memory of the world that relies on and presupposes its unveiling.

Since its reality excludes the very possibility of a memory and thus of a memory concerning it, life escapes memory in principle. At bottom,

Husserl's entire problematic of the phenomenological method, which was analyzed at length in our first section, faces the question of whether it is possible to memorize the transcendental life that is initially lost in its anonymity. It was a question of knowing how the forgetting of transcendental life that characterizes natural existence, which is intentionally oriented toward the world and absorbed in its objects, could be overcome by an act of this same thought, which would allow it to find itself in the complex and unceasingly revised process of phenomenological reduction.

We understand better now the failure of the method, and the aporia that it struggled in vain to circumvent: Both teach us what forgetting signifies when it is related to Life. Because it gives way before the gaze of thought, it is capable neither of forgetting (in the sense of being abandoned to the Sheol of non-phenomenality) nor of being recalled, by wrenching it away from the nothingness of the unconscious, and returning it to existence: No possible memory indeed. Life bathes in a radical Forgetting that grips its very essence. This forgetting is thus not an accidental or provisional state, which would be followed by a possible recall—that would take a mislaid content that was undetermined for a while, in a sort of cosmic night, and return it to consciousness in the happy light of the world. *If life escapes all memory even when it never leaves us,* it is because a memory without memory has always united us to it and always will. Always already, it has accomplished its work; always and already it has placed us in our living condition. It is this immemorial memory of life alone that can join us to Life; it is life itself in its pathos: it is our flesh.

In light of this decisive phenomenological proposition alone, the question of forgetting—by the "I can" of the Life that gives it its power—can be elucidated. This forgetting is thought's own doing, and in no way that of the "I can" itself. That is why nothing changes with regard to its condition, its phenomenological status, or the power it has from this status. If thought forgets the self-givenness that edifies the "I can," this shows only that thought is foreign to it, and that the absence of thought, far from keeping the "I can" (and thus each power of our flesh) from being deployed, is instead its condition. This is the reason why our entire practical life is carried out with the ease, facility, and freedom that one attributes to a mysterious "instinct," or to the mechanism of unconscious physiological processes. The "silence of the organs" is only a name for the radical immanence from which the "I can" draws its first power—the power to be able—which activates every power of our flesh, whether its movements are slow or rapid, with the suddenness of a lightning flash.

The phenomenological silence of our living praxis in its immediate accomplishment is irreducible to the muteness of things, and one realizes this because, *being the silence of pathos, it is heavy to bear.* Even when our daily activity is bound up with pleasure, in the happy ease that habitually characterizes all forms of spontaneity, it is however never *qua* activity, spontaneity, freedom, or "action" that it should be described. In as much as every human action bears within it as its most interior possibility an "I can" that is given passively to itself in the pathos-filled self-givenness of life, it is a *feeling of action* that is always in question. But it would still be a superficial view to interpret the pleasure that the simple fact of acting often brings us as one modality of feeling among other possible modalities, such as pain or suffering. Because the action of any kind of power presupposes the action of the "I can," this original capacity of power must first be at work on its own basis, buttressed against itself as its own ground, wresting itself away from the radical passivity in which it is given in absolute life's self-givenness: *all feeling of action is in reality*, according to Maine de Biran's extraordinary intuition, *a feeling of effort*, and this effort is precisely not some modality of our affectivity. Effort in its specific pathos marks how the "I can," with its original capacity to act shown back to its source, in the place of its generation in absolute life, and here given to itself in pathos, is in and by this pathos capable of deploying freely— itself, starting from itself, by its own strength, and at its own expense in some way—the power and strength with which it has just been invested. This original pathos, which releases a strength and endows it with the strength to be exerted from itself and according to its own strength—to be more exact, when the test of this force is exercised in these conditions and in this way—*this* is the feeling of effort.

So it is clear that the affectivity of this feeling is not that of some modality of our life. It is edified where transcendental Affectivity and Strength intersect, where, by joining it to itself, the former endows the latter with the ability to apply itself starting from itself, which alone makes it an actual force, immanent to itself in and through this Affectivity. The transcendental Affectivity that precedes every conceivable feeling is life's own. Before founding the abundance of our feelings, emotions, and sensations, it auto-affects itself according to the two phenomenological tonalities of suffering and joy in which every life arrives in itself. It is *this* Affectivity, this original Affectivity in its fundamental and no longer contingent phenomenological tonalities, that generates every strength within it, communicating to it the pure tonalities in which it reveals itself inevitably as a suffering or happy force, and raises from its suffering in the effort in which it is necessarily deployed, without which no force is set in motion.

So we see how life escapes forgetting, in its most elementary and quotidian praxis, in our simplest, most habitual, and humblest gestures: Because none of them is capable of being accomplished without recourse to the "I can," any more than it is in a position to begin anywhere but in the original phenomenological tonalities of suffering and joy in which it is put in possession of itself in the pathos of absolute Life.

Let us now consider this everyday human activity as we carry it out habitually: in the world and in its light. It is then that we discover the immense field of social activity, "social praxis," a field which is nothing other than the content of society—its economic content. Precisely because it shows itself in the world, it is interpreted from the outset as an objective content composed of a plurality of "economic objects," whose properties and laws one seeks to determine with the help of more or less arbitrary parameters. But one cannot make it so that all of these "objects" do not refer (their objectivity or ideality notwithstanding) to the work of men and women, which, according to Marx's affirmation already cited, is a "real, subjective, individual, and living work." No theory, no ideology, and no thought can muffle the voice of this carnal, effort-making, and suffering "I can." *So in its everyday praxis life does not look to thought to overcome its forgetting; it is responsible for itself, in its own pathos.*

This pathos does not assume only the expression of suffering or sadness, as it does through the great social (i.e., individual) phenomena of hunger, misery, the cynical exploitation of labor, and human distress in all its forms. For whoever endeavors to go back to the transcendental possibility of all action, rather than sticking naively to its mere effectuation—and even more naively to objective behavior, from which angle this effectuation is displayed in the world—it is precisely this transcendental possibility, the power to be able of the carnal "I can," which must be analyzed. To accomplish any movement, as we do constantly in everyday existence *by having the feeling that we can accomplish it,* this is rather reassuring. This is undoubtedly the source of the pleasure that according to Aristotle accompanies every act naturally. Nevertheless, a wholly other tonality is connected to this capacity for power inherent in every power, and it is as essential to life, perhaps, as the suffering or enjoyment of its self-revelation, and as capable as they are of wrenching it from forgetfulness: anxiety.

§37. Forgetting Life and Recalling It with Pathos in Anxiety.

Kierkegaard's genius is to have from the beginning connected the concept of anxiety to that of possibility or power.[*] In making use of such a connection, it is not only a fundamental affective tonality—as that of

---

[*] Søren Kierkegaard, *Søren Kierkegaards Skrifter*, Vol. 4, ed. Niels Jørgen Cappelørn, et al (Copenhagen: Gads Forlag, 1997) / *Le Concept de l'angoisse*, French trans. K. Ferlov and J. Gateau (Paris: Gallimard, 1935) / *The Concept of Anxiety*, ed. and trans. Reidar Thomte (Princeton: Princeton University Press, 1980).

Suffering or Joy, or even, staying within the framework of Kierkegaard's set of problems, Despair—that is brought to the center of philosophical reflection. At the same time, it is pathos in general that receives in this reflection a place it had never occupied. Recognizing this precedence in Affectivity does not isolate it in any way, however. Connected to power, Affectivity is interpreted as the principle of action, so that this action can no longer be understood except in its real motivation, which is precisely an affective motivation. Moreover, Affectivity not only provides action with its actual motivation, but also constitutes properly its essence, and this is because Affectivity constitutes the essence of reality itself. By connecting anxiety and possibility, Kierkegaard invites us to test our own thesis, according to which transcendental Affectivity constitutes the internal possibility of every conceivable force and all power, because in this Affectivity alone it is put in possession of itself, and thus becomes an actual force.

This relation between anxiety and possibility must therefore be explained. It will no longer surprise us if it is first of all a relation in thought, in light of its own conceptions. For thought, possibility is of course related to action, but it precedes action, and in some way pertains first to thought itself. Thought pro-jects action before itself, it dis-poses action before its gaze in the two-fold form of a project, precisely, that at the same time presents itself as a potential objective behavior. This is then the object of a reflection whose goal it sets and whose means it evaluates. In short, it is a question of *a representation of action*, where this prior representation, but also the behavior meant to realize it, both obey the laws of representation, which is to say in the end the constitutive phenomenological structures of the world's appearing. We face questions like these: How can this task be accomplished? What tools should be used? Where should they be applied? For how long?, etc. Thus, for calculating and for-seeing thought, the possible always pertains to its own field and competence: By projecting itself toward the possible, thought gives rise to it, just as thought is also what responds to the questions that prompt the objective presentation of the possible, whether it is a question of "realizing" it, or perhaps of dismissing it.

But here is another sort of action. Having left with his friends for a climb whose difficulty they underestimated, a man comes to a halt on the ridge separating two chasms, struck with vertigo. The possibility of falling paralyzes him, and anxiety overcomes him. Where does this possibility take place? Beside him? At the bottom of the chasm to which he feels irresistibly attracted and from which he strives to turn away? Where is the anxiety that grips him? In what do both consist? Another man (or is it the same one?) waits on the subway platform. The train arrives, and a similar anxiety comes over him. Not without intense effort, he tears himself away from the gaping possibility open before him, takes refuge on the bench in the station, and holds onto it, closing his eyes. These are "psychologically fragile" beings.

Here are two others that are more normal. He left the dance hall, and on a large adjoining balcony he contemplates the night. Later one of his partners arrives, and like him, has put her hand on the balustrade. Are they there to escape the suffocating heat of the room, the din of the music, or all the commotion? Or was it some anxiety for them too? It overtakes them on the balcony and doesn't let go.

Kierkegaard's decisive intuition, which makes him, like Descartes or Maine de Biran, the inventor of a radical phenomenology, was to cross out in a single stroke all these objective circumstances toward which our explanations stray. Kierkegaard eliminates all objectivity from the start, in a reduction that is not at all partial but complete, and he carries this out by beginning his analysis of anxiety with an analysis of innocence. For "innocence is ignorance," he says (SKS 4, I, §3, 343 / 37). It is total ignorance that does not just strike the knowledge of external circumstances (though these do not actually disappear, but now count for nothing).

Let us observe in passing that it is setting aside the objective conditions for anxiety that prompts the decisive and now famous distinction in §5 between anxiety and fear, with which it is most often confused. In fear, all the similar feelings refer to a precise fact, to something menacing, whose approach or at least probability is perceptible. Because innocence is in itself ignorance, and remains in an immediate unity with itself as if it were absorbed in this immediacy, innocence is deprived of discernment not only vis-à-vis the world of causes and effects, but even more with respect to ethics and to its fundamental determinations, good and evil. That is why Kierkegaard says that Adam, because he is still in this state of innocence when the prohibition is addressed to him, understands nothing about it.

It is true that many things have happened since Adam, and it is no longer precisely innocence that reigns in our societies. Whatever the motives may be that drove the man and woman just mentioned to meet on the balcony, neither is absolutely ignorant of them. They both "went out," like the young girl in Pavese's *The Beautiful Summer* who also slipped out into the street simply to get some fresh air, take a walk, and unwind. As for them, they undoubtedly know a bit more about this encounter. If the meeting occurred because at bottom it was more or less sought, this complies with the ordinary course of human affairs and intrigue rather than serendipity.

And can it also happen now? The *possible* in suspense—is it not thought that weighs this? That evaluates in a glance the truly narrow space that separates the hands placed side by side on the railing? It could be that, as they both are thinking, barely moving his hand the man places it on the young woman's. Would she pull hers away? Would she just "nihilate" it, like a Sartrean heroine pretending this hand was nothing, and felt nothing, since it was not hers—leaving open the way that leads to the great game of pleasure, the game of the possible?

And yet the possible that drives this game improperly called love is in no way identical with a content displayed before thought's gaze, which assuredly does not escape the protagonists of this pre-programmed adventure. This is the meaning of the reduction of objectivity Kierkegaard carries out when he makes innocence the prerequisite for the analysis of anxiety: *To situate the possible, which will become the principle of anxiety, no longer in the field of thought, but in life's radical immanence, an immanence whose innocence supplies an exemplary pathos.* Before measuring the importance of such a shift for understanding the possible that is proper to anxiety, a remark about the status of innocence in Kierkegaard's problematic is necessary.

Precisely because its pathos takes on an exemplary (in other words, universal) meaning, innocence is a state that no human existence can do without. "How sin came into the world," Kierkegaard says in a very serious proposition, "each man understands solely by himself" (SKS 4, I, §6, 356 / 51). And yet sin is characterized in the first place by the loss of innocence. We must thus translate it such that each of us learns for himself how he has lost innocence. Before it is lost, it is true, innocence knows nothing of itself. It is only when it is lost that it becomes conscious of what it was. As phenomenologists of life, we understand immediately how such propositions must be interpreted. When we say that before sin innocence knows nothing of itself, the knowledge of which it is deprived is that of thought. Innocence *does not perceive itself as innocence.* The knowledge of innocence that occurs only when it is lost is that of an impression that has toppled into the past, whose reality is destroyed and reduced to a noematic unreality. But there is nothing unreal or unconscious about innocence in itself; it is referred to this way only by the thought that believes everything that escapes its current representation is abandoned to nothingness and actually lost. Escaping thought's knowledge, innocence in reality never stops having the experience of itself in its own pathos. *Something like innocence is possible, moreover, only in this way, given in its pathos-filled immediacy and unconcerned with seeing or being seen.*

This innocence absorbed in itself, which no glance troubles, is the innocence of flesh, for example—and, more importantly, *this is what makes it flesh.* All flesh is innocent. Thus, we said, the everyday gestures that spontaneously deploy its powers without it paying them any attention unroll with such ease that common representation takes them clumsily for "instinctive," blind acts, like inert processes. In its immediacy, innocence seems to forget itself, just like flesh precisely. For this illusion to cease, however, it is enough that the most constant characteristic of praxis is felt by us: effort, the feeling of effort, what is hard about it, and all the degrees in which it intensifies right up to the point of becoming unbearable.

The phenomenology of flesh rests on the essential distinction it has established between the pretend powers whose spontaneous development everyday life expresses (seeing, hearing, moving) and, on the other hand, the transcendental possibility of applying them in an "I can" that is capable of being exerted starting from itself—the possibility of power identical to our freedom. Kierkegaard's dazzling intuition is that *this radical possibility of power is brutally revealed to us in anxiety*: "the anguishing possibility of power" (SKS 4, I, §5, 350 / 44; translation modified).

Because this profound possibility supports each elementary power of our flesh—each sequence of our most habitual activity, the most naive act—the pleasure connected to it is not as simple as the ease of its unfolding would make one think. *As innocent as innocence may be, a secret anxiety inhabits it.* Whether it be innocent because it is ignorance and knows nothing about the world, or whether the anxiety connected to the possibility of power is, according to another of Kierkegaard's decisive insights, an anxiety before "nothing," it can escape neither the fact that this possibility of power is present in it, nor the anxiety in which it is felt. Quite the contrary. Knowing nothing about what it can do only exacerbates the possibility of power; anxiety penetrates innocence entirely. It endows it with the pathos proper to it—this mix of attraction and repulsion before the unknown; this unstable state that is still not culpable because it still hasn't done anything and knows nothing of what it can do (whether good or evil)—it is already overwhelmed by the possibility of doing it, and subjected to it, and engulfed by the anxiety of this "vertiginous freedom."

We say a secret anxiety because it is shielded from the gaze—because the secret is the domain of pathos. Apart from the world, in this sort of incognito that is consubstantial with it, the feeling is experienced more strongly and increases of itself; it grows. Handed over to itself, the possibility of power is anxious about itself. Innocence had first felt its anguish as a new feeling, as an adventuresome quest, with a sort of complaisance like children have. Because, Kierkegaard says, "anxiety belongs so essentially to the child that he cannot do without it. Though it causes him anxiety, it captivates him by its pleasing anxiousness."

There is a pleasure in anxiety, but in this very pleasure anxiety is subject at the same time to the law of pathos and the vertigo of freedom. It is responsible for itself and bent under its own burden to the point it is no longer able to bear it. Fleeing itself, getting rid of itself, this is now what it projects—at the heart of its anxiety, which burns in it like a consuming fire. The inability to get rid of itself exacerbates it at the moment the possibility of power comes up against the non-power in itself that is older than it and that gives it to itself—against the powerlessness that we have shown to be the source of this power. This is when anxiety is brought to its paroxysm and increases vertiginously: Wanting to flee itself and coming up against its inability to do it, cornered by itself, the possibility of power is thrown back on itself, *which means that at the same time it is thrown back on the power that makes it possible.* So it throws itself into it, as if it were the only way out, the only possibility that remains, and takes action.

This strange and trying process of anxiety that unfolds in human action—which will always differentiate it from every material process, so that it is absurd to confuse them—takes place on the dizzying crest of the mountain, on the platform in the station, and on our dancers' balcony. One will object that, since they already lost their innocence, the dancers undoubtedly did not go through the trance we are describing. They only came looking for the pleasure of a night out, an encounter, or an adventure. *And if this pleasure were that of anxiety*—which in our world, deserted in its anonymity, could alone break its unbearable ennui—*restoring the Self to itself?* For anxiety is only the paroxysmal expression of the essence of Self, of the pathos in which, joined to itself and having thus become the Self it is, it will always be invested with this possibility of power that is its infinite freedom.

Kierkegaard was in no way mistaken about the evolution of societies; he offered a powerfully original conception of history as a history of generations, and at the same time of the relation of the individual to this history. From one generation to the next, and owing to its indefinite repetition, anxiety accumulates quantitatively ("objective anxiety"), thus aggravating the conditions in which sin becomes possible. Between these conditions and sin itself, no "transition" can be described or analyzed, because actually there isn't one, but only a "leap," the absolute position of a new "quality," which is irreducible to any condition and thus to any explanation. This leap is sin, the act itself. Hence this decisive proposition already cited, according to which, "sin presupposes itself" (SKS 4, 343, 380, 349, 338 / 42, 77, 43, 32). So the act proceeds from a radical freedom conferred on the individual in the very process of its generation in absolute Life, as the transcendental Self whose freedom is thus consubstantial with it.

This is why each generation (in the sense of a natural and not transcendental generation, in the historical sense) is confronted with the same task—each individual begins again the history of the world, in other words, that of Adam. Every phenomenological determination constitutive of the transcendental Self pertains to it and could not be dissociated from it. On the balcony, our dancers also knew innocence, and also lost it. The age at which an individual loses innocence depends only on the degree of corruption of the society to which he belongs. Nor can anxiety itself be forgotten. On the balcony, our two dancers who lost their innocence still did not part with anxiety. Perhaps they are there to find it again.

In the most depraved societies, when all moral rules and all "taboos" are abolished, and when various forms of perversion are welcomed with immense favor, where skepticism or cynicism are the only topics capable of awakening the last trace of interest, anxiety has not so much disappeared as put itself in charge. It shows itself through two series of apparently contradictory phenomena. On the one hand, a systematic reduction to objectivity by means of the objective sciences, the technologies they propose, and the interpretations that they impose (for example, the reduction of flesh to the body, or of our transcendental life to material processes, etc.)—and one waits unconsciously for this objectivity to diminish or eclipse everything that is properly human in humanity, anxiety in particular, and the phenomena connected with it, such as death, for example. Corresponding symmetrically to this, on the other hand, the systematic fabrication of objects, conditions, and conduct capable of producing it—of producing violence, indignity, infamy, and ignominy in all its forms, right up to the kind of prostitution that one might call artificial to the extent that it is no longer a question of prostituting oneself for money, but for the pleasure of prostituting oneself—for the anxiety that every form of self-abasement purveys. If anxiety confirms in every man and woman that they are this transcendental Self that is incapable as such of doing away with itself, how do they get rid of it?

The reader of Kierkegaard's extraordinary essay—a few lines of which are enough to rout all Hegelianism, and beyond it whole sectors of modern objectivist thought—cannot conceal his surprise. From §5 on, a completely different "explanation" of anxiety is advanced, which no longer refers it to the internal phenomenological structure of the transcendental Self: Suddenly the world itself seems to be its provenance.

§38. The Duplicity of Appearing and the Reduplication of Anxiety.

Immediately after disqualifying all exteriority and all consciousness of an object in the reduction to innocence and its ignorance that precedes the analysis of anxiety, it is now up to exteriority to raise anxiety in us. This happens when anxiety is related to a definition of man as a "synthesis of soul and body." Since this synthesis is said to be "unimaginable," one can see that the body in question here is the external body of the tradition in its opposition to the soul (an opposition that consists in this very exteriority). In other terms, the synthesis of the soul and the body is, as Kierkegaard denotes elsewhere, a "paradox" that belongs on the same plane as the relation of time and eternity, and in a similar way suggests an enigmatic conception of the human condition.

However, to the extent that anxiety arises from the synthesis of the soul and body, such a synthesis, however unimaginable and paradoxical it may be, must be possible. Kierkegaard entrusts this possibility to a third in which the two elements are united, and "this third is the spirit." Upon one such situation, for which the spirit (the synthesis of two irreconcilable terms) is itself the paradox, *The Concept of Anxiety* constructs a dialectic in which none of the terms can subsist in its own state—neither the body as a simple body, as brute animality, nor the spirit resting and remaining in itself ("being left to itself," "grasping itself") for as long as "it has itself outside itself," by virtue of its paradoxical relation to an external body, which is its own. It is this equivocal relation of man to the spirit, or of the spirit with itself, that is at the heart of anxiety (SKS 4, I, §5, 349–50 / 43–44).

We recognize without difficulty the phenomenological tenor of this "synthesis of the soul and the body" whose possibility is the "spirit" (and is here still interpreted by Kierkegaard within a classical system of thought, since it involves the modern dualism attributed to Descartes): *It is the duplicity of appearing.* In accordance with this, the soul, which also means our living flesh—the whole of our impressions, our sensory performances, and our various powers—is perceived from the outside as the aspect of an objective body whose configurations, parts, members, organs, and numerous particularities, which have *nothing in common with what it experiences originally, can appear to it only as incomprehensible and, to put it briefly, absurd determinations.*

Here we discover a first form of contingency, which stems from the fact that this objective body, with its organization and structures that are also objective, is the object of an empirical observation without which no truly rational explanation can account for it. Confronted with a variety of foreign organs, we can of course try to attenuate its unusual character by alleging a corresponding variety of "functions," each of which will appear as a mode of realization—and perhaps a mode of realization that is particularly ingenious or adequate. By proceeding in this way, however, we only push the problem further back. The admirable texture of a lung of course makes breathing possible, but why is it necessary that something like respiration exists?* Because it is necessary for a living organism

---

* "He is dead," Giraudoux writes of one of his heroes, "because breathing annoyed him."

in these conditions? And yet the response of science (a programmatic response) *is still only the formulation of Kierkegaard's question: Why does the spirit of mind* [l'esprit] *need to be connected to a body of this nature—to a body in general?*

One can see that what makes our objective body a contingent reality is not its singular aspect, with its characteristics that are also singular. It is not because science would be incapable of explaining it in the end that it would be absurd: It is so only in the eyes of the mind, to the extent that there is an abyss that this mind itself has never been able to cross— between what this body is in itself on one side, with its functions (nutrition, excretion, etc.) and its destiny (its laborious training, its fleeting maturity, its inevitable decline), and on the other side what the mind is in itself (whether a question of its intelligible vision of eternal truths or the joy of undergoing experiencing itself and living). Except that this abyss, this site of a radical heterogeneity, this "unimaginable" connection of elements, is precisely what defines it—that which is nothing other than this connection, a "synthesis of soul and body." What makes the spirit anxious is not having this unlikely objective system in front of it, with its unpalatable functions, its pile of molecules or blind quantitative processes; what makes the spirit anxious is *being* this.*

If we want to measure the violence of this anxiety that pertains to a new sort of explanation, we must consider more closely the objective content in whose presence it is produced. On the one hand, the properties of the objective body, as the aspect in which our invisible flesh seems to appear, are homogeneous among themselves: They are all precisely objective properties. They all take place there in front of a possible gaze (our own, or that of a third party if it is a question of the parts of our body that we cannot see immediately). Between these properties, and in spite of their common phenomenological status, a difference is revealed, and it is all the more surprising for the one who makes the discovery about himself or herself for the first time: It is a question of a man's or woman's body. It is significant that, at whatever moment such a discovery may intervene, it is the moment of anxiety. Not only does the mind perceive itself from the standpoint of an objective body with its determinations, to which only habit allows us to grow accustomed, but there is one among them that seems more incomprehensible and more contingent than all the others: the sexual determination that marks it at the depth of its being and at the same time differentiates it radically by putting it into a specific category of individuals, male or female, and defining them by a function (as

---

*In the extraordinary novella *The Metamorphosis*, Kafka exposed with great rigor and very concisely the Kierkegaardian paradox of anxiety.

"generator," or "mother," or possibly "surrogate mother"), with which it, *qua* mind, has nothing to do. This is Kierkegaard's dazzling intuition: "*The sexual is the expression for the monstrous contradiction that the immortal spirit is determined as a genus*" (SKS 4, II, §2, 373 / 69, our emphasis).

"Intuition" does not here mean understanding, or evidence (sensible or intellectual evidence). Even if the sexual were given to us in a vision, it is not a question of this, but of the enormous contradiction it expresses. And this contradiction is not given to us in "vision," any more than in our "mind," in the sense in which we usually mean it: *Its revelation happens in life's pathos, and this is anxiety*. This is anxiety's second explanatory principle, which roots it no longer in the vertiginous capacity of power proper to the Self, but in the paradoxical relation of the two modes of appearing.

Having situated the connection, relation, or "synthesis" in pathos, whose mode of accomplishment is here anxiety, Kierkegaard possesses a dialectic that was unknown to that point, a dialectic of pathos whose implications (which he develops spontaneously) are as gripping as they are novel.* The first consists in interpreting the respective situation of the irreconcilable terms related in the "mind" not as a transition from the first to the second, but as a simultaneous and vertiginous increase of the two mutually present elements. An increase that thus is nothing other than their increasingly antagonistic relation in the "mind," namely the qualitative increase of anxiety itself.

Let us follow this sort of "story" that doesn't take place in the world but occurs as a qualitative modification of pathos itself and culminates in the "leap" into sin. Because the discovery of one's own body as an objective body—and even more as an objective body marked by sexual difference—is identical to an affective disposition, the fact that such a body belongs to the mind is experienced as anxiety at the outset. At the stage of innocence, as we have seen, anxiety is already there. It is there not only because innocence bears within it this capacity for power, even when it does not know what it wants, when it is anxious at "nothing." It is there because, in its very ignorance, innocence is this synthesis of the soul and body that is constitutive of the "mind" from which it is never separated. It is this latent affective disposition that is awakened in mod-

---

*We ourselves have attempted a phenomenological elucidation of this dialectic, which, as affective, is the very dialectic of life. Cf. *The Essence of Manifestation* (Paris: PUF, 1963), §70. That such a dialectic differs entirely from Hegel's, and that Kierkegaard grasped from the beginning the profound originality of his own conception, is made evident in the formidable critique of Hegel's dialectic with which *The Concept of Anxiety* opens; cf. the introduction.

esty, when, without any need here for the involvement of a foreign gaze, "spirit is found at the extreme point of the difference of the synthesis" (SKS 4, II, §2, 372 / 68)—of this monstrous, "enormous" difference that is established in it, between itself and its sexed body.

To these prestigious analyses, the phenomenology of life is able to add two remarks. One can indeed wonder why the synthesis between the "spirit" ["*l'esprit*"] (transcendental life) and our objective body is so paradoxical that it provokes anxiety, of which modesty is a transitional phase. Because what is inexplicable and ultimately absurd is the objective body as such, and its foreign organs, or even the functions for which these organs are the means. Kierkegaard, however, never considers this objective body in itself, but only in its synthetic relation with the soul, in the mind [*l'esprit*]. We would claim that it is only to the gaze of the mind (even if there is no gaze there) that the body with its surprising configurations and sexual difference is absurd. This supposes of course not only that this body "differs" from the spirit, but also that, from its side and in itself, *the spirit is not at all absurd but quite the contrary: It is the domain of a justification and an absolute legitimation, a self-legitimation.* Only designating the spirit as life will allow us to understand this latter condition.

Our second remark is a question. If two explanations are successively proposed in the analysis of anxiety, must one not ask: Are these really heterogeneous in the same way as the two fundamental modes of phenomenalization are, to which they refer? How in any case can we understand their relation? If, as Kierkegaard claims at the end of his investigation, "possibility is the weightiest of all categories," and again, that "in possibility all things are equally possible" (SKS 4, V, 455 / 156), is this not because these two attempts at explanation overlap in some way, and refer to a single "possible," so that the anxiety connected to this is reduplicated to the point of actually intensifying, until it reaches the paroxysmal condition from which the irrepressible desire arises that will lead to the offense—to what Kierkegaard calls the leap into sin?

§39. Desire and the "Leap into Sin."

That our own objective body never exists in a separate state, but only within this synthesis with the soul which is the spirit, implies reciprocally that the spirit inhabits each of the terms of this synthesis which it itself is: Not only our soul, but also our objective body. On this condition alone can it unite in itself each of the two irreducible and irreconcilable terms of the synthesis—on the condition that it is the common element in them in which they are united. The question is thus one of knowing what this presence of the spirit in our own body means exactly, when this is defined by a set of objective properties, and in a singular way by sexual difference.

We will understand this better if we do not forget that true name of this "spirit" is transcendental life. Doesn't the clarification demanded from the phenomenology of life instead turn back against it? Isn't its principal thesis that there is no life except in Life, in its pathos-filled self-revelation, and never in the appearing of the world? How then can our objective body contain within it the Life that escapes in principle an appearing of this sort?

The phenomenology of flesh has responded with precision to this question. Our objective worldly body is animated by significations that make it precisely this living body (*Leibkörper*) whose eyes are eyes that see, whose ears are ears that hear, whose members are movable members moving freely by themselves—all significations borrowed from our original flesh, in whose reality alone the operations aimed at through these various significations draw their reality. Such a body is indeed seen in the world, and the significations that confer on it the character of being living are aimed at too, yet as unreal noematic correlates. But the reality to which they refer—that of our living flesh with all these real operations (of seeing, moving, etc.)—this reality belongs to the sphere of transcendental life's absolute immanence; and like it, this is invisible.

Thus, we said, the man who looks at himself in a mirror sees his face, his sadness, and the movement of his lips only to the extent that, jointly with this perception, the capacity to experience sensations or accomplish movements is actualized in him phenomenologically. Our worldly body does not refer only to an invisible subjectivity: Under its visible species a flesh is hidden, always present and always living, which never stops auto-impressing itself in the pathos of its night.

And this, we added, holds for the objective body of the other as well as for our own. It too conceals within it a capacity to feel, to move, to suffer and to enjoy, which hides from me, it is true, at the very time this body presents itself as invested with this two-fold, pathos-filled and dynamic potentiality. That is the difference, we will claim, that separates the knowledge I have of myself and of my own body from that which I have of the other and of his own body. As for me, while I perceive my own body in the world, *I am this hidden flesh*, which is sensing, moving, and suffering, and which endows my objective body with the characteristics it has for me as well as for others. The other's objective body also bears within it these invisible powers of its senses and movements—more profoundly, this original flesh in which all these powers are given to themselves in the "I can," that he is as well as I. *For me*, it is true, this "I can" and this flesh belonging to it are only unreal significations, differentiating his objective body from an ordinary body. This does not alter the fact that this "I am," this flesh, and this originary Life are really in him. It is solely because this Life really lives in him that these significations are "true," signifying a real life, and a real flesh—that his objective body is and can be, for him as for me, a "living" body.

Because one's own objective body (whether the other's or mine) bears a living flesh, and at the same time conceals it through the declension of its worldly appearances, *it is constituted* a priori *as a magical object*—a two-fold object, visible and invisible, inert and movable, insensible and sensible. On the one hand, it is an opaque, blind, and "material" thing, which can be enlightened by light from the outside, but can never welcome and receive it within, be illuminated by it internally, or become light itself, a seat of intelligibility, a pure crystal of appearing. On the other hand, it is a thing, whose essence is auto-appearing in the way a self-revelation is possible: in the pathos of life.

We recognize without difficulty the ambiguity of the "sensible" that we have encountered from the beginning of our investigation. There is the sensible in the sense of what we can sense (the smoothness of this fabric), but which itself senses nothing; and the sensible in the sense of what possesses this capacity to sense and is defined by it. Our objective body has the meaning of something that is able to sense, but in itself, reduced to its condition as a "thing," to its "thingly" character, it senses nothing. The eye does not see. Only our flesh—or our "soul," Descartes would say—sees. In ordinary experience, the two meanings of "sensible" are constantly superimposed and confused. On the contrary, when our thingly body is explicitly intuited as a flesh, and invested as such with the capacity to sense, then an essential modification occurs: *The sensible becomes the sensual, and sensibility is then called sensuality.*

Our objective body is a magic object, constitutively double, and beneath the surface of it offered in the light, beneath the visible span of its skin, bonded to it and inseparable from it, the invisible of our organic body unfolds, and *this* body is itself kept in the "I can" of our original flesh that unceasingly inhabits it, retains it, and moves it. For this reason, this objective body that is ours is never a sensible body; it is determined from top to bottom by *a primordial sensuality*, whose reality and true essence are nothing other than our original flesh, nothing other than life.

Thus Kierkegaard's synthesis of the soul and the body in the spirit takes place, such that the latter is present in the former, invisible life in our objective body. So that *our objective body is not a thingly body whose living character would be reducible to a field of intentional significations that confer on it the ideal capacity to sense and to move; but rather, this is what it is in truth*—it really carries within it this real ability and these real powers.

Hence this body capable of experiencing sensations can suffer and enjoy if I touch it, or move as a result of these sensations, and give rise to a formidable anxiety for the one who now has not a sensible but a sensual experience of it. It is the anxiety of the one who does not touch a thing, or a body that is similar to a thing, but a body of flesh that a real life inhabits. Of one who really can produce pleasure or pain in this body (in the sensual body of the other, for example) and thus the set of movements that will very likely follow. Who can caress its skin in such a way that the one who caresses will not only experience, on her own hand while it moves, the smooth, fresh, or tepid feeling that the other's skin will communicate to it. Shifting the hand over it, it will provoke a series of impressions on it too—of freshness or tepidity, pleasure or fright. *On the skin of the other, or more precisely beneath it,* at this moving limit of the other's organic body— while, breathing more slowly, *the latter* will arouse it, immobilize it, or take hold of it in the "I can" of its original flesh. This sensual body, which in itself is moving, suffering or enjoying, is the body of the other *in so far as it carries its spirit within it.* This is the inconceivable synthesis of a body and a spirit that takes place in front of the gaze, *beneath the hand,* of the one who questions: "Will he really hold out his hand to the magic object and place it on the living flesh that remains there next to him and seems there for the taking, and *try to feel it where it feels itself,* where its sensuality is most alive, in its sexual difference—and 'take' it, and hold it in its power?"

His anxiety then increases vertiginously. This power to attain the "spirit" of the other in its body is not only one of extending the hand to it, touching it where its sensuality is most accessible, and perhaps waiting. What the phenomenology of flesh has established is that such a power is not a mere pretend power that every flesh feels in itself at every moment. *What it feels constantly in reality is the capacity for power,* the ability to implement in itself, of itself, and starting from itself its power to touch and to take—it is the possibility of power, its ability to be able [*pouvoir pouvoir*]. It is from this possibility of power, Kierkegaard has taught us, that the formidable anxiety arises for the one who *could* fall into the chasm, hurl himself on the train rails, or grasp the young woman's hand placed next to his. And yet, *if the power to extend the hand and close it around the hand of the other is still only an unreal possibility, an object-of-thought* (indeed, what our dancer is thinking about), *the possibility of power itself is a real and always effective possibility*; it is constitutive of the transcendental Self in the ipseity whereby our flesh is placed in itself, and in each of the powers that are now its own—in the possibility of being able to exert them. Anxiety arises from this Self, only one moment with itself, wondering "if he will do it." But the question it addresses to itself is not an act of thought, it has neither subject nor object, and it does not concern the power to reach out the hand, which has never concerned thought and has always been "self-evident." The question arises from the abyssal possibility of power, and it is this possibility that is constitutive of the reality of the Self and is inseparable from it: It is its revelation in anxiety, the anxiety of its freedom. "Freedom's possibility," Kierkegaard says, "announces itself in anxiety" (SKS 4, II, § 2, 378 / 74).

It is then that the reduplication of anxiety happens: when the two "explanations" that the problematic has alternately offered for its emergence overlap. When on the plane of reality the two sources of anxiety intersect like two streams mixing their water in a single torrent that will submerge everything. When the anxiety stemming from the enormous contradiction of the spirit posited as a body with is sexual specificity increases disproportionately from the anxiety stemming from the possibility of being able to touch the former in the latter—this spirit in this body, where they united one to another, in this unimaginable synthesis in which the spirit seems accessible in this sexed body, which is its being-there. Where touching this body, this sex, would mean touching the spirit itself where it is spirit, and touching life where it undergoes experiencing itself in its own Self, irreducible to any other.

The moment anxiety is reduplicated is the moment desire is born. Desire has nothing to do with a natural phenomenon, or some kind of material (biological or chemical) process. Desire is possible only in anxiety. The world of desire is the world of anxiety. The characters, the motivations, the history, and the destiny of desire are the motivations and the destiny of anxiety. If anxiety is born in the face of the disturbing presence of the spirit in the being-there of a sensual object, which is endowed with all the sexual attributes that bring this sensuality to its limit, so that one could touch each of them where it is capable not only of being-touched, of being sensed, but of feeling itself—and if this anxiety redoubles in the anxiety that increases with the vertiginous possibility of being able to perform each of these gestures, strokes, and caresses—must one not then ask: Is desire anything other than the desire to do all this?

It is not enough, however, for desire to desire, even when the one feeling it can derive some pleasure from it (for the anxiety inherent in all desire is not itself exempt from charm). This desire is still only desire, a real "state" of course—an effective modality of life, a fundamental tonality of flesh—but one that does not bring satisfaction in itself.* How desire, not content to be desire, can want to and be able to satisfy itself—how, in other terms, anxiety succumbs to sin—is, according to Kierkegaard, something that can never be explained. At the very least, the fulfillment of desire, the leap into sin, must be possible. And the phenomenology of life, without claiming to give account in any way for each particular act in which sin happens, is able to bring to light this possibility. *The relation at whose term anxiety and desire will turn into sin, making it effective, is really only a particular case of the absolutely general and essential relation that links Affectivity and Action in principle. This relation is nothing other than our own flesh.* The phenomenology of flesh has thus spoken a lot about it. The sets of problems concerning anxiety, desire, and the "leap" are its integral parts. This is what we know.

When any modality of our life, always given to itself in its own pathos, undergoing experiencing itself and bearing itself in this pathos, feels itself suddenly as too heavy to bear, and thus no longer bears itself (the various tonalities of our life being actually nothing other than the various ways of bearing oneself or no longer bearing oneself), then, as this is unbearable, the irrepressible will to get rid of oneself arises. Yet there is nothing abstract about such a power: Given to itself in the pathos of anxiety or desire, put in possession of itself in this pathos, which is the pathos of our own flesh (our suffering and desiring flesh), it is a power of this flesh, and, even more, it is the ability to be able, the original "I can" that it inherits from life. Because, giving it to itself, Affectivity is the essence of Strength, its various affective tonalities (this anxiety, this desire) are not only the motives of all the actions our flesh is able to perform: They carry within them and identically constitute the original possibility of being able to perform them and thus the reality of all of these actions.

So when facing the other's magic body, the anxious desire to reach the life within it arouses the anguishing possibility of being able to do so—the streams of anxiety's two dark rivers have reunited indeed. Their force sweeps everything away and eliminates every point of reference. Anxiety then takes on its feminine form as weakness: Even though it comes from the Self, it crushes it and leaves it powerless, left to drift in the anxiety that drowns it. The "leap" will deliver him from this, it is thought. "At the maximum we find here the dreadful fact that *anxiety about sin produces sin*" (SKS 4, II, §2, 377 / 73, Kierkegaard's emphasis).

---

*Just as anxiety is still only anxiety and, in Kierkegaard's language, has still not carried out and will itself never carry out the "leap" that turns it into sin. In itself anxiety is not culpable. We see this well in innocence, where it already occurs and which has still not lost its innocence—in the modesty that, in a look of lust, can turn into an intolerable pride, even when there is no movement in it toward the opposite sex, and no desire.

One often designates as eroticism this anguishing world of desire and sin. And yet eroticism is complex, and elucidating it requires new analyses.

§40. Two Cases of Transcendental Flesh in the Erotic Relation. The Ego of Description.

The leap, or sin, does not deliver from anxiety—quite the contrary. And this is for two reasons. In the first place, the origin, or let us say more precisely the *agent* of the offence, the Self and its constituents (its capacity for power, its freedom, the anxiety that arises precisely from it) are always there. Accordingly, once the real act is carried out, this real presents itself again as a possible in the figure of the future; it is what I will be able to carry out once more and always once more, since the capacity to carry it out (the fundamental "I can" that I am) remains in me. And along with the vertiginous freedom of this capacity for power, the anxiety it inexorably creates too. In this respect, one can say that the sexual, which is understood here as sin, created time. And that actual time exists henceforth as the time of the possible, of the possibility of the repetition of sin. And one can well see how, instead of having been suppressed, the anxiety connected to the possible, to this real capacity for power, increases in the history of each person as it has increased in the history of the world, from generation to generation, since the sin of Adam. It is a quantitative increase of what Kierkegaard calls objective anxiety—not that anxiety would in itself be something objective, but because it is implicated in this worldly temporality, in the new objectivity it has created.

And this is the second reason why, far from putting an end to anxiety, sin prolongs and exasperates it: this modification of objectivity, of our own objective body whose latent sensuality unceasingly increases its power of fascination. In a certain way, our body is always marked by sexual difference, and yet for profound reasons that we will return to at length, this mark remains long implicit: In innocence, for example, the difference is lived in ignorance. Our sensible body may well be determined by the primordial sensuality of a flesh capable of sensing, but the consideration of this sensuality as such and for itself, and even more its use for producing certain sensations or movements in an objective body (whether this one or another), for example, sexual sensations or motions, are not present to the mind from the outset. It is this implementation, this spontaneous or reflective use of sensuality, that occurs in sin, so that the sensuality that is primarily only the phenomenological expression of the synthesis of the body with the soul in the spirit undergoes a radical upheaval that turns it into what Kierkegaard calls "sinfulness." "We do not say that sensuality is sinfulness but that sin makes it sinfulness" (SKS 4, II, §2, 377 / 73).

Capacity to sin is not sin, nor is its immediate and real possibility, which resides in the act of freedom—in other words, in sin itself, in its self-positing. But it creates this "historical milieu" that has been constructed since Adam to the point of reaching a paroxysmal state in which the repetition of sin develops from general conditions, a capacity to sin in principle that makes the incitement to sin omnipresent. This incitement consequently seems to belong to the objectivity of this environment, to the point that it becomes something objective itself, as a natural behavior that would no longer be designated as a "sin" or "offence," except from outdated prejudices.

Before returning to the future of sensuality, the capacity to sin, and sin (of what we globally and in the most extreme confusion call "sexuality") in the world today, we should deepen the study of eroticism such as it comes to be grasped in the anxiety of desire, and notably in the transformation of the sensuality it arouses. It is the other's sensuality, to be more precise, his or her objective body, that will serve momentarily as the guiding thread for our investigation, since whether one takes it from traditional philosophy or from contemporary phenomenology, it would be through his or her body that we would have access to the other. It is an access that is not first a theoretical access, or some kind of reasoning, whether a reasoning by analogy or even a "passive appresentation," but desire in its concrete, carnal, and spontaneous form.

The thematic inflection here suggested is motived by the fact that, in the analysis of anxiety, desire, and finally the "leap," we have come to the point of view of *the ego of our description*, directing our attention to the way things occur in it—thus to our dancer rather than his companion. It is in him, in the "I can" of his original flesh, that we read the increase of anxiety, the immanent transformation of this into the driving force of desire felt in the front of the other's objective body, whose sensuality (the presence of its flesh within it) was then exacerbated.

How can we misjudge any longer the unilateral character of such a presentation? To divide from the beginning the erotic relation between the ego and what is for it only the "other" is to risk falling back into the classical dichotomy of subject and object, with the ego, entirely naturally, playing the role of the former, while the "other" (the other ego) is identified with the object—especially as it is precisely in the aspect of its objective body that it presents itself to the ego's gaze, which is assumed as the principle of description (of the "subject-ego"). Is it not this classical dichotomy that serves as a substratum for the famous dialectics that claim to give account of the experience of the other, whether this be Hegel's dialectic of the struggle for recognition between consciences (of master and slave), or the simplified adaptation of it in Sartre's dialectic of the gaze? But is it not also what still determines the no less famous touching and touched chiasma, on which the later Merleau-Ponty founds his entire analysis of the "Sensible"?

And yet the critique of the chiasma has shown that it is not legitimate to install a dissymmetry between the two terms that it dissociates even while it makes a single reality of their (interlacing) unity—the reality of the Sensible understood on the basis of the Seeing/visible or Touching/tangible couplet, which refers to the very structure of our body and claims to define it. It refers to this singular structure, one term of which, a hand, touches the other, the former receiving a sort of mastery from this ability to touch, which confers on it the overhanging, domineering status of a "subject," while the other, subjected to this power, touched and sensed by it, is relegated to the rank of an ordinary thing, of a "thingly body"—of an object. But in the erotic relation, when in order to overcome and flee his anxiety, the dancer carries out the "leap," and takes hold of the young woman's hand, her hand is in no way reduced to the inferior condition of an object. *No object has ever had the experience of being touched.* The possibility of being touched is a transcendental possibility absolutely symmetrical to that of taking and touching: What is designated in the chiasma by the term "tangible," or "touched," has the same phenomenological status, the same dignity, as what is described as "touching." The young woman's hand belongs to an original flesh; only in belonging to this flesh, and never as an object or thingly body, is it capable of being touched and entering into the erotic relation. Just as the hand of the dancer touches it only in his own flesh, and not on the railing of the balcony, or in the world, where no object has ever touched another object any more than it has been touched by one.

The analysis of the set of fundamental phenomenological conditions that are immanent to the "touching" and make it possible—the original flesh of the Self given to itself in life's pathos; the "I can" that results from this self-givenness, from the self-givenness within it of every power constitutive of this flesh; the organic body that it deploys; the limit against which its effort is broken; the real content of the world that is this invisible limit)—this analysis, all these elements, must be reproduced on the side of the capacity to be touched, and inscribed in the original flesh of the young woman whose hand (on which her dance partner put his) is just like his: only an objective appearance. The only difference between the two cases of transcendental flesh (of which the two hands side by side are thus both the manifestation and the dissimulation), is that the one is "active" and the other "passive;" they are two modalities of one and the same capacity for power, so they are interchangeable, and the man and woman can exchange roles.

Because, just like the man's, the woman's hand is only an objective appearance of her carnal capacity for power—the vertiginous anxiety of a freedom increases because of this too, a freedom to leave her hand there, to neutralize it or draw it back, or to leave the balcony. And this anxiety is no less than that of her partner. Like his, it is coupled with the anxiety of having a body. And yet the woman's body is much more marked by sexual determination. The paradox of the synthesis of the body and soul in the spirit thus takes on an infinitely greater tension in her. She is more sensual than the man, and because she is more sensual, she is more anxious. Her anxiety is more "feminine" even than his, if the feminine character of anxiety denotes not the fact that it is a woman's, but the moment proper to all anxiety, where overwhelmed by it the Self loses all initiative, breaks away, and surrenders to the temptation. This is why Kierkegaard praises the Genesis narrative, which "contrary to all analogy, represents the woman as seducing the man" (SKS 4, II, §2, 370 / 66). This does not mean that she is more culpable than the man, but more anxious. Nor does this mean that she is inferior, but, on the contrary, here, she is spiritually superior—if anxiety is the sign of spirit, the sign of our heterogeneity.

We see in any case how superficial the theses are that interpret the touching/touched relation (in as much as what is touched is not a thingly body, but a sensual one) as provoking a disparity between the two terms, meaning that each of them would be referred to a different phenomenological level: Where the touching bears within it the capacity to make manifest, to "make visible" (by touching), and the touched would be in principle lacking this capacity. Even if, in a second step and in a totally incoherent way, it is the latter (the touched), promoted to the rank of the touching, that is invested with this decisive phenomenological power of showing, of which the former (the touching), struck by a blindness no less sudden, thrown back to the level of some "sensible," is suddenly deprived. But if in the relation analyzed the inversion of terms and roles in no way modifies their transcendental status in each case, if "being-touched" is a modality of our original flesh and belongs to it just like "taking," "grasping," or "caressing" does, then we must recognize that

the erotic relation is a dynamic and pathos-filled relation taking place on a plane
of absolute immanence, and that it has its site in life.

Shall we then say that, in this relation immanent to life, it is life that knows life? Except, as we know, life is nothing anonymous or universal. Incidentally, in a life of that kind, in the romantic or Schopenhaurian mode (which is also blind or unconscious) no experience of the *other* is even conceivable—because life is an "experiencing undergoing itself," and is always that of a Self. In the erotic relation, there are indeed two transcendental Selves in communication with each other. Because each of them belongs to life, and life is immanent to each of them, the question arises of knowing if in such a communication each Self attains the other *in its own life*, if it touches it *where it touches itself.* Such a question is nothing less than the metaphysical scope of the experience of the other. It asks: Is eroticism what gives us access to the life of the other? Having accounted for the implication of sexual difference for the understanding of eroticism—of its anxiety, and of the desire that takes shape there—the question refers to sexuality. Is sexuality so extraordinary that it allows us to attain the other in himself or herself, in what he or she is for themself in some way? Merleau-Ponty's observation that "for most people, sex is their only access to the extraordinary" would then be stripped of every pejorative nuance, and taken seriously.

To the decisive question of the *effective content* of the experience of the other, where the destiny of man is in play in so far as it is a question of escaping his unbearable solitude, two responses will be provided. The first, whose exposition follows, arises from a phenomenology of flesh. However, to the extent that a phenomenology of flesh refers to a phenomenology of Incarnation, a second set of problems will necessarily need to be sketched, no longer taking flesh itself as its presupposition, but our arrival in flesh in absolute life.

To remain with the limited and provisional presuppositions of a phenomenology of flesh understood in the strict sense, the response is unequivocal. In sexuality, the erotic desire to attain the other in his or her very life encounters an insurmountable failure.

§41. The Erotic Relation in Life's Immanence: Desire's Failure.

It is thus in life's immanence that the erotic relation must first be described, with respect to "being-touched" as well as to touching. When, in the immanence of its movement moving in itself, my own "I can," behaving as "touching" and deploying its own organic body, comes up against what resists it absolutely, and against which it has no power—*what is touched* by it at the invisible limit of its effort is an external body: the real content of the world. Except that this body, the content that is *external to my power, is precisely nothing external in the phenomenological sense, as what shows itself in the exteriority of the world.* This content, on the contrary, is in me; it is the practical limit of my "I can," internally lived by it, and equally invisible. With respect to what is given to it in this way, the touching suddenly becomes passive. This passivity, however, can take on two different modalities depending on whether this limit is inert (let us imagine that, closing my eyes, I touch the face of a wall) or whether it exerts a sort of counter-movement against my movement, an active pressure that I nevertheless cannot experience otherwise than *in the impeded dynamism of my "I can."*

Let us suppose that what is touched and felt in this way were the young woman's hand. In my primordial experience, this hand is nothing objective—any more than mine is. My own "hand" is an immanent power of grasping coming up against its own invisible limit, while the young woman's hand is for me nothing other than this limit, this resisting continuum opposing itself actively to my movement, while this hand, for example, exerts pressure on my own or closes over it in return.

A series of sensations settle over this original, dynamic system, and I undergo them from the term that is an obstacle to my movement, and these are precisely sensations of pressure; on the other hand, my own sensations of movement are also situated on the continuum of this invisible limit. The phenomenology of flesh has taught us to distinguish carefully original impressions and constituted impressions: Only the former are real. Thus, only the original impressions of movement are real, as well as the impressions of pressure considered in their auto-impressionality. But situated on the organic body and on its limit, they are nothing more than constituted sensations, which mix together constantly.

The phenomenology of skin presented above allows us to clarify this invisible limit between touching and "being-touched." Does the caress, which plays such an important role in the erotic relation, not offer a privileged example? But the analysis of skin intervenes (see §31 above) only at the moment when, abandoning the reduction to radical immanence in which it first takes place, the phenomenology of flesh appeals explicitly to the duplicity of appearing. Only in the world's appearing, *in it and for it*, does the invisible limit of the "I can" change into a foreign body over which it no longer has any power—into a thingly body. Only there, let us say, does this invisible limit, this thingly body, now show itself to us with the aspect of a body that is external in the phenomenological sense, in the outside itself of the world. As we have seen, our skin is nothing other than the phenomenological duplicity of this thingly body—a strange entity with two faces, ex-posing the one in the world's light, dissimulating the other in the night of our flesh.

If being-touched comes about in the immanence of an "I can" (as a passive modality of it) just like touching does (which is an active modality of it), then the original elucidation of the touching/being-touched relation, considered as an archetype of the erotic relation, must be pursued in an attitude of radical reduction that holds deliberately to the immanent sphere of life, to which the terms of the relation both belong. This is why the skin, and in a general way every phenomenon involving the duplicity of appearing, must be provisionally put out of play. Kierkegaard's analysis, by not distinguishing the two sources of anxiety whose dazzling intuition he pursues, already slips outside the reduction to the extent that the paradoxical synthesis of the soul and body in spirit surreptitiously treats this body, and particularly sexual difference, as objective determinations, referring inevitably to the world's ek-static appearing. Placed in this exteriority, sexual difference would suddenly appear absurd, and anguishing for a spirit that did not recognize itself in this.

Maintaining our attitude of reduction, we will keep for the moment to the radical dimension of life's immanence, a dimension that we will conventionally call *the lovers' night*. Not that it is a question of the obscurity that comes over the world when the sun sets, or a room where one has turned out the lights. It is a question of life's invisible. *The phenomena of the invisible are describable.** When on the balcony our dancer has taken the hand of his companion and exerted pressure on it, and it happens that she gives it to him, the rigorous analysis of these unapparent phenomena has been produced. For an "I can" to exert pressure means to deploy the resisting continuum of its own organic body up to the limit where, no longer giving way, this continuum turns into an invisible thingly body. When this resisting body, not content to stop the movement of the "I can," opposes itself actively to it as a counter-movement, what do we truly know about this? That it is the hand of the dancer who presses her hand in turn against his? Knowledge such as this, however, is only an unreal signification appended to the impression of the pressure he really undergoes, which is lived by him *as* produced by the hand of the young woman, with exactly the *signification* of resulting precisely from the movement that she brings about in turn. But *this movement, as she experiences it, in its accomplishment in the immanence of her own "I can,"* in the pathos-filled self-givenness

---

* Cf. the first chapter of this book, "The Reversal of Phenomenology," which established the possibility of this description.

of her own transcendental Self, in her own life—this is what stays on the other side of the mirror, and the dancer never feels himself. It is no more the originary impressions of this movement than the impressions constituted on her own, invisible, thingly body. So if the desire is to attain the other's life *in itself,* where it attains itself in its own original flesh, this desire does not reach its goal.

In the same fashion, this is what a phenomenology of the sexual act would show. In the lover's night, the sexual act mates two instinctual movements, each of which comes up against the resisting continuum of its own invisible thingly body. Which is thus, for each of the two drives, this moving limit obeying it, and then opposing it and pushing it back. In copulation, the two drives come into resonance, each being deployed and then ceding in turn. Nevertheless, the phenomenological situation remains as follows: Each drive, in the alternation of its active and passive modalities, only ever knows itself, its own movement together with the sensations felt at the limit of its own invisible, organic body. What the other drive feels remains beyond what the first feels. The impotence of each to attain the other in itself exasperates the tension of desire up to its resolution in the paroxysmal feeling of orgasm, in such a way that each has its own without being able to feel that of the other as the other feels it. If this is erotic desire in the sexual act, here again it is a failure.

And this failure must be grasped as what it is for everyone. It does not come from a sort of rupture of immanence, as is the case when, in the presence of the lovers' kiss, the evaluation of this tender act wrests from Rilke this disillusioned cry: "Oh how oddly the drinker escapes the act" (*Duino Elegies,* "Second Elegy"). In the amorous coupling, it is not an "escape" or a distraction that intervenes, although of course that can happen. *It is in the immanence of the drive that desire fails to attain the pleasure of the other where it attains itself;* it is in the lovers' night that, for each of them, the other remains on the other side of a wall that forever separates them. A proof of this is given by the signals lovers offer each other while carrying out the act, whether it is a question of spoken words, sighs, or varying manifestations. Such that the coincidence sought is not the real identification of a transcendental Self with an other, the recovery of two impressional flows melting into one, but at best only the chronological coincidence of two spasms powerless to overcome their division.

That even in this case the two flows of desire remain separated, the following fact, as incontestable as it is tragic, also demonstrates: At the very heart of this limit experience that the lovers expect to be not only extraordinary, but absolute, and to establish a sort of fusion or even identification between them, *the possibility of feigning remains.* How many women have made the one to whom they give themselves, out of love or for another reason, believe that they take from him a pleasure they do not feel, and perhaps will never feel?*

This is indeed the consequence of the duality of impassioned movements each following its own trajectory, each ending in its own pleasure, which despite its intensity remains in itself and leaves the other's pleasure somewhere inaccessible. To take the phenomena in the rigor of their immanence, shouldn't we speak, rather than of eroticism, of auto-eroticism?

However, to the extent that, as we have noted, signs, signals, and varying expressions intervene all along this amorous process, must one not recognize, *since these signs and signals are themselves phenomena,* that the auto-eroticism at work here differs from auto-eroticism properly speaking, where everyone is truly alone with himself, which in truth seems to express solipsism? In the impassioned coupling, on the contrary, a recognition for him or her who has produced or allowed this sort of satisfaction, however provisional, is added to the immanent phenomenon felt by each drive at the moving limit of its organic body, and to the enjoyment in which its desire results, and is indissociable from it and from the well-being it procures. The erotic relation then doubles the pure affective relation, which is foreign to the carnal coupling, and is a relation of reciprocal recognition, of love perhaps, even when this might well precede and indeed provoke the entire erotic process that results from it.

Now if evidently the affective relation is itself an immanent relation whose description, just as that of the sexual act, demands an attitude of

---

*One will perhaps object that the interpretation of desire and sexual activity as always and necessarily ending up in failure is far from being universally admitted. The question inevitably arises of knowing if, at the origin of such an interpretation, certain *a priori* have not altered or falsified the inquiry. Can one avoid thinking here of the philosophy of Schopenhauer, who explicitly identified love with sexuality and took it for an illusion? How is sexuality an illusion? Because it is reduced to sexual desire, and this is precisely what fails. Why does it fail? The only reality (the metaphysical reality of the universe) is, according to Schopenhauer, the Will—a will that has no object, and accordingly no proper object to satisfy, and that thus remains in a state of perpetual dissatisfaction—a hunger, an unquenched thirst. Thus this Will wills indefinitely, eternally, and always begins to will again without any possible stopping point. Yet sexual desire, according to Schopenhauer, is nothing other than this Will that penetrates and decimates the entire body—otherwise there would be no reality anywhere that could put an end to its dissatisfaction, a dissatisfaction that is consubstantial with it and lasts as long as it does. This is the reason why, eternally dissatisfied, sexual desire indefinitely begins its absurd cycle again. A metaphysical conception, repeated in Freud as well as most of the great creators of the late-nineteenth and twentieth centuries, one sees it determine modern pessimism, and condemn in advance the great adventure of love, reduced to sexual desire, adversity, and failure.

This immense ideological catastrophe, which stems from random assumptions, does not concern phenomenology. Phenomenology is opposed in principle to metaphysics in as much as it holds deliberately to the *phenomena as they show themselves in themselves.* This ultimately means: *as they show themselves in the world or in life.*

reduction, is not the question of the possibility for it to attain the other in itself, in recognition or love, for example, immediately posed again? This question concerning the experience of the other is not only repeated; it appears far more difficult to elucidate if the erotic relation seems in the eyes of most people the most natural means for the experience of the other to be effectively realized—if love itself, for example, looks to be fulfilled in a corporeal embrace. In this case, the failure of sexual desire, far from being able to be overcome in the affective relation to the other, on the contrary condemns this affective relation to reproduce that failure in itself, thus leading it to advance its own failure.

In the presence of these difficulties, a question arises: Would the failure—whether it be of the erotic relation or of the affective relation (that of the experience of the other in general)—*not hold for the phenomenological reduction understood as a reduction to a sphere of radical immanence* in the sense that we mean it? Such a reduction can indeed give access to essential phenomena unnoticed to that point, to the discovery of an original flesh, of its immanent power, of the organic body finally grasped in its specificity, and of the world's real content as in itself escaping the world's appearing; but this reduction would not for all that avoid solipsism. Is reducing to immanence not reducing each phenomenon to its self-givenness and thus enclosing it in itself, and erecting this "enclosure" that marks the solipsism of an irremediable powerlessness? Interpreted on the basis of this self-givenness, and considered all the more to be constituted by it, does the Self not raise up the walls of its own prison, is it not in its own immanence condemned to an unbearable solitude—forever incapable of leaving itself, opening itself to an alterity without which no other, no experience of the other, seems possible?

Must we not direct attention again to the fact that Kierkegaard's analysis leaves the sphere of immanence when it considers what we have called the second source of anxiety: the synthesis in the spirit of the soul with the body, *considered in itself and in its sexual differentiation as an objective phenomenon?* Wouldn't the disqualification of the world's appearing need to be removed if the erotic relation must be brought back to its concrete plenitude, where, perhaps, its failure would be capable of being transformed into this plenitude?

§42. The Erotic Relation in the World's Appearing. Repetition of the Failure.

In the lovers' night, when they awake from the happy satisfaction that engulfed them, absorbed in one another, does each not think of the other again? Should we not look for the other *where it is*—and not on the other side of the wall, upon which the drive broke and surged back on itself, referring to itself and drowning in its own pleasure? Where he is, and where she is, where the body of the lover is stretched out next to the body of her love. Isn't it enough for her to open her eyes in order to see him, or if it's still dark, to reach her hand toward him, squeeze his shoulder, stroke his lips again and feel his breath, or breathe it in?

To reach out her hand, to squeeze, to caress skin, to feel, or to breathe in a scent, a breath, is to open oneself to the world. It is in the world, in its appearing, that the other is really there, and that his body (to which the other is united) is there and is real. If it is a question of attaining the other beyond the limit that crushes the impassioned movement, beyond the resisting continuum in which the organic body becomes a thingly body, and beyond the invisible side that this body opposes to desire—is it not in the appearing of the world that this body now lies before the gaze, the touch, or the caress? What shows me this ungraspable "within" of the other's thingly body is its "outside," and that is what occupies me, whether it be a question of ordinary experience or of the radical modification it undergoes when the sensible body becomes an erotic and sensual body (a body capable of sensing and being touched)—when at the same time as this body, the entire world has taken on the face of anxiety.

A companion of desire, anxiety is now no longer based on the singly vertiginous capacity for power, but on the body that flaunts itself in the visible universe from which it proceeds. The second source of anxiety—one that arouses not some thingly body but a *body-in-synthesis-with-the-soul in the spirit*—thus joins with the first. And as we know this means nothing more than that a flesh, an "I can," and its freedom, inhabit this body—*anxiety inhabits it.* The anxiety of power to be touched, power to let oneself be touched, and power to experience a series of sensations that can be subjected to the power and the will of an other. So the redoubling of anxiety does not mean merely that, in addition to its anxiety in the face of its freedom, the spirit also has anxiety at being this body there in the world, with its determinations and its objective sexual configurations. Redoubling means that the anxiety that is redoubled in each one is redoubled from being the anxiety of the other—from each of the two lovers, or from those that will succumb to the temptation to become so. The possibility is wide open for each of them to touch the other at the most "sensible" point of their body, the extreme point of its sexuality—"there," which means on their own thingly body as it is shown in the world. And in the same way this is also the possibility of "being-touched": there, on the being-there of this body. The fact that this two-fold possibility constitutive of the erotic relation occurs in the world, and is indebted to it, prohibits us it seems from circumscribing such a relation in life's sphere of immanence.

The fact that the erotic relation's being-there belongs to the world can be read from numerous signs that run through human history. Let us retain just one: clothing. Beyond the practical justifications for it that depend on latitude, the seasons, or even the cultural habits of social groups, isn't its essential function to conceal what is too intimate in its paradoxical synthesis with the body that the soul risks exhibiting? Owing to this function, isn't the meaning of clothing inverted to the point that it becomes erotic itself in proportion to the eroticism it wants to hide? Isn't removing this clothing—revealing what was supposed to avoid scrutiny, an act involved in every erotic relation—responsible for all the anxiety of the world in which it originates, which originates in the anxiety of having a body whose sex is offered in its objectivity to the other? Where the other will be able to touch it and finally take it—away from the anxiety of the vertiginous power to be able to do all this—from the redoubled anxiety of the one to whom the offer is made? "To give oneself" means to expose a body where the other can indeed attain it, to invite her to do so, to put in front of his desire this fascinating body that can give rise to a series of sensations in it that will be its very life, the secret life of the one who gives his or her body and thus not only gives their body, but also this gift itself: *their freedom.*

In his commentary on the text of Genesis, the pertinence of which he constantly affirms against what seems obvious to common sense, Kierkegaard includes the famous statement that after sinning "they knew they were naked." But today—in our "historical milieu" that is marked by the quantitative increase of objective anxiety through successive generations, but also because anxiety *as such* is a result of the paradoxical synthesis, in the spirit, of the soul with a sexually differentiated objective body—doesn't nudity, in which the body ex-poses itself to the other's desire, belong to the concrete phenomenality of the process described? Doesn't the nudity precede the process as much as it follows from it? With the omnipresent being-there of the undressed, gazed upon, touched, and taken object-body, doesn't the appearing of the world extend its reign over the entire erotic relation? Is that relation intelligible without this exhibition?

From its first steps, the phenomenology applied in this book has recognized that the duplicity of appearing constitutes the arch-fact apart from which no problematic concerning the body or flesh is possible, since only this duplicity decides between the former and the latter, ensuring that no body is possible, at first glance, except in the world, and no flesh is possible except in life. In truth, the reduction to immanence has neither the aim nor the objective of challenging, in defiance of every phenomenological presupposition, the effectiveness of the world's appearing, to the extent that everything we claim is from the world, and falls within its horizon, and is part of it as such, shows itself in the world, as "opposite," or as an "object." By tracing a rigorous line of separation between what appears in the "outside itself" of this horizon and what reveals itself in life's pathos, by focusing on the latter, the reduction to immanence aims at a second division, which is no less decisive, because it rests on the first: the separation of the real and the unreal. It is in light of this essential dichotomy between reality and unreality that the entire problem of the body has been pursued, and the erotic relation must be evaluated.

Must we here have one final reminder of the analysis of "touching"? As we see better now, touching does not have a univocal meaning; it denotes not just one but two phenomena that are structurally different. On the one hand, the intentional excess of a meaning opening to something external, where it is a question of the world's exteriority. On the other hand, however, this operation of the intentional body must be considered in life. It is the latter that constitutes the reality of touching, because it constitutes the reality of intentionality. As the same time, it is the movement that draws on life's givenness for its possibility, and thus for its reality—the movement moving in itself that is inherent in touching and in every transcendental performance of our original corporeity. In its innermost possibility, intentional touching refers to this movement moving in itself, so what it touches must then be understood not on the basis of its intentionality, but on the basis of this immanent movement. What it touches is not a body ex-posed on the outside, but the invisible practical limit of a power, which is moved by it, actively deployed or passively undergone, and in this way is felt in it, by it, and by it alone.

So the pretension to grasp in their real nature the erotic relation's phases and constituents by projecting them against the horizon of the world appears pointless. This was notably the illusion of post-Husserlian phenomenology when, wanting to break through the barrier that it thought prohibited access to the other, it clearly designated what it called interiority as the obstacle to put aside—as opposed to transcendence, whose reign it turned into an absolute. Opened to the world from the outset, and defined by this opening, is man not at the same time with others within this world? Is *Dasein* as such not a *Mit-sein*? Being with others in the same world, that is the most original fact, and it doesn't have to be explained, but recognized. We will come back to this point (see §47, below).

As soon as one examines the concrete phenomena, these generalities that have only an apparent clarity go up in smoke. Desire does not proceed first from anxiety. There is no desire unless what it desires is not given in its reality, but remains beyond the given—*unless the thingly body ex-hibited in the world does not deliver the reality of its flesh in and through this ex-hibition.* This is what is desired. It is precisely because it does not show itself in the being-there of the thingly body that it is and can be desired. Yet neither is the anxiety connected with desire based on the objective being-there of a body reduced to its objectivity. Just as with desire, for the same reason, and at the same time, anxiety arises from a body shot through with sensuality, and thus a primordial capacity to sin—from a body that a flesh inhabits. Except the flesh that makes the thingly body an anguishing, desiring, desirable, and sensual body is not an unreal noematic signification. There is one circle of reality. Only real flesh, a living flesh, is capable of giving birth to a real desire, a real anxiety. *A real and living flesh that reveals itself in life's auto-impressionality, never in the outside itself of a world.* To entrust the erotic relation to the world, to look for life there, is not to overcome the failure desire knew in the lovers' night; it is to redouble it.

Even more, it is to eliminate all its conditions. For desire itself is a modality of life, just like anxiety is. When the latter emerges in the presence of an objective sexual determination, it is in the spirit that it feels anxiety at not recognizing itself in a sex. And that is because this spirit, which is nothing other than life, is actually not found there. But what never shows itself in the world is flesh itself, which is flesh only in life. What escapes the reign of the visible, not finding its possibility there any more than its satisfaction, is the Self inherent in flesh, its "I can," the capacity for power, the ability to move itself proper to every power (whether touching or being touched), the totality of original impressions—in short, the entirety of phenomenological properties that belong to flesh and thus to the erotic relation, which is a carnal and not a thingly relation.

§43. The Reduction of the Erotic Relation to Sexuality in the Time of Nihilism.

The situation is thus the following: In the lovers' night, desire fails, and is incapable of reaching the other's life in itself, and this determines its plan to seize the other's life on its naked body, which is offered in the world's appearing. Yet the failure of this endeavor is peculiar in that it does not modify the presupposition from which it follows, but on the contrary, pushes this to its limit. Since the aim to possess does not attain the life of the other on its body, which is exposed in all of its sensual potentialities and offered to desire through them, a sort of sudden metaphysical decision is left, which is at the same time a form of violence. We must state categorically that this real life (which is the other's reality as much as my own) this object of desire, *is just that*: a natural body displaying its sexual properties in the world. This life's sensuality, its capacity to feel and enjoy, are crushed onto the body, incorporated in it, identified with it, and one with it; they become what one touches, what one caresses, and what one gives joy to by touching; what is there, really in the world, the object before one's gaze, and near at hand. The erotic relation is reduced to an objective sexual relation; and that is how it now comes about, as a performance and a set of objective phenomena.

The reduction of eroticism to objective sexuality explains the importance that the act of undressing now assumes. It is no longer a question of one gesture among all those that make up the erotic process in its entirety. This gesture marks a rupture: *It defines and displays the site where the relation between two beings will now take place. In it the decisive displacement occurs whereby each living being's desire to enter into symbiosis with the life of another living being and finally to be united with it in a loving vital fusion will play out somewhere other than in life, on a terrain where there is nothing living, and where no life is possible.*

Such an upheaval, which affects the human condition itself and thus every society that submits to it (in general, the decadent societies) has two characteristics. The first is that this has nothing to do with a fact properly speaking, which it would suffice to observe in the way the natural sciences proceed, as well as the human sciences, since they now have it in mind to imitate them. Because such a fact goes against the nature of life, and stipulates that it be consummated where its very existence is simply impossible, we would claim it follows from a decision. But every decision against nature assumes the form of violence because it implies an active negation that opposes the consistency and coherence of its reality. This must be eliminated and destroyed. This active and deliberate destruction of reality, in this case life's own reality, is nihilism.

Nihilism means first a negation of all values. And yet, since the beginning of time, values regulate human actions, determining the structures of societies and the way they operate. So for nihilism to occur, several different processes—processes of destruction, indeed self-destruction—must have led to the dissolution and ultimately the elimination of all these values. Though in fact there are no values in nature. Only in life and for it, by virtue of the needs and values that belong specifically to life, are the values that correlate with these needs assigned to things. Life is a universal principle of evaluation, and this principle is singular. At the same time, life proves to be the origin of culture, in as much as this is nothing other than the set of norms and ideals that life imposes on itself in order to realize its needs and desires, which in the end are summed up or concentrated in one alone: the need for life to increase itself constantly, to increase its capacity to feel, the level of its action, and the intensity of its love.

So if life is diminished and obscured, if it is no longer the organizing principle of a society and of each one's life within it, the principle of each of its activities, then the time of nihilism has come. And it comes every time life is discarded, whether implicitly or explicitly, and for each of the activities for which it is discarded. *This is the case for the erotic relation, when torn from life's pathos, handed over to the world, reduced to what of it is shown in the world, across all the objective determinations of a thingly body; it is at the same time reduced to what in it can still become an object of desire—its sexuality.*

It is a problem of knowing how all the original phenomenological properties of a living, sensing, desiring, suffering, and enjoying flesh can mutate into those of a body that feels nothing and doesn't feel itself, desires nothing, and in itself is deprived of the capacity to will and of power—of the intoxication and the anxiety of a freedom. It is the act of undressing that brings about this extraordinary mutation. That is why it arises from a radical will and occurs as a leap. With respect to life, it is an issue of profanation. To that which is cloaked in the secret of an original modesty because it carries within it the spirit that is heterogeneous to every thing and every objectivity, it really claims: This absurd thing and indecent sex is what you are and is all you are—indecent because it has nothing in common with you, or with spirit. Only this claim is not simply an allegation, it is an act—the act that brings about a subjectivity's extraordinary metamorphosis into an inert object: the sexuality whereby life exposes itself, and thus affirms that it is nothing other, and nothing more, than that.

It is life, however, that carries out the act that denudes and exposes life in sexuality. The profanation it engages in is a self-profanation. Two correlative traits belong to the erotic relation that takes place in the world's appearing, and they are taken to their extreme degree from the beginning: sadism and masochism. It is masochism for the spirit to declare that it is nothing other than a contingent objective determination (foreign precisely to the spirit) and for it to lower itself to the rank of a thing, of a masculine or feminine sex. The other's sadism corresponds to this masochism, as its correlate, and enjoys the suffering of the one that is diminished like this, affirming in and by its display that its truth is in this poor thing, which is indeed foreign to spirit, indecent, and absurd. But the other in the relation is put in the same situation. Sadism and masochism are now indefinitely interchangeable, and become the elements that constitute the erotic relation as long as it seeks, and expects, to be realized outwardly.

To the worldly phenomenological effectuation of the erotic relation reduced to an objective sexual behavior, voyeurism is connected. It appears as a logical consequence of the act of undressing *which makes the flesh identified with a visible body* and then forces it to behave as an objective reality in the inter-subjective communication of living beings. And yet voyeurism cannot be considered a consequence of such an act except to the extent that it has the radical meaning conferred on it, not as a mere phase of the erotic process, but as bringing about in it the metamorphosis of the phenomenological properties of flesh into those of a body, in such a way that it is this body in its objective condition (seen, touched, felt, heard, and smelled) that becomes the agent of communication.

For whatever is seen, in as much as attention is focused on what is seen as such, as given in sight and thus in a world, it is for everyone to see—by all who are there, holding the same space of light in view: a room, a scene in a theater, or a television screen. Thus voyeurism is not at all limited to the two traditional actors of the erotic relation; it carries in principle the possibility of extending to everyone who will have decided to hand the erotic relation over to the world. Either to undress together and give themselves over to various sexual practices reduced to their objectivity, establishing between them no longer an "inter-subjective" relation but an "inter-objective" one, and expecting from it all the tonalities of anxiety, disgust, degradation, masochism, sadism, and enjoyment (the kind degradation provides) that these practices can bring. Or, without themselves resorting to this, then at least watching it, the possibilities of which are multiplied by the new technologies of communication, which are themselves forms of voyeurism.

This collective profanation of life is called pornography. In pornography an attempt to bring the objectivity of the erotic relation to its limit emerges, where everything is given to be seen—which then requires the vantage points on the behaviors and sexual attributes to be multiplied, as if something within sexuality were endlessly refusing this total objectification. The same radical project of objectification occurs in prostitution, which is not first and foremost a social fact, but is also a metaphysical act, whose "publicity," however limited it may be, remains the hidden *telos* (the prostitute is one who, just like money, concentrates this potential advertising in his being). Let us add that, in objectivity, anything can take the place of anything: individuals are interchangeable just like things are. That is why the logical consequence of voyeurism is "partner swapping," which often accompanies it. At this point the very particular pleasure that degradation provides, already seen in prostitution, is brought to its extreme.

One will claim that these phenomena evoked belong to all societies. At the basis of all societies is human nature, whose phenomenological structure, though it has seldom been clarified *phenomenologically*, is no less constant through the centuries. This structure is the duality of appearing. That is why the multiple modalities of existence that are connected to it and draw their final possibility from it are indeed at work everywhere there are human beings. The characteristic of nihilism is that, within this global structure of the duality of appearing, the original and fundamental mode of life's revelation is kept off limits.

It turns out that this disqualification of transcendental life occurred on the theoretical plane at the beginning of the seventeenth century and determined the entire development of modern science. It was indeed explicit when Galileo had attributed to it knowledge of the universe composed of extended material bodies, all of whose properties relative to transcendental life and in any way dependent on it were eliminated. We have exhibited (see §17 above) the nature and scope of this Galilean reduction, which had only a methodological function that was intended to circumscribe in a rigorous way a specific domain of investigation, the immense domain of objective knowledge of the material universe. To the extent that modern science has given birth to an entirely new technology, however, which tends progressively to replace life's active subjectivity with inert material processes, the entirety of modern societies (their thought as well as their "practice") is marked by this disqualification of life, and by its correlate, the undivided reign of objectivity in nihilism.

Giving the erotic relation up to the world's appearing also takes on a new meaning, which is truly exaggerated and insane, when it receives additional motivation that follows from nihilism, to the point of becoming one of its most remarkable signs. It is no longer a question then of phenomena that have taken place at all times and everywhere, in so far as they rest upon the universal structure that is the duality of appearing. That certainly remains the presupposition of everything "human," and it can occur only in a reality that is defined by this duality. In this absolute presupposition that defines the human condition, however, there is not only objectivity; this is neither its foundation nor its decisive element, in fact. That is why, in the Galilean reduction, when objectivity is detached from life and considered in itself in an abstract way, as an autonomous moment, and when a thought that is allegedly rational, scientific, and true grants it the privilege of defining the site of this truth and thus of all reality, the threat of travesty and denaturing hangs over all human phenomena.

As far as it concerns the erotic relation, the reduction of it to an objective behavior *is no longer the work of a desire* that fails to find the life of the other in its own immanence; *it is a general presupposition of modern knowledge that comes into play,* which takes objectivity as the site of reality, and the knowledge of this reality as the one and only mode of actual knowledge. The laws of erotic communication are thus the laws of the objective sexual relation it turns into; they are no longer the laws of Eros, of life's infinite Desire to return to the life of a living being, to be united with it, and to find it again in the depth of the abyss where this union is possible. These are laws that regulate objective phenomena—the biological, chemical, or physical laws that all belong to modern science. The amorous fusion reduced to its objective appearance—such that one can see it, and photograph it with its various inflections, which are intended to mask its monotony—has become the business of sexologists, psychologists, psychiatrists, and sociologists.* Only those with objective methodologies at their disposal may acquire a rigorous knowledge of it. "Fourteen percent of French women make love on the stairs." The question rationally posed in this objective context will be settled when construction begins on the next five-year housing plan, or with the progress of scientific research on AIDS.

All of the ancestral cultural forms of knowledge (religion, ethics, and aesthetics), which are born from the most original knowledge of transcendental Life in its self-revelation and from the self-development of its pathos, are "obsolete." In the time of nihilism, moreover, none of these forms of knowledge that springs from transcendental life has the right to speak, any more than this life itself does.

§44. Life Is without a Why. Life Is Good.

In considering the erotic relation, either in its immanent achievement, or in its worldly appearing, we have recognized how in each case it is wrapped in anxiety and in each case leads to failure. Further reflection has persuaded us that, despite the primordial phenomenological distinctions in play, the analysis of eroticism remains a prisoner of a decisive

---

*Medicine has never been a science properly speaking—not that it lacks rigor: Resting on the hard sciences like biology, chemistry, etc., it nevertheless remains "humanist" in principle. By this we should understand that all objective sciences in operation are shot through by a gaze that sees, beyond them, on the radiograph of a lesion or tumor, beyond the objective body therefore, *what its result is for a flesh,* for this living and suffering Self who is sick. Medicine is unintelligible without this constant reference to transcendental life as constitutive of human reality. The medical gaze is today one of the last refuges of culture.

limitation. This is because no flesh can be envisaged in itself as a sort of autonomous order, an object of a separate process of elucidation, if it is true that flesh occurs to itself only in life. This is why, as we have found repeatedly, or rather constantly, the analysis of flesh and its various constituents, as soon as it goes further, refers to what takes place before it: the most fleeting impression, to the relentless emergence of an always new impression; the power of flesh, to its original powerlessness; and finally the flesh itself, to absolute Life's arrival in itself. It is only this reference of all flesh to the Arch-possibility of Life's Arch-flesh that can say whether it is possible for a flesh to constitute the site of perdition or salvation.

And yet when we consider the relation of flesh to absolute Life as an immanent relation, we see certain characteristics of the erotic relation immediately fall away, notably the contingency and therefore absurdity of sexual difference, and above all of sexual determination as such. Thus the desire that thought that in sex it could reach the life of the other where it reaches itself, its pleasure where it undergoes experiencing itself, meets only a thingly body heterogeneous to the spirit, whose objective configuration remains incomprehensible or obscene in its eyes, and whose life in any case escapes it.

We will claim that it is the duality of appearing, and more precisely the objectivity of sexual determinations and thus of the erotic relation itself which is responsible for the absurdity of these determinations as well as for the failure of desire. Such is assuredly the case, and this is the first point that demands an explanation: Why does sexual life seem both absurd and doomed for failure in the world's appearing?

Yet the very nature of the question must first be clarified. To ask "why" assumes that *that about which and with respect to which one poses the question refers to something beyond itself*, to a horizon of exteriority against which it stands out as an external being or external object. It is on the basis of this horizon, which confers its presence upon it and within which it "is there," that one comes back to it in order to ask it why, in view of what it is there, as it is, with the properties that it has. Necessarily, a question like this has no response. Why, to what end, for what purpose this being, this object, exists, why this sex is there—only the beyond could tell it, the horizon of exteriority that has been opened by the very question, and that is nothing other than the world's appearing. As the problematic has shown at length, however, such an appearing *must uncover what it uncovers without creating it, and without in any way giving an account or a reason for it.* Thus unveiled in the objectivity of the world, naked, sex no longer offers anything more than this contingent and absurd appearance. It is a source of desire and anxiety only in so far as it has the signification of being inhabited by a flesh. But because this never dwells outside itself, and never shows itself in such a horizon, the signification is empty, and it goes up in smoke the same time the desire does.*

Life is without a why. And this is because it does not tolerate in itself any outside itself to which it would need to manifest itself in order to be what it is—to which it would have to ask why it is what it is, *why, for what purpose*, it is life. However, if life leaves outside itself no reality that is external to it, to which it would have to go cap in hand asking the reason for its manifestation and thus for its being, no horizon of intelligibility on whose basis it would have to return to itself in order to understand and justify itself, this is only because it carries within it this final principle of intelligibility and justification. This is because it self-reveals itself in such a way that it is also what is revealed in this immanent, pathos-filled revelation of itself. *Life's self-revelation is also its self-justification.* If life is without a "why," if it asks for nothing, and doesn't ask for the why of its life from anyone, from any ek-static knowledge, from any intentional thought in search of some meaning, or from any science, this is because, while undergoing experiencing itself, it is neither only nor first what it experiences when it undergoes its own experience, but is *the very fact of undergoing experiencing itself, and the delight of this experience that is its enjoyment of itself and that tells it that it is good.* This is the phenomenological root of Meister Eckhart's radical propositions: "However difficult life may be, one nevertheless wants to live [. . .] But why do you live? In order to live, you say, and yet you do not know why you live. Life is so desirable in itself that we desire it for itself." And life's supreme justification is not only what life undergoes when it always undergoes experiencing itself, but the fact of undergoing experiencing itself and of living; and life itself attests to this in as much as it subsists in every circumstance, and at the height of suffering and adversity. For an absolute justification alone, a phenomenological self-justification as self-revelation, which nothing has power against, and which thus works in every modality of life, the most awful as well as the most noble, the limit assertion of Eckhart authorizes: "Even those who are in hell, in eternal torment, whether angels or demons, do not want to lose life; for life is this noble to them [. . .]."†

Is there any need to recall here that the famous verses of Angelus Silesius—"The rose is without a why / it blooms simply because it blooms / it has no concern for itself nor any desire to be seen"—follow directly from Meister Eckhart's dazzling propositions, where the rose is

---

*This is what an analysis of auto-eroticism, properly speaking, would show.

† *Traités et Sermons*, French trans. Aubier and Molitor (Paris: Aubier, 1942) p. 48 / *The Complete Mystical Works of Meister Eckhart*, trans. Maurice O'C Walshe, rev. Bernard McGinn (New York: Herder & Herder, 2009), p. 505ff.

nothing but the name for life? What stands out here with intense clarity is that this unequalled vision of life's essence doesn't come merely from the genius of the poetic imagination, but is based on a rigorous phenomenological analysis. Because life rules out everything beyond itself for which and in which it would live, two decisive characteristics follow, which Silesius assigns immediately to life. The first: It is to its immanence that life is indebted for being life and doing everything it does: "it blooms because it blooms." The second: In its own proper native condition, it is in no way related to itself ek-statically. Neither in care, as if the immanent ipseity of life could be in care-for-itself and thus separated from itself in its Care without immediately self-destructing: "has no concern for itself." Nor in seeing, as if life could see itself by relating intentionally to itself in seeing without dissolving immediately into unreality, like Eurydice under Orpheus's gaze: "nor any desire to be seen."

This phenomenological essence of life defined positively by Eckhart and negatively by Silesius sheds its light on the erotic relation. Is it not significant to notice that all the negative characters that the human body takes on in its abandonment in the world—its neglect, its lack of justification, its strangeness, its contingency, its absurdity, and possibly its ugliness or vulgarity—disappear as soon as, lived from the inside, this body is revealed to itself as a living flesh? For if it is possible to ask why the being that we are has two eyes rather than three or one in the middle of its forehead like the Cyclops, why it has four limbs (two upper and two lower) rather than a thousand legs like the hero in Kafka's *Metamorphosis*, or ten thousand hands like Kanon's goddess, still no one has really complained about seeing, hearing, or walking. If in the world everything seems arbitrary, it is no longer the case for the transcendental performances of our senses or the other original powers of our flesh where they are revealed to themselves and take place. Quite the contrary: It is their absence or their alteration that turns out to be unbearable, as in the case of sickness or disability.

But if none of the powers of our flesh is ever in question in the question "why," for as long as, absorbed in its immanent effectuation, it feels itself immediately as "good," how can we forget that such a power presupposes a capacity for power, an "I can," a Self, and finally a flesh, which never occurs to itself except in life? But this series of implications is not the result of analysis; it refers to a form of passivity concretely felt by each of our powers in its particular operation. It is not merely the capacity for power (which it does not take from itself) that makes it passive with regard to itself, it is the specificity of this power that marks it with a definitive contingency. For why would there need to be, in these transcendental living beings that we are, something like vision, hearing, the sense of smell, motor skills, and sexual activity with its differentiation that imposes everywhere its powers of attraction and its equally-differentiated drives? Everything happens as if the world's appearing did nothing but make visible, literally stripping naked the radical contingency of a diversity of specific properties that are already inscribed in flesh. Is this diversity not secretly felt despite its immanence—the specificity and contingency exposed by the body but consubstantial to the flesh, which merely translates an older passivity? It is a question of recalling the scene of this radical passivity that extends its invisible reign everywhere, across these superimposed strata, if we are now to understand the possibility, according to the teaching of Christianity, for a flesh to constitute the way of salvation.

§45. The Degrees of Passivity: From Genesis to the Prologue of John.

Two texts will assist us, both borrowed from Scripture, Genesis and the Prologue of John. Separated by centuries, these two fragments of a process of continuous elaboration are not without relation, so that one can consider the second as a commentary on the first. A commentary, or rather a decisive deepening, where the Prologue constitutes the revelation of the essential truth buried in Genesis. When these are related, the opposition between creation and generation (to which allusion has already been made) is clarified. It is conceivable to establish such a relation, however, only if our reading of Genesis avoids the naivety usually brought to it.

To this end, we should set aside the idea that Genesis offers a sort of historical account of the origin of the world and its content—inert things or living species or human beings. Considered in this way, the text immediately loses all meaning. Thus when Adam is created he is 20 years old, and so is his spouse Eve. This Adam, created at 20 years of age, is said to be the first man. Yet from his union with Eve two children are born, one of whom, Cain, kills the other. So that driven away from the place where he is, which is already no longer Paradise, Cain wanders the earth meeting men who will be completely hostile to him. All of which assumes that these men, descending through natural generation, belong to families that have long populated the earth.

Considered in itself, the creation is no less striking if one distinguishes in it the creating act and the content created. We must then recognize that the content preexists the creating act at least with respect to its condition of existence, in this case the time in which the creating act takes place, even though that act must obviously precede it. Thus God successively created heaven and earth, light and darkness, the waters, plants, fruit trees, etc., all on the first day, then on the second . . . until the seventh day, when like a wise man he decides to rest. Certainly one can consider this circularity between the creation and the created as a metaphysical picture, which would already lead one to doubt the naivety of the account. Leaving aside an array of inadequate questions, we will come immediately to the essential.

Genesis is the first known account of a transcendental theory of man. By "transcendental," we mean the pure and *a priori* possibility of the existence of something such as man. It is a question of the essence of man, as one speaks of the essence of a circle, in other words of the internal possibility of something like a circle, without worrying about knowing when humans thought about a circle for the first time rather than something round, when they understood its ideal character, what ideality in general is, etc. In the same way, the question of the internal condition of possibility of a reality like our own has nothing to do with the historical and factual appearance of men upon the earth, or with their empirical development. At most this conception of man's *a priori* essence marks the moment where one can speak of a man for the first time. Adam is the first man in the strong sense that he is the archetype of every conceivable man, the essence of the human that one will inevitably find in every real man.

Whether the first man in this strong sense was a real man, this is something that, far from contradicting his transcendental condition, on the contrary results from it, if it is true that (unlike an ideal essence such as that of a circle, which is locked up forever in its ideality) the essence from which man draws his provenance is the essence of reality itself, the absolute that is Life. Man's essence is always the essence of a real man, and reciprocally, every real man, every living individual, necessarily has this archetypal possibility in himself, without which no man exists, and that is why the individual in Adam, as Kierkegaard says in *The Concept of Anxiety*, is never separated from the human race.

So if we want to understand the Bible as a transcendental document indifferent to the factual history of men, we must compare it to the other "transcendental" books we have available. For example, to the most famous among them, which has precisely brought the transcendental point of view to its radical point in modern thought. The *Critique of Pure Reason* is the prototype of a transcendental work in the sense that the object of analysis is the *a priori* condition of possibility of every conceivable man, which Kant calls *the condition of possibility of experience in general*, thus defining man as this condition of all experience, as phenomenological in his essence. With regard to this phenomenological structure of man constituted by the *a priori* forms of pure intuition and by the categories of the understanding, which are both modes of making-visible, it has been established that it is identically the world's phenomenological structure, whose pure exteriority defines pure phenomenality and thus "the condition of all possible experience," of all "phenomena."

Considering the Bible from this transcendental point of view (and leaving aside everything that separates a modern individual work from a collection of very ancient texts redacted in different epochs by different authors), we see what it is that places these two sets of problems in opposition, where one relates the essence of man to the world, and the other to God (in this case to Life). If, like Kierkegaard in the nineteenth century, some today can still find the Bible infinitely more profound than the *Critique of Pure Reason* (despite Kant's extraordinary conceptual power and unequalled terminological elaboration), it is only by virtue of this fundamental thematic difference, where the former alone affects us at the depth of ourselves. For in theoretical life as well as in practical life, as soon as one turns toward the world, forgetting that the path of life never opens there (even when this path consists of steps), the Essential is lost and will never return.*

In Genesis, the relation to the world is present, and it even seems to occupy a preeminent position to the extent that the creation is thought precisely as a creation of the world. In this preliminary sense, the concept of creation is decisive; it marks *a priori* the All of being, the totality of reality whatever it may be, with a radical passivity that will never be lifted. Despite its radical character, such a passivity remains marked by a fundamental uncertainty, and it even appears fallacious in so far as this divine creation of the world given as a universal process obviously concerns man, taking him up in it and now making him a being-of-the-world whose principal characteristics, notably passivity, must themselves be grasped on the basis of his own condition.

Man's passivity with respect to the world is two-fold: It is a passivity with respect to the world as such, to its ek-static horizon where things become visible, on the one hand, and a passivity with regard to the content that is shown in such a horizon, on the other. *The passivity of these two*

---

*This is what the crucial example of the transcendental Self shows, which Kant is unable to grasp in its "substance" and its own "simplicity" to the extent that these are only the phenomenological material of absolute Life in its originary phenomenalization. This is actually the tragic destiny of the *arid* problematic of the critique of the paralogism of rational psychology in the *Critique of Pure Reason*. On this point see our *Genealogy of Psychoanalysis, op. cit.*, chapter 4: "Empty Subjectivity and Life Lost: Kant's Critique of 'Soul.'"

relations lies in their sensibility. The world's content, the objects, and the material processes that compose it are not sensible in themselves: They are the inert systems that physics studies. They become sensible only because we relate to them intentionally through each of our senses, and because, more fundamentally, the intentional surpassing occurs when this pure horizon of exteriority comes outside itself. It is with respect to this horizon that we are passive, because it is given to us to sense in a primitive affection consisting in the fact that it shows itself to us, and that within it everything shows itself it turn. Thus in Kant and Heidegger, for example, we find constructed the possibility of a transcendental affection *qua* phenomenological affection by the world, one that defines our passivity as a pure sensibility that is itself transcendental.

But as we have been compelled to recognize repeatedly, when the biblical creation is presented as a creation of the world that involves man, it is a superficial reading that can only be provisional. Such a reading is shattered as soon as it is a question of man precisely, and the shocking and repeated proposition occurs in which God created man in his image and likeness. Like God, man is nothing of the world, and nothing in him can ultimately be explained by the world. Like God, man is not the product of a process that sits outside itself in the form of an image. Man has never been posited outside God. Man is not an image we could see. Man is nothing visible. No one has ever seen God, but no one has ever seen a man—a man in his actual reality, a transcendental living Self. It is only in the idolatrous process of profanation that we strive, in vain, to see him. Because life is never visible. It is because he is Life that God is invisible. And for this reason man is too. Man has never been created, he has never come in the world. He has come in Life. And it is in this sense that he is in the likeness of God, cut from the same cloth as Him, as every life and as all the living are. From the cloth that is the pure phenomenological substance of life itself.

We recognize the initiatory propositions of the Prologue of John that allow us to understand *the unity of the transcendental aim of Scripture.* This unity is laid bare when the idea of creation makes room for that of generation. Man can be understood starting from the idea of generation alone. The generation of man in the Word—note that biblical creation is itself made in the Word, in the Speech of God, which is the Speech of Life: "God said [. . .]"—repeats the generation of the Word in God as his self-revelation. This homogeneity between the generation of the Word and of man explains why, when the Word will become incarnate in order to be made man, it is not in the world that he has come, *but in a flesh,* *"to his own"*—among those who have been generated in Him and have always belonged to him. But when we try to understand all this, we have left history; nor do we need to follow the chronological development of Scripture, whose aim is also reversed. It is the concept of generation that gives exhaustive and adequate meaning to the creation; it is the Prologue of John that allows us to understand Genesis.

When the concept of generation substitutes for that of creation, the concept of passivity itself is overturned. It is no longer a question of the passivity of man with respect to the world, but an entirely different passivity, the radical passivity of his life with respect to Life. Here the final ambiguity of the concept of sensibility is fully uncovered. Sensibility and Affectivity have always been confused as if it were a question of one and the same essence, one and the same reality. Far from being identical, however, sensibility and Affectivity have a paradoxical relation, at once foundational and antinomic. On the one hand, *Affectivity founds sensibility*. The phenomenology of flesh has constantly made this foundational relation apparent: Every intentional performance (those of our senses, for example), all the operations and active or passive syntheses in which these performances take place, are possible only as given to themselves originally in the auto-impressionality of our flesh. In the field of play the distance of the world opens, it is always possible to behave in this or that way with respect to an "in-front" or an "ob-ject," to turn toward it or away from it, whereas this movement itself, as movement moving in itself in its pathos-filled self-givenness, no longer has any such possibility with respect to itself, and is on the contrary handed over to itself in the radical passivity that belongs to every modality of life because it belongs to Life itself, which overwhelms every suffering, every desire, and the most humble impression—with its own weight. This radical passivity— which in itself excludes every distance and every transcendence, and thus sensibility itself as a power of sensing different from what it senses—is the transcendental affectivity we are discussing. Here a major discovery of the phenomenology of Life appears: *the radical heterogeneity of transcendental Affectivity with respect to sensibility even within the immanent founding of the latter in the former.*

Yet this passivity, which is ultimately the passivity of every flesh, every Self, and every life with respect to itself, covers over a passivity that is far more radical still, to the extent that each of these lives is given to itself only in the self-givenness of absolute Life. In its radical character, such a passivity refers to the secret buried in every life, to its hidden source: to the arrival of absolute Life in its Word as the condition of every arrival in ourselves—of our transcendental birth, our Filial condition. It is this radical passivity that according to Christianity opens the way of salvation. Within the framework of our investigation, we will limit the analysis of this soteriological theme to certain formulations that it assumes in Irenaeus and Augustine.

§46. The Way of Salvation according to Irenaeus and Augustine.

If in Christianity salvation rests upon the Filial condition, which is originally the condition of transcendental man, and if this condition has been
lost (forgotten, but more precisely broken, in the sin of idolatry that has
substituted the idolatrous relation for the original relation to Life), then
salvation undoubtedly consists in recovering such a condition practically
and not merely theoretically. These are the adoptive Sons of whom Paul
or John speak, in whom the condition that was initially the condition of
every man has been restored. If life's radical passivity (a life such as ours,
generated in the self-generation of Life in its Word) contains the way of
salvation, it is because there is no salvation for a life so generated, other
than the generation in which it lives originally from the very life of God.
To take things in the strict sense, it is not in an indeterminate life, but a
life marked in its essence by a radical Ipseity, because our life has been
generated in the Word of God, and because, having broken this connection in the idolatry of a finite flesh toward itself, its pretend power,
and the pleasures it imagines itself to produce, it is for this reason that
re-generation assumes the coming of the Word in a flesh of this sort, and
that, according to the thinkers of Christianity, Irenaeus and Augustine
notably, the Incarnation took place.

And first, Irenaeus declares explicitly that the Incarnation of the
Word in our finite flesh must allow us to find again our initial relation to
God, and much more, to be made God: "Truth [. . .] appears when the
Word of God was made man, *making himself like man and making man like
him*" (*op. cit.*, p. 617, our emphasis). Thus Irenaeus from the beginning
comes up against the Greek aporia, if it is true that it is not only a question
of affirming the extraordinary Event of the Incarnation, but of ascertain-
ing its possibility. In a truly ingenious way, as we saw in what we called the
Christian cogito of flesh, Irenaeus refers to the in-carnate condition of
man himself in order to show how life, far from being incompatible with
flesh, is on the contrary its condition.

Nor is it implausible that, at the time of Christ, the one who took on
flesh in the Christ was not an ordinary man but the Word of God. In every
human in-carnation, *each time a life comes in a body in order to make it into
flesh*, it is precisely not an ordinary life that is able to do that, to incarnate
itself—because, after all, there is no ordinary life. A life that is capable
of giving life to a body in order to make it flesh is one that is capable of
giving itself life first in the eternal proceeding of its self-revelation in
its Word. Thus all flesh originates from the Word. "All things came into
being through him, and without him not one thing came into being"
(John 1:3). Irenaeus's proximity to the initiatory texts of the Prologue
conveys to him John's blinding intuition of *an essential affinity between*

the original creation of man and the Incarnation of the Word, such that only the second allows us to understand the first. This foundational retro-intelligibility is what Irenaeus exposes, and the Irenaean themes stand together in it.

The first, which we have exhibited at length, posits that "the flesh is capable of receiving life" for the essential reason that it originates from Life. This is exactly what the Johannine rereading of Genesis taught Irenaeus, the apperception of creation not as the positing of a worldly thing outside itself but as the generation of a flesh through the insufflation of life in a body of mud—by the breath of life that is its Spirit. Irenaeus read this explicitly in Paul: "Your body is the temple of the Holy Spirit" (I Corinthians 6:19). Because this coming of Life in a flesh defines the creation of man as his transcendental birth, a co-naturality between the divine essence and our own is established here, as Irenaeus affirms, "while we belong to God by our nature." Only a tragic history could undo the native membership that our flesh has in Life, and this history, or rather the Arch-event that dominates it and is tirelessly repeated in it, is the history of sin's Apostasy, of which we have traced the sequences abruptly broken by the "leap." It is this leap into Apostasy that has destroyed our original nature and, being unceasingly reproduced in it, unceasingly destroys it. "Apostasy has alienated us against our nature." The native membership of our flesh in the Word of Life—only the arrival of this word in a flesh like ours, its Incarnation, can reestablish it. But these are the conditions of the Incarnation that Irenaeus helps us better to understand.

And first, as we have just recalled, he helps us understand the possibility of it. By becoming incarnate in a flesh like ours, the Word really comes into what he himself generated in his Life in the beginning, into that which he made not only possible, but real. "The Word [. . .] is united to his own work that was fashioned by him." But if the Word of Life generated flesh by giving Life to it, outside of which no flesh is possible and within which every flesh abides, the Word is never absent from its creation to the extent that, in this creation, it is the generation of man in question: "He was at all times present to the human race" (*op. cit.,* respectively, p. 570, 570, 360, 360).

Another side of the possibility of the Word's Incarnation becomes clearer for us, and another Gnostic argument collapses. In its eyes, the difficulty was not only to understand how an eternal and incorporeal Logos (eternal because incorporeal) could be united to a putrescible, terrestrial body. When the relation is read in the reverse sense, where the supposed Word is to be incarnate in the Christ, the aporia reemerges. "If the Christ is born at that moment, then he never existed before." Thus Gnosticism did not read the Johannine proposal. It is the Word that is incarnate. Not only was the Incarnation of the Word possible in so far as every flesh is joined to itself in it, but the following is also true: Because according to the Johannine proposal it is the Word that is made flesh in the Christ, it is equally false to claim that the Christ, who is the Word, did not exist before his coming into history, the One in whom everything was created in the beginning, in whom all flesh has come in itself. It is of course true that the Christ has two natures, that of the Word and that of a man, and that he assumed the latter until the end, until his agony on the Cross. But *these two natures are not equal*: According to absolute Life's order of proceeding, the former generates the latter, through a superabundant love, Irenaeus claims, in complete gratuitousness.

So the Christ's "one and the same," his identity, which will be so difficult to think through the great future councils, which continue to express themselves in a Greek horizon, becomes more than intelligible when Irenaeus extends it back to the Gospel sources. Hence, on the one hand, an immense deployment of "proofs" by the Scriptures, repeatedly cited and commented on—"That John knows only one and the same Word of God, which is the only Son and which became incarnate for our salvation, Jesus Christ our Lord [. . .]," "For we do not suppose that one is Jesus and another is Christ" (*op. cit.*, p. 346; and, in the commentary on Matthew, p. 347)—and on the other, this gripping philosophical justification pushed to the very sources of Life. Beyond the transcendental possibility of the Incarnation of the Word, however, it is its reality as the foundation of salvation that matters in the end. Irenaeus first indicates unequivocally the site where this salvation must be accomplished and that can only be that of reality. And we are confronted again with the Christian paradox: The site of salvation is also the site of sin, their reality is cut from the same cloth—This is precisely our flesh, our finite flesh.

Two major phenomenological presuppositions are thereby confirmed, namely that life in its carnal, phenomenological materiality defines reality, and at the same time defines the reality of action, in as much as it is a question of real action (and not of an ideal activity like the one that consists in dealing with significations). Because it constitutes the site of every real action, the flesh also defines the site of salvation, if it is true that the latter, according to the Gospel, consists not in words but in deeds—"Not everyone who says to me 'Lord! Lord!' will enter the kingdom of heaven, but only the one who does the will of my Father who is in heaven" (Matthew 7:21)—not in a knowledge of the cognitive type but in the practical transformation of a flesh, which no longer gives itself over to the cult of itself, and henceforth will no longer live except from the infinite Life that gives it to itself in the beginning, and never stops giving itself to it even in its idolatry.

This is the reason why the Word assumed a finite flesh like ours, because it had fallen prey to sin and death. As we have shown at length, the flesh really does open the dimension where, producing upon himself in the touching/touched relation the sensations of his desire, man has the power (which he attributes to himself) to become and to make of himself what he wants. And thus he has the power to love himself doubly in this pretend power and its pleasures. It is this love of self that leads to death because what is loved—this pretend power or the sensations it procures—precisely does not have the power to give itself to itself, to give itself life. And thus by loving them, it is his own powerlessness that man loves, and it is to his own finitude and death that he entrusts himself.

By incarnating himself, the Word thus took upon himself the sin and death inscribed in our finite flesh, and he himself destroyed them by dying on the Cross. What is restored then is the original human condition, his transcendental birth in divine Life outside of which no life occurs to life. But this restoration is possible only if it is the Word himself who is incarnated in this flesh, which has become sinful and mortal, so that out of its destruction the Word itself emerges and with it our generation in Him, in the embrace of absolute Life—a generation whose first formulation is the biblical creation. Irenaeus expressed this structure of Christian salvation in many ways with the greatest clarity.* Let us retain one of them: "The one who had to put sin to death and redeemed man worthy of death was made into that very thing he was, which is to say, this man kept in slavery by sin and held under the power of death, so that sin was put to death by a man and thus man leaves death." Then the explicit resumption of the great Pauline themes: "Just as 'by the disobedience of one man,'" who was the first, molded from a virgin earth, "many were made sinners," and have lost life, thus it was necessary that, "by the obedience of one man," who is the first, born from the Virgin, "many were justified and receive salvation" (*op. cit.*, p. 366–67, cf. Romans 5:12–18).

Augustine leads this Christian structure of salvation, which we find in all the Fathers as well as in the councils, to its furthest point, where the becoming-man of God, which makes possible in turn the becoming-God of man, must be taken literally—as meaning deification, the identification with incorruptible Life that alone allows man to escape death. Augustine seeks to lay bare the possibility of this identification in principle

---

*"He [the Lord] gave his flesh for our flesh [. . .]. He has favored us with incorruptibility by the communion we have with himself." "How would we actually have part in the adoptive filiation towards God, if we had not received, through the Son, this communion with God?" "And how would we have received this communion with God if his Word had not entered into communion with us by making us flesh?" (*op. cit.*, respectively, p. 570, 366, 572).

by explaining one of John's most enigmatic propositions, relating the words of Christ in his final prayer to the Father. This text that unveils the mysteries of Christ's mission on earth puts into play a two-fold relation: of Christ to his Father, and of Christ to those whom his Father has entrusted to him for their salvation. Let us recall several elements from the Johannine context: "I am not asking you to take them out of the world, but I ask you to protect them from the evil one. They are not of the world, just as I am not of the world [. . .]. As you have sent me into the world, so I have sent them into the world *and for them I sanctify myself, so that they also may be sanctified*" (17:15–19, our emphasis). From this immense text, all of whose components it is not possible to analyze here, let us retain the proposition on which Augustine meditates: "And for them I sanctify myself."

Implied in this proposition, on the one hand, is the relation to men of the operation Christ carries out ("For them"—he performs it for them), and on the other hand, the operation itself ("I sanctify myself"). Augustine understands this from the outset as the identity of the Christ and of men. For how, he asks, could Christ sanctify men by sanctifying himself *unless it is because men are in him*: "Because they themselves are me." It is indeed evident that if a sanctification takes place in the Christ, those who are in him will be sanctified at the same time. "Sanctified" in a radical sense, meaning not to become holy ones, but this One who alone is Holy: God. Sanctified, that is, deified, and only as such saved. We will return in §48 to this identification of Christ with men on which Augustine's explanation of the mystical body of Christ is based.

The second implication, indeed the founding implication, is presented like an enigma: It is Christ's operation, the sanctification that he accomplishes himself, but *with respect to himself*, a sanctification concerning him, directed toward him, and having Christ as its object. "No one justifies himself," the Christ had conceded to the doctors, scribes, priests, and high priests who addressed him, in a dialogue of tragic tension that the Synoptic gospels and the Johannine text recount, a very serious reproach that also conforms to the Law. Christ's response consisted in a radical declaration that can only aggravate his case: That it is not he, but God, who makes him justice—which presumes between Him and God a relation so intimate that it already contains blasphemy. By transposing to sanctification what has just been said of justification (*are not sanctification and justification the Same?*), could we not think in an analogous manner: "No one sanctifies himself"—and yet this is what the Christ affirms.

Augustine ventures an explanation of this sanctification of Christ by himself, and he does it on the basis of Incarnation and as the explanation of the Incarnation itself. Indeed, since it is the Word (who is God, who is in the beginning with God) who becomes incarnate (that is, who was made man by taking on the flesh of a man) so he sanctifies this man in whom he becomes incarnate in this unique person of the Christ who was made Word and man. Or, to consider matters not from the point of view of the Word but of the man in whom he is incarnate, he has been sanctified from the beginning of his historical existence in as much as it is the Word that has taken on flesh in him, in his own human flesh. In brief, as Word, the Christ sanctifies himself as man. This is Augustine's explicit declaration: "He thus sanctified himself in himself, that is, man in the Word, because the Christ is one, Word and man, sanctifying man in the Word."*

In Augustine's admirable analysis, an obscure core remains. To say that the Word sanctifies the man Jesus by being incarnate in him (because then this man is the Word himself) indeed makes the Word the foundation of salvation, but it does not truly explain the internal possibility of this relation of the Word and man. Word and man are juxtaposed in the person of Christ, in such a way that this juxtaposition, this dual nature, recurs as the central problematic of the great councils, fixing dogma while remaining, as Cyril of Alexandria for example says in his second letter to Nestorius at Ephesus, "inexpressible and incomprehensible."

Yet in the Johannine text, which evidently repeats the words of Christ, the coexistence of the Word and man in the Christ is at no time presented as an assemblage of two opaque and irreducible realities. On the contrary, one and the same principle of intelligibility or rather Arch-intelligibility runs through the Word and man in order to unite them in the Christ. This Arch-intelligibility is absolute Life's self-revelation. It commands the phenomenological relation of reciprocal interiority between the Father and the Son because absolute Life's self-revelation is its self-revelation in the Self of the First Living. The phenomenology of Incarnation has shown at length that the Arch-passibility of this Arch-revelation is, in its phenomenological effectuation, the Arch-flesh presupposed in every flesh. But all of this is said in John's text, which presents a formal structure of the type "just as . . . so . . . ," whose ambition to give account can hardly be disputed. And what it accounts for is the structural similarity between the phenomenological relation of reciprocal interiority of absolute Life and its Word, on the one hand, and the relation of reciprocal, phenomenological interiority between the Word and all the living in the Christ, on the other. Between all these equivalent pronouncements that refer to a radical Elsewhere, to this Other-than-the-

---

*St. Augustine, *Oeuvres completes* (Paris: Librairie Louis Vivés, 1869) t. X (*Tractatus*, CVIII, "Sur Jean"), p. 364ff / *Tractates on the Gospel of John*, trans. John Rettig (Washington, DC: The Catholic University of America Press, 1994), p. 279ff.

world, which is absolute Life in the Parousia of its radical self-revelation that is its "glory" ("They are not of the world just as I am not of the world"), let us retain the last: "The glory that you have given me I have given them, so that they may be one as we are one: I in them and they in me, that their unity may be perfect" (17:22–23).

But this is a question of the mystical body of Christ. This unity of all men in the Christ is precisely Augustine's first presupposition ("They themselves are me"), which is also the first condition of salvation, since it is only if all men are in Christ, one with him, if they are Christ himself, that, sanctifying himself, the Christ sanctifies all in himself, and at the same time saves them all.

The mystical body of Christ where all men are one in him is a limit form of the experience of the other; as such, it refers to this. From the phenomenological point of view, the mystical body is possible only if the nature of the relation that men are capable of having among themselves can attain this limit point, truly, where they are one, in such a way that, according to the presuppositions of Christianity, which are equally those of a phenomenology of Life, the individuality of each one is preserved, indeed, exalted, and in no way abolished in such an experience, if it must still be an experience of *the other*.

The experience of the other has become one of the major themes of phenomenology. Let us indicate, as briefly as possible, the theses of the phenomenology of Life on this problem, which here takes on a decisive importance.

§47. The Experience of the Other in a Phenomenology of Life.

When philosophical reflection encounters an essential question, the first topic it investigates must be the phenomenological presupposition that provides the basis and ultimate possibility for the reality it examines. In this respect, the phenomenology of Life has taught us this: When the reality in question is life, its phenomenological presupposition is never the one in which the question itself moves. The presupposition of philosophical questioning is always thought, intentionality, and ultimately the distance of a world, which life escapes by reason of its own phenomenological presupposition, and this is nothing but life: its Arch-revelation in the Arch-passibility of an invisible pathos. Thus the question of language is totally renewed when the phenomenological basis of the appearing of the world, which we have ascribed to language since Greece, cedes place to the "Logos of Life." Thus the conception of the body is itself over-

238

turned when this body (to the extent that it is a question of our own) is no longer a worldly body, but a living flesh, which occurs only in life, in accordance with its proper and original mode of phenomenalization. The same holds true for the experience of the other.

This has been a subject of recent interest, notably on the part of phenomenology. A word should be said about the traditional conception, however, which seems at first glance foreign to phenomenological analysis. In classical thought, the possibility of communication between people comes from the presence of the same Reason within them. This explains how different individuals, despite their diverse spheres of personal existence, are able to understand one another and communicate—beyond the sensations they have (that according to psychology are given only to one of them), they think the same thing and understand the same truths, in so far as the same Reason thinks in them. In fact, it is not only the same truths (in the sense of rational truths) that they have in common, it is one and the same world they are open to, so that in the end it is this opening to the world, in which they relate to the same things, that unites them. Thus, as most often happens, classical analysis rests upon a phenomenological presupposition that is not thematized for itself—and this is precisely what phenomenology endeavors to do.

In contemporary phenomenology, the retro-reference of the experience of the other to a phenomenological foundation is constant. For Husserl, it is intentionality that gives us access both to others and to everything that for us can be asserted as being. It was this same intentionality, moreover, which claimed to unveil our own transcendental life, whether this be in the intentional auto-constitution of the flux of consciousness which alone produced its spontaneous self-appearing (its *Selbsterscheinung*), or in the methodical reflection of the phenomenological reduction. It is not at all striking that the failure intentionality comes up against in the case of our own transcendental life is repeated in the case of the experience of the other, if the other proves to be originally and in itself nothing other than what I am myself: a living Self. In Husserl's problematic, the failure thus stems simply from the fact that, far from being able to attain the life of the other in itself (such as it is itself attained in itself), intentionality can only confer on the other the signification of bearing such a life within it—and confer on its body the signification of being a flesh, a "living body" (*Leibkörper*).

According to Heidegger, the failure of the philosophies of intentionality is not attributable to intentionality itself, or more precisely to *the essence of the phenomenality* in which it unfolds. Heidegger himself knows no other kind of phenomenality than this, specifically this original self-externalization of pure exteriority that he calls by different names, for example the ek-static horizon of temporality, in the second part of *Sein und Zeit*. What Heidegger in a very clear way criticizes Husserl for, in his final Zähringen seminar, for example, is inserting intentionality into a "consciousness," or into a "subjectivity," and maintaining, thanks to these inadequate concepts, an "interiority" that one will never succeed in truly escaping, in order to find the original Object in itself as it is, and do justice to its way of showing itself to us in the clearing of Being. It is true that for Husserl, in the case of the experience of the other that interests us here, the other is enveloped in this type of interiority that is proper to consciousness in classical thought, such that only the appearing of its body in the world (albeit the world reduced to its "sphere of belonging") gives itself to an effective perception, while its own life escapes us, since it is never more than "appresented" with this body, in the form of an intentional (and as such unreal) signification.*

By setting aside the concepts of "consciousness" and "subjectivity," and by eradicating definitively every form of "interiority," Heidegger's *Dasein*, which is no more than "being-in-the-world" (*In-der-Welt-sein*), furnishes a long-sought solution to the problem of the experience of the other. *Da-sein* (the fact of being-there) is by itself a "being-with," and in this way a being-there with others. *Dasein* is not a "being-with" because, opening us to the world, it opens us to others along with everything that shows itself in the world, in the same immediacy, without there being any need to leave any individual sphere in which we would be initially enclosed. It is not because, *in fact*, we are with someone in the world, or with many, that we are this "being-with." Whether we are alone or with others, "being-with" always precedes. Solitude, for example, is possible only on the foundation of this "being-with," and as a privative modality of it. We could never feel alone if the other did not *lack* us, and he would never lack us if we were not originally with him.†

We are acquainted with these remarkable analyses. All the modalities of our experience of the other, whether of his presence or absence, do suppose the priority of "being-with," without which none of them would be possible. *But it is the possibility of this priority itself, of "being-with"*

---

*On this point, see our work *Phénoménologie matérielle* (Paris: Presses Universitaire de France, 1990), III, 1 / *Material Phenomenology*, trans. Scott Davidson (New York: Fordham University Press, 2008).

†In §64 of *Sein und Zeit*, Heidegger offers a theory of Ipseity whose possibility is sought in Care (in the "outside itself") and in the existential modalities of its fulfillment, depending on whether it loses itself in the One or finds consistency (the "substance" and "simplicity" of the Kantian soul) in the resolute decision in view of death. In this authenticity or inauthenticity of the Self of care, the ipseity of the Self constantly presupposed is not even perceived as a problem.

as such, that must be established. Can one read it in *Dasein* itself and as identical with it? If we look with closer attention at how Heidegger proceeds in order to reach this final condition for the experience of the other, it must be recognized that it is not an immanent analysis of *Dasein* itself that clears the way toward "being-with": It is indeed the world and, furthermore, the beings showing themselves in it ("interworldly" beings) that serve as the point of departure. Because these beings are not pure objects, but "tools," and because they inevitably have a relation to the other as constitutive of their being, this relation functions as an initial situation, and apart from it no "tool" exists. Thus if I see a boat at anchor on the shore, it refers to someone who uses it for excursions—"but even if it is 'a boat which is strange to us', it is still indicative of Others." Thus in the *very content* of the world, a content constituted by a context of "tools ready-to-hand," the other is present as the user or producer of the tool—not as if this tool in itself preexisted its user (the other), but *the tool implies in itself and thus shows in itself the other as preexisting it,* even if the latter is not there. The other, others, or more precisely a *Dasein,* is thus itself present *a priori* in the world of tools, "they are there too and there with it." And this occurs in such a way that, as Heidegger declares with great force, "if one wanted to identify the world in general with entities within-the-world, one would have to say that Dasein too is 'world'." (SZ, §26, 118 / 111; translation modified). With this omni-presence of others even in the things of the world, is it not "being-with" as such that regulates our opening to the world and is thus identified with *Dasein?*

And yet, according to Heidegger himself, the world can in no way be identified with an inter-worldly being; on the contrary, it differs from this to such an extent that the manifestation of the being, which is the world itself, consists in this Difference. The world unveils the being, but as we have seen, does not create it, and thus is unable to account for it in its infinite diversity. By referring to a user or producer, an inter-worldly tool, far from showing in itself an "other," and thus our original being with the other, it is only this original "being-with" that makes possible something like a "tool," and like this context of tools, which is the ontic content of the world. One cannot therefore read "being-with" onto a being that itself can be recognized as a tool only on the foundation of "being-with." Heidegger's explanation turns in a circle. But it turns in a circle only because it is incapable of grasping "being-with" while legitimating in some way the meaning it gives it.

Many difficulties are hidden here. For a phenomenology, to grasp "being-with" means to elucidate the mode of manifestation proper to it, which in turn can mean two things: either to clarify the mode of manifestation in which "being-with" is given to us; or to regard "being-with" as constituting its mode of manifestation as such, and, even more, every mode of manifestation in general. These are the two meanings Heidegger confers on it. This is indeed the import of the repeated affirmation whereby *Dasein* (= the fact of being there as being-in-the-world) and *Mitsein* (= "being-with") are one. From there he brings out clearly that the transcendental possibility of "being-with," *qua* ultimate phenomenological possibility, is in the opening to the world as such. What remains wide open is the question of *the reality with which* we are related in this opening. One can think that it is a question of another reality in general, if it is true that pure exteriority means a pure alterity. But what is the content of this pure alterity? Or else it is a question of the horizon of the pure world, which by itself still has no content, since it is only an empty form, where there is still neither boat nor user of the boat—no one else in the sense of the other, of another "self" like mine. If "being-with" must mean a "being-with-the-other," one cannot pull this out of a hat. This is Heidegger's two-fold sophism, when he thinks he reads the other from the relational totality of tools that form the content of the world, even though there are tools only if the other (not "being with" in general) is already presupposed, and even though "being-with" as an opening to the world never explains anything about its content or about this relational, instrumental system that is supposed to show itself in it. The circle in which one always presupposes what one claims to give account of is masked by a final equation that for Heidegger is self-evident: the other is another *Dasein*, another "being-in-the-world." From then on being-in-the-world is everywhere, and is as much in "being-with" as in *that with which* we are related in "being-with": the other that itself is only being-in-the-world.

We should therefore examine again and directly the possibility for being-in-the-world to be a "being-with" *qua* "being-with-the-other"—where the other is no longer any "other" in general, and still less alterity as such, but the other: an other who is what I am myself, an other self [*moi*]. Through *Sein und Zeit* runs an affirmation that is formulated only in passing, as also being self-evident: "*Das Dasein ist je-meines*" ("*Dasein* is always mine"). To be mine means to belong to me, which presupposes 1) a self; 2) that this self is mine, is what I am—or that what I am is a self; and 3) and precisely the one I am and no other, no other self that otherwise displays, as a self, all the characteristics of my own self. But as we have demonstrated at length, something like a "self" always presupposes an original Ipseity, an "experiencing undergoing itself" in which every conceivable Self [*Soi*] consists and which occurs to itself only in life's arrival in itself in its pathos-filled self-revelation—never in the exteriority of an Ek-stasis. It is even a problem of knowing if in such an exteriority a "relation" is still possible. Was it not Heidegger himself who reminded us that, in the world, "the table does not touch the wall"? What is not the table's doing, is this not the privilege of *Dasein*: the primordial phenomenological possibility of a "relation to" as such? But touching, as the phenomenology of the "I can" has established, assumes the moving-in-itself of the movement of touching, the Self immanent to this movement and hidden in it, and a Self without which no movement of any sort would be possible and which exteriority's process of externalization is incapable of founding.

Faced with the massive failure of a phenomenology of pure exteriority to come to grips with the problem of the relation to the other, should we not substitute here again, as an ultimate phenomenological presupposition, the self-revelation of Life for the appearing of the world? All the elements that are constitutive of one such relation are then given, not as simple "facts," but in their transcendental possibility, and all the aporias of classical thought or contemporary phenomenology then dissipate. Is the experience of the other not what an ego [*moi*] has of another ego [*moi*]? For each of them, is it a question of anything other than having access, not only to the other's thought, but also to his or her very life, of living from it in a certain way? Is this not the reason why, always and everywhere, such an experience is first affective, so that in each one it is affectivity that opens her to this experience, or closes her to it? In this pathos that constitutes the phenomenological material of communication and at the same time its object, doesn't the flesh also play a major role (and not only in the case of the amorous relation)? But don't these elements constitutive of the experience of the other originate in each one from his transcendental birth—from life in its specific mode of revelation?

One will perhaps object, and not without reason, that in the classical philosophy of consciousness as well as in Husserlian phenomenology, it is the fact of anchoring the relation in an ego [*moi*] as an inevitable point of departure, and prescribing it a destination "inside" an ego—as impenetrable as a circle, Kandinsky says—in brief, that in both cases the "monadic" presuppositions of the analysis block the comprehension and effectuation of a true experience of the other that is capable of sharing with the ego a same "content," a same reality. Doesn't the analysis of eroticism that the phenomenology of the flesh offers remain a prisoner of this limitation? Hasn't it shown, even when set within the immanence of a desiring drive, that at the boundary of the organic body and its deployment this drive stumbled into the real body of the universe, in this case the other's body, like an insurmountable wall, without the power to go through or reach beyond it, its own living flesh, its desire, or its pleasure—where they undergo experiencing themselves?

But the phenomenology of flesh has itself unceasingly recognized its own limitation, and has been compelled in each of these analyses to carry out a kind of movement or question in return—*from the flesh to what comes before it.* That which comes before every flesh is its own arrival in itself, its own incarnation—which is never its doing, and occurs only in absolute Life's arrival in itself. Because absolute Life comes in itself in its original Arch-passibility, every finite flesh generated like this, arriving in itself in it, is made passible, flesh. Because this arrival of absolute Life is identically its arrival in the Ipseity of the First Self, every flesh is identically the flesh of an equally finite Self. *Thus one must never start from this Self, and even less from an I* [*moi*] *or an ego conceived as the point of departure, the source point of intentionality.* The inevitable reference the phenomenology of flesh makes to the phenomenology of Incarnation presents us with the following evidence: *Every relation from one Self to another Self requires as its point of departure not this Self itself, an I* [*moi*]—*my own or the other's*—*but their common transcendental possibility, which is nothing other than the possibility of their relation itself: absolute Life.*

In the experience of the other, it is indeed a question of recognizing its inescapable precondition, "being-with" as such, in its radical phenomenological possibility. This is precisely not the world but absolute Life. In absolute Life, "being-with" is not constructed like a formal and empty relation, so that nothing in it allows us to understand how and why such a relation is established between a plurality of egos [*moi*], presupposing them all without explaining any of them. Undergoing experiencing itself in the Ipseity of the First Self, absolute Life generates in its transcendental possibility every Self and thus every conceivable I [*moi*]. It generates them as living Selves and egos [*moi*] and at the same time generates in them the transcendental possibility of their relation. For this relationship of the living to one another consists of nothing other than Life in each one. Not exactly in its finite life, in its Self or its finite I [*moi*], where each would still be only himself, alone with himself and without any possibility of joining another. The relation of transcendental living Selves takes place in them before them, precisely in their transcendental possibility, in the place of their birth, in the proceeding of absolute life in which they arrive in themselves and in which they remain for as long as they are living. In as much as they are living in one and the same Life, and are Selves in the Ipseity of one and the same Self, they are and can be each with the others in the "being-with" that always precedes them, which is absolute Life in its original Ipseity.

In this way every conceivable community is born and is formed in its original phenomenological possibility. Such a community has certain essential characteristics as a result. The first concerns what is in common in this community, or if one prefers, its content: It is transcendental life. One thereby sees that a content of this sort is not originally (and thus not necessarily) a "rational" content. Reason, in the sense that we mean it, is not that which gathers originally: It isolates just as well. It is rightly said that the fool is someone who has lost everything except reason. And it is not only on the individual plane that reason can prove to be destructive. One has only to consider what happens today under our eyes in order to measure at what point reason handed over to itself, to a pure objectivism, to the calculating abstraction of modern technology, can strike at what is most proper to the heart of man and threaten his "humanity," and at the same time humanity in its entirety, to the point of leading it to ruin. The content of every community is all that belongs to Life and has its possibility in it. Suffering, joy, desire, or love each carry a gathering power infinitely greater than what one attributes to "Reason," which properly speaking has no power to gather, in as much as one cannot deduce the existence of a single individual from it, or anything that must be gathered in a "community."

Because what is in common in every community is Life, the community indeed presents another essential characteristic, as being a community of the living (in the sense of transcendental living Selves), to the extent that in such a community alone such Selves are possible; and reciprocally, it is not possible without them, without the primordial Self in which it comes into itself, and which contains the potential and indefinite multiplicity of all possible selves [*moi*]. We see here how ridiculous it is to oppose, as one does today, society and individuals. If society is something other than a collection of "individuals" reduced to their objective appearance and treated as separate entities—if society is precisely a community—then community and individual are each connected by a relation of reciprocal phenomenological interiority that is nothing other than the relation of the living to Life, emptying of meaning *a priori* the idea of any sort of "opposition" between them.

But it is life's third characteristic that must here be emphasized: Before it defines the content of what is in common, Life in its original Ipseity constitutes the transcendental possibility of being-in-common of what is in common—relation as such, "being-with" in its precedence. However, it can no longer be a question here of life in general, a finite life like our own, but of absolute Life.

From these brief reminders, it follows:

1) That every community is by essence religious, as the relation between transcendental Selves presupposes in all respects and in every way the relation of each transcendental Self to absolute Life, the *religious bond (religio)*. Not that each of them as a bearer of this bond generates his

relation to the other, but on the contrary, because it is from this bond that he has his own Self and at the same time the possibility of being related to the other.

2) That every community is by essence invisible. Of course, like our own life, our Self, and our flesh, it has its "appearance in the world," but here again this appearance is only a simple semblance cut from reality. Thus even more than our life, our Self, or our flesh, the visible community carries with it the possibility of dissimulation and deception. Is it not the place where indifference and all other shameful sentiments are constantly masked by social ritual?

3) As invisible, foreign to the world and to its phenomenological categories, to space and time, the reality of the community opens a field of paradoxical relations, and these form the nucleus of Christianity, of which Kierkegaard had the brilliant intuition. Thus a real relation can be established between transcendental Selves that never see one another and that belong to different epochs. A man can see his life turned upside down by reading a book from another century whose author is unknown. An individual can become the contemporary of an event that happened two thousand years ago. The presuppositions of a phenomenology of Life here prove themselves as an introduction to the decisive intuitions of Christianity, and notably to its extraordinary conception of intersubjectivity.

§48. The Relation to the Other According to Christianity: The Mystical Body of Christ.

This relation to the other, in the sense of another Self, is expressed in the initiatory texts of early Christianity in a way that had never yet been envisaged by the human spirit. Whatever may be the difficulty for the Christian thinkers of the following generations to conceptualize within the Greek horizon the nature of such a relation, this decisive fact remains: It is this relation to the absolute Other Self who is God that is constantly actualized in the liturgical and sacramental practices brought by the new religion.

From the phenomenological point of view, it is worth recalling that a relation of this kind must be grasped where it occurs: apart from the world, before it. What happens before the world? We know the answer: It is the reciprocal phenomenological relation of interiority between absolute Life and the First Living in as much as it puts itself to the test [s'eprouve] in the One who puts himself to the test [s'eprouve] in it. To undergo experiencing oneself, to enjoy oneself, is to love oneself in such a way that this *self-enjoyment is produced in absolute Life as its generation of the first Self in which it feels itself and thus loves itself*—for the one who undergoes experiencing himself in this absolute Life that loves itself in Him, it happens that *each one loves himself in the "other" who (with every exteriority here out of play) is never external to him, but on the contrary internal and consubstantial.* This is how the extraordinary relation we are discussing occurs: "You loved me before the foundation of the world."

The Johannine context affirms continuously, even in its formal structure, that this relation of phenomenological interiority between absolute Life and the First Living is reciprocal. In its formal structure, the phenomenological interiority of the Father to the Son is constantly formulated as the interiority of the Son to the Father: "As you, Father, are in me and I am in you"; "The Father is in me and I am in the Father"; "Do you not believe that I am in the Father and the Father is in me?" (John 17:24; 17:21; 10:38; 14:10, respectively).

It is striking, as we have had occasion to observe, that the proceeding of absolute Life's internal structure (as a relation of phenomenological interiority between Life and its Word) is repeated in the relation between this absolute and man, in this case between its Word and every conceivable transcendental Self. Doesn't an abyss nevertheless separate the infinite Life that brings itself about as such in its Word, and a life, a Self like ours, incapable of bringing itself into life by itself, and so is destined for a certain death? Here Incarnation in the Christian sense intervenes. Only by the Incarnation of the Word in the flesh of a man—who has as such "come from God," is "sent by him," namely the Messiah, or the Christ—does the union that overcomes this abyss take place. This union has been called a deification because, since the reciprocal phenomenological interiority of Life and its Word is repeated when *the Word itself is made flesh in the Christ*, every union with this is identically a union with the Word, and, in this, with absolute Life. *But how could man be united to the Word if not because, in the Word itself, in the original Ipseity of the Arch-Son, every transcendental Self is joined to itself, and given to itself as the Self that it is?* In this way, undergoing experiencing himself in the original self-trial Life undergoes in its Word, it has become like it, like God.

As a way open for the salvation of man, the incarnation now appears, according to the intuition of Irenaeus, as a *restoration*, the restoration of his original condition, in as much as man was created by God *in his image*, so this creation is his generation in absolute Life's self-generation in its Word—his transcendental birth. That this birth be contingent, and that this contingence be the sign of an original finitude, does not change anything about the essence of Life in it, about the fact that in it and in it alone it is a transcendental living Self having part in the self-enjoyment this Life confers on it. Rather, this finitude crushes it against the foundation of life within it. For if a life like ours is incapable of giving life to itself, if it is only in the absolute and infinite Life of God that it is given to itself in order to enjoy itself in life, then this life of God remains in our finite life, as the latter remains in God for as long as it lives. Thus the repetition of the reciprocal phenomenological interiority of Life and its Word in each of the living takes place as the phenomenological interiority of this living being and absolute Life.

This reciprocal phenomenological interiority of the living and absolute Life in the Word of God allows us to understand what is important for us now: the original relation established between all men and women, the experience of the other in its final possibility. If the Word is the condition in which every living, carnal Self comes into and can come into itself, *is it not at the same time the condition of every living, carnal Self other than my own—the way one must necessarily follow in order to enter into relation with him, with the other?* Here absolute Life proves to be, in its Word, the phenomenological access to the other Self, as it is for me the access to mine: the Ipseity in which I am given to me and come into me, in which the other is given to himself and comes into him. Thus it is in this sense that Life is "being-with" as such, the original essence of every community: being-in-common as well as what is in common. For we could never know what is of the other, and first of all that it is a living Self, if we did not first know what Life is that gives us to ourselves. It is thus indeed *from what comes before the self, from its arrival in itself—never from itself*—that one must begin if being-with-the-other and being-with-others must be possible. And indeed it is never this as a "projection" of the self in the other, a projection that, far from being able to found the latter, on the contrary presupposes it.

And so we see well how this "being-with," which is absolute Life in its Word, differs from the Greek Logos, from the Reason of classical thought or from Heidegger's world. For Reason presupposes pure exteriority where these e-vidences are always formed as well as its capacity to speak, if it is true that one speaks only of what one can see, by signifying it when it is not seen—this pure exteriority which is the world of *Sein und Zeit*, this exteriority where neither Ipseity nor Self are possible.

Since the self-givenness of absolute Life in its Word, in which the transcendental Self that I am is given to itself, is God's life alone, it is in *that* one and the same Life that the Self of the other is given to itself in an identical way—in it every possible Self, future, present, or past, has been, is, or will be given to itself so as to be the Self that it is. For every carnal, living, transcendental Self, being-together in the Word's one and absolute life (in the Arch-passibility of its Arch-flesh) is what constitutes the concrete phenomenological tenor of every relation between men, allowing them to understand one another before they meet, and allowing each to understand the other as he understands himself—not after the fact, at the end of a history, but *in the place of his birth, in as much as it is identically the birth of the other*, anywhere in the world, and at any time in history. It is Life in its Word, the way it has come in its Word, before the world, that unites all living beings, yesterday, today, and tomorrow, and makes their encounter possible as its sole precondition. It is this precondition that makes possible in turn every form of historical, trans-historical, or eternal relation between them.

But in Christianity there is something radically original in relation to the other great forms of spirituality: This absolute unity between all living Selves, far from signifying or implying the dissolution or destruction of the individuality of each one, is on the contrary constitutive of it, in as much as each of them is joined to himself or herself in the phenomenological effectuation of Life in its Word, and generated in themselves as this irreducibly singular Self, irreducible to any other. This is one of the decisive meanings of the ageless utterance of Meister Eckhart: "God engenders himself as myself" (*op. cit.*, p. 146). Thus one of the great paradoxes of Christianity is clarified. *Maintaining each one, the most humble, and the most insignificant, in its own irreducibly singular individuality, in its condition as a transcendental Self that is by essence this one or that one forever—far from needing or being able to be overcome or abolished anywhere, this alone can snatch humankind from nothingness.*

It is this irreducibility of each one that motivates the extraordinary attention the Christ gives them. Eliminating every consideration pertaining to a professional, economic, social, intellectual, ethnic, or other condition, behind every empirical characteristic of a given individuality, and even its individual condition (man according to the "Rights of Man," for example), discloses what is unique in each one. Thus, as Cyril claims: "Neither Paul, for example, can be or be called Peter, nor can Peter be or be called Paul."* Thus again in his first letter John designates the Christ himself as *He* (where it is an issue of living "as He lived" (I John 2:6), even when it is in his view a question of the principle of all things. That each one's irreducible singularity is generated within the very principle of

---

*Cyrille, *Traité sur saint Jean*, Book XI, ch. 11, on John 17:20–21 (PG, 74, 551–562, 934–1000). Louis Laneau comments on this text in his *De la déification des justes* (Geneva: Ad Solem, 1993), p. 137–45. One finds in this work, written in the seventeenth century by a Jesuit missionary imprisoned in Siam, a remarkable synthesis of converging interpretations of the doctrine of the mystical body of Christ in the Fathers and of salvation as identification with God. I am grateful to the poet Franck Veillart for having made me aware of this book of exceptional clarity and depth.

every generation, and, even more, that this comes to each one and takes hold of him in absolute Life's Bottomless proceeding, this is undoubtedly one of Christianity's most extraordinary intuitions.

Is phenomenology capable of giving an account of this identity between the principle that unifies Life and makes it possible, and the one that diversifies a multiplicity of living beings within it? Paul formulated in an abrupt assertion the rejection of every difference, in the sense of a discrimination between all of these transcendental living Selves: "Neither Greek nor Jew, nor master nor servant, nor man nor woman" (Galatians 3:28). Whatever may be the ethical perspectives opened by these grandiose propositions—which draw from the direct teaching of Christ, moreover—whatever the upheaval that they have also produced in history, a question remains. Is it possible to disregard certain characteristics in human beings that establish a difference between them as important as sexual difference, for example? We cannot push this aside under the pretext that it occurs on the "natural" plane and concerns objective bodies. On the one hand, this objective difference provokes anxiety, which thoroughly determines the erotic relation; on the other hand, it is in the immanence of our flesh that sexual difference reveals itself originally in the form of distinct, pure impressions, some proper to female sensibility, unknown to male sensibility, and vice-versa. Isn't an essential incommunicability now set up between transcendental Selves, to the extent that impressions inhabit them that are proper to some and unknown to others?

Such questions lead back in a naive way to a phenomenology of flesh, as if this could be abstracted from the trying process in which it comes into itself—as if every Self, every flesh, and every impression could give itself as an autonomous content that would be closed on itself and would in its specificity elude every conceivable being-in-common. But if being-in-common precedes the Self as its internal condition of possibility and if this transcendental condition is a phenomenological condition in a radical sense, in the sense of the Arch-revelation apart from which no phenomenon is possible, then the problem is completely reversed. Posed in a rigorous way, the question was the following: If we were to suppose a specific impression of female sensibility, and equally a specific impression of male sensibility, what could these two impressions have in common? *Being given to themselves in absolute Life's self-givenness.*

But what holds for these impressions holds *a fortiori* for each flesh, of which they are only modalities, and for each of the transcendental Selves that are consubstantial to these cases of flesh. Thus each living, carnal, transcendental Self, given to itself and being with itself only in absolute Life's self-givenness in its Word, is in that Word, with Him. It is now in Him with all those who also are given to themselves only in this

Word in which I am myself given to me. So each transcendental living Self is in the Word before being with itself, and in this Word, it is with the other before the other is given to itself. And the other is in the same situation of being in the Word before being with itself or with me (in the Word in which it is with itself as with me) who am myself with him and with myself in this Word. Thus, especially, since each transcendental Self is with the other where it is given to itself, it is with the other before every subsequent determination—before being man or woman.

But these are the immediate phenomenological presuppositions of the doctrine of the mystical body of Christ. This body indeed supposes all of them, some as founding relations, others as relations founded on the first, and having in it both their origin and the principle of their development—as an immanent development taking after the force of this origin, which remains within it as its invincible consistency. Thus we can distinguish, at least in an abstract way, successive phases within this construction or growth of the body of Christ, because there is always within it an element that edifies and an element that is edified.

The element that edifies, the "head" of this body, is Christ. Its members are all those who, sanctified and deified in him and by him, belong to him from then on, to the point of becoming parts of this body itself, precisely its members. To the extent that he is the *real* Incarnation of the Word, the Christ first edifies each transcendental living Self in his originary Ipseity, which is absolute Life's own—he joins it to himself. Giving each Self to itself, it gives it to grow from itself in a trying process of continuous self-growth, which makes it a becoming (the opposite of a "substance" or a "thing")—a proceeding that is at bottom nothing but absolute Life's proceeding. Our critique of Husserl's problematic concerning the Impression has shown that if "an impression is always there anew" in the flux of the internal consciousness of time, it is never by virtue of the Impression itself. Always and already the pathos-filled trial of absolute Life's self-givenness is at work, so that this flux, which in itself is foreign to every intentionality, is neither linear nor undetermined: As impressional, it is first carnal, by the authority of Life's Arch-possibility; next, it obeys an evident affective dichotomy, in as much as this Arch-possibility becomes phenomenal in the original phenomenological tonalities of pure Suffering and of the pure Enjoyment born of this Suffering. Thus, finally, this flux, this seemingly absurd parade of modest pleasures and oppressive thoughts, is secretly oriented toward an agony, toward the ultimate transition from the ultimate suffering of despair to the eruption of an unlimited joy, as evidenced by the Parousia concealed on the wood of the Cross.

Each transcendental Self's givenness to itself—a givenness in which that Self is edified within, as growing from itself and thus from its own becoming—is the operation of the Word, and the Word repeats it in each conceivable transcendental Self, whether past, present, or future. Thus the mystical body of Christ grows indefinitely from everyone who is sanctified in Christ's flesh. In this potentially indefinite extension, the mystical body of Christ is construed as "the common person of humanity" and "that is why it is called the New Adam."* Because this edification does not proceed by an accumulation of added elements, as "stones" properly speaking, in an edifice constructed by human hands, but on the contrary because in Christ the edification occurs in the Word, it continues as transcendental Self-edifications, each of which, given to itself in the Word, and one with it, is at the same time given to itself in the same unique Life of the same unique Self in which all other Selves are given to themselves. Thus it is one with all of them in Christ, and because Christ is not divisible (being the only Life that holds the power to live), neither are they separated, but, on the contrary, are one in Him, with Him, and they are, in an identical way, in Him, one with all others who are equally in Him. Thus the "universal person" of humanity, as the Fathers also say, is precisely this "common person" Cyril speaks of: *The reciprocal phenomenological interiority of all the living in the one Self of absolute Life, in the reciprocal phenomenological interiority of this Self and this Life, of the Father and the Son.*

Because we cannot fail to distinguish in this common person that which edifies and that which is edified, the head and its body, we must say with Augustine that "the head saves and the body is saved." But because that which edifies penetrates everywhere that which is edified, because the head and the body are one, and because this body composed of all the living who are united in him thus becomes "the entire body" of Christ, that which was still not completed in Christ is given to this body to accomplish and complete. Hence Paul's extraordinary declaration, giving his own sufferings—experienced through numerous tribulations and persecutions endured in the service of Christ—as sufferings still lacking in Christ's own body: "I am completing what is lacking in Christ's afflictions for the sake of his body" (Colossians 1:24). Thus it is up to Paul to complete this body, to finish it—in the radical sense, however, that these sufferings of Paul are the sufferings of the Christ himself, and belong to his body. And this is possible because Christ remains in his grown body, in his "entire" body, which the Fathers also call his Church. He remains in this "entire" body, which is his mystical body, as that which gives each of its members to itself. What he gives to each of its members is thus himself. It is not for everyone, it is true, to live as his God what gives him to himself.

* Cyril, *Traité sur saint Jean, op. cit.*, Book I, ch. 9, p. 173.

The majority live like idolaters: They hardly care at all about the power that gives them life, and live in it only for themselves, and care, in all things and in others, only for themselves. To the members of his body, to each of them who, given to themselves in the self-givenness of the Word, will live only from the infinite Life that is put to the test in this Word, *to those who love one another in Him in such a way that it is Him they love in them, Him and all those who are in Him,* eternal Life will be given, so that in this Life that has become theirs, they are saved.

Beyond Phenomenology and Theology: Johannine Arch-Intelligibility.

We have reserved for this conclusion the task of deciding between what in our essay comes within the competency of philosophy, in this case phenomenology, and what from theology. Philosophy and theology do not compete, but are given as two different disciplines. The difference consists in what theology takes as a point of departure, and more than that, as the very object of its reflection: Scripture, that is, texts that are deemed sacred. "Sacred" does not mean that they speak of what is sacred, of God, but that they come from Him, that *they are his Speech.* It is thus in all respects a question of a Speech of Truth. This is the decisive advantage of theology: To base itself in this Truth, which is given as absolute. If theology relies immediately on the Speech of God, it is precisely because this is the Speech of Truth.

Philosophy then appears singularly destitute and indigent, initially in a situation of wandering, knowing neither what Truth is nor how to go about reaching it. Far from being in possession of a self-assured beginning, it is a prisoner of aporia. It must begin its investigation from a true point of departure, without knowing where to go to have a chance of coming across it, and without knowing, in the case that it does have this chance, how it could recognize it. Descartes's universal doubt echoes the ancient skepticism from which Platonism emerged. The genius of Descartes was to discover in this doubt itself the beginning sought, and at the same time Truth itself, in as much as it resides in this beginning and in the certainty proper to it. Truth and beginning are one, just as in theology. The Truth is in the beginning if the beginning must do without every justification prior to it and other than it, if it must itself prove itself, and must be itself the True of which we must say, *verum index sui.* In short, a truth that is dependent on nothing other—the absolute Truth from which theology starts and of which it speaks.

Will one say that in philosophy, man finds the foundation he must start from through reflection, which comes from himself and from his own thought—while in the case of theology, exegesis rests on a dogmatic content that comes to us from the outside? The autonomy of the former is opposed to the heteronomy of the latter, which is enough to devalue it and turn it into the object of a belief and thus a possible unbelief, indeed a legend instead of the Truth that can found itself, and as such can be Reason, the only veritable Reason whose internal justification and autonomy are the dignity of man. We will come back in a moment to the relevance of this opposition.

For the moment, let us reflect further on the difference in method that is supposed to separate philosophy and theology: There isn't one. The opposition of the points of departure does not change the fact that *in both cases the method consists in a movement of thought,* which by developing a series of evidences, and through the play of their implications that are themselves evident, arrives at results that are all progressive gains constitutive of a theory always in the making. What the whole of our investigation has established is that this movement encounters an insurmountable failure if it must grasp life in some kind of evidence—in the opening of the world in which Life never appears. If the profound reality of man must escape a hardly conceivable unconscious, analogous to what is attributed to brute matter, rocks, stars, or quanta, it is only because this reality does not reside originally in a thought that is dislocated from the power to bring itself into phenomenality. Only absolute, unique, transcendental, phenomenological Life—whose property is precisely revealing itself to itself in its pathos-filled self-affection, which owes nothing to anyone or anything else—can define human reality as phenomenological in its essence. If thought itself is possible, in the sense of a phenomenological thought like ours and not a thought unconscious in itself (which is only a chimera) it is precisely because this thought is revealed to itself in Life. Thus it is not thought (intentionality, being-in-the-world) that gives us access to life, it is Life that gives us access to thought, in as much as thought is only a mode of life, and it is Life in it that reveals it to itself in revealing itself to itself. Thus the aporia of the phenomenological method that Husserl came up against is removed—which in the same way seemed to block the research into a phenomenology (i.e., thought) of life undertaken here—since it is transcendental Life itself that provides all thought and every form of intentionality with the primitive self-givenness in which, put in possession of themselves, they are able to do their work. These remarks developed at length obviously hold for theology as well as for philosophy, which are both forms of thought.

Thought, the distancing of the ek-static horizon where it moves—nature as the primitive "outside itself," contemplation of Ideas, representation, the subject-object relation, intentionality, being-in-the-world—has been since Greece the phenomenological basis for, and thus the essence of, intelligibility. To the extent it comes before any intelligibility of this sort, *Life's original coming in itself is an Arch-intelligiblity*. In its precedence to the intelligibility that governs western philosophy, this is not defined in a negative way. Before the world and its "appearance," Arch-intelligibility has always opened the phenomenological dimension of the invisible—which is anything but a negative concept (the concept antithetical to the visible). *Invisible is the original revelation that carries out the work of revelation with respect to itself*—before everything else. For appearing can make something other than it appear only if it appears first in itself and as such. Only absolute Life carries out this self-revelation of the Beginning. It is here that the pretension of human thought to attain Truth *by the force of its own thinking* goes up in smoke. It is here that the phenomenological intuitions of Life join together with those of Christian theology—*recognizing a common presupposition that is no longer that of thought.* Before thought, thus before phenomenology and theology alike (before philosophy or any other theoretical discipline), a Revelation is at work, which owes them nothing but which they all equally assume. Before thought, before the opening of the world and the unfolding of its intelligibility, absolute Life's Arch-intelligibility fulgurates, the Parousia of the Word in which it is embraced.

We are thus presented with Life's paradox: Only its Arch-intelligibility allows us to understand what in us is the most simple, most elementary, most banal, and most humble, and which, as an effect of this Arch-intelligibility whence we originate, reaches us in the heart of our being. In the heart of our "being": where all the living come to life, where Life gives it to itself in the Arch-intelligibility of its absolute self-givenness—in our transcendental birth, and where we are Sons. We have referred several times to the striking sequence of thought in the Fathers of the Church and the great councils. The crucial character of the problem posed by the body—substituting for the material body the living flesh that we really are and that it is up to us to rediscover today despite the reigning objectivism—in at least an implicit way for the thinkers of early Christianity (in an explicit way for Irenaeus), is to make possible the Incarnation of the Word, the only thing that matters to them and the foundation of Christian salvation.

But for us here, us post-Husserlian (which is to say non-Greek) phenomenologists, the Christian presupposition acquires a decisive meaning. It does not only help us to refuse the ruinous and absurd reduction of our body to an object, an object offered to scientific investigation and then handed over to technological and genetic manipulation, and at the limit to the practices opened by Nazi ideology. Nor is it enough for us to interpret this object-body as a subjective body, as long as this subjectivity is identified with intentionality and ultimately with the "outside itself" of the world's appearing. What we are claiming is that the new intelligibility that the elaboration of the question of the body demands, *in as much as our body is not a body but a flesh*, is totally foreign to what we have always understood intelligibility to be. This is only the worldly perception of our body as a body of flesh (*Leibkörper*), the perception of an object-body clothed with the signification of not being an ordinary thingly body, but a body capable of sensing, which comes from the intelligibility of Platonic contemplation or its modern substitutes. Again, this intelligibility is only ever derived, and presupposes one entirely other than it. *Originally and in itself, our real flesh is arch-intelligible, revealed to itself in the revelation from before the world, proper to the Word of Life of which John speaks.*

Two decisive consequences follow. The first is that the Greek aporia of the coming of the intelligible Logos in a material, putrescible body— and as a condition of a salvation that is then identified with death— dissipates like a mirage in the Johannine Arch-intelligibility. Totally different from the Greek Logos that denotes at once Reason and the possibility of the language that men speak, which consists in the formation of ideal and as such unreal significations, the Word of Life is the radical and final, transcendental, phenomenological condition of every possible flesh. In it alone, as we have seen, every living flesh is given in its pathos-filled auto-impressionality: in the Arch-passibility in which Life and its Word love each other eternally. The Christian Word could come in a flesh. In the Arch-pathos of its Arch-passibility, it alone can join to itself what in its auto-impressionality is properly flesh. This is the invincible motive for which (since the flesh and its phenomenological properties have their final phenomenological possibility in this Arch-passibility of the Word) the phenomenology of flesh referred us constantly to a phenomenology of Incarnation.

Prior to every flesh, as its arrival in itself (its in-carnation), the Incarnation of the Word is not only that in which the Word was made flesh, the extraordinary Event from which Christ's disciples await salvation—if it is true that, according to the abrupt formulation of the Prologue, it is in the Word itself that *being made flesh* is accomplished, and outside of which no flesh, no carnal living Self, and no man has ever been possible. This is why the Prologue spreads its dazzling clarity behind it onto the text of Genesis. It allows us to understand the divine creation not only as the arrival of the world outside, its objectivation, according to the phenomenological interpretation of Jakob Böhme that would dominate German Idealism. What Böhme had also understood, and what we also have rediscoved in many of our developments, is that this horizon of light that according to him is the Wisdom of God is still unable to create its content—whose specific creation, the creation of matter, the biblical God undertakes.

But when God creates man in his image and likeness, it is no longer an inert and blind matter that he throws outside himself—it is a flesh that he generates in himself, apart from the world, in the proceeding of his self-generation in his Word. "Everything was made in him and without him nothing was made that was made." God has indeed taken the mud, but he has breathed into it the Breath of Life which gives life, the Life that remains in this thingly body, not as its own property but as the Principle of all life, the common Spirit of the Father and the Son that inhabits every flesh and makes it alive, and without which the body would not even be a cadaver. A flesh that has never preexisted itself has become flesh by its transcendental birth in the Arch-passiblity of Life and its Word, in their reciprocal phenomenological interiority that is their common Spirit. According to the word of the Apostle already cited: "Your body is the temple of the Holy Spirit." The man of the biblical creation is thus earth and flesh at once, but in him everything that is body is body, a focal point and heap of material processes. But also everything that is flesh is flesh, there is not an ounce of matter in it: It is a pure phenomenological material, crystal of appearing, substance of suffering and joy, a bit of phenomenality that is foreign to light, invisible, and filled with pathos—a revelation that is not brought about in itself in its pathos-filled impressionality, and is not given to itself in this way, except in absolute Life's Arch-passibility.

This is the extraordinary concept of flesh unveiled in Christianity. A flesh that is sensible only in the secret of its affective tonalities and its invisible, pathos-filled determinations. And which is *intelligible* only in the empty, external appearance of a material determination (never as flesh, therefore, but only as an inert object). And its essence is the Johannine Arch-intelligibility of God himself and of his Spirit. The Parousia of the absolute shines in the depth of the simplest impression. That is why the flesh does not lie. It does not lie like truthful thought does when it says what it sees or thinks it sees, even when there is nothing there, as in dreams. It is not a thought that doesn't lie, but also could, whether intentionally or inadvertently, or even out of ignorance. Flesh does not lie because it cannot lie, because at bottom, where it is gripped by Life, it is Life that speaks, Life's Logos, the Johannine Arch-intelligibility.

In the Fathers, and before them in the initiatory texts, we find an even more decisive correlation added to the correlation between flesh and an Arch-revelation foreign to the world, which itself had been unthought until then (where, far from being reduced to a blind body that can be illuminated only from the outside by the light of the world, that never penetrates it and is indifferent to it, the flesh, like fire, ignites as the substance of its own revelation). This new correlation not only concerns every incarnation and every flesh, but precisely the event without measure that is the Christian Incarnation. Since it occurred, it has always been lived by Christians as the Revelation of God himself. How must this Revelation proper to the Incarnation of the Word in Christ be understood in the end?

For as long as flesh is confused with the body, the Incarnation of the Word is its coming in a body and thus in the world. *Revelation is entrusted to the world's appearing.* We have already encountered in Athanasius the thesis in which the Incarnation of the Word signifies its coming in a visible body and in this way the Revelation of God in this world. We have already recognized the difficulty it raises. If God must reveal himself in the form of this worldly man whose corporeal appearance he has assumed, how is this to be distinguished from the corporeal appearance of other men—how can we know or believe that this is precisely the Word? Like every man in his external aspect, is the Christ not a prisoner of the incognito that appealed so much to Kierkegaard, and that never gives up its secret to the unbelieving—which in any case makes every act of belief so difficult? We have seen how the *De incarnatione* removes the difficulty by showing that this ordinary man, of humble appearance, like others, all of a sudden differs from them by words and acts that are so extraordinary that he proves to be no longer a man but, in the violence of the contrast, the absolute of justice and truth in which many will recognize the Messiah.

It is permissible to think, however, that the Incarnation accomplishes the Revelation of God otherwise than by means of this contrast, however gripping it may be. Is it not enough to recall a final time that the Incarnation of the Word is not its coming in a body but in flesh? Or, to say it in a more rigorous way, that its coming in this body that some have seen was not dissociable from the coming of absolute, invisible Life in its Word. And that it is this Word in its Arch-passibility that was made flesh, not dissociable from this flesh itself, and like our own, destined to suffer and also to die. Its hidden reality now takes place in the Coming of the Word in its visible body, the eternal generation of the Only Son, first born in absolute Life's self-generation. Incarnation reveals the reciprocal phenomenological interiority of the Father and the Son. "Do you not know, Philip, that I am in the Father and the Father is in me?" Visibly, Philip has difficulty seeing and understanding what the Christ says to him.

But what are we ourselves? *Are we not a flesh that in its reality is like the one the uncertain gaze of Philip questions?* An invisible flesh generated in absolute Life's self-generation in its Word, in the Arch-passibility from which every conceivable flesh draws its pure phenomenological material, its pathos-filled auto-impressionality? When the biblical God breathed into us the Breath of Life that made each of us living, it is this generation that takes place. The Incarnation reveals to us our own generation in life, our transcendental birth. It reveals to us that our human condition is Filial, and, tearing it away from all our illusions, refers it to its unfathomable truth.

It is this restoration of our original condition that Irenaeus strives to explain, in difficult texts that constantly affirm the identity between the biblical creation of man by the insufflation of life in a piece of matter, and on the other hand the Johannine generation of flesh in the Word. "[. . .] In these last days, He [the Word] was made man, even though *he was already in the world and invisibly sustained all created things.*" From then on, the historical Incarnation of the Word in a visible body has the goal of reminding man that it is in this Word that he had been made in the beginning, in the image and likeness of God: in the invisible. The incarnation makes manifest to man his invisible generation. "In ancient times it was indeed said that man had been made in the image of God, but this did not appear because the Word was still invisible, the one in whose image everything had been made." It is also the Word's invisible condition that had made man lose his "image," this self-revelation of Life that is the Word in which every transcendental Self is given to itself in its Johannine generation. Hence, according to the reasoning of Irenaeus, when the Word is incarnate in the flesh of Christ, and becomes visible to men in the world, it makes visible to everyone that he is this Word in whose image they have been made—he manifests their divine condition. "But when the Word was made flesh, he made the Image appear in all truth, by becoming himself that which was itself its Image." This means that, when he was incarnated, he showed himself to other men *as man who is the image of God*, he showed them in this man that he was the original Image in the image of which man was made, he showed them the Word in him. He told them that like Him, generated in Him, they bear this Word in them that he himself is, that they were of divine origin. Thus thanks to the Incarnation, man was reestablished in his dignity as a son of God. "And he reestablished the likeness in a stable way by making man plainly like the invisible Father by means of the Word henceforth visible" (*op. cit.*, respectively p. 625, our emphasis, and pp. 617–18, 618). *What the Incarnation of the Word in the human condition spoke, therefore, was ultimately the transcendental generation of every living, carnal Self in this Word; it was the transcendental truth of man.*

Philip's hesitation remains. *How can we overcome the paradox that entrusts to the visible the revelation of the Invisible?* In order for the Word that has become visible in its Incarnation to allow us to see in this Incarnation the Word in whose likeness we have been made, must we not presuppose that the One that we see, or rather that they have seen, and also testify that they have seen, is precisely the Word? Must we not already believe in him? *Then what does it mean to believe when believing means believing in the Christ?*

We speak quite badly about belief as long as we have not performed the prior work that consists in recognizing the ultimate phenomenological foundation of what we're talking about. Thus we spontaneously treat the act of belief as an act of thought—an act capable of making visible what it thinks (its *cogitatum*); so that by making it visible in the clarity of evidence we would no longer be able to doubt it.[*] Related to and treated as a mode of thought, belief can never be more than an inferior form of it, to the extent that it never succeeds in having a clear evidence of what it believes. When the content of belief vanishes in front of belief itself, as *identified with an act of thought,* doesn't this lead us back to the ultimate phenomenological foundation we are looking for, to the place that is foreign to the world, to every sight and every thought, where belief and faith are possible, where everything is given without separation or distance: in absolute Life's self-revelation in its Word?

"I believe in Christ" means: "I am certain of the truth which is in Him." And in as much as every relation among transcendental Selves— among "egos" ["*moi*"]—is edified in life, "I am certain of the truth which is in Him" means "I am certain of the Truth which is in You." But how can I be certain of the truth which is in the One to whom I say "You," unless it is because His own Truth is in me? This presupposes in the first place that since the truth that is in me—my own certainty—is the truth that is in Him, *it is homogeneous with him, and is indeed neither thought, nor the certainty of a thought, but the truth proper to the Word, the Truth of Life, the Arch-intelligibly we're talking about.*

How then is the Truth of the Word in me, in each transcendental living Self? In its arrival in itself in the arrival in itself of absolute Life in its Word—in its transcendental birth. Only the one who hears within him the sound of his birth (that undergoes experiencing himself as given to himself in absolute Life's self-generation in its Word), the one who, given to himself in this self-givenness from the beginning, no longer undergoes experiencing himself, properly speaking, but undergoes experiencing within him only this Self that gives him to himself, only *that* one can say to this Self of the Word: "I am certain of the truth which is in You."

"I am certain of the truth which is in You" now means: I draw my certainty, my truth from the truth that is in You, I draw my life from yours, "it is no longer I who live, it is you who live in me." Because "God engenders himself as myself," and because "God engenders me as himself," then, truly, because it is his life that has become my own, my life is nothing other than his own: I am deified, according to the Christian concept of salvation.

---

[*] On this ruinous misinterpretation of Descartes's cogito, see §18 above.

Only the one who believes in Christ, who says, "I am certain of the truth that is in You," *that* one alone understands and can understand the Speech of the Scriptures, the Speech of Life that tells him: It is in me that you have life, "you are my Son." This Speech is what he reads in the Scriptures, but he can read it there only because that is who speaks in it, who speaks to him. The one who speaks to him in the speech that gives Life to him. "Who speaks to him": who generates him in itself as that which, undergoing experiencing itself in it, suddenly undergoes within it only its Parousia.

The Johannine Arch-intelligibility in which every Self experiences itself in the one firstborn Son in whom absolute Life undergoes its own trial and enjoys itself—this intelligibility that comes before the world's "outside itself," before every intelligibility that sees in it, before every form of knowledge and science, before what we have always called a "knowing," a "gnosis"—must it not then be called an Arch-gnosis? A superior form of knowing, a knowing of the third kind, which is given only to those who are raised up to it by an extraordinary effort of the intellect or by exceptional gifts?

We must recognize that Christianity is an Arch-gnosis. Irenaeus, for example, in no way criticizes gnosis as such, but only "gnosis falsely so-called," that which, instead of the truth, which it simply ignores, was only able to develop dangerous, imaginary, extravagant, speculative constructions, the product of mere fantasies. In its words, which are foreign to the truth of the world and which will not pass away when the world passes away, in its texts, which we have called initiatory, doesn't Christianity actually initiate us into the secret hidden since the origin of the world, into this great secret that we are? This secret is the Johannine Arch-intelligibility in which we are initiated into what we are in our transcendental generation in Life.

But because Arch-intelligibility is an Arch-passibility—the Arch-passibility in which God eternally loves himself in the infinite love of his Word—because it is also in this Arch-passibility that this Word has taken on flesh and that every flesh is possible (ours as well as his own), then it truly inhabits all flesh, shattering the idea that we have of this. Our flesh is not the opaque body that everyone hauls with them from the time they are said to be born—the body on which without surprise, but in anxiety and throughout his existence, they will watch for every particularity, every quality and every defect, every modification, every decline, and every wrinkle that draws invincibly on the face of man or woman the stigmata of its decrepitude and death. Our body is not an object incapable of drawing from itself and assuring itself of its own promotion to the rank of a phenomenon—it is not an object handed over to the world, obliged to ask the world to illuminate it with its fugitive glow, and for the time to appear in it and then to disappear. Our flesh bears the principle of its manifestation within it, and this manifestation is not the world's appearing. In its pathos-filled auto-impressionality, in its very flesh, given to itself in the Arch-passibility of absolute Life, it reveals this, which reveals it to itself, and it is in its pathos Life's Arch-revelation, the Parousia of the absolute. In the depth of its Night, our flesh is God.

We had never before asked flesh to hold the principle of knowledge within it, and supreme knowledge, which is even more. That is why it disconcerts and defies the wisdom of the wise and the science of the scholars, and every form of knowledge that arises from the world, which thinks, measures, and calculates from it every thing that we have to think, to do, and to believe. We had never before asked flesh to hold the principle of our knowledge and our action, but itself has never asked anything of anyone—or anything other than to enlighten it, to enlighten it about itself and to tell us what it is. When in its innocence each modality of our flesh undergoes experiencing itself, being nothing other than itself, when suffering says suffering and joy joy, it is actually flesh that speaks, and nothing has power against its word. There is flesh, however, only as the effect of its arrival in itself, in an in-carnation, in the Incarnation of the Word in the Arch-passibility of absolute Life.

Thus John's Arch-intelligibility is implicated everywhere there is life, it extends even to these beings of flesh that we are, taking into its incandescent Parousia our paltry wants and our hidden scars, as it did for the wounds of Christ on the Cross. The more each of our sufferings happens in us in a way that is pure, simple, stripped of everything, and reduced to itself and to its phenomenological body of flesh, the more strongly the unlimited power that gives it to itself is felt in us. And when this suffering reaches its limit point in despair, the Eye of God looks upon us. It is the unlimited intoxication of life, the Arch-pleasure of its eternal love in its Word, its Spirit, that submerges us. All who are brought low will be raised. Happy are those who suffer, who perhaps have nothing left but their flesh. Arch-gnosis is the gnosis of the simple.

Index

Absolute, the, 6, 8, 45, 123, 135, 167, 179–80, 227, 257, 262
action, 46, 101, 137, 146, 150–52, 160, 161, 166, 172, 183, 187–89, 203, 233, 262
Affectivity, 61–63, 71, 121, 142, 187, 189, 203, 230
All, the, 179, 228
Alquié, Ferdinand, 104
animals and animality, 3, 6, 11, 100, 117n
anxiety, 188–97, 201–4, 207, 210, 213–17, 222; distinguished from fear, 190
Apelles, 11, 132
Arch-intelligibility, 18–20, 26, 30–31, 86–87, 90–91, 124, 134–35, 170, 236, 255–56, 261–62
Arch-passibility, 169–70, 171, 175, 236, 250, 256, 258, 261–62
Aristotle, 8–9, 188
"arrival" (la venue), xvi, 5, 85, 88, 93, 120–21, 124–25, 137, 165–66, 169–70, 208, 223, 230, 243, 256, 260, 262
Athanasius, 10, 16, 17, 258
attention, 32, 59, 78, 156, 220
Audi, Paul, 139n
Augustine, 231, 234–37, 251
auto-eroticism, 166–67, 212
autonomy, 66, 106, 183, 249, 254

becoming, 6, 13, 63, 76, 85, 250–51
Being, 8, 20, 27, 44n, 239; cogito and, xiii
"being-in-common," 14, 244, 247, 249
"being-in-the-world," 40, 239, 241, 254
"being-with" (Mitsein), xv, 216, 239–41, 243, 244, 247
belief, 48, 254, 258, 260
Bergson, Henri, 116

Bible, 228
Old Testament: Genesis, 7, 121, 129, 133, 183, 207, 215, 226–30, 232, 256–57; Exodus, 8
New Testament: Matthew, 233; John, 5, 10–11, 14, 16, 17–20, 26, 32, 55, 67, 88–89, 121, 125–26, 167, 170–71, 173, 175, 229–32, 235–37, 246, 256, 259; Acts, 7, 177; Romans, 171–72, 176, 234; 1 Corinthians, 171, 177, 232, 257; 2 Corinthians, 176; Galatians, 249; Colossians, 251; 1 John, 10, 18, 248; 2 John, 10n
birth, 125–30; transcendental, 230, 232, 234, 242, 243, 246, 255, 257, 258, 260
body. See flesh: distinguished from body; objective body; "scientific body"; "sensible bodies"; subjective body; transcendental body
Böhme, Jakob, 44–45, 46, 256

capacity, 113, 169, 178, 187–88, 197, 201, 204–7 passim, 217–19
care, 225, 239n
causality, 46, 95, 103, 124
certainty, 69, 89–92, 105, 253, 260
Christianity: alleged contempt of the body, 10n, 167; community and, 245; early development, 6–12, 122, 126–31, 245, 255; heresies, 10, 11, 126, 129, 131–32; historical Jesus, 15, 236; Incarnation, 5–20, 41, 125–28, 131–33, 166, 167, 170–71, 231–36, 246–47, 255–59; individuality and, 248–49; mystical body of Christ, 14, 131, 235, 237, 250–52; sanctification of Christ, 235; transcendence, 122–23; the Trinitarian God of, 171
cogito, cogitatio. See Descartes, René

Michel Henry (1922–2002) was a leading French philosopher and prize-winning novelist. His books previously translated into English include *Barbarism* (2012), *Material Phenomenology* (2008), and *Genealogy of Psychoanalysis* (1993).

Karl Hefty currently holds an Arthur J. Ennis, O.S.A. Postdoctoral Fellowship at Villanova University in Pennsylvania.